Construction Grammar

What do speakers of a language have to know, and what can they 'figure out' on the basis of that knowledge, in order for them to use their language successfully? This is the question at the heart of Construction Grammar, an approach to the study of language that views all dimensions of language as equal contributors to shaping linguistic expressions. The trademark characteristic of Construction Grammar is the insight that language is a repertoire of more or less complex patterns – constructions – that integrate form and meaning. This textbook shows how a Construction Grammar approach can be used to analyse the English language, offering explanations for language acquisition, variation and change. It covers all levels of syntactic description, from word-formation and inflectional morphology to phrasal and clausal phenomena and information-structure constructions. Each chapter includes exercises and further readings, making it an accessible introduction for undergraduate students of linguistics and English language.

THOMAS HOFFMANN is Professor and Chair of English Language and Linguistics at the Catholic University Eichstätt-Ingolstadt as well as Furong Scholar Distinguished Chair Professor of Hunan Normal University. Notable publications include *Preposition Placement in English* (CUP, 2011), *English Comparative Correlatives* (CUP, 2019) and *The Oxford Handbook of Construction Grammar* (co-edited with Trousdale, OUP).

CAUTION
CONSTRUCTION AHEAD

Construction Grammar

In This Series:

Construction Grammar
The Structure of English

THOMAS HOFFMANN

Katholische Universität Eichstätt, Germany
Hunan Normal University, China

CAMBRIDGE
UNIVERSITY PRESS

CAMBRIDGE
UNIVERSITY PRESS

University Printing House, Cambridge CB2 8BS, United Kingdom

One Liberty Plaza, 20th Floor, New York, NY 10006, USA

477 Williamstown Road, Port Melbourne, VIC 3207, Australia

314–321, 3rd Floor, Plot 3, Splendor Forum, Jasola District Centre, New Delhi – 110025, India

103 Penang Road, #05-06/07, Visioncrest Commercial, Singapore 238467

Cambridge University Press is part of the University of Cambridge.

It furthers the University's mission by disseminating knowledge in the pursuit of education, learning, and research at the highest international levels of excellence.

www.cambridge.org
Information on this title: www.cambridge.org/9781107013490
DOI: 10.1017/9781139004213

First published 2022

A catalogue record for this publication is available from the British Library.

Library of Congress Cataloging-in-Publication Data
Names: Hoffmann, Thomas, 1976- author.
Title: Construction grammar : the structure of English / Thomas Hoffmann.
Description: Cambridge ; New York, NY : Cambridge University Press, 2022. | Series: Cambridge
  textbooks in linguistics | Includes bibliographical references and indexes
Identifiers: LCCN 2021046270 (print) | LCCN 2021046271 (ebook) | ISBN 9781107013490 (hardback) |
  ISBN 9781107601123 (paperback) | ISBN 9781139004213 (epub)
Subjects: LCSH: English language–Syntax. | Construction grammar.
Classification: LCC PE1361 .H64 2021 (print) | LCC PE1361 (ebook) | DDC 425.01/836–dc23/eng/
  20211105
LC record available at https://lccn.loc.gov/2021046270
LC ebook record available at https://lccn.loc.gov/2021046271

ISBN 978-1-107-01349-0 Hardback
ISBN 978-1-107-60112-3 Paperback

Additional resources for this publication at www.cambridge.org/HoffmannEnglish

To Moni, Sammy and Jonny

Construction Grammar: The Structure of English

A central property of human cognition is symbolic thinking, that is the ability of our minds to pair a string of sounds ([hɑːt] or letters <heart>) with an arbitrary meaning ('♥'). All speakers of English have stored thousands of such form-meaning pairings (also known as 'words') and are thus able to communicate with each other about topics as diverse as love, life, football or quantum mechanics. Now, all linguistic theories agree that words are one of the central units of any language. In addition to words, however, most theories postulate additional mechanisms for the combination of words into utterances (combinatory syntactic rules that have no access to meaning). In contrast to this, Construction Grammar holds that form-meaning pairings are not only a useful concept for the description of words, but that all levels of grammatical description involve such arbitrary and conventionalized form-meaning pairings. This extended notion of the Saussurean sign has become known as the 'construction' and includes morphemes, words, idioms, as well as abstract phrasal patterns.

The present textbook shows how a usage-based Construction Grammar approach can provide an explanatory as well as descriptively adequate analysis of the English language. It covers all levels of syntactic description, from word-formation and inflectional morphology to phrasal and clausal phenomena and information structure constructions. Moreover, it outlines how constructionist approaches can account for language acquisition, variation and change. Finally, it also offers an in-depth comparison of the differences as well as similarities of the many constructionist approaches that are currently being employed by Construction Grammar researchers.

Contents

Figures

Tables

Preface

The present book has taken an awful lot of time to write. When I first submitted my proposal for it to Cambridge University Press, I thought I would be able to deliver the manuscript within two years without any problems. Then we had our first child, I changed jobs, commuted for a couple of years and finally moved the whole family to Osnabrück, where I was working as a tenure-track assistant professor at the time. After that, however, I thought I would be able to quickly write up this textbook. Then we had our second child, I changed jobs, commuted for a couple of months and finally moved the whole family to Eichstätt, where I now work as a tenured professor. Finally, I was able to finish the textbook! Well, eventually I did, after serving as head of department, then head of my school and various other fun admin jobs. Believe it or not, all this time has done the book a lot of good – after teaching its content for more than a decade now, it is definitely a better read than the one I would have originally written.

Thanks, as always, first and foremost, go to my wonderful family, Moni, Sammy and Jonny. You are my world and without your love, support and understanding none of this would be possible, or even worthwhile. I spent ages in my study at home, typing away at this book and especially Sammy and Jonny did not quite get why daddy was 'wasting his time' like this. Still, I hope that when you grow up you will always feel that I stopped whatever I was doing whenever you needed to talk to me – or for a quick two-against-one football match.

This book owes a lot to the wisdom and knowledge of many wonderful colleagues, many of whom I am fortunate enough to call friends. I have benefited greatly from many challenging and stimulating discussions with Alexander Bergs, Hans Boas, Thomas Brunner, Bert Cappelle, Nik Gisborne, Thomas Herbst, Martin Hilpert, Graeme Trousdale, Mark Turner, Peter Uhrig and Alexander Ziem. Moreover, I, obviously, could never have written this textbook without the ground-breaking work on Construction Grammar by Bill Croft, Chuck Fillmore, Adele Goldberg and Ivan Sag. I am indeed standing on the shoulders of giants!

I would like to thank everyone at Cambridge University Press for their continued support in publishing this book. Publishing with Cambridge University Press is an honour as well as a privilege and, on top of that, always a pleasure. In particular, I am indebted to Andrew Winnard for considering my book a possible contribution to the excellent *Textbooks in Linguistics* series in the first place – and for his patience waiting for the final manuscript. I would also like to express my gratitude to Isabel Collins, for her continuous support throughout the entire publication process.

Finally, I would like to thank my student assistants, Matthias Mugratsch for his help during the early stages of the project and Sina Damköhler for all the meticulous and invaluable work she has put into the final layout of the book.

A textbook such as the present one cannot be written without drawing on one's own previous research. Astute readers will notice that parts of the book particularly draw on my following, earlier publications:

- Hoffmann, Thomas. 2017a. From constructions to construction grammar. In: Barbara Dancygier, ed. *The Cambridge Handbook of Cognitive Linguistics*. Cambridge: Cambridge University Press, 284–309.
- Hoffmann, Thomas. 2017b. Construction grammars. In: Barbara. Dancygier, ed. *The Cambridge Handbook of Cognitive Linguistics*. Cambridge: Cambridge University Press, 310–29.
- Hoffmann, Thomas. 2017c. Multimodal constructs – Multimodal constructions? The role of constructions in the working memory. *Linguistics Vanguard* 3,s1: 1–10.
- Hoffmann, Thomas. 2018. Creativity and construction grammar: Cognitive and psychological issues. *Zeitschrift für Anglistik und Amerikanistik* 66,3: 259–76.
- Hoffmann, Thomas. 2019a. *English Comparative Correlatives: Diachronic and Synchronic Variation at the Lexicon-Syntax Interface*. Cambridge: Cambridge University Press.
- Hoffmann, Thomas. 2019b. Language and creativity: A construction grammar approach to linguistic creativity. *Linguistics Vanguard* 5,1: 379–96.
- Hoffmann, Thomas. 2020. What would it take for us to abandon Construction Grammar? Falsifiability, confirmation bias and the future of the constructionist enterprise. *Belgian Journal of Linguistics* 34: 149–161.
- Hoffmann, Thomas and Graeme Trousdale. 2011. Variation, Change and Constructions in English: Introduction. *Cognitive Linguistics* 22,1: 1–23.
- Hoffmann, Thomas and Graeme Trousdale. 2013. Construction Grammar: Introduction. In: Thomas Hoffmann and Graeme Trousdale, eds. *The Oxford Handbook of Construction Grammar*. Oxford: Oxford University Press, 1–12.

So much for the Preface – now, after all this dilly-dallying – it is high time to start with our usage-based Construction Grammar analysis of the English language.

1   Introduction

Language is arguably the most important cultural tool that humans have ever invented. In this book, using English as our specific object of choice, we will look at the cognitive basis of language and discover how all aspects of it, from inventing new words to uttering full sentences, rest on one central cognitive unit: the construction. As we will see in this chapter, a core property of languages is that they are complex sign systems. As part of this, I will first introduce the classic definition of words as linguistic signs, that is, as arbitrary pairings of form and meaning. Next, we shall see that even morphemes or abstract syntactic patterns are best analysed as form-meaning pairings. All of these different types of signs will be captured by the notion of the *construction*. Besides, instead of a strict dichotomy of words and rules, we will treat language as a system that ranges from simple word constructions to complex syntactic constructions. Finally, we will explore the basic assumptions shared by all approaches that consider the construction the basic notion of syntactic analysis (so-called Construction Grammars) and outline how these differ from Chomskyan Mainstream Generative Grammar.

1.1   Constructions as Linguistic Signs

Speaking a language is an incredibly useful skill. If you meet someone who also speaks your language you can tell them about all the major events in your life, such as the birth of your child, last night's episode of *Doctor Who* or what kind of food you like. You can make predictions about next week's football scores or discuss last year's World Cup final. Language allows you to talk about the past or the future, fictitious people and events (think *wizards*, *unicorns* or *Quidditch*), your own feelings (*I like this book!*) or that of others (*You're really enjoying this book?*). Yet, how can we actually achieve all that? What is the secret property of languages that enables us to do all of these things?

The answer that I will give in this book is that all aspects of language, from inventing new words to uttering full sentences, rest on one central cognitive process: symbolic thinking (Deacon 1997) – our ability to arbitrarily store pairings of form and meaning. As we all know, different languages have different names for the same concept. What we call *apple* in English is known as *Apfel* in German or *alma* in Hungarian. Yet, since we assume that English, German or Hungarian speakers all have similar concepts of apples, it seems necessary to distinguish two levels when we speak about words: the level of meaning (the concept associated with a word, its 'signified' or '*signifé*', which we shall conventionally mark by single quotation marks, e.g., 'apple') and the level of form (the phonological sound side of a word, its 'signifier' or '*signifiant*', which I am going to represent via IPA transcription; details on all phonetic symbols used in this book are freely available from the IPA's website[1]). Thus, English uses the sounds /ˈæpl/ as the signifier to express a meaning that in German is linked to the signifier /ˈapfl/ and in Hungarian is associated with /ˈɑlmɑ/.

This insight that words are best analysed as parings of form and meaning goes back at least to Ferdinand de Saussure (1916), one of the most famous linguists of the twentieth century. He called this combination of form/signifier and meaning/signified '*linguistic sign*' and pointed out that it has two important characteristics: first of all, the relationship of form and meaning is arbitrary. In other words, there is no reason why an 'apple' should be called /ˈæpl/ in English, since other languages use completely different signifiers. The second property of linguistic signs immediately follows from the first: if the choice of form is completely arbitrary, then a speaker cannot guess it, she must learn it. Besides, all speakers of a speech community must subconsciously agree on the signifier of a sign. If I decide to call an apple /ˈɑlmɑ/ in English and you call it /ˈapfl/, then we would not know what the other person is saying even if we both wanted to talk about apples. The relationship between signifier and signified is thus arbitrary and therefore needs to be conventionally agreed upon in a speech community and stored in the mental lexicon of the individual speaker.

In (1.1) you can see a schematic representation of the arbitrary and conventional relationship of signifier and signified:

(1.1)

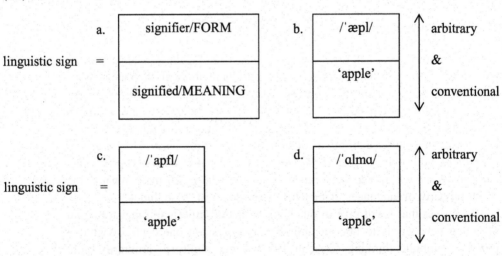

---

[1] See www.internationalphoneticassociation.org/IPAcharts/IPA_chart_orig/IPA_charts_E.html [last accessed 01 July 2021]. You can also find reliable information on the IPA symbols on Wikipedia: https://en.wikipedia.org/wiki/International_Phonetic_Alphabet [last accessed 01 July 2021].

Example (1.1a) gives the FORM and MEANING pole that any linguistic sign has, while examples (1.1b–c) show the analysis for *apple*, *Apfel* and *alma*, respectively. Note that 'apple' is supposed to be a shorthand notation for the complex mental concept that speakers have of apples. This mental representation of *apple* is not a simple picture of an apple. Instead, our mental prototype of an apple is going to include, amongst other things, its typical shape, colour, smell as well as other cognitive associations (e.g., that apples are considered healthy; cf. Bergen and Chang 2005, 2013; Hudson 2010: 34–7 for the complex properties of concepts). However, since mental concepts are rich and complex and difficult to capture in a few words, for the sake of convenience, I will represent these by single quotation marks throughout this book (trusting that you will always interpret them as the rich concept that they are).

As we will see, the notion of the linguistic sign is crucial to modern linguistics. It is, for example, not only relevant for the analysis of words. Take the examples in (1.2):

(1.2) a. unfair
     b. untrue
     c. unreal
     d. unfaithful

All the words in (1.2) consist of the prefix *un-* plus an adjective and their meaning is always the opposite of that adjective (*unfair* = 'not fair', *untrue* = 'not true', etc.). As these examples show, the morpheme *un-* is a linguistic sign, but one which contains an adjective slot (ADJ) on its form level:

(1.3)   FORM: $[/\Lambda n_1\text{-}/ADJ_2]_{ADJ3}$
          $\Leftrightarrow$
          MEANING: 'NOT$_1$ A$_2$'$_3$

Instead of the box notation of (1.1), (1.3) uses a double arrow '$\Leftrightarrow$' to signal the symbolic relationship between the two poles of a sign. This has the advantage that we can also easily present (1.3) in a horizontal format in the running text: FORM: $[/\Lambda n_1\text{-}/ADJ_2]_{ADJ3}$ $\Leftrightarrow$ MEANING: 'NOT$_1$ A$_2$'$_3$. In the rest of the book, I will, therefore, use the format in (1.3) to represent FORM-MEANING pairs (and only draw boxes around a construction if the relationships between several constructions are illustrated in a single example).

The linguistic sign in (1.3) is also an arbitrary and conventional pairing of FORM and MEANING. In German, e.g., the etymologically related prefix *un-* has a slightly different FORM (using a different vowel /un/-ADJ) and in Hungarian it is a suffix (ADJ-*tlan* / ADJ-*tlen*) that is used to express a similar MEANING (cf. *sportszerű* 'fair' vs *sportszerűtlen* 'unfair'). On top of that, since we now have a complex sign consisting of more than one element, I use subscript numbers to keep track of the individual components across the FORM-MEANING levels (following Jackendoff's 2002 Parallel Architecture model as well as constraint-based approaches such as, for example, Boas and Sag 2012;

Kim and Michaelis 2020; Pollard and Sag 1994; see Chapter 7 for more details). You can think of these subscripts as links that, if you click them, should take you to the corresponding element on the other plane: since the /ʌn/-part of the FORM side clearly corresponds to the meaning 'NOT', both receive the subscript '1' to indicate that they are one FORM-MEANING subunit within the sign (and if you 'click' on the '1' of /ʌn$_1$-/, it will take you to 'NOT$_1$' on the MEANING pole, and vice versa). Likewise, the A$_2$ on the meaning level of (1.3) stands for the meaning of the ADJ$_2$ that is inserted in the second slot of the sign and consequently carries the subscript '2'. Finally, since the whole complex sign is used like an adjective (it can be used predicatively; cf. *That was unfair.* as well as attributively *That was an unfair question.*), its entire form is subscripted with 'ADJ$_3$' and symbolically linked to the meaning of the whole unit ' '$_3$. (Similarly, the *Apple*-construction above would have to be modified to include the information that *apple* is a noun in English: /'æpl/$_N$ ⇔ 'apple')

The FORM level in (1.3) therefore does not only include phonological information like the classic Saussurean sign but also morphosyntactic information (e.g., that the open slot has to be filled by an adjective). Yet, in order to capture the similarity of words and morphemes, we need a term that covers both types of FORM-MEANING pairings. We therefore use the term 'construction' for any arbitrary FORM-MEANING pairing that must be stored in the mental lexicon, regardless of whether it is a 'classic' Saussurean sign like *apple* or a morpheme like *un-*. 'Constructions' can thus be defined as in (1.4; for a more precise cognitive definition see Section 2.1.3):

(1.4)   **Construction (first working definition):**
         a construction is an arbitrary pairing of (phonological/syntactic) FORM and
         MEANING that is stored in a speaker's mental lexicon

Since constructions are FORM-MEANING that are stored in the long-term memory of speakers, we need another term for the actual utterances that are the output of our minds. Spoken or written performance data that we can record and analyse empirically are, of course, the products of our minds. In Construction Grammar, we call these authentic tokens of use 'constructs'[2] and in this book we will also explore the question of how our mental constructions combine to produce complex, authentic constructs.

Constructions are not only a helpful concept for the analysis of the word and sub-word (that is, morphological) level. As we shall see in this book, all levels of

---

[2] Most Construction Grammar approaches use the term 'construct' in this sense (as a single token of performance that is the result of construction interaction). The only approach that does not follow this usage is Sign-Based Construction Grammar SBCG (Boas and Sag 2012; Michaelis 2010, 2013). In SBCG, 'constructs' is instead the technical name used for a special constraint (namely, a type constraint on local trees). In almost all other constructionist publications, however, people use the term as explained in the text.

syntactic analysis from the morpheme to the sentence level can be successfully described using constructions. Take the following example:

(1.5)   It's both a cliche and a major regret to me,
             but **I** most certainly **took my mother for granted**.[3]

Example (1.5) contains the structure *TAKE for granted*, whose meaning is not completely compositional; that is, it does not simply follow from adding up the meaning of the individual words: *I . . . took my mother for granted* does not simply mean 'I + . . . + took + my + mother + as + given'. Instead, the speaker also wants to express that she didn't value her mother enough and that she regrets this. Non-compositional items such as *TAKE for granted* are called 'idioms' and must be learnt by all speakers of English in order to use and understand them correctly. In other words, it is a construction since it is an arbitrary pairing of FORM and MEANING. So, we do not only need word- (*apple*) and sub-word-level constructions (*Un*-ADJ) but also constructions that are bigger than single words.

Note that, like the *Un*-construction above, the idiomatic *TAKE for granted* construction is not completely phonologically fixed:

(1.6) a.   . . . MPs took their constituents for granted[4]

     b.   We took our success for granted.[5]

While some elements (*for* and *granted*) reoccur unchanged in (1.5), (1.6a) and (1.6b), others can be filled by various items. Thus, all three examples have different subjects (*I, MPs, we*) and objects (*my mother, their constituents, our success*). Now, the parts of a construction that have a fixed phonological form (i.e., [fə] and [ˈgɹɑːntɪd]) are called **substantive** elements (Croft and Cruse 2004: 255). The *Apple*-construction (1.1b), for example, only consists of one such substantive element ([ˈæpl]), while the *Un*-construction in (1.3) has a substantive element [ʌn] – which is followed by a single slot. Such slots that can be filled by various elements (cf., e.g., *fair, true, real* and *faithful* in (1.2)) are termed **schematic** elements (Croft and Cruse 2004: 255; Goldberg 2003: 220; Jackendoff 2002: 176). The *TAKE for granted idiom* has schematic subject and object slots as the examples in (1.5) and (1.6) show.

On top of that, the *TAKE for granted* construction also has one element that is partly substantive and partly schematic, namely its verb slot:

(1.7) a.   . . . sometimes in life I **take** things for granted[6]
     b.   . . . she **takes** things for granted
     c.   . . . we **took** things for granted

In (1.7), like in (1.5) and (1.6), the verbal slot of the idiom is filled with the lexeme TAKE. However, in these examples the precise phonological realisation

---

[3] Source: www.huffingtonpost.co.uk/helen-spencer [last accessed 02 January 2021].
[4] Source: www.guardian.co.uk/politics/2011/feb/18/nick-clegg-alternative-vote-change [last accessed 02 January 2021].
[5] Source: www.digitalspy.co.uk/music/news/a365743/ [last accessed 02 January 2021].
[6] Source: http://playstoprewind.co.uk/index.php?section_id=4 [last accessed 03 March 2012].

of TAKE (its so-called word-forms) depends on factors that apply to all verbal constructions in Standard English and therefore do not have to be specified by the *TAKE for granted* construction: subject–verb agreement in English, for example, requires finite verbs (i.e., those that are specified for the grammatical features person, number and tense) in present tense sentences to agree in person and number with the subject:

(1.8) a.   she sings / he kisses the bride / she gives him a kiss
      b.   they sing / you kiss the bride / I give him a kiss

In (1.8a) the subjects (*she, he*) are all [3rd person] [singular] and consequently require a finite verb form that is also marked for these grammatical features (cf. the 3rd person singular suffix *-s* in *sings*, *kisses* and *gives*). Thus, **she sing / *he kiss the bride / *she give him a kiss* would all be considered ungrammatical (in Standard English; here and below an asterisk '*' signals that a structure is ungrammatical). In contrast to this, the majority of English verbs do not show any overt agreement marker for 3rd person plural subjects (*they*) or 1st (*I / we*) and 2nd person (*you*) singular and plural subjects (cf. 1.8b).

We will return to the issue of subject–verb agreement in Chapter 3. Right now, it is only important to understand that it is a constraint that applies to all English sentences and one that we therefore do not necessarily need to encode in the *TAKE for granted* construction. Similarly, tense, that is whether a verb is, for example, used in the present tense (1.7b) or past tense (1.7c), is also a grammatical category that is marked on all verbs (cf. *She sang / He kissed the bride / she gave him a kiss*) and that we do not need to specify in the *TAKE for granted*-construction (see Section 5.2 for a discussion of English tense and aspect constructions).

Taking all of the above observations into account, we can now give a first constructional representation of the *TAKE for granted* idiom:

(1.9)   *X TAKE Y for granted* construction
         FORM: [SBJ$_1$ TAKE$_3$ OBJ$_2$ fə$_3$ ˈɡɹɑːntɪd$_3$]$_{idiom4}$
         ⇔
         MEANING: 'A$_1$ [doesn't value]$_3$ B$_2$'$_4$

As with the *Apple-* and *Un-*construction, substantive elements are phonologically fixed and therefore given in IPA transcription. Moreover, schematic slots are put in CAPITALS, with the SBJ and OBJ slot only being specified for their syntactic function (i.e., subject and object – don't worry if you are not yet 100 per cent sure how to identify these, we will cover this in Chapters 3, 4 and 5). In contrast to this, the verb slot has to be filled with a word-form of the lexeme TAKE. Finally, subscript numbers indicate FORM-MEANING subparts of the constructions (TAKE$_3$ fə$_3$ ˈɡɹɑːntɪd$_3$, e.g., can be said to correspond to [doesn't value]$_3$ on the meaning side). As we will see in Section 4.3, idioms such as (1.9) are not the only type of idiom construction (they are qualitatively different from idioms like

KICK the bucket 'to die') and we will discuss how to capture the commonalities and differences of idiom constructions.

So far, we have focused on constructions that had at least one substantive element. There are, however, also completely schematic templates:

(1.10) a. Could **he shriek himself unconscious** ...?
           (BNC W_fict_prose CJJ)
      b.   **Firefighters cut the man free** ...
           (BNC W_newsp_other_report K55)
      c.   **he had** often **drunk himself silly**
           (BNC W_fict_prose CDN)

Shriek is normally an intransitive verb (one that does not require an object; cf. *Leila laughed and shrieked* BNC W_fict_prose AD9), yet in (1.10a) it has two obligatory post-verbal complements (*himself* and *unconscious*) that seem to depend on each other: while *he shrieked himself unconscious* is fine, neither **he shrieked himself* nor **he shrieked unconscious* would be grammatical. *Cut* and *drink*, on the other hand, can be used transitively, that is, with an object (cf. *I cut my fingernails all the time* BNC W_fict_drama FU6 or *he drank a large whisky* BNC W_fict_poetry FAS). Yet, the use of *cut* and *drink* in (1.10b,c) is clearly different from these transitive uses: while in *I cut my fingernails*, the fingernails are actually cut, the firefighters (hopefully!) do not cut the man in (1.10b). Similarly, you can drink a whisky, but not yourself (as in (1.10c)). On top of that, all the sentences in (1.10) also give the effect that the shrieking, cutting and drinking action has on the object (it falls asleep, is set free or loose).

The examples in (1.10) seem to follow a pattern that takes a verb and describes the result that the verbal action has on an object. One way to analyse this pattern is to postulate the following abstract Resultative construction (Boas 2003, 2005a; Goldberg 1995, 2006; Goldberg and Jackendoff 2004)

(1.11)   Resultative construction
          FORM: $[SBJ_1\ V_2\ OBJ_3\ OBL_4]_{Resultative\ Construction5}$
          $\Leftrightarrow$
          MEANING: 'A_1 CAUSES B_3 TO BECOME C_4 BY V_2-ing'$_5$

The construction in (1.11) is completely schematic; it only consists of syntactic slots for the subject (SBJ), verb (V), object (OBJ) and result (OBL, which includes adjective phrases like the ones in (1.10)). Besides, its meaning includes parts ('CAUSES ... TO BECOME') that are not associated with any element on the formal level. This part of the 'resultative' meaning is therefore an arbitrary property of the construction and another reason why one might postulate that it is a stored template. (Semantic properties such as CAUSE or BECOME are basic relations that appear in the MEANING pole of many constructions. In the following such semantic features are highlighted by SMALL CAPS; see Section 2.2.1 for details.).

An important issue concerning the Resultative construction is how the verbal arguments are incorporated into it. As mentioned above, *shriek* is an intransitive verb that only brings a 'shrieker' to the subject slot of the construction. The object (*himself*) and oblique (*unconscious*) parts must be provided by the context. These and other issues will be explored in depth in Chapter 5, which deals with the so-called argument structure constructions, of which the Resultative construction is one type.

Finally, there are also constructions that go beyond the clause-level. Take, for example, the following football (aka soccer) chant (Bergs and Hoffmann 2018; Hoffmann 2015):

(1.12)   Are you England?
          Are you England?
          Are you England in disguise?
          Are you England in disguise?[7]

In 2009, the Northern Ireland football team rather surprisingly beat Spain 3–2 in a friendly match. During their celebrations the Northern Ireland fans did not pick a chant that mentioned Spain, but the one in (1.12) about their arch-rival England.

As you can probably guess, the chant is supposed to mock the current opponents by referring to them as one's least favourite rival team. Yet, it is not only the Northern Ireland fans that use this chant:

(1.13)   Are you Villa?
          Are you Villa?
          Are you Villa in disguise?
          Are you Villa in disguise?[8]

(1.14)   Are you Andorra,
          Are you Andorra,
          Are you Andorra in disguise?
          Are you Andorra in disguise?[9]

West Bromwich supporters use the chant in (1.13) to mock opponents (when they are not playing Aston Villa) and (1.14) is the creative outburst of an England fan that mocks the Croatian team.

The chant therefore is a widely used one and, when we take into account the pattern in (1.12)–(1.14), seems to have the following constructional template:

(1.15)   *Are you* FOOTBALL TEAM *in disguise* construction

          FORM:[10]   /ɑː juː [FOOTBALL TEAM]$_1$
                      ɑː juː [FOOTBALL TEAM]$_1$

---

[7] Source: www.youtube.com/watch?v=HDrzfIOxh0A&feature=related [last accessed 02 January 2021].
[8] Source: https://www.fanchants.com/football-songs/west_bromwich_albion-chants/are-you-villa-in-disguise/ [last accessed 26 June 2021].
[9] Source: www.youtube.com/watch?v=5wH4B2z0fpY [last accessed 02 January 2021].
[10] An anonymous reviewer asks why (1.15) does not have a SYNTAX pole (which would have to specify agreement between *you* and *are*). Maybe some speakers have stored such a more detailed representation, but I guess for most football fans (1.15) is an idiomatic chunk that except for the slot of the FOOTBALL TEAM is not parsed. Just because we as linguists see two words here that agree, it doesn't mean that speakers actually have such complex underlying representations.

ɑː juː [FOOTBALL TEAM]$_1$ ın dıs'gaız,
ɑː juː [FOOTBALL TEAM]$_1$ ın dıs'gaız/$_{chant2}$
TUNE: Bread of Heaven$_2$

⇔

MEANING:　'our current opponents play like X$_1$
and X$_1$ is a crap football team'$_2$

The form part has the substantive elements /ɑː juː/ and /ın dıs'gaız/ as well as a slot for the name of a football team that is repeated four times. Another property of the construction's form, not shown in detail in (1.15), is that it has a fixed tune associated with it (the religious hymn 'Cwm Rhondda', or 'Bread of Heaven'; Shaw 2010: 7). While not all constructions are to be sung, we will see that the linguistic equivalent of the tune, prosodic information, can also be a crucial form property of a construction. The construction's meaning is complex and requires some social background knowledge for its interpretation. The football team that is inserted in the schematic slot cannot be the current opponent. Instead, it is a particular disliked team that is ridiculed as playing badly. On top of that, the current opponent is mocked by insinuating that they play as badly as the team mentioned in the song.

As we have seen, constructions are a useful tool for describing all linguistic levels from morphemes over words and idioms to schematic syntactic templates and football chants. This insight has led many researchers over the past thirty years to explore constructional analyses of many languages. Out of these, all approaches that subscribe to the view that constructions are the central building blocks of grammar are called **Construction Grammar**s (Bergen and Chang 2005, 2013; Boas and Sag 2012; Croft 2001, 2012; Fillmore and Kay 1993, 1995; Goldberg 1995, 2006; Kim and Michaelis 2020; Steels 2011, 2013). While there are many different Construction Grammar approaches and frameworks (see Chapter 7), all would subscribe to the definition in (1.4). On top of that, many Construction Grammar approaches claim that constructional analyses model the linguistic mental competence of speakers; that is, that constructions are what speakers draw on to produce and understand sentences. Moreover, they argue that it is a constructional account that can best explain how children can acquire this mental system. This view is, of course, in sharp contrast to the other major linguistic theory of our time, Mainstream Generative Grammar (Chomsky 1995, 2000; Radford 1997, 2004), and we will take a closer look at this controversy in Section 1.2. In this book, however, we will mainly focus on English grammar and see what a constructional analysis of English syntax looks like and what the advantages of such an approach are. Before we take a closer look at English, however, next I shall first present the core assumptions shared by Construction Grammar approaches.

As we will see in Section 2.1.2, this is particularly important to keep in mind when analysing child language data during acquisition.

1.2   Basic Assumptions of Construction Grammar Approaches

There are four assumptions that all Construction Grammar approaches share (Goldberg 2013).

1.2.1   The Lexicon-Syntax Continuum

Many grammatical theories assume a strict division between the lexicon as a repository of meaningful words and morphemes, on the one hand, and meaningless syntactic rules which combine these words into sentences, on the other hand (cf., e.g., Radford 1997, 2004 and Section 1.3 below). As we saw above, however, Construction Grammarians do not uphold this strict lexicon-syntax distinction. Instead, all levels of grammatical knowledge involve FORM-MEANING pairs, that is, constructions. The only difference between lexical constructions (such as the *Apple* construction (1.1b)) and phrasal/grammatical constructions (such as the Resultative construction (1.11)) is the degree of schematicity: while the former are fully substantive (have their phonological form filled), the latter are schematic (and thus contain slots that can be filled by various lexical constructions). Moreover, Construction Grammarians point out that the grammatical knowledge of a speaker does not only consist of these two extreme types of constructions. Instead, fully substantive and fully schematic constructions only lie at the opposite ends of a cline. In-between, we find constructions that have both substantive and schematic parts (such as the *Un*-construction (1.3) or the *X TAKE Y for granted* construction (1.9)). A central claim of the constructionist approach is therefore that 'all grammatical knowledge in the speaker's mind [is stored], in the form of ... constructions' (Croft and Cruse 2004: 255). The full list of constructions that make up a speaker's mental grammatical knowledge is then referred to as the '*constructicon*' (in analogy to the lexicon, which in other theories only comprises words and morphemes; Fillmore 1988; Jurafsky 1992).

1.2.2   Taxonomic Network Organization and Inheritance

The constructicon is not seen as an unstructured list of constructions. Instead, all versions of Construction Grammars agree that the constructions of a language form a structured inventory, which can be represented by (taxonomic) networks (cf. Croft and Cruse 2004: 262–5).

To see how that works, consider a non-linguistic example: there are lots of conceptual categories by which we can classify humans. For example, we classify them according to their gender (whether they are male, female or non-binary), their marital status (single, married, widowed ...) or their profession (plumber, miner, doctor ...; many more could be added but for the sake of simplicity, I shall limit myself to those three here). If we arrange these categories together with their various options in a taxonomic network, we get something like Figure 1.1

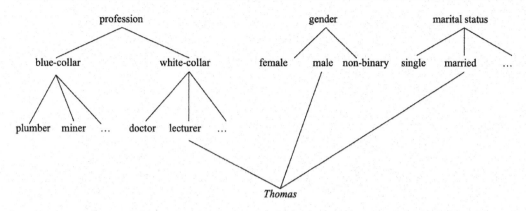

Figure 1.1 *Using taxonomic networks to represent information*

In many Western societies, Gender is now constructed as having three options (male, female and non-binary), which are, therefore, given as three subordinate categories of this concept in Figure 1.1. Professions, on the other hand, are often subdivided into those that require manual labour ('blue-collar jobs') and those that are considered more intellectually demanding ('white-collar jobs'). Finally, your marital status can be single, married or a number of less frequent alternatives (widowed, if you once were married but your spouse has passed away, or celibate; that is you have consciously decided not to get married).

Instead of just independently listing concepts such as male, married or lecturer, the advantage of such a taxonomic representation is that it groups together more closely related items (such as male, female and non-binary) under a single umbrella (gender). Moreover, this seems to model pretty well how the mind seems to be organized. If I say *couch* and ask you to come up with other related terms as quickly as possible, chances are that many of you will say *sofa*, *table* or *chair*; that is, other pieces of furniture. Similarly, if you read the word *insect* in a text and then come across *bug*, you would probably think of the animal. Yet, if the preceding sentence was about spies, you might think of an electronic device to surreptitiously tap people's conversations. In psychology, this phenomenon is called 'priming' (one meaning primes another one) and it has been taken as an indication that the mind stores information in a way that connects related concepts and ideas together (cf., e.g., Bock 1986a, 1968b; Bock and Griffin 2000; Hudson 2010: 75–6).

As you can see in Figure 1.1, I have also outlined how the network can be used to classify me (Thomas): I am a male, married human working as a lecturer. Now an important property of a taxonomic network is that it is a convenient way of storing information. Once you have a concept 'male' (which includes biological sex but also other stereotypical features you and your culture associate with 'maleness' and that might be changing through time), you do not have to list all of these for each individual (e.g., me, Noam, Bill, Fred, Jeff . . .). Instead, you can save the relevant information once in the taxonomy (in a node 'male') and each individual that is linked to that node will automatically be assumed to show all of these features (a phenomenon that is called 'inheritance', since you can be said to inherit these properties from the more abstract category).

Figure 1.1 shows something else, namely the fact that you can inherit features from more than one category. I, for example, inherit features from the concept male, but also from lecturer (that I work and teach at university, write textbooks ...) and am married (have a wife). In cases where this is possible, we speak of multiple inheritance networks, and a great many Construction Grammar approaches believe that the construction is arranged in such a multiple inheritance network (Booij 2010; Diessel 2019; Fillmore, Kay and O'Connor 1988; Goldberg 1995; Hudson 2007b; Lakoff 1987; Langacker 1987; Wierzbicka 1988). Moreover, the majority of Construction Grammarians assume so-called default inheritance networks (cf., e.g., Croft and Cruse 2004: 262–5; Ginzburg and Sag 2000: 5–8; Goldberg 2003: 222–3). This captures the idea that normally (by default) a subordinate construction will inherit all properties from its superordinate construction, but that a more specific construction can also override inherited properties. In my case, this means that by default I inherit all properties of being male, married and a lecturer. Yet, at the same time, I am afraid of spiders and occasionally sad movies can make me cry, two things you might not normally consider very manly. So, while I inherit properties such as having lots of facial hair and a love of football, which are typical of (our social construct of) men, I also override others such as avoiding the public display of emotion or not being afraid of tiny animals.

Figure 1.2 illustrates how multiple inheritance networks might work for a sentence like (1.7b) above.

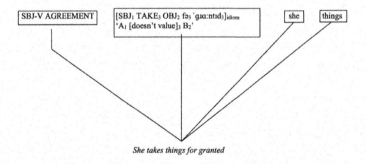

Figure 1.2 *Taxonomic network analysis of (1.7b)* She takes things for granted.

Figure 1.2 shows how the sentence (1.7b) inherits from various constructions: the main frame is provided by the *X TAKE Y for granted*-construction (1.9), into which the word constructions *she* and *things* are inserted, while the Subject–Verb Agreement construction ensures concord, that is identity, of the subject and the verb's person and number features. Different Construction Grammar approaches have different analyses for the Subject–Verb Agreement construction – we will therefore have to take closer look at these in Section 3.2.

Inheritance networks thus allow constructs such as *She takes things for granted.* to be freely formed as long as the constructions they consist of do not conflict (cf. Goldberg 2006: 22). Consequently,

> [c]onstructional approaches share with mainstream generative grammar the goal of accounting for the creative potential of language (Chomsky 1957, 1965). That is, it is clear that language is not a set of sentences that can be fixed in advance. Allowing constructions to combine freely as long as there are no conflicts, allows for the infinitely creative potential of language (Goldberg 2006: 22).

Note, however, that there are also cases that cannot easily be explained by inheritance and which therefore require an alternative constructional analysis (Müller 2006, 2010; Sag, Boas and Kay 2012: 9–14). Take e.g., the *great* $N_{kinship}$ construction (Kay 1973):

(1.16) a.   great grandfather
    b.   great great grandfather
    c.   great great great grandfather
    d.   great great great great grandfather ...

(1.17) a.   great grandmother-in-law
    b.   great great grandmother-in-law
    c.   great great great grandmother-in-law
    d.   great great great great grandmother-in law ...

(1.18)   *great*-$N_{kinship}$
    FORM: $[\text{ɡɹeɪt}_1\ N_{kinship2}]_{N3}$
    ⇔
    MEANING: 'Kinship (at one further generation of ancestry)$_1$
              than kinship$_2$'$_{N3}$

Grandmother and *grandfather* are already stored in a speaker's mind and do not have to be created using (1.18). As (1.16) and (1.17) show, however, you can draw on (1.18) to add *great* to existing kinship terms like *grandfather* or *mother-in-law* to express other generations of ancestry (so your *great grandmother* is one of your parents' *grandmother*, your *great great grandmother* is one of your parents' *great grandmother*, and so on). Now, it is, of course, possible to provide an analysis of the *great*-$N_{kinship}$ construction (1.18) along the lines we have outlined for other constructions above: on the FORM level, the construction has a substantive element $[\text{ɡɹeɪt}]_1$ that has a MEANING of 'at one further generation of ancestry$_1$'. On top of that, there is a schematic $N_{kinship2}$ slot that provides the generation and kinship information that the full construction shifts back by a generation. Using constructional inheritance, we can then account for words such as *great grandfather* (1.16a), which can be said to inherit from the lexical construction *grandfather* as well as the *great*-$N_{kinship}$ construction (1.18). But what about words such as *great great grandfather* (1.16b), *great great great grandfather* (1.16c) and so on? As it turns out, these cannot easily be explained by an inheritance approach: as you can see in Figure 1.2, so far we have treated inheritance as an 'all-at-once' phenomenon, that is all constructions from which a specific construct inherits apply simultaneously. However, when you only have two constructions, the *great*-$N_{kinship}$ construction (1.18) and an $N_{kinship}$ construction (such as *grandfather*) inheritance is only going to get you the construct *great grandfather*. If you add that as a lexical construction to your constructicon, then you can, of course, inherit *great great grandfather* from the *great*-$N_{kinship}$ construction (1.18) and this new $N_{kinship}$ *great grandfather* construction. Yet, there comes a point when, for whatever reason, you want to talk about your *great great great grandmother-in-law* (who for the sake of argument you have just found out was a famous artist), despite the fact that you never before even for a second thought of your *great grandmother-in-law*, let alone your *great great grandmother-in-law*. In order to do this, we must find a way to apply our constructions recursively, that is as part of licensing the construct *great great great grandmother-in-law* we need to license the following steps:

(1.19)   *grandmother-in-law* construction + *great* $N_{kinship}$ construction
          = *great grandmother-in-law*
      → *great grandmother-in-law* + *great* $N_{kinship}$ construction
          = *great great grandmother-in-law*
      → *great great grandmother-in-law* + *great* $N_{kinship}$ construction
          = *great great great grandmother-in-law*

Thus, we need a constructional template that will allow us to loop through all of the processes in (1.19) without assuming that the intermediate steps (*great grandmother-in-law* and *great great grandmother-in-law*) have been previously stored in the construction. We will see in Chapter 3 how we need to adjust our representations of constructions in order to license such recursive phenomena.

Maybe you are thinking right now that the *great*-$N_{kinship}$ construction is a fairly marginal phenomenon and that this is not an important issue. Yet, as we will see in later chapters, there are many phenomena that cannot be captured by a simple 'all-at-once' inheritance of all constructions involved. If we want to claim that Construction Grammar is a psychologically plausible theory, we need to model how speakers can license all types of constructs (and make sure that our model actually works!). Now the different approaches to Construction Grammar differ greatly with respect to the degree of their formalization of the theory (and also with respect to several fundamental assumptions; see Chapter 7). Some, like Embodied Construction Grammar (Bergen and Chang 2013), Fluid Construction Grammar (Steels 2013) or Sign-Based Construction Grammar (Boas and Sag 2012; Michaelis 2013) try to rigorously formalize their results and are therefore better at spotting problems when the combination of constructions causes unexpected issues. As Pollard and Sag rightly point out, 'as theories become more complicated and their empirical consequences less straightforwardly apparent, the need for formalization arises' (1994: 6). Nevertheless, all of these formal Construction Grammar models are fairly complex and the learning curve of these formalisms is pretty steep. In addition to that, the three formalisms also differ greatly from each other. Besides, an open question is also whether their formal mechanisms can be shown to correlate with mental processes; that is, whether the mind works like a computer (see also Chapter 7). For the present book (following Hilpert 2019 and Ziem and Lasch 2013), I have therefore chosen to present my analyses using a less formal Usage-based Construction Grammar approach (influenced by insights from Cognitive Grammar (Langacker 2005), Radical Construction Grammar (Croft 2001) and Cognitive Construction Grammar (Goldberg 2003, 2006; Lakoff 1987)). In the next chapter, I will argue that such a usage-based approach receives great support from acquisition studies as well as psycholinguistics. Throughout the book, however, I will also incorporate insights from formal constructionist approaches and discuss their approach to various phenomena. I do this because I believe that a model has to be internally consistent and working before we can even start to worry about its psychological plausibility. At the end of the day, though, it is also important to remember that all constructionist approaches share the same main goals and the majority of differences are notational in character. In order to show you this, you will find a concise comparison of approaches in Chapter 7 (where I will also illustrate how the FORM and MEANING are represented in the various approaches and give a brief introduction to and comparison of the various types of Construction Grammar formalisms).

1.2.3   Surface Structure-Orientation

Mainstream Generative Grammar (Chomsky 1995, 2000; Radford 1997, 2004) advocates a view of language in which phonology, syntax and semantics are three independent modules. In this approach, abstract syntactic representations are manipulated independently by transformations or derivations and only once these syntactic operations are completed is the semantics of the output computed. This is in stark contrast to Construction Grammar approaches, which, as we saw above, treat linguistic elements and structures as holistic pairings of phonological/syntactic FORM and semantic/pragmatic MEANING. As a result of this holistic view, Construction Grammar places much more emphasis on surface structure, that is, the concrete utterances that a hearer is exposed to, than Mainstream Generative Grammar (which is much more inter-ested in invisible syntactic operations that cannot be directly observed in the output; Culicover and Jackendoff 2005; Goldberg 2003).

1.2.4   Cross-linguistic Variability and Generalization

Since constructions are arbitrary pairings of form and meaning, it should not be surprising to find that phrasal and clausal constructions – just like word constructions – vary greatly across languages. At the same time, this does not mean that Construction Grammarians deny that a great number of cross-linguistic generalizations exist. Yet, unlike other approaches, Construction Grammar claims that these generalizations derive from domain-general cognitive processes and the functions constructions have to fulfil (Boas 2010; Croft 2001; Evans and Levinson 2009; Haspelmath 2008).

1.3   Summary

Constructionist approaches emphasize the fundamental role that symbolic thinking plays for language. Unlike other linguistic theories, however, Construction Grammar does not only treat words as arbitrary form-meaning pairings. Instead, all grammatical knowledge, from morphemes to clausal structures and beyond is said to consist of pairings of form (phonology and syntax) and meaning (semantics/pragmatics).

In this book, we will explore what a constructional analysis of English looks like. As part of this, we will look at the role of constructions in phonology, morphology, semantics and syntax. I mentioned above that there are various constructionist approaches and formalisms. The approach I have chosen for this textbook is a form of Usage-based Construction Grammar. This type of approach emphasizes that it is actual, authentic data that constitute the prime input for our mental constructicons. The next chapter will show how such an approach receives considerable support from language acquisition studies.

Exercises

1.1 How is the notion of the construction similar to the classic Saussurean linguistic sign and in which way does it extend it?

1.2 Try to identify the construction underlying the following examples (and mark which elements are substantive, i.e., phonologically fixed, and which are schematic, i.e., slots): *deafen* 'to make deaf', *widen* 'to make wide', *sweeten* 'to make sweet'.

2 Usage-Based Construction Grammar

In the last chapter, we learnt that the basic units of a Construction Grammar analysis are FORM-MEANING pairings of varying degrees of schematicity. In this chapter, we will see that for most Construction Grammarians constructions are not just descriptive tools for linguistic analysis. They also maintain that constructions are in fact the basic unit of our mental grammars. This obviously raises the question of how people in general, and children in particular, acquire constructions. The majority of constructionist approaches answer this question by claiming that people acquire constructions through actual language use and with the help of general cognitive processes. Such approaches are known as 'usage-based'. In this chapter, we will explore a Usage-based Construction Grammar account of language acquisition, survey the types of data sources used in such approaches and discuss how we have to refine our definition of constructions in light of the results of usage-based studies.

2.1 Learning Constructions: Usage-Based Approaches

2.1.1 Innate Grammar?

In Chapter 1, I gave you a preliminary definition of constructions as arbitrary pairings of (phonological/syntactic) FORM and MEANING that are stored in a speaker's mental lexicon. Yet how do constructions actually 'get' in your mind? The majority of constructionist approaches would subscribe to the idea that '[c]onstructions are understood to be learned on the basis of the input and general cognitive mechanisms' (Goldberg 2003: 219). Goldberg's quote summarizes the central tenets of all so-called usage-based approaches (Bybee 2010, 2013; Diessel 2013, 2015; Hopper 1987; Langacker 2008): these claim that all you need in order to acquire a language is domain-general cognitive processes such as, for example, categorization or chunking/automatization that are also at work in other cognitive domains (such as vision or neuromotor processing) as well as a sufficient amount of authentic input. This view is obviously in sharp contrast to the idea of an innate language faculty ('Universal Grammar') that has been endorsed by Principles-and-Parameters theories (cf., e.g., Chomsky 1965, 1995, 2000; Radford 1997, 2004). Usually, the main reason for the postulation of an innate language faculty depends on the 'poverty of stimulus' argument:

> It seems clear that many children acquire first and second languages quite successfully even though no special care is taken to teach them and no special attention is given to their progress. It also seems apparent that much of the actual speech observed consists of fragments and deviant expressions of a variety of sorts. Thus it seems that a child must have the ability to 'invent' a generative grammar ... even though the primary linguistic data that he uses ... may ... be deficient in various respects.   (Chomsky 1965: 200–1)

Chomsky thus assumes that input alone cannot explain why language acquisition is such a fast and uniform process, which means that children must be genetically predisposed to acquire languages (which in the end led him to postulate Universal Grammar).

This is, of course, an empirical issue that requires a closer look at the kind of input children actually receive as well as the structures they produce. Pullum and Scholz (2002), for example, have shown that the positive input children are exposed to is in fact far richer than assumed by Mainstream Generative Grammar. Take, for example, the declarative sentence in (2.1), which has a corresponding yes-or-no question (2.2a) but not (2.2.b):

(2.1)   The child that is$_1$ alone is$_2$ unhappy.

(2.2) a.   Is$_2$ the child that is$_1$ alone unhappy?
   b.   *Is$_1$ the child that alone is$_2$ unhappy?

Most English declarative sentences with auxiliaries (*He should*$_{\text{auxiliary1}}$ *be*$_{\text{auxiliary2}}$ *unhappy.*) correspond to a yes-or-no question in which the first auxiliary is placed before the subject (*Should*$_{\text{auxiliary1}}$ *he be*$_{\text{auxiliary2}}$ *unhappy?* but not **Be*$_{\text{auxiliary2}}$ *he should*$_{\text{auxiliary1}}$ *unhappy?*). Mainstream Generative Grammar textbooks often claim that '[c]hildren learning English probably never hear any sentences of this type [TH: i.e., (2.2a)]' (Cook and Newson 1996: 13). Thus, they argue that if children only relied on surface similarities in the input, they might be tempted to overgeneralize this pattern and form a yes-or-no question in which the first auxiliary of (2.1) appears clause-initially as in (2.2b). Yet, not only is (2.2b) ungrammatical (i.e., native speakers would all agree that it is 'wrong'). Children do not produce patterns such as these. Mainstream Generative Grammar, therefore, argues that on top of input, children must also have access to an innate Universal Grammar that prevents them from making such mistakes. Note that such an analysis only works if you ignore the semantics of the sentences involved: in (2.1) and (2.2a), [*the child that is$_1$ alone*] as a whole acts as one chunk – a chunk that has a semantic function called reference: it picks out an entity in the real world (not just any child, but one that is alone and that can be uniquely identified by the hearer – and if the hearer cannot identify it, her next question is going to be *What child?*). Informally, we can represent the meaning of (2.2) as '(child =$_1$ alone) =$_2$ unhappy?'. Thus, if children want to ask a question like (2.2) why should they front the syntactic element linked to the first equal sign '$=_1$' if they really want to know whether the 'alone child' is ('$=_2$') unhappy? Now, Mainstream Generative Grammar (Chomsky 1965, 1995, 2000; Radford 1997, 2004) separates phonology, syntax and semantics into independent modules, which means that syntax operates independently of semantics (and phonology). For them, such a semantic explanation is therefore not an option, which explains why Mainstream Generative Grammarians entertain the hypothesis that, based on input, children should generalize a rule that leads to ungrammatical structures such as (2.2b). As I pointed out in Chapter 1, Construction Grammar rejects this modularity hypothesis, emphasizing instead that language is an integral part of human cognition (Hollmann 2013: 493) and that various linguistic levels of description (including phonology, syntax, semantics, pragmatics and information structure (for an overview, see Goldberg 1995, 2011, 2013)) interact in a non-modular fashion.

Beside this theoretical issue, the poverty-of-stimulus argument also has another drawback: as Pullum and Scholz were able to prove, children actually do receive positive input for auxiliary-initial sentences such as *Where's the other dolly that was in here?* by their caregivers (2002: 44). Furthermore, they also show that children encounter positive evidence for other structures usually deemed absent from their input (e.g., irregular plurals in noun–noun compounding such as **mice**-*eater* or auxiliary sequences such as **must have been** *dreaming*; cf. Pullum and Scholz 2002: 24–36).

The primary linguistic input thus appears rich enough for children to build their mental grammars.[1] Not only that, child-directed speech, the specific kind of talk that parents and caregivers use when speaking with babies and small children (which is characterized by, for example, higher pitch, slower tempo, greater rhythmicity, longer pauses and greater amplitude; Clark 2009: 32–50) has also been shown to facilitate language acquisition. But how then do children actually acquire language? How can they move from a mere imitation of what they have heard to a creative use of language that allows them to say things they have never heard before? (So that, when they are adults, they can creatively come up with things like 'I'm all about that bass', 'Heart-breakers gonna break, break, break, break, break' or 'Out on the road today, I saw a DEADHEAD sticker on a Cadillac' – sentences that the writers of these lyrics in all likelihood coined and did not just copy from their parents or peers.) As it turns out, in order to answer these questions, we need to think about why human language evolved in the first place. Or put differently, why humans ended up communicating with constructions.

---

[1] There are also researchers working within the Construction Grammar paradigm, notably Culicover and Jackendoff (2005) that believe that at least some aspects of language are genetic (see Jackendoff (2002: 69–103) for an overview of the arguments for this position, and Tomasello (2003: 284–90) for a critical view). Besides, note that even within the Principles-and-Parameters approach there have been considerable changes as to which purely linguistic features are postulated to be innate (cf. Hauser, Chomsky and Fitch 2002, who claim that only recursion is part of the narrow faculty of language).

2.1.2   Language Acquisition: First Constructions

As recent research has shown (for an overview cf. Tomasello 2014), humans coordinate and communicate with each other in ways that cannot be observed in any other species. Other great apes also exhibit complex social interaction, but a closer analysis of their behaviour reveals that their motivation is ultimately always driven by individuals' personal gains. In contrast to this, even three- or four-year-old children already cooperate with peers in a collaborative way that is not just driven by their own advantage. From an evolutionary perspective, humans thus seem to have evolved as an 'ultra-social animal' (Tomasello 2014): mutual interdependence for survival gave rise to the cognitive ability of shared intentionality, the idea of acting on and understanding the world 'as a kind of plural subject' (Tomasello 2014: 193). Even before linguistic communication emerged, humans evolved two types of cognitive abilities that allowed them to share intentions and that proved vital for the emergence of language (Tomasello 2003, 2009): intention reading and pattern finding. Intention reading means that we as humans are predisposed to understanding that other people do not necessarily think like us and that different people might have different intentions. An important step that helps us guess what another person's intentions might be is to establish joint attention (by pointing at something or looking in the same direction). If we know what another person is focusing on at a specific moment in time, it becomes (slightly) easier to guess what they are thinking. Joint attention is thus an important first step in establishing someone else's intention – and it is also the first important step that every child must take when acquiring his or her first language (cf. Clark 2009: 27–32).

Nevertheless, as we all know, joint attention alone is not enough to guess what someone else is thinking. Another major evolutionary innovation was our ability to communicate with symbols (Deacon 1997; Tomasello 1999); that is, arbitrary and conventional linguistic signs (aka constructions; see Chapter 1). Using speech sounds (forms) to express mental meanings obviously made it much easier to share our intentions with others. Other cognitive evolutionary developments clearly also contributed to the emergence of constructions. That we are able to associate FORM and MEANING as a single holistic unit, a construction, rests to a great extent on a general cognitive process called cross-modal association (Bybee 2013). Despite the fact, for example, that shape, colour and smell are processed in different parts of our brain, we perceive a fragrant red rose as a single object (not to mention the fact that we also imbue it with additional social meanings such as that is considered a token of love in most Western cultures). The use of FORM-MEANING pairings as holistic symbols to share our intentions was thus also supported by the ability of cross-modal association.

Constructions provided a considerable evolutionary advantage. Yet, we still have not answered the question of how children acquire the constructions of their mother tongue or how they end up using language in a creative way that goes beyond the input that they have encountered. This is where the second cognitive ability mentioned above, pattern finding, comes in: from a very early age onwards, humans are really good at detecting patterns. Even three- to four-month-old babies can, for example, already notice that, in general, different types of cats look more similar to each other than to dogs (Rakison and Lawson 2013: 599–602): when babies have been familiarized with cats only, they will spend more time looking at a new dog than at a new cat. Since babies focus longer on new objects than on ones that they are already familiar with, this shows us that even these small children already seem to have formed a mental category for cats based on the similarities of all the cats that they have encountered. While a new cat can quickly be identified as an instance of this mental category, a new dog does not match the previous experience as well and therefore is more interesting and receives more attention.

Next, let us see how intention reading and pattern finding interact in first language acquisition: as Tomasello (2003, 2006, 2009) notes, language acquisition studies (cf., e.g., Diessel and Tomasello 2000; Diessel 2006; Lieven et al. 2003; for an overview Diessel 2013, 2015) show that children first (around the age of fourteen months) use short constructions such as *Bike!* or *More!*. This stage is sometimes called the 'one-word-stage', but this term is actually a bit misleading. Children do not just utter simple word constructions (in which a phonetic FORM such as /baɪk/ is paired with a context-independent, i.e., semantic, MEANING 'bycycle'). Instead, they use these linguistic symbols to express their intentions with respect to a specific situation (cf. Tomasello 2006: 23). When a child says *Bike!*, it might mean that it wants to ride a specific bike. By uttering *More!*, it maybe wants to 'request or describe the recurrence of objects or events' (Tomasello 2003: 37). While the precise meaning of these uses might be child-specific, the prime function of these first constructions (which are also known as 'holophrases') is generally pragmatic: they are an expression of the children's intention, addressed to a specific hearer in a given communicative situation. This is a first indication that the meaning pole of constructions should not just be limited to semantic (that is context-independent) meaning but will also have to include pragmatic (context-dependent) meaning. Later in the book, we will also discuss constructions used by adults that clearly also carry pragmatic information.

Continuing with the development of child language, the next step occurs around the age of eighteen months, when children start tweaking utterance level constructions to fit their communicative needs. They achieve this by one of the following three ways (Tomasello 2003: 308–9):

(a)   taking a substantive construction that they first used as a fixed formula such as *wanna ball* and replacing one of its constituents with a slot (*wanna _*), so that they can express new intentions with this new **item-based construction** (*wanna toy*, *wanna bike*, etc.);

(b)   adding a new element at the beginning or end of an utterance-level construction they have already acquired (e.g., *Throw it!* and *here* becomes *Throw it **here**!*);

(c)   inserting a constituent into an utterance-level construction they have already acquired (German children, for example, insert *auch* ['too'] into positions where nothing else has previously appeared).

From the point of view of linguistic creativity, the most interesting phenomenon is the sudden rise of (a) item-based constructions around the age of 18–20 months. These constructions exhibit the first traces of syntactic marking such as word order or inflectional morphology that signal the role of a participant in a scenario (e.g., 'hitter' and 'hit-object' in *X hit Y* or 'broken entity' in *Y broken*). Importantly, however, Tomasello (2003, 2009) points out that these constructions can have more than one open slot but are always centred on a fixed substantive lexical item (thus only *hit* and not *beat* or *punch* might be used for a scenario where 'X hits/beats/punches Y'; cf. Tomasello 2006: 24). Only later, in the late preschool period do children exhibit utterance-level constructions of adult-like abstractness (such the Passive construction; cf. Tomasello 2003: 316, 2006: 24).

Let us take a closer look at some authentic examples of item-based constructions, which in earlier language acquisition studies were also known as 'pivot schemas/pivot words' (cf. also Diessel 2013, 2015). Number (2.3) and (2.4), for example, give two typical item-based constructions from a child called Andrew (Braine 1963):

(2.3)   Constructs licensed by the *More* X construction (Braine 1963; cited in Braine 1976: 7)
  a.   more car (meaning: 'I want to drive around some more.')
  b.   more cookie (meaning: 'I want another cookie.')
  c.   more hot (meaning: 'I want another hot thing.')
  d.   more read (meaning: 'I want you to keep reading.')
  e.   more sing (meaning: 'I want you to keep singing.')
  f.   . . .

(2.4)   Constructs licensed by the *No* Y construction (Braine 1963; cited in Braine 1976: 7)
  a.   no bed (meaning: 'I don't want to go to bed!')
  b.   no down (meaning: 'Don't put me down!')
  c.   no mama (meaning: 'I don't want to go to mama!')
  d.   no pee (meaning: 'I don't need to pee!')
  e.   no wet (meaning: 'I'm not wet!')
  f. . . .

Andrew clearly uses the *More X* construction in (2.3) to express the desire for something to reoccur. Occasionally, he also seems to have used the construction to simply signal the observed reoccurrence of a thing or event (then *more fish* could mean something like 'there is another fish'). For now, let us just focus on the uses in (2.3). For these we can postulate that Andrew had acquired the following item-based construction in (2.5):

(2.5)   *More X* construction of Andrew (Braine 1963)
        FORM: $[\text{mɔː X}]_1$ ⇔ MEANING: 'I want X to reoccur'$_1$

Andrew's use of the *No* construction in (2.4) is in line with what other acquisition studies (for an overview cf. Clark 2009: 214–17) have observed: children use constructions with *no* quite early to negate some preceding proposal (e.g., in (2.4a) as a reply to the suggestion that he should go to bed or in (2.4d) in response to a suggestion that he should go to the toilet). The item-based construction underlying the constructs in (2.4) is therefore something like this:

(2.6)   *No Y* construction of Andrew (Braine 1963)
          FORM: $[n\text{ə}u\ Y]_1 \Leftrightarrow$ MEANING: 'I do not want Y'$_1$

The two item-based constructions in (2.5) and (2.6) illustrate the step-wise fashion by which more abstract, schematic constructions arise during language acquisition: children do not jump from fully substantive to completely schematic constructions that just contain slots. Instead, they are fairly conservative, keeping at least one substantive item as an anchor/pivot (Gerken 2006; Lieven, Pine, and Baldwin 1997; Tomasello 1992, 2000, 2003; cf. the discussion in Diessel 2015). This does not mean that these first constructions are not creative. As Braine (1976: 8) already pointed out, the constructs in, for example, (2.3a) *more car* 'I want to drive around some more.' or (2.4b) *no down* 'don't put me down' are utterances that children have probably not heard in their input. These item-based constructions thus allow children to express meanings for which the adult language uses more complex constructions that the children have not yet acquired.

   As pointed out above, another way in which children can express more complex meanings is by combining two utterance-level constructions they had previously used independently under a single intonation contour (Clark 2009: 152–5; Diessel 2013: 352). Tomasello (1992: 336–7; see also Clark 2009: 172–4) noted, for example, that his daughter first used *spill-it* as a holophrase after spilling some liquid. Then, after a period of about two months, she combined this utterance-level construction first with single nouns specifying the place of the spill (e.g., *spill-it couch*, *spill-it leg* or *spill-it table*) and a month later with nouns denoting the person who spilled something (e.g., *I spilled-it*). Finally, only after adding the thing that was spilled (e.g., *spilled wheezer milk* 'spilt cat's milk') did she produce more complex patterns in which the verb was combined with two roles of the event (e.g., I_{SPILLER} *spilled the blackboard*$_{\text{LOCATION}}$ 'I spilled (sth.) ?on/?by the blackboard'). Cases such as these where the substantive pivot is a verb (here *spilled*) are also called **verb-island constructions** by Tomasello (2003, 2006, 2009).

   Earlier, we noticed that many of the first pivot constructions that children produce, such as the *More* X or the *No* Y construction, mainly had a pragmatic meaning with which they express requests. Verb-island constructions such as the various *spill-it* constructions discussed by Tomasello are probably also used by children in a similar way (after all, during the first few months, it is the adults who will have to clean up the mess). In addition to this, it turns out that children construct their first two-part verb-island constructions in a way that combines an element that contains given information (and links to what another person just said) and adds new information that the child wants to express (e.g., when a child is asked what it wants to play, it might reply *play*$_{given}$ *MUSEUM*$_{new}$; Clark 2009: 162–6). Consequently, verb-island constructions fulfil a discourse-informational function, allowing children to link their contributions with what their interlocutors said. Finally, verb-island constructions are also interesting because they allow children to express another central aspect of human language: 'the encoding of events and their participants in a clause' (Croft 2012: 1). To illustrate this, imagine a scene in which someone knocks over a cheval glass mirror in a shop that then shatters into a million pieces. Adult speakers of English have multiple ways of encoding this event linguistically. They might, for example, tell a friend who was not there about this event using any of the following sentences (I include here the names of the underlying abstract argument structure constructions that are used to encode important aspects of events and their participants, and which will be discussed in depth in Section 5.1):

(2.7) a.   He broke the mirror. (Transitive construction)
      b.   The mirror broke. (Intransitive construction)
      c.   He broke the mirror into pieces. (Resultative construction)
      d.   The mirror is broken. (Passive Transitive construction)
          (modelled on Diessel 2013: 357)

As we can see in (2.7a–d), English affords adult speakers many competing constructions that essentially describe the same event. The Transitive construction in (2.7a) focuses on the subject (*he*) causing something to happen to the object (*the mirror*). So does the Resultative construction but it also explicitly adds the resulting state of the affected object (ending up in pieces). In contrast, (2.7b) and (2.7d) focus on the affected entity (the mirror) but differ as to whether they highlight the process of it breaking (the Intransitive construction (2.7b)) or the state of it being broken after the event (the Passive Transitive construction (2.7d)). Note that all four sentences can be considered to be true in this case (they all faithfully describe the event as it happened in the real world). The only difference is how speakers end up conceptualizing or construing this event cognitively – how they express their viewpoint ('construal'; Croft 2012: 13–19).

Interestingly, the first verb-island constructions acquired by children also seem to be tied to specific event construals; that is, specific types of argument structure constructions (Diessel 2013: 357; Tomasello 1992: 108–9): Tomasello's daughter, for example, at first only used *break* in the Transitive constructions but not the Intransitive construction or the Resultative construction. The same seems to be true for other type of argument structure constructions. Take, for example, the following three argument structure constructions (adopted from Goldberg 2003: 73; a more detailed analysis of these can be found in Section 5.1):

(2.8)   Intransitive Motion construction
        FORM: $[SBJ_1\ V_2\ OBL_3]_4$
        $\Leftrightarrow$
        MEANING: 'X_1 MOVES$_{BY\ MANNER=V2}$ $Y_{PATH/LOC3}$'$_4$

Examples:
He$_1$ ran [out of the house]$_3$.
[The fly]$_1$ buzzed [into the room]$_3$.
[People]$_1$ strolled [along the river]$_3$.

(2.9)   Caused Motion construction
FORM: [SBJ$_1$ V$_2$ OBJ$_3$ OBL$_4$]$_5$
⇔
MEANING: 'X$_1$ CAUSES Y$_3$ TO MOVE Z$_{path/loc4}$ BY V$_2$-ING'$_5$
Examples:
She$_1$ kicked [her shoes]$_3$ [under the sofa]$_4$.
He$_1$ blew [the foam]$_3$ [off the cappuccino]$_4$.
They$_1$ drove [him]$_3$ [to Texas]$_4$.

(2.10)   Ditransitive construction
FORM: [SBJ$_1$ V$_2$ OBJ$_3$ OBJ$_4$]$_5$
⇔
MEANING: 'X$_1$ CAUSES Y$_3$ TO RECEIVE Z$_4$ BY V$_2$-ING'$_5$
Examples:
She$_1$ sent him$_3$ [an email]$_4$.
Jack$_1$ passed her$_3$ [the salt]$_4$.
[The waiter]$_1$ served them$_3$ [their dinner]$_4$.

The Intransitive Motion construction (2.8) describes a scene in which the subject moves along a path or to/from a location; the Caused Motion construction (2.9) depicts an event in which a subject causes an object to move along a path or to/from a location; and the Ditransitive construction portrays a situation in which the subject causes the object to receive something (2.10). As the examples in (2.8)–(2.10) illustrate, the mental grammars of English adult native speakers seem to license quite a range of different verbs in these argument structure constructions (e.g., *ran, buzzed, strolled* in (2.8), *kicked, blew, drove* in (2.9) and *sent, passed* and *served* in (2.10)). In fact, preliminary research indicates that adult argument structure constructions do not exhibit strong verb-island effects: Stefanowitsch and Gries (2003) for example found that no single verb accounted for more than 10 per cent of all instances of any argument structure construction they investigated (cf. also Goldberg 2006: 76–7).

Children, on the other hand, clearly display a strong preference of verb-island constructions when they first produce argument structure constructions: the verb pivots for their initial Intransitive Motion, Caused Motion and Ditransitive construction are highly frequent general-purpose verbs, namely, *go, put* and *give*, respectively (Clark 2009: 170; Goldberg 2006: 77–9). Instead of fully abstract argument structure constructions such as (2.8)–(2.10), they instead appear to rely on the following verb-specific argument structure constructions:

(2.11)   GO Intransitive Motion construction
FORM: [SBJ$_1$ GO$_2$ OBL$_3$]$_4$
⇔
MEANING: 'X$_1$ MOVES_BY_GOING$_2$ Y$_{path/loc3}$'$_4$

(2.12)   PUT Caused Motion construction
          FORM: $[SBJ_1\ PUT_2\ OBJ_3\ OBL_4]_5$
          $\Leftrightarrow$
          MEANING: 'X_1 CAUSES Y_3 TO MOVE Z_{PATH/LOC_4} BY PUTTING$_2$'$_5$

(2.13)   GIVE Ditransitive construction
          FORM: $[SBJ_1\ GIVE_2\ OBJ_3\ OBJ_4]$
          $\Leftrightarrow$
          MEANING: 'X_1 CAUSES Y_3 TO RECEIVE Z_4 BY GIVING$_2$'

So, argument structure constructions arise first from more specific verb-island constructions such as (2.11)–(2.13) that are centred on highly frequent verbs. The meaning of these verb pivots also seems to provide a gateway to the abstract meaning of the argument structure construction: the prototypical meaning of *go* involves movement of a participant, *put* denotes placing an object somewhere and *give* entails someone causing another person to receive something. *Go*, *put* and *give* therefore act as highly frequent anchors that due to their prototypical meaning provide a stepping stone for the acquisition of more abstract argument structure constructions (Goldberg 2006: 77; Slobin 1985 – though note that in Section 5.1 we will have to ask ourselves if speakers really need abstract constructional templates such as (2.8)–(2.10) or whether adults simply have more verb-specific argument structure constructions than children).

On top of that, there is also evidence that input plays a role here: unlike in adult-to-adult communication, where no verb-islands were found (see above), the child-directed speech of parents and adult caretakers exhibits a tendency to also employ *go*, *put* and *give* more frequently than other verbs in their respective prototypical argument structure construction: Goldberg, Casenhiser and Sethuraman (2004), for example, examined the different verbs used in Intransitive Motion, Caused Motion and Ditransitive constructions that mothers produced when interacting with their children. They found that:

• 39 different verb types were used in the Intransitive Motion construction, but that *go* was by far the most frequent one (accounting for 39 per cent of all Intransitive Motion tokens);

• 43 different verb types were used in the Caused Motion construction, but that *put* was by far the most frequent one (accounting for 38 per cent of all Caused Motion tokens);

• 13 different verbs were used in the Ditransitive construction, but that *give* was by far the most frequent one (accounting for 20 per cent of all Ditransitive tokens).

(adapted from: Goldberg 2006: 76)

These results obviously raise the question whether parents and caretakers unconsciously adjust their language to provide children with the optimal input for the step-by-step acquisition of more abstract constructions. From a usage-based perspective, a very important issue therefore concerns the frequency of structures that children are exposed to as well as the cognitive mechanisms that allow them to abstract more general templates from their input.

2.1.3   Exemplar Storage and Usage-Based Construction Grammar

So far, we have seen that input plays a very important role in language acquisition, but that there also comes a time when children move beyond reproducing things they have heard before (moving from holophrases to more and more abstract constructions). How can Usage-based Construction Grammar approaches explain these findings? In order to answer this question, we need to first look at how humans store specific instances of experience (seeing a specific cat, say a British Shorthair) and how they generalize from similar types of experience (seeing several other cats, for example a Burmilla or a Cornish Rex[2]) to create an abstract mental category ('cat') that allows them to say for any future animal they meet whether it is a cat or not. In a similar way, after encountering numerous specific utterances such as *He gave her a book.* and *They sent me a present.*, English speakers are able to construct and understand new utterances such as **you can WhatsApp me the pics** and *I'll upload the pics for you*[3] ('You$_1$ can causes me$_3$ to receive [the pics]$_4$ by_WhatsApping$_2$') probably because they had earlier created an abstract category for the Ditransitive construction (2.10).

Remember that from an early age onwards, babies and small children are already really good at detecting patterns and therefore seem to start building up their first mental categories (Rakison and Lawson 2013: 599–602). As their name already suggests, so-called **exemplar models** of classification (Nosofsky 1988, 2011) argue that these categories are actually based on large clouds of stored exemplars: in these approaches, it is assumed that each experience you make leaves a detailed trace in your memory: for any cat you encounter, you store detailed information on what that cat looked like, what it did, how it smelled, where and when you saw it, etc. Similarly, for any linguistic utterance that you encounter, you also store very detailed information:

> This information consists of phonetic detail, including redundant and variable features, the lexical items and constructions used, the meaning, inferences made from this meaning and from the context, and properties of the social, physical and linguistic context.   (Bybee 2010: 14)

How is all this linguistic information stored in our minds? Drawing on neurological and psycholinguistic evidence, Goldberg recently argued that

> constructions are understood to be emergent clusters of lossy memory traces that are aligned within our high (hyper!) dimensional conceptual space on the basis of shared form, function, and contextual dimensions.   (Goldberg 2019: 7)

---

[2] For pictures of these different breeds of cats, cf. http://en.wikipedia.org/wiki/List_of_cat_breeds [last accessed 02 January 2021].

[3] Source: www.windowcleaningforums.co.uk/topic/32731-help-advice-on-equipment-new-starter/ [last accessed 28 June 2021].

In other words, constructs lead to complex memory traces that associate a FORM (which includes rich phonetic data) with MEANING (including its function as well as social and physical context features). Moreover, memory is, of course, always selective and not all aspects of experience are completely recorded (Goldberg 2013: 27). So, these memory traces are only partial abstractions of the actual experience, and like all aspects of memory susceptible to being forgotten ('lossy') over time if they do not receive sufficient activation. From this perspective, the FORM-MEANING constructional templates used in this book can be seen as simplified representations of this complex neurological network of memory traces. (Besides, Section 5.1, e.g., explores the question of how abstract the representation of argument structure constructions have to be to explain the observed patterns of usage.)

According to exemplar models, linguistic (as well as non-linguistic) memories thus require substantial storage capacity since some apparently redundant information that you do not need for future recognition of an exemplar of a category is also stored (for example where you saw a cat or whether a Ditransitive construction is uttered by a male or female speaker seem irrelevant – though the latter will become important again when we think about the cognitive basis of sociolinguistic variation in Chapter 7). Luckily for us, human neural storage capacity is much greater than previously believed (Bybee 2013: 54). Moreover, as we all know, humans are also really good at forgetting irrelevant detail. The way we do this is by getting rid of information that is not reinforced by repetition or recency (Bybee 2013: 54). In other words, since most cats that we encounter will have a similar shape, this information will be strengthened in all exemplars in our mental cloud, while the specific location that you only ever saw one cat at (say in front of your house) will become less important for the entire exemplar cloud (see also Goldberg 2006: 45–9, 2019). Besides, depending on your experience, your idea of what a prototypical cat looks like might differ from that of other people: if the majority of the cats you encounter have fur, then you will expect your average cat to also have fur. If you have encountered mostly hairless cats, then fur will not be a prototypical feature for you. Finally, if as a child you only encounter one type of cat in your neighbourhood (for example Bombay cats[4]) then your mental category of cats will require them to have black coat, toes and nose. In these cases, we say that one specific type of exemplar (here Bombay cats) has a **high token frequency** (you see that one type over and over again). Instead, if you encounter many types of differently coloured cats you will have a more abstract prototype that will not be limited to one colour only. We then say that a category has a **high type frequency** (that is, you frequently encounter many different types).

---

[4] Cf. http://en.wikipedia.org/wiki/Bombay_cat [last accessed 02 January 2021].

Repetition and recency are therefore important factors that shape your exemplar categories and potentially lead to prototype effects. This is true for non-linguistic knowledge and, in line with usage-based linguistic approaches, should also be true for linguistic knowledge; that is, the storage of constructions. Consequently, type and token frequency are also expected to play a role for the mental storage of constructions (which is often also referred to as the cognitive **entrenchment** of constructions): take, for example, greeting formulas in English. In similar situations (early in the day and late in the day, respectively), people will hear greetings such as *Good morning* and *Good evening* over and over again. All of the individual constructs that speakers encounter will be stored as exemplars, with people registering for example recurring pragmatic constraints concerning the time of day at which either formula is conventionally acceptable in their speech community. At the respective time of day, these formulas thus have a high token frequency (Croft and Cruse 2004: 292–3; Langacker 1987: 59–60), but – like the Bombay cat example above – do not display any variation (in Standard English, for example, people do not frequently utter *Happy morning* or *Nice morning* as alternative ways of greeting each other – and if they do, then it usually a marked choice that in itself is meaningful). As we saw above, Ditransitive constructs, on the other hand, have a high type frequency, that is, they can be encountered with many different lexicalizations (such as *John gave Bill a book*, *Peter sent Mary a letter*, *She forwarded him the mail ...*), all of which share a common meaning ('X causes Y to receive Z by V-ing'). This variation of types therefore seems to be the key to the entrenchment of abstract grammatical patterns (Goldberg 2006: 39, 98–101; see also Bybee 1985; Croft and Cruse 2004: 308–13): since native speakers encounter many different types of verbs as well as participants in these exemplars, they start schematizing each structural position for which they can identify a form slot that is symbolically associated with a corresponding meaning element (resulting in the abstract Ditransitive construction (2.10) FORM: $[SBJ_1 \; V_2 \; OBJ_3 \; OBJ_4]_5 \Leftrightarrow$ MEANING: 'X_1 CAUSES Y_3 TO RECEIVE Z_4 BY V_2-ING'$_5$; a more detailed discussion of argument structure constructions is given in Section 5.1).

As we have seen in the previous section, children do not start schematizing all parts of a substantive construction in one go. Instead, keeping some parts phonologically fixed (so-called pivot/verb-island positions), they only gradually schematize other slots of a construction (mainly those expressing the participants of an event). The first argument structure constructions that children, for example, produce are verb-specific ones in which high frequency, prototypical verbs (*go*, *put* and *give*) act as verb-islands while the participants are schematic slots (which already allows children to use these verb-specific constructions as templates to talk about a range of Intransitive Motion, Caused Motion and Ditransitive events). Earlier, we noted that this to a certain degree reflects the specific input that children receive: argument structure constructions in the child-directed speech of parents and adult caretakers

exhibit considerable type frequency (that is, many different types of participants as well as verbs are used by adults with Intransitive Motion, Caused
Motion and Ditransitive constructions). At the same time, while there is
variation in verb slot, the child-directed speech of adults shows a strong
preference for high frequency, prototypical verbs (*go*, *put* and *give*) – a much
greater preference than can be observed in adult-to-adult speech. In other
words, while children encounter argument structure constructions with a high
type frequency, their input also has one type with a verb that can be considered
the prototypical instantiation of the construction in question that has a high
token frequency.

Children might, therefore, first produce item-based constructions because the
input that they receive favours such partly schematic, partly substantive generalizations. In addition to illustrating again the importance of the interaction of input
and domain-general cognitive principles, this observation led Casenhiser and
Goldberg (2005) to raise an interesting hypothesis: could it also be that this
specific type of input – high type frequency of a pattern together with a high
token frequency of one prototypical pivot/verb-island construction – actually
helps children create more abstract and schematic constructions? In order to
answer this question, they designed the following ingenious experiment.

They wanted to test how different types of input frequency affect how
successfully children learn a novel construction. For this experiment, they could
obviously not use existing English constructions, since they would not have been
able to rule out that all children taking part in the experiment had not previously
learnt this construction (or at least that some had already heard it from an adult,
while others had not – in this case the results from the study would have been
impossible to interpret since you could never be sure whether they just depend on
the variables tested in the experiment or on previous experience with the
construction by some subjects). So, in order to test their hypothesis, they had
to test a novel, non-English construction:

(2.14)   non-Standard English Appearance construction
            FORM: [NP$_1$ NP$_2$ NONSENSE$_{V3}$-*o*-TENSE^5]$_4$
            ⇔
            MEANING: 'NP$_1$ TENSE(appear$_3$) on/into/etc. NP$_2$'$_4$
            (adjusted from Casenhiser and Goldberg 2005: 502)

The non-Standard English construction in (2.14) thus describes an event in which
the first participant (NP$_1$) appears, for example, on the second participant (NP$_2$).
(2.15a) and (2.15b) give two examples constructs of this construction that were
used as stimuli in the experiment (from Casenhiser and Goldberg 2005: 502):

(2.15) a.   The rabbit the hat **moopo**ed
             'the rabbit **appear**-ed **on** a hat'

---

[5] In the experiment, stimuli sentences contained present tense nonsense verb forms (for example,
moopo-s) as well as past tense verb forms (for example, *moopo-ed*).

b.   The sailor the pond **neebod**
  'the sailor **sailed onto** the pond (from out of sight)'

For the experiment they recruited fifty-one children (aged 5–7). In order to see how well these learnt the novel construction, they first ran a short training session, which took less than three minutes. In this session, the children were split into three experimental groups. All children in all groups twice saw eight short movie clips with puppets that depicted various appearance events that fitted the construed meaning of (2.14) (for example, a rabbit occurring on a hat or a frog dropping onto a box[6]). The difference between the three groups only concerned the type of input the children received for the novel, non-Standard English Appearance construction (cf. Casenhiser and Goldberg 2005: 502–3):

• The children in Group 1 (called BALANCED FREQUENCY) saw the eight films and heard corresponding descriptions of the events using constructs of the non-Standard English Appearance construction. The input these children received was characterized by high type frequency, since it contained a balanced set of five different novel verbs.
• The children in Group 2 (called SKEWED FREQUENCY) saw the eight films and heard corresponding descriptions of the events using constructs of the non-Standard English Appearance construction. The input these children received was characterized by high type frequency as well as high token frequency of a prototypical pivot, since it contained a set of five different novel verbs of which one occurred four times.
• Finally, the children in Group 3 (called CONTROL) only saw the eight films without any verbal input.

Group 3 was therefore a classic control group that enabled Casenhiser and Goldberg to establish a baseline for the results for children that received no input of the tested construction. More interestingly, the other two groups allowed them to test whether the special type of input frequency observed in child-directed speech (high type frequency plus high token frequency of a prototypical pivot; represented in the experiment by the SKEWED FREQUENCY Group 2) actually helps children learn a construction better than just high type frequency (represented in the experiment by the BALANCED FREQUENCY Group 1).

Table 2.1 illustrates this difference of the two groups by listing the actual stimuli used in the training session. As you can see, the children in the BALANCED FREQUENCY group encountered three verbs in two constructs (*moopo*; *vako*; *suto*) and two verbs once (*keebo*; *fego*), while the SKEWED FREQUENCY group heard one verb four times (*moopo*) and the other four verbs only once (*vako*; *suto*; *keebo*; *fego*):

---

[6] See https://youtu.be/BcNSzJTc3gE?t=477 [last accessed 12 NOVEMBER 2021] for an example clip that was used in the study.

Table 2.1 *Training stimuli (adapted from Casenhiser and Goldberg 2005: 503)*

Scene displayed on video	BALANCED FREQUENCY (2 *moopo*; 2 *vako*; 2 *suto*; 1 *keebo*; 1 *fego*)	SKEWED FREQUENCY (**4** *moopo*; 1 *vako*; 1 *suto*; 1 *keebo*; 1 *fego*)
The rabbit appears on a hat.	*The rabbit the hat moopoed.*	*The rabbit the hat **moopoed**.*
The monster wiggles out from under a cloth.	*The monster the cloth keeboed.*	*The monster the cloth keeboed.*
The frog drops down onto a box.	*The frog the box vakoed.*	*The frog the box **moopoed**.*
The king drops down into a chair.	*The king the chair vakoed.*	*The king the chair vakoed.*
The sun rises into the sky.	*The sun the sky fegoed.*	*The sun the sky fegoed.*
The queen rolls onto the stage.	*The queen the stage sutoed.*	*The queen the stage sutoed.*
The bug appears on a table.	*The bug the table moopoed.*	*The bug the table **moopoed**.*
The ball rolls into the room.	*The ball the room sutoed.*	*The ball the room **moopoed**.*

Casenhiser and Goldberg then proceeded to the main part of the experiment in which all three groups saw 'two *new* film clips presented side-by-side on the screen and heard a sentence describing one of the clips' (Casenhiser and Goldberg 2005: 503). On one screen, a character appeared in the scene (a scenario that fits the meaning construal of the non-Standard English Appearance construction; clip A). On the other screen, a character performed an action while remaining in constant view (a scenario that did not fit the new construction; clip B). All in all, there were twelve trials: six in which subjects heard a description of the appearance event depicted in clip A 'using a new novel verb (i.e., one that was not heard during training) in the appearance construction (e.g., 'the sailor the pond neebos')' (Casenhiser and Goldberg 2005: 503), and six in which the children heard a novel verb in a Standard English Transitive construction frame (NP_1 NONSENSE$_V$-o-TENSE NP_2). In order to see which constructions the subjects matched with which event, the children were instructed to touch the screen that they thought they heard an audio description of.

So how successful were the three groups in matching the right input (the non-Standard English Appearance construction) to the right scene (the screen depicting an appearance event)? Example (2.16) summarizes the main result:

(2.16)   Main results from Casenhiser and Goldberg (2005: 504):
          control < balanced frequency < skewed frequency

On average, the CONTROL group correctly chose just about three out of the six non-Standard English Appearance constructions. Since they had not heard the construction during the training phase, this result is as expected: we would not expect them to get more than 50 per cent right (in an experiment where they have a 50:50 chance to start with, since they are forced to click on one of two screens). The BALANCED FREQUENCY group already performs significantly better than the CONTROL group, a result that, at first, seems unspectacular. Remember, however, that the training phase of the experiment only ran for less than three minutes, which shows how little input appears to be needed for children to create an exemplar cloud for a number of similar constructions. Besides, since new verbs were used in the experiment that the children had not heard in the training phase, they could not just rely on the specific constructs they had previously encountered but needed some type of constructional abstraction to make the correct choices. Finally, the SKEWED FREQUENCY performed even significantly better than the BALANCED FREQUENCY group – a first, impressive result that the special kind of input (high type frequency including one high token frequency prototypical pivot) provided by parents and caretakers might actually (unconsciously) be ideally tailored to the needs of children. As Casenhiser and Goldberg's experiment showed, however, this special kind of input is a sufficient but not a necessary condition for learning abstract constructional templates, since these also seemed to emerge in the BALANCED FREQUENCY group that was just exposed to a high type frequency of the construction (cf. also Goldberg 2006: 89–90). High type frequency, on the other hand, can be said to be a sufficient and necessary condition for the entrenchment of an abstract, schematic construction (though as we will see in Chapter 3, even patterns with a low type frequency can sometimes be extended provided they exhibit a high degree of semantic coherence; cf. Barðdal 2008).

Type and token frequency of the linguistic input, therefore, facilitate the mental schematization and categorization of more abstract constructions. Another domain-general cognitive process that is also at work during this process is **analogy** (Tomasello 2003: 297–300, 2009: 86): 'analogical mapping involves recognizing a common relational system between two situations and generating further inferences guided by these commonalities' (Gentner and Smith 2013: 669). Let me return to the Ditransitive construction to illustrate the effect analogical mapping has on learning constructions:

(2.17) a.   FORM: [The lawyer]$_1$ sent$_2$ [his client]$_3$ [a letter]$_4$.
      $\Leftrightarrow$
      MEANING: '[The lawyer]$_1$ CAUSED [his client]$_3$ TO RECEIVE [a letter]$_4$
            BY SEND$_2$-ING'

b.   FORM: [Romeo]$_1$ sent$_2$ Julia$_3$ [a rose]$_4$.
      $\Leftrightarrow$
      MEANING: '[Romeo]$_1$ CAUSED [Julia]$_3$ TO RECEIVE [a rose]$_4$
            BY SEND$_2$-ING'

When speakers are exposed to two verbalizations of different sending events such as (2.17a) and (2.17b), they detect the similarities between the constructs via analogical mapping: in both utterances, the sending event is initiated by a sender (SBJ$_1$) that causes a recipient (OBJ$_3$) to receive some kind of entity (OBJ$_4$). As trivial as this may seem, this process already helps speakers to learn about how sending events are construed in their language. If you think about it, any sending event in real life involves much more than just the three participants mentioned in (2.17a) and (2.17b): it takes place at a specific time (*I sent the letter* *to you last week*$_{\text{TIME}}$.[7]) and the entity being sent is usually transferred from one place to another (*I sent wood from Illinois*$_{\text{SOURCE}}$ *to California*$_{\text{GOAL}}$.[8]). Yet, in English, the information that is given in most verbalizations of sending events includes the sender, the recipient and/or the entity that is sent, but not the time of sending or the source[9]. Adopting a Frame Semantic view (cf. Croft 2012: 11–13; Croft and Cruse 2004: chapter 2; Fillmore 1977, 1982, 1985), many Construction Grammar approaches assume that this kind of knowledge is represented cognitively in so-called **semantic frames**: knowledge structures that contain information on those participant roles that are highlighted or 'profiled' by a concept (e.g., the sender, recipient and entity that is sent in the SENDING frame) as well as all semantically presupposed, 'background' information of event types (including, e.g., the fact that sending events involve transfer from a source, a fact that normally is not verbalized in English; cf. Croft 2012: 11).

Similarly, upon an analogical comparison of the participants of (2.18a) and (2.18b), speakers are able to conclude that HAND Ditransitive constructions describe an event in which a person instigating the action (SBJ$_1$) causes a recipient (OBJ$_3$) to receive something (OBJ$_4$):

(2.18) a. FORM: [She]$_1$ handed$_2$ [me]$_3$ [a glass of cider]$_4$.[10]

⇔

MEANING: '[She]$_1$ CAUSED [me]$_3$ TO RECEIVE [a glass of cider]$_4$ BY HAND$_2$-ING'

b. FORM: [I]$_1$ handed$_2$ [him]$_3$ [two new pound notes from my purse]$_4$.[11]

⇔

MEANING: '[I]$_1$ CAUSED [him]$_3$ TO RECEIVE [two new pound notes from my purse]$_4$ BY HAND$_2$-ING'

In a next step, an analogical comparison of the participant roles of (2.17a,b) and (2.18a,b) reveals further similarities: in both semantic frames, SBJ$_1$ acts as an active source that causes a recipient (OBJ$_3$) to receive something (OBJ$_4$). Thus, analogical mapping[12] of the specific types of participant roles of SENDING and HANDING/GIVING frames triggers generalizations of roles that characterize the common semantic properties of elements of more abstract constructions, leading

---

[7] Source: https://framenet2.icsi.berkeley.edu/fnReports/data/frameIndex.xml?frame=Sending&banner= [last accessed 02 January 2021].

[8] Source: https://framenet2.icsi.berkeley.edu/fnReports/data/frameIndex.xml?frame=Sending&banner= [last accessed 02 January 2021].

[9] Cf. https://framenet2.icsi.berkeley.edu/fnReports/data/frameIndex.xml?frame=Sending&banner= [last accessed 02 January 2021].

[10] Source: https://framenet2.icsi.berkeley.edu/fnReports/data/lu/lu8905.xml?mode=lexentry [last accessed 02 January 2021].

[11] Source: https://framenet2.icsi.berkeley.edu/fnReports/data/lu/lu8905.xml?mode=lexentry [last accessed 02 January 2021].

[12] As Traugott and Trousdale (2013: 37–40) point out, there is an important difference between analogical thinking (recognizing similarities in two structures) and what they call 'analogization', the actual cognitive mechanism that leads to the entrenchment of a new structure (for more details cf. also Chapter 7).

to abstract semantic roles such as agent, recipient and theme for the abstract Ditransitive construction (2.10): FORM: $[SBJ_1\ V_2\ OBJ_3\ OBJ_4]_5 \Leftrightarrow$ MEANING: 'AGENT$_1$ CAUSES RECIPIENT$_3$ TO RECEIVE THEME$_4$ BY V$_2$-ING'$_5$.

On top of an analogical generalization of semantic roles, the comparison of constructs such as (2.17a,b) and (2.18a,b) also allows learners of a language to form generalizations about the types of elements that appear in the schematic slots of a construction: a so-called **functionally-based distributional analysis** (Tomasello 2003: 301) of the types of syntactic elements that, for example, appear in the subject SBJ$_1$ slot of the various Ditransitive constructs above reveals that these include, *inter alia*, proper nouns (*Romeo* (2.17b)), pronouns (*she* (2.18a), *I* (2.18b)) as well as *the* + noun sequences (*the lawyer* (2.17a)). Due to the fact that all these elements in the same schematic slot share a similar communicative function in utterances (they are all referring expressions that allow hearers to pick out entities in the real word), a paradigmatic category such as 'Noun Phrase' gradually emerges (see Chapter 4). Since speakers will also come across Noun Phrases such as *the lawyer* and *he* in other types of constructions (for example, *The lawyer yawned. / He yawned.*), this paradigmatic category will become entrenched independently of the constructions it was first detected in.

So far, we have seen how children can use the constructs in their input to generalize to more abstract and creative schematic constructions through type and token frequency, categorization, analogy and functionally based distributional analysis. Yet, how do they manage not to go overboard and generalize too much beyond their input? There are, for example, constructs that are currently not possible in English, despite the fact that both type frequency as well as domain-general cognitive principles seem to point towards a possible realisation of a construction (Tomasello 2009: 81–4). Take, for example, the pairs of sentences in (2.19) and (2.20) (adopted from Tomasello 2009: 81; cf. also Goldberg 2006: 26–33, 2019):

(2.19) a.   He gave/sent/bequeathed his books to the library.
             (construct licensed by the Caused Motion construction)
       b.   He gave/sent/bequeathed the library his books.
             (construct licensed by the Ditransitive constructions)

(2.20) a.   He donated his books to the library.
             (construct licensed by the Caused Motion construction)
       b.   *He donated the library his books.
             (construct **not** licensed by the Ditransitive constructions)

As we can see in (2.19) verbs from the semantic frame of GIVING[13] such as *give*, *send*, *bequeath* can, amongst other contexts, appear in two constructions that differ slightly as to how they construe a GIVING event: (2.19b) are all instances

---

[13] Cf. https://framenet2.icsi.berkeley.edu/fnReports/data/frameIndex.xml?frame=Giving&banner= [last accessed 02 January 2021].

of the Ditransitive construction (2.10: FORM: [SBJ$_1$ V$_2$ OBJ$_3$ OBJ$_4$]$_5$ ⇔ MEANING: 'X$_1$ CAUSES Y$_3$ TO RECEIVE Z$_4$ BY V$_2$-ING'$_5$), while (2.19a) are instances of the Caused Motion construction (2.9: FORM: [SBJ$_1$ V$_2$ OBJ$_3$ OBL$_4$]$_5$ ⇔ MEANING: 'X$_1$ CAUSES Y$_3$ TO MOVE Z$_{PATH/LOC4}$ BY V$_2$-ING'$_5$). While the verbs in (2.19a,b) all activate the GIVING frame, only the examples in (2.19a) thus imply a caused motion to a location (the construal of this construction emphasizes that the book must physically be taken from one place to another and the instances in (2.19a) are therefore similar in meaning to other Caused Motion constructs such as *She sent the book to Chicago*.; Goldberg 1995, 2003: 221, 2013: 20).

This, first of all, explains why English speakers possess two alternative ways of expressing the same event type: while (2.19a) and (2.19b) are roughly synonymous, the two options crucially differ as to their construal of the GIVING frame (the Ditransitive construction emphases actual or metaphorical transfer, while the Caused Motion construction highlights caused motion to a location). What it does not explain is the syntactic behaviour of the verb *donate* in (2.20): the meaning of *donate* clearly draws on the GIVING frame.[14] Yet, unlike the verbs in (2.19), *donate* can only occur in the Caused Motion construction but not in the Ditransitive construction (2.20b). The answer to this question seems to be that this is just an idiosyncrasy of the lexeme *donate* (it is an arbitrary convention that has been entrenched in the speech community). However, if type frequency and domain-general process interact in the way we have seen, why do adult speakers not occasionally produce constructs such as (2.20b) via analogy with the other GIVING verbs in (2.19)? And what about children, do they produce such patterns?

Well, sometimes adult speakers do in fact occasionally produce *donate* Ditransitive constructs:

(2.21)   A FOUR-YEAR-OLD boy with cerebral palsy who was left heartbroken when Comet refused his £500 iPad gift card is celebrating – after **a pensioner donated him the cash**.[15]

Nevertheless, Ditransitive constructs with *donate* such as (2.21) appear much less frequently compared to *donate* Caused Motion constructs. Consequently, the Caused Motion uses of *donate* will have a higher type/token frequency, which means that they are much more deeply entrenched. Technically speaking that is not really an explanation (if *donate* is conventionally realised in the Caused Motion construction, then it is no surprise that this use is the much more frequent one). This is just an arbitrary fact of English grammar that has to be learnt by native speakers and second language learners alike.

---

[14] In FrameNet terms, it is a **lexical unit** that evokes this frame: https://framenet2.icsi.berkeley.edu/fnReports/data/frameIndex.xml?frame=Giving [last accessed 02 January 2021].
[15] Source: www.thesun.co.uk/archives/news/1028292/ [last accessed 02 January 2021].

Still the question remains how children can avoid making too many 'mistakes'; that is overgeneralize, beyond what is considered acceptable by adult native speakers. The simplest answer would be that 'children only learn verbs for the constructions in which they have heard them' (Tomasello 2009: 82). Children would therefore be highly conservative learners that do not generalize beyond the input they receive. We have already seen that this is not completely true (cf., e.g., the non-adult pivot constructions (2.3a) *more car* 'I want to drive around some more.' or (2.4b) *no down* 'don't put me down' above). Yet, first language acquisition research suggests that it is at least true for the earliest stages of language learning (Diessel 2013: 357; Tomasello 2009: 82). Later, particularly during the age of three to five years, children overgeneralize systematically. Take, for example, the following attested utterances from Bowerman (1982; cit. in Diessel 2013: 358):

(2.22) a.   Kendall **fall** that toy. (child aged 2;3 [= 2 years and 3 months])
     b.   Who **deaded** my kitty cat? (child aged 2;6)
     c.   Don't **giggle** me. (child aged 3;0)

In (2.22), the child clearly overextends intransitive verbs (verbs used without an object; cf. *The toy falls. / My kitty cat is dead. / He giggles.*) to transitive scenarios (in which a subject causes the toy to fall, the cat to die and the child to giggle, respectively). If you go back to the examples in (2.7), you will see that there are indeed English verbs that can appear in the Intransitive as well as the Transitive construction in this way (cf. *The vase broke.* vs *He broke the vase.*). So, once children move beyond their initial conservative use of one verb-island that is tied to one type of argument structure construction, they do exhibit the kind of overgeneralizations expected by analogical mapping.

After the age of five, however, the number of such non-adult overgeneralizations decreases significantly. A major reason for this is the existence of another cognitive process called **pre-emption** that restricts schematization and analogy (Boyd and Goldberg 2011; Goldberg 2006: 94–8, 2011, 2019; Tomasello 2003: 300): if there are two different ways, Form X and Form Y, of expressing a message and a speaker uses Form X, the hearer will assume that 'there was a reason for that choice related to the speaker's specific communicative intention' (Tomasello 2003: 300). For the constructs above this simply means that children at one point will notice that the events for which they expect constructs such as (2.22), adult speakers actually use alternative constructions that must therefore be conventionally used in the speech community:

(2.23) a.   Kendall **dropped** that toy.
     b.   Who **killed** my kitty cat? (child aged 2;6)
     c.   Don't **tickle** me. (child aged 3;0)

Similarly, for the GIVING verb *donate*, children will unconsciously register that this verb is used in the Caused Motion construction even in cases where there is no implication of a caused motion to a location meaning; that is, when they would expect a Ditransitive construction: cf., for example, *He donated his money to charity.*, in which charity does not denote a specific location, but merely the abstract recipient of the money. Consequently, they will refrain from using *donate* in the Ditransitive construction.

Finally, on top of entrenchment and pre-emption, some constructions have language-specific semantic constraints (Pinker 1989; Tomasello 2009: 82–3) that children will have to infer from the input. English, for example, does not allow all types of motion verbs in the Caused Motion construction (examples (2.24) and (2.25) adapted from Tomasello 2009: 82):

(2.24) a.   I walked the dog to the station.
       b.   I drove my car to New York.

(2.25) a.   *He came her to school.
       b.   *She falled him down.

As the above examples show, verbs that denote 'manner of locomotion' (e.g., *walk* and *drive* in (2.24a,b)) can be used in the Caused Motion construction. In contrast to this, verbs denoting 'motion in a lexically specified direction' (e.g., *come* and *fall* in (2.25a,b)) cannot combine with this construction (Tomasello 2009: 82–3). As with all other constructional properties, children must learn such semantic constraints via an interaction of input frequency, pre-emption and analogical generalization of the meaning of the constructs observed in this construction.

Domain-general cognitive processes such as entrenchment via type and token frequency, categorization, analogy and functionally-based distributional analysis thus allow children to generalize beyond the input they receive. Their generalizations, however, are constrained first (up until the age of about three) by a conservative use of entrenched patterns. After a period of overgeneralization, from the age of about four, two other cognitive mechanisms, namely pre-emption and knowledge of semantic subclasses of verbs then start to constrain the extension of constructional schemas (Brooks and Tomasello 1999a, 1999b; Brooks et al. 1999; Tomasello 2009: 83–4).

2.2   Usage-Based Constructions

2.2.1   The Internal Structure of Constructions

In Chapter 1, we defined constructions as 'an arbitrary pairing of (phonological/syntactic) form and meaning that [are] stored in a speaker's mental lexicon'. After we have looked more closely at how speakers, and children in particular, actually store constructions in their mind, we are now in a position to refine our definition of these mental FORM-MEANING pairings. In contrast to simple Saussurean signs, the mental representations of constructions deriving from the abstraction and generalization of input data are much richer (Goldberg

2019). In Chapter 1, for example, we already saw that the FORM pole of constructions includes phonetic and phonological detail (concerning the pronunciation of substantive elements or the intonation contour of a construction), morphological (for example, whether a morpheme combines with adjectives or nouns) as well as syntactic information (for example, whether a slot in an argument structure construction functions as subject or object). Similarly, the MEANING pole of a construction can contain not only semantic but also pragmatic properties (for example, concerning the intention/illocution of a speaker that is expressed by a construction; take for example the request pivot constructions in (2.3) and (2.4)) or whether a noun phrase introduces a new referent to the discourse or refers to an entity already given; cf. [*A man*]_{new information} *enters a bar.* vs [*The man*]_{given information} *enters a bar.*; see Chapter 4).

At this point, it is important to emphasize again that different Construction Grammar approaches use different types of notation systems and formalisms to represent the internal properties of constructions. In Chapter 7, I will familiarize you with the most important approaches, so that you are able to read and understand publications that use the major notation systems currently in use. However, I agree with Goldberg (2013) that the differences between all these approaches are actually fairly superficial and mostly just notational in character. All of these approaches share the central tenets of Construction Grammar (cf. Section 1.3) and analyses from one approach can more often than not easily be transferred to or interpreted in another one.

In this book, I have therefore chosen to represent constructions using a fairly informal notation system of a type that is often found in Usage-based Construction Grammar. As mentioned above, in Chapter 7, I will then outline how this system translates into more formal representations (as used by, for example, Embodied Construction Grammar, Fluid Construction Grammar or Sign-Based Construction Grammar). Moreover, note that the following list of constructional features is not necessarily exhaustive and that some researchers suggest that a fully realistic Construction Grammar will need to also add several other linguistic properties (cf. Fried and Östman 2005; Trousdale and Östman 2013: 486–9).

In the following, the FORM pole of constructions includes at least the three levels mentioned above: PHONOLOGY, MORPHOLOGY and SYNTAX. Yet, concerning the latter two levels, you will remember that I mentioned in Section 1.3.1 that Construction Grammar does not uphold a lexicon-syntax distinction. Thus, following Jackendoff and Audring (2016, 2020), we will collapse these into a single-level MORPHOSYNTAX. Moreover, when we talk about written language constructions, PHONOLOGY will be replaced by ORTHOGRAPHY (with elements on this level appearing in angled brackets and orthographic representations rendered by italics, for example, *<apple>*):

- PHONOLOGY will contain the phonetic/phonological representation of substantive elements using the International Phonetics Association's alphabet (in slashes / /). The order of elements on this

level also specifies the linear order (word order) of the utterances
licensed by a construction.

- MORPHOSYNTAX includes information such as the word class of
items (e.g., N(oun) or V(erb)) as well as the form (phrasal status, for
example, NP, VP, etc.) and the function (for example, SBJ, OBJ,
etc.) of syntactic elements. In Chapter 3, we will see how morphological constructions can be described using these features, while
Chapter 4 and 5 outline constructional analyses of constructions more
at the syntax end of the lexicon-syntax cline. Brackets ([ ]) will be
used on this level to indicate elements that function as a unit (e.g., as
an NP or VP).

The MEANING pole provides SEMANTICS, as well as, whenever needed,
PRAGMATICS information (all of which, obviously, are always part of the
'high- (hyper!) dimensional conceptual space' (Goldberg 2019: 7) of a
construction.)

- SEMANTICS: throughout this chapter, we have seen that the semantics of constructions is not truth-conditional in nature (as, advocated
by model theoretic approaches to semantics; cf. Croft 2012: 4–19):
constructional meaning does not just encode the conditions under
which a construct licensed by a schema describes an event that has
happened in the real world. Instead, from a cognitive point of view,
meaning is how speakers view ('construe') an event. As we have
seen, one and the same event can be encoded by many different
construals in a language that focuses on quite different characteristics
of a scene (cf., for example (2.7)). Since paraphrasing the construal
meaning of a construction can become fairly complicated, we will
use the following shorthand notation: the SEMANTICS part of the
overall meaning of constructions will be put into single quotation
marks (' '). The idiosyncratic meaning of constructions will be given
by informal paraphrases, while the semantic properties that appear
across several constructions will be represented by means employed
by truth-conditional approaches (though remember that we only use
these as shorthand notations for the rich, mental meaning which
speakers will have entrenched in their minds): events that express a
relationship between argument roles (*eat*, for example, entails 1.
someone who eats 2. something.) that can be filled by many different
participants (*I eat an apple.* / *Ferris eats a pizza.* / *They eat meat.*) are
put into a predicate logic notation (e.g., 'eat(X, Y)', which we intend
to stand for 'complex force-dynamic event in which X ingests Y'.
Despite the model theoretic flavour of these representations, we thus
only take them as shorthand for the complex, cognitive construal of
events. Whenever necessary, I will also make explicit reference to the
cognitive construals of these events by drawing on Frame Semantic

definitions (using the FrameNet website https://framenet.icsi.berkeley .edu, an electronic database of semantic frames as well as the lexical units that evoke them; Boas 2005b; Fillmore, Lee-Goldman and Rhodes 2012). For the event encoded by *eat*, FrameNet,[16] for example, mentions that it evokes the INGESTION frame:

Ingestion Frame
An Ingestor consumes food or drink (Ingestibles), which entails putting the Ingestibles in the mouth for delivery to the digestive system. This may include the use of an Instrument. Sentences that describe the provision of food to others are NOT included in this frame.
Moreover, the FrameNet definition also provides more detailed information on the two argument variables that are conceptually necessary for the INGESTION frame (its so called 'Core Frame Elements (FEs)'):

Core FEs
Ingestibles   The Ingestibles are the entities that are being
[Ingible]   consumed by the Ingestor.
Ingestor [Ing]   The Ingestor is the person eating or drinking.

Semantic Type: Sentient
Since FRAMES and FRAME ELEMENTS are semantic properties that occur across many constructions, they will be put in small caps (just like event properties such as BECOME or CAUSE). As we shall see, the more detailed and cognitively more adequate Frame Semantic representations will become particularly helpful in our discussion of argument structure constructions (Section 5.1). In addition to that, once we also take into account issues of tense (for example, present tense *I eat an apple* vs past tense *I ate an apple*) and aspect (for example, simple present *I eat an apple* vs present progressive *I am eating an apple*), we will also require a more fine-grained analysis of events. The details of this analysis (following Croft 2012) will also be presented in Chapter 5.

• PRAGMATICS: the pragmatic level contains all aspects of meaning that are dependent on the specific situational context in which a construction can be used. This includes information on the SPEECH ACT expressed by a construction (whether it is, for example, intended as a request (2.5) or expressive in nature (2.6)) as well as CONTEXTual constraints on the use of constructions (cf. the interpretation of deictic elements such as *here* and *now*, which depend on where and when someone utters them – your 'here

---

[16] Cf. https://framenet2.icsi.berkeley.edu/fnReports/data/frameIndex.xml?frame=Ingestion [last accessed 02 January 2021].

and now' when reading this book is clearly different from my 'here and now' when writing this book). As with the SEMANTIC properties, PRAGMATIC constraints will be given by informal paraphrases. Moreover, not only the speaker's construal of events influences how events are encoded. Another important factor is the speaker's assessment of the activation of information in their interlocuter's mind. Take, for example, the two constructs in (i) and (ii):

(i) John broke the vase.

(ii) It was John who broke the vase.

The event described in the two sentences is the same. Yet, while speakers might use (i) for a fairly neutral description of the event, they will employ the verbalization in (ii) to add contrastive information (it was John, and not someone else, who broke the vase). Thus, (ii) can be used in a situation where the speaker, for example, assumes that the hearer thinks that someone other than John broke the vase. PRAGMATICS, therefore, includes an informal representation of properties relating to the INFORMATION STRUCTURE (IS) of constructions (for example, the status of information as given-accessible-new, which will be of relevance in our discussion of NPs in Chapter 4; note, however, that not all approaches would put INFORMATION STRUCTURE under PRAGMATICS).

In addition to these properties, constructions can, for example, also encode other contextual information such as, for example, whether a construction is linked to certain speakers or text types and genres (see Trousdale and Östman 2013: 488). In the present book, we adopt a very wide definition of PRAGMATICS (as covering all aspects of social, textual as well as discourse-functional meaning in a specific situation). In Section 6.1, we will particularly look at the role of SOCIAL information (the gender, age or class of a specific speaker, which we will also subsume under our broad definition of PRAGMATIC meaning).

Finally, as mentioned in Chapter 1, variables receive co-index subscript numbers to identify the individual components across the form-meaning levels (following Boas and Sag 2012; Jackendoff 2002; Pollard and Sag 1994). Below, (2.26) illustrates the notation system employed in the rest of this book for the *Un*-ADJ construction, which had preliminarily been analysed in (1.3):

(2.26)

Un-ADJ construction (revised)

FORM: PHONOLOGY: $/ \ʌn_1\text{-}X_2 /_3$
           MORPHOSYNTAX: $[\text{UN-}_1 \text{ ADJ}_2]_{\text{ADJ3}}$

$\Leftrightarrow$

MEANING: SEMANTICS: $\text{'NOT}_1 \text{ A}_2\text{'}_3$
          PRAGMATICS:

First of all, note that not all FORM and MEANING properties in (2.26) receive a value. The *Un*-ADJ construction does not possess any characteristic properties on the PRAGMATICS level, so that we can leave these unspecified. Second, indices allow us to tie together information from the different levels (thus the index '1' symbolically links the phonological string $[\text{ʌn}]_1$ and the morphological information that it is a bound prefix $\{\text{UN-}\}_1$ to the semantic meaning of 'NOT_1').

As mentioned above, the present notation system is admittedly somewhat idiosyncratic. It will allow us, however, to combine insights from many different Construction Grammar approaches and, as you will see in Chapter 7, it is in a format that can easily be translated into virtually any of the currently available formalizations and notation systems in use.

2.2.2   When Can We Postulate that Something Is a Construction?

So now we know how to analyse the complex internal structure of constructions. But how can we tell whether something is a construction?

Basically, all Construction Grammar approaches treat a pattern as a construction if it constitutes an arbitrary pairing of FORM and MEANING that cannot be licensed by other constructions already stored in the construction. In addition to that, based on language acquisition research and studies on actual language use, usage-based approaches to Construction Grammar postulate that even if a construct can be accounted for by the combination of other constructions, it can become entrenched in the mind of speakers if they encounter it with sufficient frequency. As Goldberg (2006: 5) puts it:

> Any linguistic pattern is recognized as a construction as long as some aspect of its form or function is not strictly predictable from its component parts or from other constructions recognized to exist. In addition, patterns are stored as constructions even if they are fully predictable as long as they occur with sufficient frequency.   (Goldberg 2006: 5)

In light of this, (2.27) presents the usage-based definition of the construction that we will use throughout the rest of this book:

(2.27)   **construction (final usage-based definition)**
1.   a construction is an arbitrary pairing of FORM and MEANING:
      FORM ⇔ MEANING
      – FORM includes phonetic/phonological, morphological and syntactic
        information
      – MEANING includes semantic and pragmatic (including social
        meaning) information
2.   a construction is acquired through language use and is stored in a
      speaker's mental constructicon
      – either if some aspect of its FORM or MEANING is unpredictable from
        its components or other constructions
      – or if the construction is frequent enough in language use to become
        entrenched.

2.2.3   Data in Usage-Based Construction Grammar

As Section 2.1 highlighted, research indicates that first language acquisition is clearly usage-based. Consequently, usage-based oriented research must analyse authentic, natural, observational data to adequately assess the quality as well as quantity of linguistic input that speakers receive. Methodologically, this means that most Usage-based Construction Grammar studies draw on corpus data (Gries 2013: 97–101).

In modern linguistics, a corpus is defined as 'a finite-sized body of machine-readable text, sampled in order to be maximally representative of the language variety under consideration' (McEnery and Wilson 1996: 24). Corpora are there-fore samples of authentic, naturally occurring speech or writing that – and this is a very important point – are considered representative for a speech community. For English, the Internet, for example, is probably the biggest database currently available. Yet, its use as a linguistic corpus is not unproblematic because of the heterogeneity of the population that keeps adding English texts to it: nowadays, English is a global language (Crystal 2003). For many English sentences on the web, we just do not know whether they come from a British or American first language speaker, an African or Asian second language speaker or a European foreign language speaker of English. From a Usage-based Construction Grammar point of view, it would be highly interesting to see the respective language use of all of these groups. However, since their constructions (as well as the functional domains as well as overall frequency of use) of English will differ greatly, we would not want to make any claims about the constructions of, say, a British English speaker based on data from a German foreign language speaker.[17]

Methodologically, corpus data have the advantage of being authentic, natural, observational data (Gries 2013: 94–6) that can be considered objective as well as valid and reliable data sources of linguistic usage (Hoffmann 2011: 10). Like all data sources, however, corpus data also have their limitations (Hoffmann 2011: 9–14): (1) There is the 'positive data problem': just because an utterance occurs in a corpus does not automatically mean that it is grammatical (since it can also be a performance phenomenon; e.g., a false start or self-repair structure). (2) In addition to this, there is the 'negative data problem': the absence of a structure from a corpus does not entail its ungrammaticality (since it might be missing due to mere chance or register effects). Nevertheless, the great advantage of corpus data is obviously that they provide natural, authentic data that can be analysed for frequency and context effects.

Still, while corpora thus constitute an important data source for the investigation of language use of a speech community, the question remains whether they allow us any insight into the degree with which an individual has entrenched a construction. Some (for example, Blumenthal-Dramé 2012; Schmid 2020)

---

[17] For each of the web-based examples of the book, I therefore double checked whether it was possible to ascertain the native speaker status of the source by, for example, limiting the search to .uk domains and by also gleaning as much information as possible about the speaker/writer by carefully surveying each single website.

argue that as aggregate data from several different speakers, corpus data alone are not suitable for the study of entrenchment. Instead, they only provide information about the conventionalization of constructions across speakers in a speech community (Schmid 2020). As Stefanowitsch and Flach (2017: 122) concede, corpus data are not 'typically representative of the input, let alone the output of a particular individual'. Nevertheless, following Schmid's 'from-corpus-to-cognition principle', they point out that text frequency 'instantiates entrenchment in the cognitive system' (2000: 39) in two complementary ways: first of all, there is the 'corpus-as-output' view that argues that, taking into account the effects of domain-general principles, authentic corpus data can be used to draw 'inferences about the mental representations underlying this behavior' (Stefanowitsch and Flach 2017: 102–3). Second, the 'corpus-as-input' view advocates that corpus data can be taken as a representative sample of the input that speakers of a speech community are exposed to and which consequently shape their mental construction networks (Stefanowitsch and Flach 2017: 103).

Corpus data can thus be said to offer one, but obviously not the only window onto the entrenchment of constructions. Psycholinguistic experiments, without doubt, offer a more direct access to the entrenchment of structures in the individual, but also have disadvantages (due to their unnatural setting and the unnatural types of stimuli and responses that are often used; see Gries 2013: 94–5). In light of this, several studies have argued for complementary data sources to be used as converging or corroborating evidence and these have, indeed, shown that the results from experimental and corpus-based studies often converge (Hoffmann 2011; Stefanowitsch and Flach 2017: 121).

In light of the above, it is not surprising that the evidence used in constructionist studies is drawn from complementary data sources such as 'child language, psycholinguistic experiments, speakers' intuitions, distribution in corpora and language change' (Bybee 2010: 10). Now, throughout this book, I will point you to studies that have relied on all of these data sources and that provide support for Construction Grammar as a psychologically and cognitively valid theory of mental grammar. Besides, in order to illustrate authentic instances of various constructions, I will particularly draw on the following corpora, many of which are freely available (so that you can test many of the claims made in this book yourself):

(a)   BROWN corpus family (1 million words each / only written data):
         – BROWN corpus
           (1960s written American English; Francis and Kučera 1979)
         – Lancaster-Oslo/Bergen corpus
           (LOB; 1960s written British English; Johansson, Leech and Goodluck 1978)
         – Freiburg-Brown Corpus of American English corpus
           (FROWN; 1990s written American English; Hundt, Sand and Skandera 1999)
         – Freiburg-LOB Corpus of British English corpus
           (FLOB; 1990s written British English; Hundt, Sand and Siemund 1998)

(b)   British English segment of the International Corpus of English
            (ICE-GB; 1-million words of 1990s spoken and written British
            English, http://ice-corpora.net/ice)
(c)   British National Corpus
            (BNC; 1970s-1993, spoken and written British English data,
            100 million words, www.english-corpora.org/bnc/)
(d)   Corpus of Contemporary American English
            (COCA; 1990-2012, spoken and written American English, >1
            billion words, www.english-corpora.org/coca/).

Remember that even though all of the above corpora have been very carefully
compiled as representative samples of the respective varieties, we cannot assume
that any result we obtain from them will hold for all speakers of the speech
community in question: from an exemplar-based view, no two people will ever
be exposed to input that is 100 per cent identical. Consequently, we expect some
individual differences between speakers. Yet, overall, corpus data are currently
the best proxy for what the average input for a speaker of a certain population
should look like. This explains why corpus data are the most widely used data
source in Usage-based Construction Grammar studies – and why we will make
use of them as much as possible in the following chapters.

2.3   Summary

        In this chapter, we saw how children acquire the construction of their
language in a step-wise fashion starting with FORM-MEANING holophrases
and then moving via item-based constructions to completely schematic argument
structure constructions. As it turns out, the input that children receive is much
richer than previously claimed and there is thus no need to postulate an innate
Universal Grammar. Instead, we noted that domain-general cognitive processes
such as entrenchment via type and token frequency, categorization, analogy and
functionally based distributional analysis play a huge role in providing the tools
that allow children to generalize beyond their input and to creatively use language to say things they have never heard before. At the same time, there are also
cognitive constraints, namely entrenchment, pre-emption and knowledge of
semantic subclasses of verbs, that delimit this creativity.

    In light of the phenomena discussed in the chapter, we then realised that we
have to postulate a more elaborated internal structure for constructions. As we
saw, the FORM pole includes properties concerning PHONOLOGY/
ORTHOGRAPHY and MORPHOSYNTAX. The MEANING pole comprises
information on the SEMANTICS as well as PRAGMATICS of constructions.

    Finally, we addressed the issue of when we can claim that a construction is
stored in a speaker's mind: all Construction Grammar approaches warrant the
postulation of a construction if it exhibits arbitrary properties on any constructional level. In addition to that Usage-based Construction Grammar approaches
assume that a perfectly regular, compositional construct that could be said to be

licensed by other, independent constructional templates can be stored if it is encountered with sufficient input frequency. In light of the overwhelming evidence for the usage-based nature of language acquisition presented in this chapter, we will adopt a Usage-based Construction Grammar approach in the rest of this book. The major data source for such an approach are, as I argued above, linguistic corpora. The next chapter will now show how such an approach can explain the major properties and phenomena of English morphology.

Exercises

2.1 What are the major arguments against an innate Universal Grammar?

2.2 What are the main claims of Usage-based Construction Grammar?

2.3 Explain the role that the following domain-general cognitive processes play for the emergence of a speaker's constructicon:

(a) entrenchment via type and token frequency

(b) categorization

(c) analogy

(d) functionally-based distributional analysis.

2.4 A good example that illustrates how children move from holophrases via item-based constructions to more adult-like complex constructions comes from data on the acquisition of WH-questions. Dąbrowska (2000) investigated this issue and found that English-speaking children first produce frozen holophrases without any schematic slots such as *What-s-that?* or *How-do-you-know?*. As they get older, they step-by-step schematize these constructions. In other words, they only gradually add slots to make their constructional templates more and more adult-like. Consider for instance the examples in (2.i) to (2.ix) from Dąbrowska (2000) that illustrate the development of a particular type of WH-question in the speech of a two-year-old child named Naomi (for a more in-depth discussion cf. Diessel 2013).

(2.i)	What doing? (many times)	1;11.11 [i.e., 1 year, 11 months, 11 days]
(2.ii)	Whats Mommy doing? (many times)	1;11.21
(2.iii)	Whats donkey doing? (4 times)	2;0.18
(2.iv)	Whats Nomi doing? (2 times)	2;0.18
(2.v)	Whats toy doing?	2;0.18
(2.vi)	Whats Mommy holding?	2;0.26
(2.vii)	Whats Georgie saying?	2;1.19
(2.viii)	What is the boy making?	2;11.17
(2.ix)	What is Andy doing?	2;11.18

2.4.1 What kind of construction underlies the children's earliest question utterances?

2.4.2 Give a Usage-based Construction Grammar account of how the constructions change gradually from (2.i) to (2.ix).

3   Morphological Constructions

In the last chapter, we discussed evidence supporting a Usage-based Construction Grammar approach. Now, we move on to looking at the various types of constructions needed for a full analysis of Present-day English. We start with what is normally considered to be the smallest type of FORM-MEANING pairings, morphemes and investigate the various parameters according to which these can be classified. In particular, we will see to what degree the classic Structuralist distinction between grammatical and lexical morphemes makes sense from a Construction Grammar point of view. Then we will look at the various ways in which Present-day English can license new words, outlining a Construction Grammar approach to word-formation.

3.1   Morphemes: The Smallest Types of Constructions?

Let us start our exploration of Present-day English by asking what the smallest constructions in our constructicon are. Intuitively, you might be inclined to say 'well, words are clearly the smallest pairings of form and meaning'. Already in Chapter 1, however, we came across constructions that seemed to be smaller than words:

(3.1) a.   untrue
     b.   unfair
     c.   unreliable

We probably all agree that *untrue*, *unfair* and *unreliable* are perfectly acceptable English words. On top of that, since they are pairings of FORM and MEANING (e.g., *unfair* = FORM: /ʌn₁ˈfeə₂/ ⟺ MEANING: 'NOT₁ fair₂') we can call them constructions. Yet, as we noted in Chapter 1, we cannot only say what the whole words mean, but that we can also identify subparts of (3.1a–c) that are FORM-MEANING pairings: *true* (3.1a), *fair* (3.1b) and *reliable* (3.1c) are also constructions that can appear independently without anything else added to them (they are words themselves[1]). On top of that, the examples in (3.1) also contain the

---

[1] The definition of 'word' underlying this simple statement is one by Bloomfield, who defined words as 'minimal free forms'. According to this view, words are the smallest meaningful elements of a language that can stand by themselves. As we will see, this is a helpful heuristic, but, as always, things are slightly more complex than this (see Section 4.3).

element *un-*, which cannot appear by itself (it always needs to attach to another element), but which nevertheless is clearly a meaningful element (it always means 'NOT'; FORM: $/\text{ʌn}/_1$ ⇔ MEANING: 'NOT$_1$'). Elements such as *un-*, *true* or *fair* that cannot be divided into smaller meaningful parts are called '**morphemes**' in virtually all modern linguistic theories (by the same type of analysis, ignoring orthography, *reliable* can be split up into two morphemes, namely *rely* and *-able*). Since morphemes are defined as the smallest units that carry meaning, we might thus be tempted to say that they are the smallest types of constructions in our constructicon – but things are slightly more complex than this, as we shall see in a second.

A standard way of classifying morphemes is to distinguish **free morphemes** (those that can appear independently, e.g., *free* or *true*) from **bound morphemes** (those that need to attach to another element, e.g., *un-*):

(3.2)   VOTE: Aberdeen named Scotland's most dismal town. Fair or unfair?[2]

Whatever your view on Aberdeen, what (3.2) illustrates is that words like *fair* or *unfair* can appear on their own. In contrast to this *un-* cannot do so (*Aberdeen named Scotland's most dismal town. Yes or *un-?*), but must instead always attach to another linguistic element. From a Construction Grammar point of view, the main difference between bound and free morphemes is one of schematicity and phonological independence: while free morpheme constructions are fully substantive and phonologically independent (their phonology is fully specified and contains no slots; cf. (3.3)), bound morpheme constructions are partly substantive, partly schematic and their phonological FORM indicates that they obligatorily need to attach to another element. In other words, the part that is usually identified as the bound morpheme in many non-constructionist analyses is phonologically fixed, but these constructions also contain a variable phonological slot (cf. (2.26), whose salient features are given in (3.4)):

(3.3)   *free* construction
FORM: PHONOLOGY: $/\text{fɹiː}/_1$
             MORPHOSYNTAX: ADJ$_1$
             ⇔
             MEANING: SEMANTICS: 'free'$_1$

(3.4)   *un-*ADJ construction (revised)
FORM: PHONOLOGY: $/\text{ʌn}_1\text{-X}_2/_3$
             MORPHOSYNTAX: [UN-$_1$ ADJ$_2$]$_{\text{ADJ3}}$
             ⇔
             MEANING: SEMANTICS: 'NOT$_1$ A$_2$'$_3$

When you look at (3.4), it becomes clear that morpheme constructions are actually not as 'small' as we might expect from the classic definition of morphemes given above (as the smallest linguistic units that have meaning).

---

[2] Source: www.pressandjournal.co.uk/news/aberdeen/478626/ [last accessed 02 January 2021].

The reason for this is that constructionist approaches subscribe to a word-based model of morphology and not a classical morpheme-based one (cf. Haspelmath and Sims 2010: 40–53). In a morpheme-based approach, the lexicon entry for {*un-*} would look something like (3.5) (curly brackets '{ }' are often used as a notational device to identify morphemes):

(3.5)   morpheme-based lexicon entry for {*un-*} (adapted from Haspelmath and Sims 2010: 43)

$$\begin{bmatrix} /\text{ʌn}/ \\ -\text{ADJ} \\ \text{'not'} \end{bmatrix}$$

At first glance, (3.5) might look pretty similar to (3.4): the entry of the morpheme provides information on its phonology (/ʌn/), meaning ('not') and combinatory potential (a hyphen '–' indicates where the morpheme has to be inserted; in (3.5) in front of an adjective). Importantly, however, while (3.4) is a constructional template for a full word, (3.5) is only a single morpheme. This difference will become clearer once we look at how complex words are produced in the two approaches:

(3.6)   (non-constructionist) Morpheme-based approach
          {un-} + {ADJ} → {*un*-ADJ}

(3.7)   Constructionist word-based approach

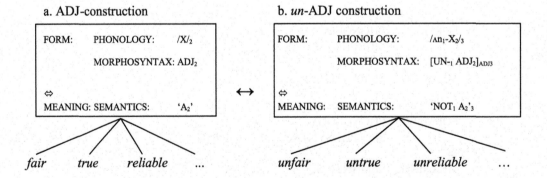

a. ADJ-construction

FORM:	PHONOLOGY:	$/X/_2$
	MORPHOSYNTAX:	ADJ_2
⟺		
MEANING: SEMANTICS:		'A_2'

          fair   true   reliable   ...

↔

b. *un*-ADJ construction

FORM:	PHONOLOGY:	$/\text{ʌn}_1\text{-}X_2/_3$
	MORPHOSYNTAX:	$[\text{UN-}_1\ ADJ_2]_{ADJ3}$
⟺		
MEANING:	SEMANTICS:	'$\text{NOT}_1\ A_2$'$_3$

          unfair   untrue   unreliable   ...

In morpheme-based models, complex words are derived by the concatenation of morphemes. As the morphological rule in (3.6) shows, {*un-*} and {ADJ} are simply combined to yield {*un*-ADJ} (e.g., {-*un*} + {*fair*} → {*unfair*}). The single arrow → in such rules indicates directionality: {*un-*} and {*fair*} are the input, and {*un*-ADJ} is the output of this rule. The constructionist word-based representation differs from such a rule account in one crucial aspect: (3.7) is not a production rule but simply a morphological correspondence (Haspelmath and Sims 2010: 47). Both the ADJ-construction as well the *un*-ADJ construction are constructional schemas that arise independently due to a high type frequency of individual constructs (see Chapter 2): once speakers have encountered and stored words such as *fair*, *true*, *reliable* and so on, they (subconsciously) detect their common properties and can entrench a more schematic ADJ-construction such as (3.7a). Similarly, the *un*-ADJ construction (3.7b) arises as an abstraction over specific tokens that are encountered such as *unfair*, *untrue*, *unreliable*, etc. Thus, importantly, the construction (3.7b) is not directly derived from (3.7a) in this approach. Instead, both constructional schemas enter the constructicon independently due to the input frequency of tokens that instantiate them. Once they are part of the constructicon, speakers will obviously note the many correspondences between the two constructions (including the fact that the phonological, morphological and semantic information of the ADJ is identical in both constructions, but that the *un*-ADJ construction means exactly the opposite of the ADJ construction). Unlike unidirectional rules, these correspondences are bidirectional (which is why a bidirectional arrow ↔ in (3.7) is used to express the mutual morphological correspondence between the two constructions): once you have established the morphological correspondence between these two constructional schemas you can also add constructional tokens by analogy from either direction. Say, for example, you come across a new construct licensed by the *un*-ADJ construction for the first time, such as *that was so **un-gucci***.[3] Now it is extremely possible that previously you have not heard anyone describe something as *that was so Gucci*. Yet, you will nevertheless (roughly) know what they are trying to say (that something does not exhibit qualities associated with the label Gucci – whatever these might be). Consequently, you will have added *un-gucci* to your constructicon first by making reference to your *un*-ADJ construction schema. On top of that, the morphological correspondence in (3.7) will then allow you to add *gucci* as an instance of the ADJ-construction. Note that in morpheme-based approaches you could not adopt such an analysis that goes from the output to the input side (since the rule is one-directional and complex forms always have to be created by combining smaller morphemes[4]). Unlike morpheme-based approaches that focus more on the alleged input side of their rules, usage-based approaches to morphology, therefore, put more emphasis on the role of 'output' schemas, which is why they are also said to be '**output-based**' or '**product-oriented**' (cf. Croft and Cruse 2004: 300–2).

At this stage you might be wondering whether the two approaches are basically just two different ways of doing the same thing. After all, both can explain how speakers end up with words like *unfair* or *unfriendly*. Yet, when we

---

[3] Source: https://twitter.com/littlemix_pride [last accessed 02 January 2021].
[4] That is not to say that morpheme-based theories cannot analyse such examples, but their analysis will have to rely on additional auxiliary assumptions.

look more closely at the way English (as well as many other languages) creates new words, we see that many formations cannot be explained by simple concatenative input-based rules that combine morphemes. Take, for example, the following sets of words in (3.8) and (3.9) (from Haspelmath and Sims 2010: 49):

(3.8)   V   N   ADJ
          attract   attraction   attractive
          suggest   suggestion   suggestive
          prohibit   prohibition prohibitive

(3.9)   V   N   ADJ
          –   illusion   illusive
          –   aggression   aggressive

From a morpheme-based view, the verbs in the first column of (3.8) seem to be the input of two morphological rules that either creates nouns (3.10) or adjectives (3.11):

(3.10)   (non-constructionist) {-*ion*}-rule
          {/X/}$_V$ + {-*ion*}   →   {X-*ion*}$_N$
          'do(x)'   'action of doing(X)'

(3.11)   (non-constructionist) {-*ive*}-rule
          {/X/}$_V$ + {-*ive*}   →   {X-*ive*}$_{ADJ}$
          'do(x)'   'prone to doing(X)'

So, if you take the verb *attract* and feed it into the rule in (3.10), the morpheme {-*ion*} will be added and you get the noun *attraction*. If you put *attract* into (3.11), {-*ive*} will be attached to it and the result is the adjective *attractive*.

When you carefully pronounce the words *attract* and *attraction*, however, you will already notice that these cannot be the result of the simple rule given in (3.10): while *attract* ends in a *t*-sound (that is an alveolar stop, cf. [ə'tɹækt]), the corresponding sound in *attraction* can be orthographically represented as something like *sh* (a post-alveolar fricative [ə'tɹækʃən]). So, in order to maintain a rule-based explanation, we would have to introduce an additional constraint to (3.10) that would specify that a *t*-sound in the input becomes a *sh*-sound in the output. While this would make the morphological rule slightly more complicated, it can, of course, be done. The words in (3.9), however, pose a more serious problem for input-based approaches: there are no English words **illus* or **agress*, so we have no input for the morphological rules in (3.10) and (3.11) to create *illusion/illusive* and *aggression/aggressive*.

Instead of assuming the two morphological rules above, a constructionist account would adopt an output-based approach in which the three constructional schemas for the verbs, nouns and adjectives in (3.8) and (3.9) are connected via the following morphological correspondences (adapted from Haspelmath and Sims 2010: 50):

(3.12)

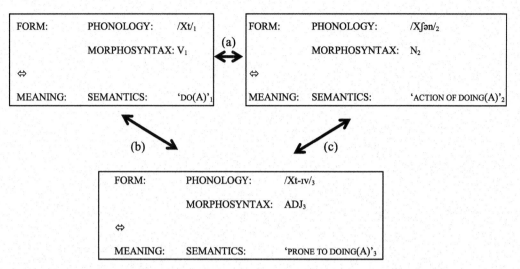

As you can see in (3.12), we postulate a construction for each of the three types of words (a schematic verb construction, a schematic noun construction and a schematic adjective construction). All of these share information on their FORM as well as MEANING level: all three constructions share a substantial part of their phonology (the /X/-part) and have a meaning that includes a common core (relating to 'DO(ING) (A)'). In addition to that, there are morphological correspondences that link the verb and the noun construction (3.12a) as well as the verb and the adjective construction (3.12b). These two correspondences are similar to the morphological rules in (3.10) and (3.11), except for the fact that their relationship is bidirectional and that they link output-based schemas (and do not derive one type from the other). On top of that, however, (3.12) also contains a direct link between the noun and the adjective construction (3.12c), something that we would not get in a morphological rule approach. This morphological correspondence link thus helps to explain why we can have adjective-noun pairs such as *aggressive-aggression* and *illusive-illusion* in (3.9) even in cases where we do not find a corresponding verb. (Note that *aggressive* and *illusive* do not contain a /-t-/, but with respect to all other properties match the ADJ-schema, which means that they can be seen as non-prototypically members of the construction that override this single phonological property.)

Throughout this chapter, I will point out several other word-formation phenomena in English that are problematic for morpheme-based approaches, but that receive a straightforward and cognitively plausible explanation in word-based constructionist analyses. Before taking a more detailed look at English word-formation, I would, however, like to return to a point raised earlier: the issue of recursiveness and constructional inheritance. As I mentioned in Chapter 1, the *great*-N$_{kinship}$ construction (Kay 1973) can be applied recursively so that you can refer to virtually any member of the ancestor line of your parents:

(3.13) a.   great grandfather
     b.   great great grandfather
     c.   great great great grandfather
     d.   great great great great grandfather ...

Back in Chapter 1, I also pointed out that it is not possible to license such recursive structures by constructional inheritance only: if we, as we did back then, postulate a *great*-N$_{kinship}$ construction and an N$_{kinship}$ construction (such as *grandfather*), then we can get a construct like *great grandfather* by inheriting from these two input constructions. What we cannot license are structures like *great great grandfather* or *great great great grandfather*. Why is that? Well, all you can inherit from the *great*-N$_{kinship}$ construction is a constructional skeleton that has a single N$_{kinship}$ slot. It does not matter how often you click that particular button of your mental fruit machine, when you throw in a *grandfather* coin, you will only get the schematic *great*-N$_{kinship}$ template to combine with it to yield *great grandfather*. In order to recursively license structures such as (3.13b–d), we need a way to feed our initial output (our *great grandfather* coin) back into the fruit machine. In other words, we need a way to recursively apply the *great*-N$_{kinship}$ construction and constructional inheritance alone will not help us with that.

    Constructional inheritance is essentially a vertical link in the constructicon: it is, for example, the relationship between a more schematic superordinate construction such as the *un*-ADJ construction and its more substantive, subordinate constructs such as *unfair, untrue, unfaithful* (3.7b). In order to license recursive structures such as *great great great grandfather*, however, we also need horizontal links in the constructicon that allow us to take the output of constructional inheritance (for example *great grandfather*) and feed it back into a constructional template. Fortunately, the morphological correspondence rules that we introduced earlier in this chapter allow us to do this. Take, for example, a look at the morphological correspondence link between the N$_{kinship}$ construction and the *great*-N$_{kinship}$ construction in (3.14):

(3.14)

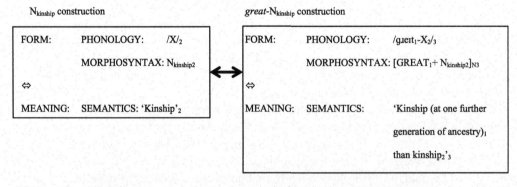

Once *great grandfather* is licensed by the *grandfather* construction and the *great*-N$_{kinship}$ construction, we can treat it as another instance of the N$_{kinship}$

construction (since its FORM and MEANING are subsumed by this more abstract template and since the bidirectional link allows us to go back to the 'input' construction). Once we have identified it as an $N_{kinship}$ construction, however, we activate the morphological correspondence link in (3.14) and feed *great grandfather* into the *great*-$N_{kinship}$ construction to yield *great great grandfather*. The morphological correspondence link thus enables us to take the 'output' of a morphological construction and use it again as the 'input' for further recursive applications of a construction.

In the following parts of this chapter, I will provide you with a constructionist overview of all the ways in which English can license new words via constructional templates, morphological correspondences as well as other strategies. First, however, we will turn to another classical topic in morphology – inflectional morphology.

3.2   Inflectional Morphology

In addition to the bound–free morpheme distinction discussed above, classical morphological theory usually also distinguishes **lexical** from **grammatical morphemes**. Lexical morphemes, such as *un-* (3.4), *great-* (3.14) *-ive* or *-ion* (3.12), are considered to create new lexical items; that is, new form-meaning pairings ('new words'). In contrast to this, grammatical morphemes, also known as **inflectional morphemes**, are only seen as making a word fit into its syntactic context without changing its basic meaning (creating 'new word forms' of one word). To illustrate these properties of inflectional morphemes, take a look at the following examples:

(3.15) a.   I love her.
     b.   You love her.
     c.   We love her.
     d.   They love her.
     e.   He|she|it loves her.
     f.   The old man loves her.

The meaning of the verb *love* in all of the above examples is obviously the same. Yet, if there is a third person singular subject as in (3.15e) or (3.15f) then in Standard English a present tense verb has to appear with the suffix *-s* added to it. So, what the *–s* suffix does is to tell us something not about the verb itself but about another element that it co-occurs with in the clause (the subject). Moreover, the presence of the word form *loves* instead of *love* in (3.15) seems to be the result of an obligatory syntactic rule. If you do not follow it, by for example combining *$They_{PL}$ $loves_{SG}$ her*, the result is a sentence that speakers of Standard English consider incorrect. In cases such as these where grammatical information is marked identically on two syntactic elements, we speak of

agreement or **concord**. In (3.15e,f), for example, both subject and verb agree in their person and number features (the verb *loves* and the pronouns *he*, *she*, *it* are all [3rd person] [singular]).

How can we model agreement in Construction Grammar? For our purposes, the simplest way to capture agreement is via a constraint such as (3.16) (which is a highly simplified version of the subject–verb agreement constraint in Fluid Construction Grammar (Steels and de Beule 2006: 220)):

(3.16)   SUBJECT: $NP_{[NUMBER:\ n]\ [PERSON:\ p]}$
               PREDICATE: $Verb_{[NUMBER:\ n]\ [PERSON:\ p]}$

In (3.16) the values for the grammatical categories NUMBER and PERSON are identified as the variables 'n' and 'p', respectively. This constraint simply ensures that the NUMBER or PERSON values of the subject NP are identical to those of the finite verb (if 'n' is 'PLURAL' on the subject NP, this constraint requires that the verb also is marked for 'PLURAL', and so on).

Example (3.16) is only a syntactic constraint that has no MEANING pole, so technically it is not a construction. As Croft (2001) argues, however, agreement does in fact have a language-specific, semantic function in that it allows the identification of the roles that participants play in a specific construction (with different languages marking different participants in semantically equivalent constructions; cf. Croft 2001: 209–13; cf. also Barðdal 2008). Even if we use a special word order in which both subject and object precede the verb, such as *Bagels he loves!*, the verbal agreement marker *-s*, for example, automatically helps us identify the 3Ps. sg. pronoun *he* as the subject and 'EXPERIENCER' of this emotion instead of *bagels* (which just express the 'CONTENT' of the emotion in the EXPERIENCER_FOCUSED_EMOTION frame evoked by the verb *love*).[5] Now, English has a fairly fixed word order and only a very limited number of inflectional markers. Yet, languages that employ a greater number of inflectional morphemes can even use the agreement marker alone to identify the subject participant, something that seems to support Croft's hypothesis: in Hungarian, for example, if you want to say 'he loves beer' you can either say $ö_{3PS.SG.}$ *szeret-i*$_{3PS.SG.}$ *a sört* 'he$_{3PS.SG.}$ love-$_{3PS.SG.}$ the beer' or just *szeret-i*$_{3PS.SG.}$ *a sört* 'love-$_{3PS.SG.}$ the beer' without the subject pronoun. In such so-called pro-drop languages, a participant role of the verb (here the EXPERIENCER) is therefore solely expressed by the inflectional agreement marker. In these cases, agreement information can be said to be semantically meaningful.

The treatment of agreement in Construction Grammar is a controversial issue and different approaches offer radically different answers to this

---

[5] Source: https://framenet2.icsi.berkeley.edu/fnReports/data/frameIndex.xml?frame=Experiencer_focused_emotion [last accessed 23 June 2021].

question. The details of this discussion are, however, beyond the scope of the present book (and I refer the interested reader to Hoffmann 2013: 310–12 for further details).

3.2.1   Verbal Inflectional Constructions

For English, however, there is another important detail that we need to take into account: the verbal *-s* marker does not only express agreement, it is also a tense marker:

(3.17) a.   She loves him.
     b.   They love him.

(3.18) a.   She loved him.
     b.   They loved him.

As the examples in (3.17) and (3.18) show, in English agreement is normally only overtly marked in present tense clauses where we see a different verbal word form for 3PS.SG subjects (*loves* in 3.17a) and non-3PS. SG subjects (*love* in 3.17b). In contrast to this, in past tense contexts (3.18) the same word form (*loved*) is used with 3PS.SG subjects (3.18a) and non-3PS.SG subjects (3.18b). (There are, of course, also irregular forms such as $I_{1PS.SG}$ *am/was*$_{1PS.SG}$ vs. *you*$_{2PS.SG/PL}$ *are/were*$_{2PS.SG/PL}$, which we will discuss in more detail below.) Now in languages that employ independent agreement and tense markers, the above question of whether agreement should be modelled as a meaningless syntactic constraint remains. In English, on the other hand, we now have another alternative: tense, that is whether we construe an event as happening now or having happened in the past is obviously very meaningful (see also Section 5.2). Consequently, from a word-based constructionist point of view, speakers of English will be able to detect the following morphological correspondences in their verb paradigms:

(3.19)   V   ↔   V-*s*   ↔   V-*ed*

V	V-*s*	V-*ed*
(present: non-3PS.SG)	(present: 3PS.SG)	(past)
kick	kicks	kicked
love	loves	loved
wish	wishes	wished
. . .	. . .	. . .

As before, we can argue that the paradigmatic relationships in (3.19) lead to three word-based construction templates[6] that are connected via morphological correspondence links similar to the one given in (3.12):

---

[6] Croft calls these MVerb-TA constructions (Croft 2013: 219; Croft and Cruse 2004: 288).

(3.20)   The morphological correspondence links between inflected V constructions (simplified)

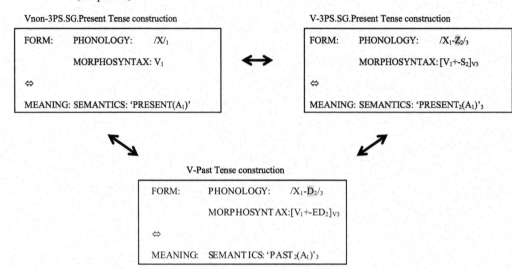

Vnon-3PS.SG.Present Tense construction

FORM:	PHONOLOGY:	$/X/_1$
	MORPHOSYNTAX: V_1	
$\Leftrightarrow$		
MEANING: SEMANTICS: 'PRESENT(A_1)'		

V-3PS.SG.Present Tense construction

FORM:	PHONOLOGY:	$/X_1\text{-}Z_2/_3$
	MORPHOSYNTAX: $[V_1\text{+-}S_2]_{V3}$	
$\Leftrightarrow$		
MEANING: SEMANTICS: 'PRESENT$_2(A_1)$'$_3$		

V-Past Tense construction

FORM:	PHONOLOGY:	$/X_1\text{-}D_2/_3$
	MORPHOSYNTAX:$[V_1\text{+-}ED_2]_{V3}$	
$\Leftrightarrow$		
MEANING: SEMANTICS: 'PAST$_2(A_1)$'$_3$		

As before, the three constructional templates in (3.20) are output-based generalizations, which arise through the encounter of numerous different types instantiating them (3.19). They all share common elements (particularly a schematic phonological slot X_1 that is identified morphologically as a verb V_1 with the semantic meaning given by the variable A_1). On top of that, both the Vnon-3PS.SG.Present Tense construction and V-3PS.SG.Present Tense construction give the present tense meaning of A_1, while the V-Past Tense construction provides its past tense meaning.

However, (3.20) only offers a first approximation of the V-3PS.SG.Present Tense and the V-Past Tense construction. As you will have noted, the former construction still needs to specify that it can only co-occur with 3PS.SG subjects. On top of that, however, there is another issue that concerns the exact phonetic realisation of the two morphological elements {-S} and {-ED}, respectively (which is why I gave their corresponding phonological form element a grey shaded capital letter, Z and D, respectively – placeholders whose exact phonetic value we still need to identify). Let us start by taking a closer look at various verb tokens instantiating the V-3PS.SG.Present Tense construction:

(3.21) a.   John **loves** ice cream.
  b.   Everybody **lies**.
  c.   He **feels** ill.

(3.22) a.   A ghost **haunts** this castle.
  b.   He **walks** his dog.
  c.   She always **laughs** at his jokes.

(3.23) a.   Usain Bolt **kisses** his gold medal ...[7]

---

[7] Source: www.theguardian.com/sport/2012/aug/10/usain-bolt-olympic-200m-final [last accessed 02 January 2021].

b.   Niagara Falls **freezes** over as temperatures plummet.[8]
c.   This is the way he **washes** his clothes.[9]
d.   Amazing moment marine creature **camouflages** itself against a reef is captured on video[10]
e.   Fish **catches** man after he dangles his arm above water.[11]
f.   Luke Shaw **nudges** ahead of Ashley Cole.[12]

Orthographically, the 3PS.SG present tense inflection is realised similarly in (3.21)–(3.23) as <-(e)s>. However, when you listen carefully to native speakers pronouncing the various sentences, you will notice that there are actually three separate, albeit similar phonetic realisations: in (3.21) the <-(e)s> is realised as a voiced alveolar fricative /z/, in (3.22) it becomes a voiceless alveolar fricative /s/, and in (3.23) it is pronounced as /ɪz/. Which of the three must be realised depends on the phonetic context:

- All the verbs in (3.21) end in a voiced sound (cf., e.g., the voiced sounds /v/, /aɪ/ and /l/ in *love*, *lie*, and *feel*, respectively) and the inflectional ending is consequently also a voiced /z/.
- The verbs in (3.22) end in a voiceless sound (cf., e.g., the voiceless sounds /t/, /k/ and /f/ in *haunt*, *walk*, and *laugh*, respectively) and the inflectional ending is also a voiceless /s/.
- Finally, the verbs in (3.23) all end in one of the six sounds classified as sibilants (/s/, /z/, /ʃ/, /ʒ/, /tʃ/, /dʒ/; cf. *kiss*, *freeze*, *wash*, *camouflage*, *catch*, *nudge*, respectively). In this case, the inflectional ending becomes /ɪz/.

While the first two forms are clear-cut cases of assimilation (the voicing of the ending assimilates to the final sound of the base it attaches to), the third realisation can be seen as a case of dissimilation. The reason for this dissimilation lies in the phonetic shape of the inflectional ending: if you realised *kisses* and *freezes* according to the two assimilation patterns, the result would be /kɪs/+/s/ = /kɪs:/ and /fɹiːz/+/z/= /fɹiːz:/. In other words, the final segment of *kiss* and *freeze* would simply be held longer (so you would have to say *kisssss* or *freezzzzze*). These forms would, however, not be distinctive enough from the non-3PS.SG forms *kiss* and *freeze*. So, in order to keep the meaningful distinction between *kiss-kisses* and *freeze-freezes*, an extra ('epenthetic') vowel /ɪ/ is inserted (which is voiced and thus followed by a voiced /z/).

The three realisations of the inflectional ending are therefore in complementary distribution, which means that context decides which one must be used and that

---

[8] Source: www.telegraph.co.uk/travel/destinations/northamerica/usa/11422250/Niagara-Falls-freezes-over-as-temperatures-plummet.html [last accessed 02 January 2021].
[9] Source: www.mojim.com/usy189271x8x8.htm [last accessed 23 June 2021].
[10] Source: www.dailymail.co.uk/sciencetech/article-2939261/ [last accessed 02 January 2021].
[11] Source: www.thesun.co.uk/archives/news/410485/ [last accessed 02 January 2021].
[12] Source: www.telegraph.co.uk/sport/football/teams/england/10678940/England-v-Denmark-Luke-Shaw-nudges-ahead-of-Ashley-Cole.html [last accessed 02 January 2021].

where one occurs you cannot use the other. Classical morphological theories call these concrete realisations of an abstract morpheme 'allomorphs'. From a usage-based constructionist point of view, the various types instantiating these three patterns thus do not lead directly to an abstract V-3PS.SG.Present Tense construction. Instead, in a first step, speakers will generalize to the following three more specific constructions:

(3.24)

$V_{voiceless}$-3PS.SG.Present Tense construction

FORM:	PHONOLOGY:	$/X_{voiceless1}\text{-}S_2/_3$
	MORPHOSYNTAX:	$[V_1\text{+-}S_2]_{V3}$
$\Leftrightarrow$		
MEANING:	SEMANTICS:	'PRESENT$_2$(A$_1$)'$_3$

V_{voiced}-3PS.SG.Present Tense construction

FORM:	PHONOLOGY:	$/X_{voiced1}\text{-}Z_2/_3$
	MORPHOSYNTAX:	$[V_1\text{+-}S_2]_{V3}$
$\Leftrightarrow$		
MEANING:	SEMANTICS:	'PRESENT$_2$(A$_1$)'$_3$

$V_{sibilant}$-3PS.SG.Present Tense construction

FORM:	PHONOLOGY:	$/X_{sibilant1}\text{-}IZ_2/_3$
	MORPHOSYNTAX:	$[V_1\text{+-}S_2]_{V3}$
$\Leftrightarrow$		
MEANING:	SEMANTICS:	'PRESENT$_2$(A$_1$)'$_3$

Since these three inflectional constructions share a significant amount of their information on the formal as well as meaning level, in a next step it seems possible to assume that speakers generalize beyond them to an even more abstract construction (3.25):

(3.25)   *3PS.SG.Present Tense*-V construction (revised)

FORM:	PHONOLOGY:	$/X_1 - Z/_3$
	ORTHOGRAPHY:	$<Y_1\text{-(e)}s_2>_3$
	MORPHOSYNTAX:	$[V_1\text{-}S_2]_{V3}$
		$V_3<$SBJ[NUMBER:3,PERSON:SG],
		$(\dots)>$
$\Leftrightarrow$		
MEANING:	SEMANTICS:	'PRESENT$_2$ (V$_1$)'$_3$

As before, the precise phonetic realisation of the ending is not specified in (3.25) (after all, the only phonological generalization is that it must contain an alveolar fricative, but whether it is voiced, voiceless or needs to be preceded by an epenthetic [ɪ] depends on the context specified by the subschemas in (3.24)). Finally, (3.25) also contains information that will be part of all the subschemas in (3.24) (and has only been omitted so far for the ease of presentation): the agreement information that this verb form requires a 3PS.SG subject (specified here on the MORPHOSYNTAX level by giving the syntactic arguments of the verb V_1 in pointed brackets and specifying that the subject has to have the features [NUMBER:3,PERSON:SG]; (...) stands for optional additional complements if the verb is transitive). In addition to that, literate speakers will also have acquired the ORTHOGRAPHIC information that the ending is rendered as <-(e)s> in writing.

In morphology, an important question concerns the productivity of morphological processes. In this context, productivity is normally defined as the property of a pattern to license new formations (cf., for example Bauer 2001: 13; Plag 2003: 52; for a discussion of various quantitative measures of productivity and their application within a Construction Grammar framework; cf. Hilpert 2013: 127–33). Inflectional endings are normally seen as maximally productive (Haspelmath and Sims 2010: 90–3) and the 3PS.SG.Present Tense-V construction (3.25) is thus probably one of the most productive constructional templates of English. If you, for example, coin a new verb in English, you will almost automatically be able to also create its 3PS.SG.Present Tense-V form: say you come up with new verbs such as *to strug*, *to blist* or *to knidge* (all three non-sense verbs that are phonotactically well-formed, that is they obey the sound sequences found in other English words). Drawing on the abstract constructional templates in (3.24), you will be able to create the new 3PS.SG present tense forms in the sequences *he strugs*, *she blists* or *it knidges*. Moreover, since the three words end in a voiced ([g] in *strug*), voiceless ([t] in *blist*) and sibilant ([dʒ] in *knidge*) sound, you will also be able to choose the adequate subschema for each word and realise the ending as [z], [s] and [ɪz], respectively.

Interestingly, once we take a closer look at the V-Past Tense construction, we can detect a similar kind of allomorphic realisation pattern:

(3.26) a.   John **loved** ice cream.
      b.   Everybody **lied**.
      c.   Smoking **killed** him.

(3.27) a.   Usain Bolt **kissed** his gold medal.
      b.   He **walked** his dog.
      c.   She always **laughed** at his jokes.

(3.28) a.   A ghost **haunted** this castle.
      b.   They **loaded** the van.

In (3.26) the <-(e)d> is realized as a voiced alveolar stop [d], in (3.27) it becomes a voiceless alveolar stop [t], and in (3.28) it is pronounced as [ɪd].

Again, the first two patterns constitute a case of assimilation (*love*, *lie* and *kill* end in a voiced sound (3.26); *kiss*, *walk* and *laugh* have a voiceless final consonant (3.27)). Since the past inflectional ending is encoded by an alveolar stop, an epenthetic [ɪ] is only added in cases where a verb already ends in an alveolar stop and the assimilation process would result in a loss of the past tense information ((3.28); cf. *haunt+ed* [hɔːnt]+[t]=*[hɔːnt:] and *load+ed* [ləʊd]+[d]=*[ləʊd:]). As before, we therefore assume that speakers of English must have entrenched three subschemas to correctly produce this allomorphic pattern:

(3.29) $V_{voiceless}$-Past Tense construction

FORM:	PHONOLOGY:	$/X_{voiceless1}\text{-}t_2/_3$
	MORPHOSYNTAX:	$[V_1\text{+-}ED_2]_{V3}$
⇔		
MEANING:	SEMANTICS 'PAST$_2$(A$_1$)'$_3$	

V_{voiced}-Past Tense construction

FORM:	PHONOLOGY:	$/X_{voiced1}\text{-}d_2/_3$
	MORPHOSYNTAX:	$[V_1\text{+-}ED_2]_{V3}$
⇔		
MEANING:	SEMANTICS: 'PAST$_2$(A$_1$)'$_3$	

$V_{alveolar\ stop}$-Past Tense construction

FORM:	PHONOLOGY:	$/X_{alveolar\ stop1}\text{-}Id_2/_3$
	MORPHOSYNTAX:	$[V_1\text{+-}ED_2]_{V3}$
⇔		
MEANING:	SEMANTICS: 'PAST$_2$(A$_1$)'$_3$	

So again, from a usage-based point of view, we assume that people first encounter specific tokens of the regular past tense formation (3.26)–(3.28). These will be stored in the speaker's long-term memory (unless you never hear a specific form again, then, like all other long-term memory traces, it can also be forgotten). Once speakers have unconsciously learnt that these forms pattern in the allophonic way outlined above, three abstract schemas (3.29) for each of the three possible pronunciation patterns emerge. Finally, once the three schemas are entrenched, an even more abstract and schematic superordinate construction (cf. 3.20) will be added to the constructional network. Figure 3.1 illustrates what this part of the constructional network for the regular past tense constructions looks like:

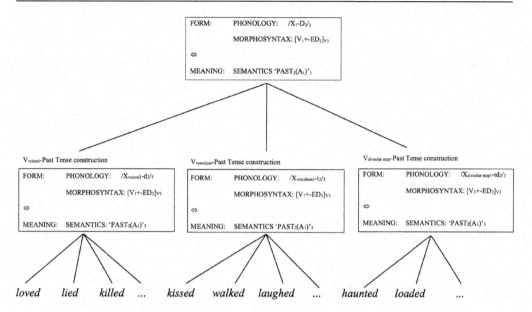

Figure 3.1 *The Usage-based V-Past Tense construction network for regular verbs*

One of the most important tenets of usage-based approaches is that each token of input, each exemplar, will lead to the entrenchment of a construction the more deeply, the more often you encounter it. As a result of this, for each speaker specific past tense verbs such as *loved* or *haunted* will be entrenched to a different degree. If you read a lot of love stories, then you might encounter *loved* more often and it will become more and more deeply entrenched. If you read a lot of ghost stories, *haunted* might be more deeply stored in your constructicon.

Have we got any empirical evidence that even specific, regular past tense verbs are stored in this way? Well, Joan Bybee (2000), for example, carried out a study on *-t/-d* deletion in American English that showed that we store words, even regularly inflected past tense verbs, in an exemplar fashion. In several varieties of English, it has been observed that the final dental stop in words such as *hold* or *test* can either be deleted (/hoʊl/ and /tes/) or not (/hoʊld/ and /test/). Now, if speakers only stored words once without registering how often they encountered them, word frequency should not affect *-t/-d* deletion. Speakers might have a general tendency (towards retention or deletion), but how frequently they had observed a particular word previously should not matter (the decision regarding retention or deletion would be made each time without any memory of previous decisions). In contrast to that, usage-based approaches would assume that words that are used more frequently might for that reason end up more frequently with the final alveolar stop being deleted. Since each of these deleted forms will also leave a memory trace (see Section 2.1.3), highly frequent words have more

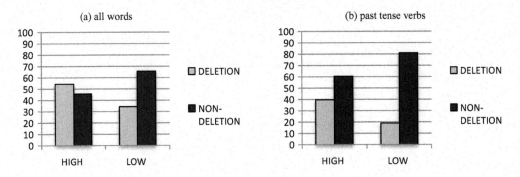

Figure 3.2 *–t/-d deletion in all words (a) and past tense verbs (b) in (figures for graphs from Bybee 2000: 70, 78)*

deleted variants stored that will also be active the next time the word is used. As a consequence, a usage-based approach would predict that high frequency words show a higher degree of deletion than low frequency words (because each deleted variant is stored, and the more often a word is used, the more of these deleted exemplars will be entrenched).

For past tense verbs such as *loved* or *kissed*, previous research had shown that deletion is actually disfavoured, since the final alveolar stop in these cases overtly marks past tense information (which would be lost if the alveolar stop is omitted). Bybee, however, predicted that even for these past tense verbs a slight frequency effect should be observable (so that more frequent ones exhibit more deletion than low frequency ones).

Figure 3.2 summarizes Bybee's (2000) results for deletion vs non-deletion in all words (a) as well as for past tense verbs in particular (b).[13] It shows the expected overall exemplar effect: high frequency words exhibit proportionally more deletion than low frequency words (and Bybee showed that this effect is statistically significant; Bybee 2000: 70). Remember that if all words were only stored once, both high and low frequency words should have the same proportion of deletion/retention. Thus, the overall data clearly show that a higher frequency leads to a greater entrenchment of (deleted) exemplars. In contrast to this, both high frequent as well as low frequent past tense verbs (Figure 3.2b) disfavour deletion (as expected, since deletion in these cases leads to the omission of the overt past tense marking). Nevertheless, as a closer look at Figure 3.2b reveals, even there we can detect a frequency effect (Bybee 2000: 78): despite the overall dispreference of deletion, the statistical analysis revealed that high frequency past

---

[13] Bybee (2000: 70) classified forms as having a high or low frequency by checking their frequency in a reference corpus of authentic American English (the BROWN corpus). The threshold between the two groups was 35 per one million words, since psycholinguistic studies (Sternberger and MacWhinney 1988) had reported that it is the median frequency for a one million corpus (with 50 per cent of all words having a higher, and 50 per cent of all words having a lower frequency).

tense forms again exhibited a significantly higher proportion of deleted tokens than low frequency past tense forms (39.6 per cent vs 18.9 per cent). So even for regularly inflected past tense forms, we find evidence for an exemplar-based storage model. Thus, this supports our claim that the different exemplar past tense verb constructions, such as *loved*, *killed* and *haunted*, are stored on top of the three more abstract allomorphic constructions as well as the maximally schematic superordinate V-Past Tense-construction. Due to the great number of types instantiating these more abstract constructions, we expect these to be competing with the exemplar verb constructions. The lower the level of entrenchment of the exemplar verb constructions, the more likely it is that the more abstract allomorphic constructions might be activated first. These findings are in line with psycholinguistic research (cf. Plag 2003: 49–51) that has found that complex words can be accessed in the mental lexicon either via the whole-word route (their stored exemplar such as *loved*), or via the decomposition route (the creation of the complex word via the more abstract schematic past tense verb construction (3.20) and its morphological correspondence with the related present tense verb form *love*).

For regular verbs, we therefore have a dual route of processing. English, however, also has a set of irregular verbs that do not fit the schemas for regular verbs and definitely have to be stored in an exemplar-based way. Take, for example, the various finite present tense word forms of the lexeme *be*:

(3.30)   a. $I_{1PS.SG}$ $am_{1PS.SG}$ happy.
          b. $You_{2PS.SG}$ $are_{2PS.SG}$ happy.
          c. $He/she/it_{3PS.SG}$ $is_{3PS.SG}$ happy.
          d. $We_{1PS.PL}$ $are_{1PS.PL}$ happy.
          e. $You_{2PS.PL}$ $are_{2PS.PL}$ happy.
          f. $They_{3PS.PL}$ $are_{3PS.PL}$ happy.

Since *be*, unlike regular verbs, has distinct agreement forms for 1PS.SG (*am*; 3.30a), 3.PS.SG (*is*; 3.30c) as well as 2PS.SG/1-2-3PS.PL (*are*; 3.30b, d–f), we need to postulate the following three present tense constructions for it (3.37):

(3.31)

BE-1Ps.sg.PresentTense-V construction

FORM:	PHONOLOGY:	$/æm/_1$ **or** $/əm/_1$
	ORTHOGRAPHY	$<am>_1$
	MORPHOSYNTAX:	$V_1<SBJ[Number:1,Person:sg], (...)>$
⇔		
MEANING: SEMANTICS:		'PRESENT(BE)'$_1$

BE-3Ps.sg.PresentTense-V construction

FORM:	PHONOLOGY:	/ɪz/₁ **or** /z/₁
	ORTHOGRAPHY	<*is*>₁
	MORPHOSYNTAX:	V₁<SBJ[Number:3,Person:sg], (…)>
⇔		
MEANING:	SEMANTICS:	'PRESENT(BE)'₁

BE-2Ps.sg.|1-2-3PS.pl.PresentTense-V construction

FORM:	PHONOLOGY:	/ɑː/₁ **or** /ə/₁
	ORTHOGRAPHY	<*are*>₁
	MORPHOSYNTAX:	V₁<SBJ[Number:2,Person:sg], (…)>
		or V₁<SBJ[Number:1.2.3,Person:pl], (…)>
⇔		
MEANING:	SEMANTICS:	'PRESENT(BE)'₁

In (3.31), optional variants are introduced by a bold-faced '**or**'. The standard, unstressed realisation of *am*, for example, is /əm/ (or even just /m/ as in *I'm happy.*), but there is also a stressed strong realisation /æm/ (which is used in situations when you want to stress the verbs, as in the following exchange: Father: *You are not ill.* Child: *I AM ill.*). Similarly, *is* and *are* have strong (/ɪz/ and /ɑː/, respectively) as well as weak forms (/z/ and /ə/, respectively). Note that *are* can co-occur with 2PS.SG (3.30b) as well as all types of plural subjects (3.30d,e,f). We could capture this by four different independent *are* constructions. Instead, we assume a single constructicon entry as in (3.31) that specifies that it can agree with 2PS.SG subjects (V₁<SBJ[Number:3, Person:sg], (…)>) as well as all types of plural subjects (V₁<SBJ [Number:1.2.3,Person:pl], (…)>).

Similarly, the past tense forms of *be* also differ distinctly from the ones licensed by the regular abstract V-past construction:

(3.32) a.   I₁PS.SG was₁PS.SG happy.
  b.   You₂PS.SG were₂PS.SG happy.
  c.   He/she/it₃PS.SG was₃PS.SG happy.

d.   We$_{1PS.PL}$ were$_{1PS.PL}$ happy.
e.   You$_{2PS.PL}$ were$_{2PS.PL}$ happy.
f.   They$_{3PS.PL}$ were$_{3PS.PL}$ happy.

As we can see in (3.32), there are two word forms of *be* with a past tense meaning: *was*, which can co-occur with 1PS.SG (3.32a) and 3PS.SG subjects (3.32c), and *were*, which agrees with 2.PS.SG as well as all three types of plural subjects (3.32d–f)). In light of this distribution, we need the following two types of past tense constructions for the verb *be*:

(3.33)

BE-1Ps.sg.PastTense-V construction

FORM:	PHONOLOGY:	/wəz/$_1$ **or** /wɒz/$_1$
	ORTHOGRAPHY	<was>$_1$
	MORPHOSYNTAX:	V$_1$<SBJ[Number:1/3,Person:sg], (…)>
⇔		
MEANING:	SEMANTICS:	'PAST(BE)'$_1$

BE-2Ps.sg.|1-2-3Ps.pl.PastTense-V construction

FORM:	PHONOLOGY:	/wɜ:/$_1$ **or** /wə/$_1$
	ORTHOGRAPHY	<were>$_1$
	MORPHOSYNTAX:	V$_1$<SBJ[Number:2,Person:sg], (…)>
		or V$_1$<SBJ[Number:1.2.3,Person:pl], (…)>
⇔		
MEANING:	SEMANTICS:	'PAST(BE)'$_1$

Be is obviously amongst the most highly frequently used verbs in English. Once speakers have stored these forms, they will pre-empt the application of the regular V-Past Tense construction (to create present tense *be-s* or past tense *be-ed*). In other words, the forms in (3.31) and (3.33) will have such a high resting activation (Plag 2003: 49) that they will always be accessed faster than the decomposition route with the regular V-Present Tense and V-Past Tense constructions.

The schematic 3PS.SG present tense {-s} and past tense {-ed} constructions are the only verbal constructions that overtly mark tense, person and number in English. Verbs that are marked for these grammatical categories are called finite verbs.

In addition to these two finite verb forms, English also has three non-finite ones. Table 3.1 gives an overview of all the various finite as well as non-finite verb forms that are relevant for English by providing the various paradigms with selected verbs:

Table 3.1. *The finite and non-finite forms of selected English verbs*

V-Infinitive	V-3PS.SG.Present Tense	V-Past Tense	V-Present Participle	V-Past Participle
(to) kiss	She kisses her child.	She kissed her child.	She is kissing her child.	She has kissed her child
(to) go	He goes to school.	He went to school.	He is going to school.	He has gone to school.
(to) sing	She sings.	She sang.	She is singing.	She has sung.
(to) sting	The bee stings him.	The bee stung him.	The bee is stinging him.	The bee has stung him.
(to) be	He is boring.	He was boring.	He is being boring.[14]	He has been boring.
(to) have	She has a baby.	She had a baby.	She is having a baby.[15]	She has had a baby.
(to) do	He does his homework.	He did his homework.	He is doing his homework.	He has done his homework.

In Chapter 4, we will see that there is good reason to have an extra category for the forms in the first column that cannot be preceded by *to* (we will call these the base form V-base construction). The second and third column list the 3PS.SG.Present Tense and Past Tense verb forms. For a regular verb like *kiss*, we expect the forms *kisses* and *kissed* either to be licensed by the abstract morphological constructions (3.24) and (3.29) or by two specific exemplar constructions *kisses* and *kissed* (that can become entrenched and active if encountered frequently enough). All the other verbs in Table 3.1, like the verb *be* above, exhibit irregular past tense forms that cannot be licensed by the abstract V-Past Tense constructions (3.29) (cf., for example, *went*, *began* and *stung*, instead of **go-ed*, **sing-ed* and **sting-ed*). For all of these verbs, speakers must therefore have stored their past tense forms as specific constructions (similar to the past tense constructions that we postulated for *be* (3.33) – though no other word in English has two past tense forms, so one type of (an exemplar cloud-type) construction will suffice for, *went*, *sang*, *stung*, etc.). Just to give you an idea of the amount of data that speakers can easily store in their mental constructicons, reference grammars of English list more than 250 such verbs with

[14] *He talks and talks, then stops suddenly and announces that **he is being boring**, before setting off again.* Source: www.independent.co.uk/news/people/profiles/2134208.html [last accessed 02 January 2021].

[15] *I've read that **she is having a baby**.* Source: www.theguardian.com/uk/2010/oct/16/alan-sugar-interview [last accessed 02 January 2021].

irregular past tense forms (cf., for example, Quirk et al. 1985: 115–20). Yet, despite this fairly large number, native speakers have no problems recalling the past tense forms of verbs such as *awake, beat, draw, fly, get, run, sit*, etc.).

Most of these irregular forms, however, form their 3PS.SG present tense form in a regular way so that *goes, sings* and *stings* (as well as *awakes, beats, draws, flies, gets, runs, sits*, etc.) can be licensed by the abstract morphological constructions in (3.24). As always, from a usage-based perspective, we also expect the present tense tokens of these verbs to be stored on top of the abstract construction (these being more deeply entrenched, the more often they are encountered). Since *do* and *have* show irregular 3PS.SG present tense forms (*does* is realised as /dʌz/ and not /duːz/; *has* is pronounced /hæz/ and not /hævz/), their forms definitely have to be stored by specific (exemplar cloud-type) constructions.

The infinitive (first column in Table 3.1) and the present participle (fourth column in Table 3.1), on the other hand, exhibit a straightforward morphological correspondence that all regular and irregular verbs show and that, consequently, can be captured by the two constructional templates in (3.40):

(3.34)

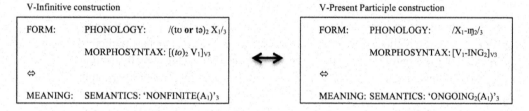

The V-Infinitive construction contains the optional infinitive marker (the two variants full form [tʊ] and weak form [tə]) as well as the phonological slot X_1 that corresponds to the same variable in the V-Present Participle construction (where the additional ending [-ɪŋ] is added). This captures the transparent morphological correspondence between these two constructions (cf. *(to) kill-killing, (to) go-going, (to) sing-singing, (to) be-being*, etc.). Note that the V-Infinitive construction in (3.34) might look similar to the Vnon-3PS.SG.Present Tense construction (3.20) (and for all English verbs, except for *be*, the resulting constructs are identical in phonological form; c.f. *to have-I have, to do-You do, to sing-We sing*, etc.). The crucial difference, however, is that Vnon-3PS.SG.Present Tense constructs are marked for present tense (as well as number and person of their subject). V-Infinitive constructs, on the other hand, are non-finite forms that receive their temporal interpretation from the syntactic context they are embedded in (which in (3.34) is encoded by 'NONFINITE( )' on the SEMANTICS level):

(3.35) a.   He attempted to kiss the bride.
      b.   He is going to kiss the bride.

In (3.35a) the (attempted) kissing event took place at an earlier point in time, while in (3.35b) it has not happened yet (but will probably happen in the future).

The temporal interpretation in these cases is therefore determined by the main verb that selects the infinitive verb (*attempted*PAST vs BE *going to*FUTURE). Besides, note that the *to*-infinitive marker is also selected by the main verbs in these cases. Other verbs, such as the modal verb *may*, only select the V-Infinitive without *to* (cf. *He may kiss the bride.* vs * *He may to kiss the bride.*).

Similarly, the V-Present Participle construction is also not a finite verb construction, since its temporal interpretation depends on the tense of the finite verb:

(3.36) a.   He is kissing the bride.
       b.   He was kissing the bride.

Before discussing the MEANING pole of the V-Present Participle construction, however, we will first have to take a closer look at the V-Past Participle construction:

(3.37) a.   He kissed the bride.
       b.   He had kissed the bride.
       c.   The bride is kissed.

(3.38) a.   He broke the vase.
       b.   He had broken the vase.
       c.   The vase is broken.

As I mentioned above, for regular verbs such as *kiss*, the past tense and the past participle form are identical in form (cf. past tense *kissed* (3.37a) vs past participle *kissed* (3.37b,c)). Irregular verbs such as *break* indicate that we are actually dealing with two different constructions here (cf. past tense *broke* (3.38a) vs past participle *broken* (3.38b,c)). This view receives further support when we look at the temporal interpretation of the two forms: while the finite past tense forms are always interpreted as having happened before the time of speaking, the temporal interpretation of the past participle form depends on the main verb. In (3.37b/3.38b), *had* is marked for past tense, while in (3.37c/3.38c) *is* is marked as present tense.

The precise interaction of these verb forms with the tense and aspect constructions they combine with will be discussed in detail in Section 5.2. Upon comparing the regular V-Past Participle construction with the V-Present Participle construction, we can, however, already establish their morphological correspondence link and contrast their semantic meaning:

(3.39)

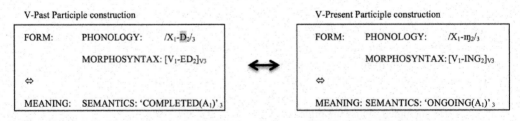

V-Past Participle construction		
FORM:	PHONOLOGY:	$/X_1\text{-}D_2/_3$
	MORPHOSYNTAX:	$[V_1\text{-}ED_2]_{V3}$
⇔		
MEANING:	SEMANTICS:	'COMPLETED(A_1)'$_3$

V-Present Participle construction		
FORM:	PHONOLOGY:	$/X_1\text{-}ıŋ_2/_3$
	MORPHOSYNTAX:	$[V_1\text{-}ING_2]_{V3}$
⇔		
MEANING:	SEMANTICS:	'ONGOING(A_1)'$_3$

The PHONOLOGY FORM of regular V-Past Participle constructs is computed identically to the V-Past Tense constructions in (3.29) (cf. with final [-t] in *He has kissed her.*, [-d] in *He has killed her.*, and [-ɪd] in *He has haunted her.*; as before the 'D' is a shorthand notation for the underlying three allomorphic realisations). Concerning their semantic interpretation, neither the V-Past Participle nor the V-Present Participle construction contains temporal information. The only difference between them is that the V-Present Participle construction tends to construe the event described by the verb as ongoing at the time specified by the main verb (present tense in (3.36a), past tense (3.36b)). In contrast to this, the past participle construction has a construal that sees the event as completed (at the time specified by the tense of the main verb; past tense in (3.37b/3.38b), present tense in (3.37c/3.38c)). As mentioned above, a more detailed constructionist analysis of tense and aspect will be provided in Section 5.2.

There is one more final point concerning Table 3.1 that I would like to draw your attention to that has important theoretical implications. Assuming that similarities on the FORM and MEANING level might lead to the generalization of a more abstract construction, the following set of irregular verbs in (3.40) seems to give rise to the morphological construction correspondence in (3.41):

(3.40)	V-Infinitive	V-Past Tense	V-Past Participle
	cling	clung	clung
	fling	flung	flung
	slink	slunk	slunk
	sling	slung	slung
	sting	stung	stung

(source: Quirk et al. 1985: 115–20)

(3.41)

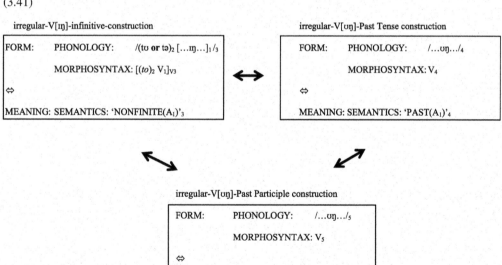

Thus, while the pattern in (3.40) is not very frequent (only a handful of English verbs exhibit it), we can nevertheless give the precise properties of this morphological correspondence network: irregular verbs that have the nucleus vowel /ɪ/ in their infinitive followed by the velar nasal /ŋ/ have a corresponding irregular past tense/past participle form with the nucleus /ʊ/ followed by the nasal /ŋ/.[16]

To make things slightly more complex, English also has another set of irregular verbs with a similar, yet also distinctly different, morphological correspondence set:

(3.42)   V-Infinitive   V-Past Tense   V-Past Participle
              drink   drank   drunk
              ring   rang   rung
              sing   sang   sung
              sink   sank   sunk
              spring   sprang   sprung

These verbs thus appear to support the following constructional correspondence set:

(3.43)

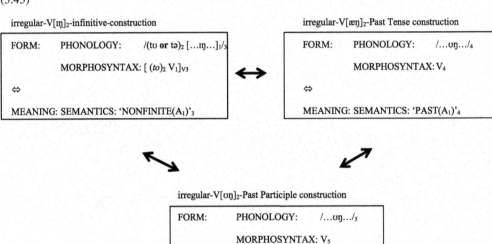

Remember that with regular verbs, we asked whether on top of the productive, general schematic constructions, specific tokens should also be stored. For the above irregular verbs, it is the other way round: we can be sure that people must store the irregular forms; but do they really need to have generalized these to the more schematic constructions in (3.41) and (3.43)? After all, they will not help you predict the right past tense form even if you know that you have an irregular verb with /ɪŋ/ in its infinitive (since it could contain either /ʊŋ/ or /æŋ/). On top of that, there are verbs that would appear to be eligible members for either set (*bring*), but that end up displaying a completely different paradigm (*brought-brought*).

---

[16] The '…' indicates that the onset slot before the vowel is variable (cf. [kl-], [fl-], [sl-] and [st-] in (3.46) and that the nasal can be followed by other consonants; e.g., [-k] in *slink*).

Many researchers have therefore argued that speakers subconsciously register the various similarities on the FORM as well as MEANING level between the words in (3.40) and (3.42), but that they do not actually encode these in the form of an abstract rule or correspondence set such as (3.41) and (3.43) (cf., for example, Jackendoff 2002: 165–7). As I mentioned above, there are only a small number of verb types that display these two irregular patterns. Nevertheless, Bybee and Moder (1983) were able to show that occasionally these patterns can become productive (in the sense of licensing new items): in an experiment they asked native speakers to give them the past tense form of novel verbs such as *spling*, *krink* and *vin*. For verbs such as *spling*, which are very similar in form to existing irregular verbs of the above paradigms (cf. *sling* and *spring*), about 80 per cent of their subjects produced irregular past tense forms such as *splung* or *splang* (cf. also Pinker 2002). For *krink*, which would also fit the abstract generalization schemas in (3.41) and (3.43), but which differs more distinctly from the existing exemplar types in (3.40) and (3.42) (none of which, for example, exhibit an initial /k-/), only about 50 per cent of the subjects gave an irregular past tense form *krank/krunk*. Finally, *vin*, which only shares its nasal nucleus with the verbs in (3.40) and (3.42), led only to about 20 per cent of irregular forms. Thus, the (occasional) productive use of these irregular patterns seems to depend largely on the (gradient) surface similarity of a target verb to the existing irregular verb exemplars. This is in stark contrast to the behaviour of regular verbs: as, for example, Prasada and Pinker (1993) in a different experiment showed, subjects readily produce regular past tense forms even for novel words that do not follow the phonotactic rules of English (and for which no existing exemplars can thus serve as overt models such as *ploamph*). We, therefore, have independent psycholinguistic evidence for the postulation of the highly productive regular past tense construction. In contrast to this, it might very well be the case that the abstract morphological constructions in (3.41) and (3.43) are not actually entrenched in the minds of speakers. Instead, they would only be notational devices to capture the FORM as well as MEANING similarities that would link the various specific exemplar verb constructions in the mental constructicon. Throughout this book, I will follow the position advocated by Jackendoff (2002), Hilpert (2013) and others, that abstract constructional schemas such as (3.41) and (3.43) should only be postulated if we have independent empirical support for them. Similarly, however, I take it that the psycholinguistic evidence on irregular and regular verb forms also shows that a speaker's constructicon does not only consist of fully substantive exemplars. As we have seen, there is evidence that speakers also generalize to more abstract schematic constructions.

3.2.2   Nominal Inflectional Constructions

In contrast to verbs, nouns are morphologically only marked for two grammatical categories, namely PLURAL and POSSESSIVE. Starting with the former, (3.44) gives a correspondence set for the regular plural formation in English:

(3.44)   Noun$_{SG}$ Noun$_{PL}$
    a.   dog   dogs
             (also: bee-bees, butterfly-butterflies, caterpillar-caterpillars)
    b.   cat   cats
             (also: ant-ants, giraffe-giraffes, snake-snakes)
    c.   horse   horses
             (also: prize-prizes, bush-bushes, mirage-mirages, church-churches,
                 language-languages)

If you pronounce the words in (3.44) carefully, you will note that we find the
same allomorphic distribution as with the 3PS.SG.Present Tense construction:

•   All the nouns in (3.44a) end in a voiced sound (cf., for example, the voiced
           sounds /g/, /iː/ and /aɪ/ in *dog*, *bee*, and *butterfly*, respectively) and the
           inflectional ending is consequently also a voiced /z/.
•   The nouns in (3.44b) end in a voiceless sound (cf., for example, the voiceless
           sounds /t/, /f/ and /k/ in *cat*, *giraffe*, and *snake*, respectively) and the
           inflectional ending is also a voiceless /s/.
•   Finally, the nouns in (3.44c) all end in one of the six sounds classified as
           sibilants (/s/, /z/, /ʃ/, /ʒ/, /tʃ/, /dʒ/; cf. *horse*, *prize*, *bush*, *mirage*, *church*,
           language, respectively). In this case, the inflectional ending becomes /ɪz/.

Consequently, we have to assume the following three regular allomorphic plural
constructions for English:

(3.45)

N$_{voiceless}$-Plural construction

FORM:	PHONOLOGY:	/X$_{voiceless1}$-S$_2$/$_3$
	MORPHOSYNTAX: [N$_1$+-S$_2$]$_{N.PL3}$	
⇔		
MEANING:	SEMANTICS: 'PLURAL$_2$(A$_1$)'$_3$	

N$_{voiced}$-Plural construction

FORM:	PHONOLOGY:	/X$_{voiced1}$-Z$_2$/$_3$
	MORPHOSYNTAX: [N$_1$+-S$_2$]$_{N.PL3}$	
⇔		
MEANING:	SEMANTICS: 'PLURAL$_2$(A$_1$)'$_3$	

N$_{sibilant}$-Plural construction

FORM:	PHONOLOGY:	/X$_{sibilant1}$-IZ$_2$/$_3$
	MORPHOSYNTAX: [N$_1$+-S$_2$]$_{N.PL3}$	
⇔		
MEANING:	SEMANTICS: 'PLURAL$_2$(A$_1$)'$_3$	

Moreover, as with the three allomorphic 3PS.SG.Present Tense constructions, we might also consider postulating a superordinate, more schematic construction:

(3.46) N-Plural construction
        FORM: PHONOLOGY: $/X_1 -Z_2/_3$
                              ORTHOGRAPHY: $<Y_1\text{-(e)s}_2>_3$
                              MORPHOSYNTAX: $[N_1\text{+-}S_2]_{\text{N.PL}3}$

        $\Leftrightarrow$

        MEANING: SEMANTICS: 'PLURAL$_2$(N$_1$)'$_3$

Note, however, that if we apply the same criteria as we did with the irregular verb constructions (3.43), we might be tempted to conclude that neither the abstract N-Plural construction (3.46) nor the *3PS.SG.Present Tense*-V construction (3.25) or the abstract V-Past Tense construction (Figure 3.1) are psychologically real. After all, all new constructs of these constructions can be licensed by the various allomorphic constructions. This even applies to words that speakers have not encountered before including nonce formations. If you are asked for the plural of *wug* /wʌg/ or *heaf* /hiːf/, you will have no problems coming up with *wugs* /wʌgz/ and *heafs* /hiːfs/ (or *heaves* /hiːvz/, if you do not use the allomorphic construction but draw on the analogy of the irregular noun *leaf-leaves*). In fact, when Jean Berko posed the same question to a group of four- to seven-year-olds in her classic experiment (1958), most of them had no problem coming up with the correct plural form.[17] Yet, in order to do this, all they would have needed were the N$_{\text{voiceless}}$-Plural and N$_{\text{voiced}}$-Plural construction. Still, in each of these cases, the three allomorphic constructions obviously share many similarities on their FORM as well as their MEANING level and it is therefore relatively easy to say what a potential superordinate construction looks like. Besides, we should not forget the impact of literacy. Once children have learnt how to read and write, the graphematic similarity of the three allomorph constructions (that they are all spelled <-(e)s>) will obviously also support the entrenchment of a superordinate construction such as (3.46) (and correspondingly of the 3PS.SG.Present Tense-V construction (3.25) or the abstract V-Past Tense construction). If in a fantasy book, you come across an alien that is identified as *a Trxtptlm!b%* then you have no problem understanding that *the Trxtptlm!b%s* is referring to a plural group of these aliens – even if, like me, you do not know how to pronounce them. In this case, it is therefore at least doubtful whether pre-literate children have entrenched an abstract construction such as (3.46). For literate speakers of English, however, we have more reasons to assume that such superordinate abstract morphological constructions are part of a speaker's mental constructicon.

---

[17] The children in the study, however, did not seem to have entrenched the N$_{\text{sibilant}}$-Plural allomorphic construction, yet. Even though they correctly produced the plural of *glass* (*glasses*), their response to *one tass, two* ...? was simply *tass* (Berko 1958: 163). Thus, they neither drew on the N$_{\text{sibilant}}$-Plural construction nor on the analogy to *glasses*. Instead, they seemed to have taken an output-based perspective: if a word ends in [s] or [z], then they seemed to match it to their N$_{\text{voiceless}}$-Plural and N$_{\text{voiced}}$-Plural construction, respectively (in other words, if a word ends in a voiceless or voiced alveolar, they treat it as if it is a plural verb since it fits their output-based constructional templates).

As with verbs, nouns also exhibit irregular word correspondences. Examples (3.47)–(3.51) summarize the most frequent patterns (examples from Quirk et al. 1985: 305–14):

(3.47)   Noun$_{SG}$ Noun$_{PL}$
     a. foot   feet
     b. goose   geese
     c. man   men
     d. mouse   mice

(3.48)   Noun$_{SG}$ Noun$_{PL}$
     a. brother[18] brethren
     b. child   children
     c. ox   oxen

(3.49)   Noun$_{SG}$ Noun$_{PL}$
     a. house   houses
     b. knife   knives
     c. mouth   mouths

(3.50)   Noun$_{SG}$ Noun$_{PL}$
     a. deer   deer
     b. sheep   sheep

(3.51)   Noun$_{SG}$ Noun$_{PL}$
     a. stimulus stimuli
     b. corpus   corpora
     c. erratum   errata
     d. appendix appendices
     e. analysis   analyses
     f. criterion criteria
     g. libretto   libretti
     h. bureau   bureaux or bureaus

While (3.47)–(3.50) contain more or less everyday words of English, the ones in (3.51) are foreign loan words (of Greek, Latin and Romance origin) that are associated with specific, fairly formal registers (for example, *corpus* is a linguistic term, *appendix* is a medical term and *libretto* is a musical term). All of these nouns and their irregular plural forms, however, must be learnt in an exemplar-based fashion; (3.52)–(3.56) provide sample constructionist analyses for each of the various patterns in (3.47)–(3.51):

The corresponding constructions for *foot-feet* is shown in (3.52). In such word pairs, the category plural is expressed by the alternation of the stem vowel (a phenomenon known as umlaut). While this is not a productive process in Present-day English, it can, however, be observed in some of the most frequent nouns of English (cf. *man-men* or *mouse-mice*):

---

[18] In the sense of 'fellow member of a religious society' (Quirk et al. 1985: 307).

(3.52)

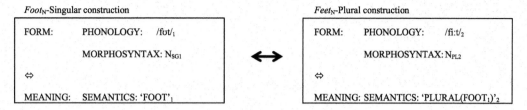

Next, the constructions for *child-children* are provided in (3.53):

(3.53)

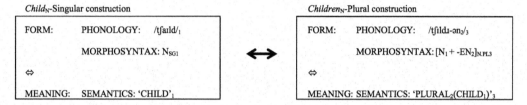

Note that due to the similarity with *ox-oxen* (3.48c), we are able to identify *-en* as a recurring element that carries the meaning PLURAL in (3.53). A closer look at *child-children* (as well as *brother-brethren* (3.48a)) reveals, however, that, on top of that, we cannot simply copy the pronunciation of the singular noun here. Instead we have to specify the irregular stem vowel alternation on the PHONOLOGY level (and for *children* have to add an extra *r* that is not present in *child*).

Similarly, in the *house-houses* set we can identify the part [ɪz] as potentially expressing PLURAL. Yet, since the final voiceless consonant of the singular noun corresponds to a voiced one in the plural form, we cannot simply derive the latter via the regular abstract (3.46) N-Plural construction. The constructional representations of such words must therefore be as follows:

(3.54)

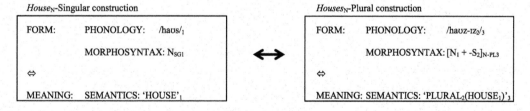

The animal names in (3.50) that have an identical singular and plural form can be captured straightforwardly by (3.55):

(3.55)

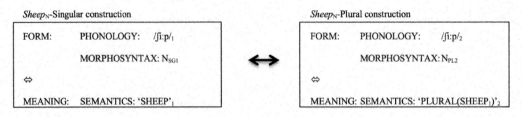

Finally, the loanwords in (3.51) exhibit various patterns. (3.56) only gives a sample analysis for the pair *corpus-corpora*:

(3.56)

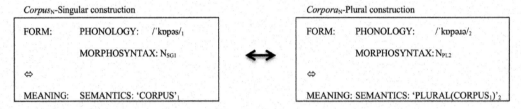

Maybe by now you might feel that the preceding example analysis was a bit dull. After all, it was just listing various irregular constructions. Yet, as I said before, all linguistic theories will have to assume that the above noun pairs must be stored by native speakers in their mental lexicon. At this point, we have already encountered twenty irregular noun pairs ((3.47)–(3.51)) in addition to the over 270 irregular verbs discussed earlier. If speakers can easily memorize that many irregular word pairs, then adding the fifteen abstract constructions we have postulated so far does not seem like a huge problem. Remember that, when we later ask ourselves how many constructions we think a single speaker has to have stored in their constructicon.

For nouns, there is one other morphological correspondence pair that we need to account for:

(3.57) a.   the cat's toy
       b.   the dog's toy
       c.   the horse's toy

All the three nouns in (3.57) are marked for the grammatical category genitive/possessive, which in English is marked orthographically by an apostrophe followed by *s* <'s> if the noun is singular and the reverse order if the noun is plural <s'>:

(3.58) a.   the cats' toy
       b.   the dogs' toy
       c.   the horses' toy

Regardless of whether the noun is singular or plural, though, the pronunciation of the genitive ending again follows an allomorphic pattern that you have probably already detected. I therefore leave it to you to provide a constructional analysis of the N-Possessive construction (cf. Exercise 3.2 below).

More interesting at this stage is the fact that English does not only express possessive relationships with the N-Possessive construction. Competing with this morphological construction is the PP$_{OF}$-Possessive construction:

(3.59) a.   the toy of the cat
     b.   the toy of the dog
     c.   the toy of the horse

In (3.59a–c) the same possessive meaning is expressed by the *of*-PP as in (3.57a–c). Now, in line with Goldberg's **Principle of No Synonymy** (1995: 67–8), we expect that speakers will not randomly have to choose between two structures with a similar meaning. Instead, a functional differentiation will emerge in which certain contexts will lead to the preference of one construction over the other. For the competition between the N-Possessive and the PP$_{OF}$-Possessive construction (which is sometimes also referred to as 'genitive alternation'), several studies have repeatedly confirmed that the N-Possessive construction is favoured if the possessor is animate and the possessum phrase is longer (cf., *inter alia*, Szmrecsanyi 2010). Thus in (3.60) where the possessor is animate (*girl*) and the possessum contains several words (*brand new skateboard*), the N-Possessive construction (3.60a) should sound better to you than the PP$_{OF}$-Possessive construction (3.60b).

(3.60) a.   the girl's brand new skateboard
     b.   the brand new skateboard of the girl

The PP$_{OF}$-Possessive construction, on the other hand, is preferred if the possessor noun ends in a sibilant and the possessor phrase is complex. Thus, in (3.61), which has a possessor noun with a final sibilant (*horse*) and a possessor phrase that is several words long (brand new horse), the PP$_{OF}$-Possessive construction (3.61b) should be judged better than the N-Possessive construction variant (3.67a):

(3.61) a.   the brand new horse's stable
     b.   the stable of the brand new horse

None of these effects is categorical in nature. Even the dispreferred variants (3.60b) and (3.61a) are still grammatical structures licensed by the grammar. So, how can we incorporate these findings into our mental architecture of grammar? First of all, it is important that the two variables that we just discussed (animacy and the length of constituents) are not just at work in the genitive alternation. Cognitively, it seems that speakers generally prefer to place animate before inanimate entities (so that *I gave the man*$_{ANIMATE}$ *a book*$_{INANIMATE}$ should be preferred over *I gave a book*$_{INANIMATE}$ *to the man*$_{ANIMATE}$ – though as we will see in Section 5.1, the choice between these two constructions is also affected by a set of additional factors; cf. also Bresnan and Ford 2010; Bresnan and Hay 2008; Mukherjee and Hoffmann 2006). This can partly be explained by psycholinguistic research that has found that animate/human referents are more accessible; that is, more easily retrieved from memory (Bock, Loebell and Morey 1992; Prat-Sala and Branigan 2000; cited in Ellis 2013: 384). A general processing preference of the human brain seems to be to leave more complex information for later and deal with simpler information first (Hawkins 1994, 2004). This principle also underlies the length effect outlined for the genitive alternation, since in both cases the construction is chosen that allows speakers to put a longer, more complex phrase at the end of the construction (the possessum in the NP-Possessive construction and the possessor in the PP_{OF}-Possessive construction). This effect, which seems to depend on the sheer length of a constituent, has also been observed in several other constructions (and is known as 'end-weight'; Behaghel 1909/1910; Wasow 2002; cit. in Szmrecsanyi 2010).

All of these findings are therefore in line with the tenet of usage-based approaches that domain-general cognitive processes crucially affect the mental constructicon. If we, furthermore, take into account insights from exemplar-based linguistics, then we can assume that these domain-general factors will also show their effect in the exemplar clouds representing the N-Possessive and the PP_{OF}-Possessive construction. Thus, the N-Possessive construction will contain a great number of animate possessives and comparatively longer possessums, while the PP_{OF}-Possessive construction will comprise longer possessives and a greater number of possessors that end in a sibilant.

Domain-general processes and the constructicon can therefore be argued to interact in accordance with Hawkins's (2004) **Competence-Performance Hypothesis**: if one of two structures is cognitively simpler than the other then it has a greater chance of being chosen by a speaker during production. As a result, it will also be encountered more frequently in the input of the hearer, leading to a deeper entrenchment of the pattern. Next time the two structures compete, the cognitively simpler one will be even more likely to win since on top of its processing advantage it is also more deeply entrenched. Under this view, there is no clear-cut distinction between the mental grammar of a speaker (her competence) and her performance. Instead, usage is tightly constrained by domain-general processes and each resulting token of usage/performance leaves a trace in the mental constructicon.

As a finale note on the N-Possessive and the PP_{OF}-Possessive construction, we could again ask whether these two abstract constructions are generalized to a superordinate Possessive construction. Yet, while it would be straightforward to describe the MEANING level of this superordinate construction, it is difficult to say what the FORM level should look like. For in the N-Possessive construction a genitive noun precedes the head noun, while in the PP_{OF}-Possessive construction a possessive PP follows the head noun. Since we cannot even sketch what the FORM level of a potential superordinate construction should contain, it seems best in this case to simply assume that the two types of constructions are strongly linked (and competing) due to their common possessive semantics. It does, however, not seem feasible to postulate a superordinate macro-construction for these two constructions.

3.2.3   Adjectival and Adverbial Inflectional Constructions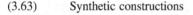

Moving on, there is one final set of inflectional endings that English has that appear on adjectives and adverbs:

(3.62)   ABSOLUTE   COMPARATIVE   SUPERLATIVE
    a.   clever   cleverer   cleverest
    b.   clever   more clever   most clever

Example (3.62) gives the two options for adjective (and adverb) comparison in English (Quirk et al. 1985: 458): either the inflectional endings *-er* and *-est* are added to an adjective to express the grammatical categories comparative or superlative synthetically; or the free forms *more* and *most* are put in front of the absolute form to yield analytic comparative and superlative forms, respectively.

A constructional analysis of the analytic comparative/superlative forms is given in (3.64), while (3.63) details the constructional correspondence for the synthetic forms:

(3.63)   Synthetic constructions

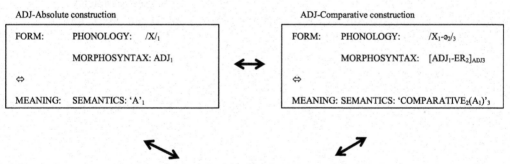

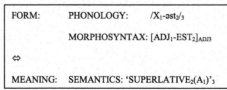

(3.64)   Analytic constructions

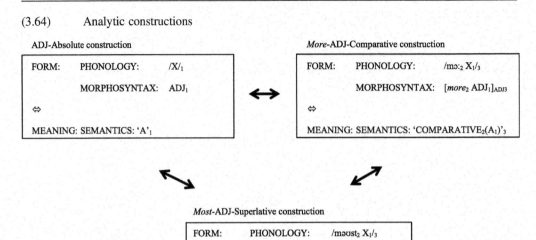

ADJ-Absolute construction

FORM: PHONOLOGY: /X/$_1$

          MORPHOSYNTAX: ADJ$_1$

⇔

MEANING: SEMANTICS: 'A'$_1$

More-ADJ-Comparative construction

FORM: PHONOLOGY: /mɔ:$_2$ X$_1$/$_3$

          MORPHOSYNTAX: [*more*$_2$ ADJ$_1$]$_{ADJ3}$

⇔

MEANING: SEMANTICS: 'COMPARATIVE$_2$(A$_1$)'$_3$

Most-ADJ-Superlative construction

FORM: PHONOLOGY: /məʊst$_2$ X$_1$/$_3$

          MORPHOSYNTAX: [*most*$_2$ ADJ$_1$]$_{ADJ3}$

⇔

MEANING: SEMANTICS: 'SUPERLATIVE$_2$(A$_1$)'$_3$

As you can see, the MEANING levels of the analytic and synthetic comparative and superlative constructions are identical, the only difference concerns the way these grammatical categories are expressed on the form level (either as endings in the synthetic constructions or as *more/most* in the analytic constructions).

Whether an adjective participates in the analytic or synthetic correspondence construction network depends on many factors: Quirk et al. (1985: 463), for example, argue that word length is important: short, monosyllabic adjectives tend to favour synthetic comparative and superlative forms over analytic formations (e.g., *greater/greatest, faster/fastest, older/oldest* vs *more/most great, more/most fast, more/most old*). In contrast to this, trisyllabic (and longer) adjectives prefer the analytic comparative and superlative constructions (e.g., *more/most beautiful, more/most troublesome, more/most unfaithful* vs *beautifuller/beautifullest, troublesomer/troublesomest, unfaithfuler/unfaithfulerst*). Disyllabic adjectives are claimed to be variably used in either the analytic or synthetic construction set (e.g., *politer/politest* vs *more/most polite*; Quirk et al. 1985: 462). Recent research (Hilpert 2008; Mohndorf 2003, 2009) has pointed out, however, that length is only one criterion affecting the choice of the comparative/superlative construction type in English. On the one hand, phonological factors play an important role in that adjectives ending in a linking *r*[19] prefer the analytic

---

[19] In British English, the final *r* sound in the sequence [ə⁺] is only pronounced if a word with an initial vowel follows: cf. *an austere car* vs *an austere object*)

constructions (*more/most austere* vs *austerer/austerest*). Similarly, adjectives with a final consonant cluster such as *apt* also favour analytic forms over synthetic ones (*more/most apt* vs *apter/aptest*). In both cases, the pronunciation of the analytic form is easier than the synthetic forms and it therefore appears that such purely formal constraints also influence the choice of construction type. On the other hand, however, Hilpert (2008) has shown that input frequency also plays an important role in that adjectives that have frequently been encountered in a specific construction (e.g., *more glad*) tend to prefer these formations even if their phonological form would make them eligible candidates for the competing comparative and superlative constructions (*gladder*).

Finally, as with the other morphological construction sets above, we can also find irregular formations that will definitely need to be stored on top of the schematic constructions in (3.63) and (3.64).

(3.65)

	ABSOLUTE	COMPARATIVE	SUPERLATIVE
a.	bad	worse	worst
b.	good	better	best

Again, I leave it to you to draw the correspondence construction network for these irregular adjectives (see Exercise 3.3 below). At this point, I just want to draw your attention to a couple of adjectives ending in a velar nasal [-ŋ] (Quirk et al. 1985: 461):

(3.66)

	ABSOLUTE	COMPARATIVE	SUPERLATIVE
a.	long	longer	longest
b.	strong	stronger	strongest
c.	young	younger	youngest

If you pronounce the adjectives in (3.66), you will notice that the synthetic constructions in (3.63) cannot be used to license them. Take, for example, *long* /lɒŋ/, instead of the expected comparative /lɒŋə/ and superlative /lɒŋəst/, we get forms that have a velar plosive /g/ inserted after the final velar nasal (/lɒŋgə/ and /lɒŋgəst/). The reasons for this odd distribution lie in the history of the English language. Up until the Middle English period, the words *long*, *strong* and *young* all ended in /-ŋg/, but then were affected by a sound change that led to the loss of word-final /g/ when it followed a velar nasal (a change that also affected nouns such as *ring* and *thing*, which originally also ended in /-ŋg/). In the comparative and superlative forms, on the other hand, the /ŋg/ sequence appeared word-internally and therefore was not affected by this sound change. Most Modern English speakers do, of course, not know about this historical explanation and will therefore have to simply generalize the following semi-regular construction correspondence set for these irregular adjectives ending in a velar nasal:

(3.67)   Synthetic constructions

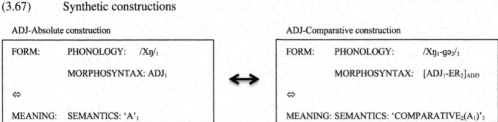

ADJ-Absolute construction

FORM:	PHONOLOGY: /Xŋ/$_1$
	MORPHOSYNTAX: ADJ$_1$
⇔	
MEANING:	SEMANTICS: 'A'$_1$

ADJ-Comparative construction

FORM:	PHONOLOGY: /Xŋ$_1$-gə$_2$/$_3$
	MORPHOSYNTAX: [ADJ$_1$-ER$_2$]$_{ADJ3}$
⇔	
MEANING:	SEMANTICS: 'COMPARATIVE$_2$(A$_1$)'$_3$

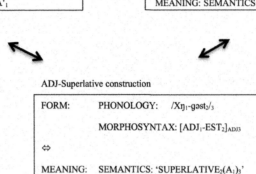

ADJ-Superlative construction

FORM:	PHONOLOGY: /Xŋ$_1$-gəst$_2$/$_3$
	MORPHOSYNTAX: [ADJ$_1$-EST$_2$]$_{ADJ3}$
⇔	
MEANING:	SEMANTICS: 'SUPERLATIVE$_2$(A$_1$)$_3$'

This concludes our overview of English inflectional constructions. As you saw, on top of a number of regular constructional templates (the V-Infinitive, V-3PS.SG.Present Tense, V-Past Tense, V-Present Participle, V-Past Participle, N-Plural, N-Genitive, as well as the analytic and synthetic adjective comparative and superlative constructions), we virtually always also had to postulate the storage of high frequent irregular constructions. Moreover, instead of morphemes, we saw that constructionist approaches postulate inflectional morphological correspondence links between the various inflectional construction templates of the various words.

Finally, however, there is one important theoretical point that we need to think about: at the start of this section, I said that inflectional morpheme constructions make a word fit into its syntactic context, while lexical morpheme constructions create new lexical items. Or as Haspelmath and Sims (2010: 90) put it: 'Inflection is relevant to the syntax; derivation is not relevant to the syntax.' This definition clearly assumes a categorical difference between syntax and lexicon – a difference that, as I have mentioned over and over again, constructionist approaches claim does not exist. So, do Construction Grammarians still assume a distinction between inflectional and derivational constructions and does that have any implications for the architecture of our mental grammar? When we think about the distribution of inflectional and derivational constructions then there is indeed a difference: the most prototypical inflections mark syntagmatic, that is horizontal, relationships between the schematic slots of constructions: subject–verb agreement, for example, establishes concord between the subject slot and the verb slot (3.68). Derivational constructions such as the *un*-ADJ construction, on the other hand, create new items that can be paradigmatically, that is vertically, substituted in a single slot (3.69):

(3.68)   Subject–verb agreement: syntagmatic relationship across two schematic slots

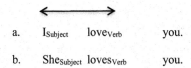

    a.   I$_{Subject}$ love$_{Verb}$ you.

    b.   She$_{Subject}$ loves$_{Verb}$ you.

(3.69)   *un*-ADJ construction: paradigmatic relationship in one schematic slot:

    He is ...

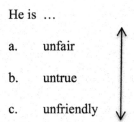

    a.   unfair

    b.   untrue

    c.   unfriendly

At the same time, note that throughout this section we have represented inflectional constructions in exactly the same way as derivational constructions: as FORM-MEANING pairings that are part of morphological correspondence networks. So, despite their different functions in the larger constructions that they appear in, both inflectional as well as derivational elements are stored in the same format – as constructions. Moreover, just as expected from the constructionist notion of the lexis-syntax cline, we also find inflectional constructions that are not as clearly syntagmatic in nature as subject-verb agreement. Tense constructions, for example, are also in a largely paradigmatic relationship (Haspelmath and Sims 2010: 92):

(3.70)

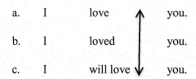

    a.   I   love   you.

    b.   I   loved   you.

    c.   I   will love   you.

The choice of tense obviously (partly) depends on the relationship between the time at which a speaker produces a sentence and the time of the event that is talked about (for more details; cf. Section 5.2). Besides, if additional temporal information is present (such as *yesterday* or *next year*), it will have to 'agree' with the tense of the verb (cf. **I will love you yesterday.* or **I loved you next *year* – yet, this is not a case of grammatical agreement, since again the time of speaking will determine whether the described event has already happened or still is to happen and this will determine the choice of temporal adjuncts).

Finally, it is important to note that morphological research has discussed a great number of features that potentially distinguish inflectional from derivational forms (Haspelmath and Sims 2010: 90–8, for example, list eleven such features). Once all of these features are taken into account, the distinction between inflection and derivation turns out to be more of a cline than a strict dichotomy (Haspelmath and Sims 2010: 98–100) – a result that fits in well with the constructionist tenet that syntax and lexicon only form two opposite poles of a cline of constructions. As argued in the section above, the inflectional system of English can straightforwardly be captured by a constructionist approach.

3.3   Word-Formation

Now that we have had an extensive look at the inflectional constructions of Modern English, let us move on and explore the various ways in which new words are created. The three most frequent and productive word-formation processes of English are derivation, compounding and conversion.

3.3.1   Derivational Constructions

In classical morphological word-formation theories, derivation is defined as the combination of a free morpheme and a bound morpheme. As we saw above (cf., e.g., (3.10) and (3.11)), from a constructionist point of view, bound morphemes are in fact constructional schemas that are partly schematic and partly substantive and whose substantive element does not correspond to a word construction that is used freely (without having to attach to another element):

(3.71)   Derivation: e.g., the bound *-able* construction (Booij 2013: 255–8)
    a.   acceptable
    b.   affordable
    c.   comparable

In (3.71), we can see several highly frequent words of English that probably all speakers of English have stored as constructions (in the 100 million-word BNC corpus, *acceptable* appears 3,576 times, *affordable* 387 times, and *comparable* 1,857 times). At the same time, these constructions also share many similarities: on the FORM level, they all have a transitive verb in initial position (cf. *to accept something, to afford something, to compare something*) and all end in /-əbl/. On the MEANING level, their semantics can be summarized as 'PROPERTY(can be V-ed)' ('can be accepted', 'can be afforded', 'can be compared'). Due to the great type frequency of this pattern (cf. also *believable, doable, approachable*, etc.), we can postulate the following constructional template to have emerged from these more specific constructions (based on Booij 2013: 256):

(3.72)

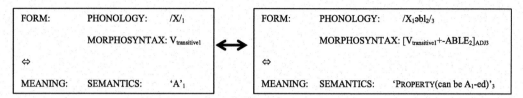

As always, (3.72) provides the morphological correspondence link between the morphologically simpler ($V_{transitive}$) and the more complex (*-able*) construction. Once speakers have entrenched this derivational *-able* construction, they can use it to license new constructs such as the following examples of *–able* adjectives, all of which only occur once in the BNC (and therefore can be extrapolated to occur with a low overall frequency in British English, which might mean that they are not stored by many speakers of English):

(3.73)   About 40% of the potentially **farmable** sea water identified by the White Fish Authority in the whole of the United Kingdom is in the Western Isles. (BNC: AL9:W_misc)

(3.74)   So this is as big as we could get without it falling apart, so it's a nice **handleable** book, though a little heavy. (BNC: KRT:S_Brdcast_news)

(3.75)   Glows through the **crackable** walls of the once big room. (BNC: J0X: W_fict_poetry)

As another example, take the word *skypeable*. The BNC only covers written and spoken texts collected from 1980 to 1993. Since the program *Skype* was first launched in 2003,[20] it is not surprising to find no hits for *skypeable* in the BNC. Once the program was launched, people were able to skype each other (see below for a constructionist analysis of this conversion from *Skype*NOUN > *to skype*VERB). In a next step, speakers were then able to coin the word *skypeable* (with the expected meaning 'can be skyped') with the help of the abstract schema in (3.72). A Google search, for example, shows, that now you can at least find something like 1,350 instances of *skypeable* on the web.[21]

In addition to words like *skypeable*, which clearly inherit all relevant properties from the constructional schema in (3.72), we also, however, find word constructions that only partly match their superordinate construction: the first element in *laughable* does not correspond to a transitive verb. *Laugh* is normally

---

[20] Source: http://en.wikipedia.org/wiki/Skype [last accessed 02 January 2021].
[21] The search string 'skypeable' (www.google.com [last accessed 10 December 2020]) yielded 1,350 hits.

used intransitively (c.f. *He laughed the matter.) and only by combining it with the preposition *at* can you, for example, *laugh at the matter*. Yet the meaning of *laughable* is fully compatible with the superordinate schema (3.72) (cf. *It was a laughable matter*[22] = 'a matter that can be laughed at'.), despite the fact that there is no transitive verb *laugh* (and that the derived adjective does not contain the preposition *at*). This is, therefore, another example that cannot easily be captured by a rule-based approach (which assumes that you need a transitive verb *laugh* first before creating the more complex *laughable*). Instead, we can analyse it as a case of default inheritance: *laughable* is created by the abstract constructional schema in (3.72), but has the idiosyncratic property that it exhibits a morpho-logical correspondence link to a prepositional verb *laugh at* (and not, like most other instances of this schema, an intransitive verb). Similarly, *agreeable* is derived by linking (3.72) to the prepositional verb *agree on/to/with* (cf. Booij 2013: 257). Other idiosyncratic exceptions to the prototypical constructional link in (3.72) include *applicable*, which links to a verb with a phonologically different stem (*apply*, which contains no final [k]), *clubbable*, which is derived from the noun *club* and means 'worthy of membership of a club', as well as adjectives such as *tractable*, which do not link to any existing English verb at all (cf. *to tract*) (Booij 2013: 257). Due to their idiosyncrasies, speakers will have to store all of these exceptions to the general *-able* pattern in the mental lexicon. Yet, a default inheritance Construction Grammar approach allows us to maintain that these are stored in the same way as the regular *-able* instances (such as *playable* or *readable*). They will all be linked vertically to the superordinate abstract *-able* schema and inherit their properties from it. The only difference is that these idiosyncratic instances have individual properties that override some of the properties of the superordinate type. This view of storage is therefore inspired by prototype approaches (which acknowledge that categories can have better as well as less typical exemplars) and allows us to capture more regular as well as less regular phenomena as instances of the same schema.

3.3.2   Compounding Constructions

Another word-formation process of English, and probably the typo-logically most frequent one (Bauer 2009), is compounding, the combination of two words into a single one. Several examples of English noun–noun (NN) compounds are given in (3.76):

(3.76) a.   armchair
     b.   daylight
     c.   steamboat
     d.   tablecloth

---

[22] Source: www.independent.co.uk/arts-entertainment/films/features/2288454.html [last accessed 02 January 2021].

An *armchair* is 'a chair with arms', *daylight* is 'the light of day', a *steamboat* is 'a boat propelled by steam' and a *tablecloth* is 'A cloth intended to cover and protect a dining table during meals' (all definitions taken from www.oed.com). As you can see in these examples, compounding is a word-formation process that combines two (free) word constructions. Besides, (3.76a–d) also illustrate the most common way in which English compounds are interpreted: the second noun in all of these complex word constructions is the semantic head (an *armchair* is a kind of chair, *daylight* is a kind of light and so on). In such cases, where one of the two elements clearly acts as the head, we speak of endocentric compounds.

From a constructionist point of view, we can capture NN compounds by the following morphological correspondence links:

(3.77)

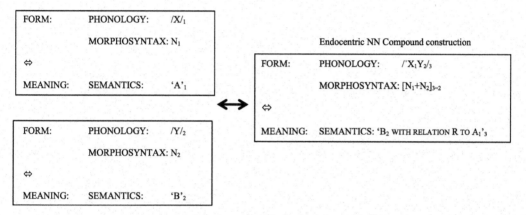

The Endocentric Compound construction obviously makes reference to the two N constructions that it consists of. On the PHONOLOGY level, it adds the information that compounds have their main stress ' on the first element X_1.[23] On the MEANING level, we see that in this abstract NN compound template the second element (indexed by the subscript '2' across the various levels of the construction) is the semantic head: a *tablecloth* thus is a 'cloth WITH RELATION R TO a table'. The reason why the meaning of the compound construction in (3.77) is so vague is that the 'specific interpretation of the relation variable R is provided by conceptual and encyclopedic knowledge, and is conventionalized for existing, listed compounds' (Booij 2013: 258–9). What Booij means by this is that it is hard to predict what exactly the meaning relation between the parts of a compound is going to be. After all, while a *tablecloth* is a cloth that is put on a table, a *steamboat* is not a boat that is put on steam. Once we know what a tablecloth is used for, it is, of course, easy to see why people created that

---

[23] For exceptions, cf. Plag (2003: 137–42).

compound. Yet, it would also be possible to call a cloth with which you wipe a table a tablecloth. There is, thus, always something idiosyncratic about the meaning of compounds and their exact meaning depends on our conceptual as well as encyclopaedic knowledge (the various possible relationships we construe between tables and cloths, out of which we select the one that we want to conventionally talk about by lexicalising the complex NN Compound construction).

In (3.77), we also specify on the morphological level that the compound construction has the same word class as the second noun ('3=2'). For NN compounds this might not seem important (since both components are nouns, so it is unsurprising that the compound is also a noun). Once we look at compounds with elements from different word classes, however, it becomes clear that the second element of an endocentric compound is not only the semantic but also the syntactic head of the compound:

(3.78) a.   blackbird
     c.   greenhouse
     b.   short story

The compounds in (3.78) are created by the Endocentric ADJ-N Compound construction that can be modelled similarly to the NN Compound construction:

(3.79)

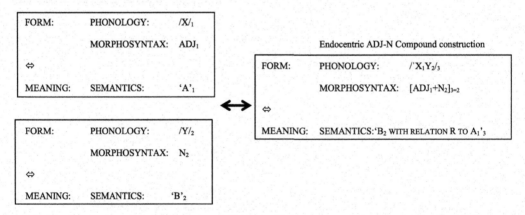

When we combine *black* and *bird* in the compound *blackbird* (3.78a), we get a complex noun (cf. *the blackbird* and *two blackbirds*) and not an adjective (cf. **He was very blackbird*). Thus, the semantic head is also the syntactic one. Moreover, we see again that the meaning of a compound is only partly predictable from its components: while *blackbirds* are black, not every bird that is black is automatically also a *blackbird* (it denotes a specific subspecies of birds, the *Turdus merula*[24]). As we shall see in Chapter 4, English also has a phrasal noun phrase construction that combines *black* and *bird* into *a black bird*, whose

---

[24] Cf. https://en.wikipedia.org/wiki/Common_blackbird [last accessed 02 January 2021].

meaning is any bird that is black. The difference between this phrasal construction and the compound construction is not only that they differ in how the semantic relationship of the two elements is computed: in contrast to compounds, this phrasal construction normally has the primary stress on the second element (cf. *a black 'bird* vs a *'blackbird*). In addition to that, adjectives in the phrasal construction can be modified (*a very black bird*), while those in compounds cannot (cf. **a very blackbird*). Finally, the combination of adjective and noun in the phrasal construction is not as tight as in compounds, since it allows for intervening words (cf. *a black, little bird* vs * *a blacklittlebird*).

Due to their slightly idiosyncratic meaning, most compounds will have to be stored by speakers of English (since they will have to learn which black birds they can refer to as blackbirds and which not). At the same time, a schema such as (3.77) allows speakers to create new compounds such as *Facebook friend* (which denotes a special kind of friend that you probably only interact with via Facebook). On top of very productive Endocentric Compound constructions, English also has other types of compound schemas (examples (3.80) from Plag 2003: 145):

(3.80) a.   redneck
       b.   loudmouth
       c.   greybeard

A *redneck* is not a neck, but instead denotes a person (as does *loudmouth* and *greybeard*). The semantic head of these compounds (a type of person), therefore, lies outside of the two compound elements. These types of compounds are called exocentric compounds. For this moderately productive pattern (Plag 2003: 146), we therefore need another constructional template:

(3.81)

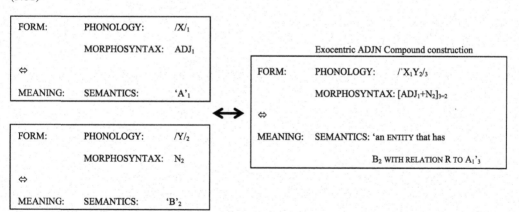

What the Exocentric ADJ-N Compound construction tries to capture is the possessive relationship of these compounds: a *loudmouth* is an entity that has a loud mouth, a *redneck* is a person that (as the stereotype has it) has a red neck. Again, however, the specific meaning of the compound goes beyond the straightforward interpretation (not all people with a red neck would be called a *redneck*).

Furthermore, while these exocentric compounds prototypically denote people, sometimes they can also refer to other types of entities (cf., for example, *greenback*; Plag 2003: 146). At the same time, like the endocentric compounds above, the second element determines the word class of the compound (cf. *a loudmouth* vs he is *very loudmouth*). For other types of non-endocentric types of English compounds, see Exercise 3.4 below.

3.3.3   Conversion Constructions

The third, very frequent word-formation pattern of Modern English is conversion, that is a change of word class, without any formal changes to a word construction:

(3.82) a.   a bottle > to bottle someone
     b.   a bridge > to bridge a gap
     b.   a stage > to stage a play

In (3.82a–c), a noun is turned into and used as a verb: it is no longer preceded by a determiner and can participate in the inflectional paradigm of verbs, cf. *He is bottling someone.* or *He has bottled someone.* Yet, apart from the different types of inflectional endings, there is no formal change that coincides with this word-formation pattern:

(3.83)

N-to-V Conversion construction

FORM:	PHONOLOGY:	$/X/_1$		FORM:	PHONOLOGY:	$/X_1/_2$
	MORPHOSYNTAX:	N_1	⟷		MORPHOSYNTAX:	$[N_1]_{V2}$
⇔				⇔		
MEANING:	SEMANTICS:	'A'$_1$		MEANING:	SEMANTICS:	'ACTIVITY IN RELATION R WITH A$_1$'$_2$

The template (3.83) gives a constructional representation of noun to verb conversion. While the PHONOLOGY level of the noun and the corresponding verb are identical, the converted element has a different word class and a meaning that is no longer nominal, but verbal in character. As with the compounding constructions above, the meaning of a converted verb depends on both conceptual and encyclopaedic knowledge. After all, *to bottle someone* could also mean to provide someone with a bottle or to fill someone up like a bottle, but instead it means to hurt someone by hitting them over the head with a bottle.

While conversion is a highly productive word-formation process in English (cf. also verb to noun conversion such as *to draw a card* > *the draw of cards* or adjective to verb conversion such as *a dry shirt* > *to dry a shirt*; cf. Plag 2003: 107–8), it also exhibits rather peculiar constraints and idiosyncrasies: while you can *winter in Spain*, you apparently cannot **spring* or **autumn in Spain* and complex nouns ending in, for example, *-ness* cannot easily be converted into verbs *Jane curiousnesses every day* (Plag 2003: 115). The various types of conversion constructions of English, therefore, will have to be specified for these usage constraints. While this is by no means easy to do, it is much simpler than an alternative analysis of conversion that assumes no special construction, but instead would see the examples in (3.88) as nouns that are simply used in a syntactic frame for verbs. Under such a view, the noun construction *bottle* would not be made to fit the syntactic context in advance, but it would be the context that would force us to reinterpret a noun as a verb (a phenomenon that is known as coercion; for an overview cf., for example, Lauwers and Willems 2011). At first sight, such a coercion approach might seem like a viable alternative to our conversion construction (3.83). Yet, if it is the context that coerces a word construction into a new word class then why does this not work for *to autumn in Spain* or *Jane curiousnesses every day*? The difference between the two approaches is that we can easily add idiosyncratic constraints to our conversion constructions (and word-formation processes are very often characterized by such idiosyncratic properties). In a coercion approach, on the other hand, we have no straightforward way to account for the fact that sometimes context can change the word class of an item and sometimes it cannot.

3.3.4   Clipping, Backformation and Blending Constructions

Conversion, derivation and compounding are the most productive word-formation processes of Modern English. In addition to these, we also find various other processes, including three types of shortening existing word constructions:

(3.84)   Clipping
  a.   advertisement ➔ ad
  b.   examination ➔ exam
  c.   airplane ➔ plane

(3.85)   Backformation
  a.   editor ➔ to edit
  b.   baby-sitter ➔ to babysit
  c.   typewriter ➔ to typewrite

(3.86)   Blending
  a.   breakfast + lunch ➔ brunch
  b.   motor + hotel ➔ motel
  c.   smoke + fog ➔ smog

Looking at the elements that are omitted by clipping and blending, we can see that most of these could not be analysed as morphemes: neither *-vertisement* of *advertisement* (3.84a) and *-ination* of *examination* (3.84b), nor *-eakfast* in *breakfast* and *l-* in *lunch* (3.86a) or *-tor* and *h-* in *motor* and *hotel* (3.86b) can be assigned any meaning. Backformations also only on the surface appear to involve morphemes: *editor* (3.85a), for example, was not created by the morphological correspondence link between verbs and action nouns (e.g., *conduct* ↔

conductor 'someone who conducts'). Instead, the OED (www.oed.com) tells us that *editor* was borrowed directly from Latin in the seventeenth century and that *edit* was created considerably later (it first appears in the eighteenth century). Remember that from a morphological rule-based perspective such examples would be extremely difficult to explain, since in this case (as well as for *baby-sitter* (3.85b) and *typewriter* (3.85c)) the 'output' existed before an 'input' morpheme entered the language. For constructionist approaches, however, this is not a problem since morphological correspondence links between constructions are bidirectional:

(3.87)

V-to-N Action Noun construction

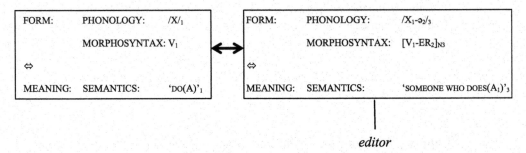

editor

As you can see in (3.87), after it was borrowed into English, *editor* became vertically linked to the superordinate schema of V-to-N Action Noun constructions. This happened due to formal as well as semantic similarities that it exhibited with other micro-constructions of this schema (e.g., *conductor*, *writer*, *player*, *singer*, etc., all of which orthographically end in the grapheme sequence <-or>/<-er> that is pronounced as [ə] and have the meaning of 'SOMEONE WHO DOES SOMETHING'). Once it was part of this constructional network, the corresponding verb *edit* was formed analogically (since all other nouns of this schema have a corresponding verb *to conduct, to write, to play, to sing*).

Backformations are classically defined as analogical creations that are derived by deleting something that looks like a suffix (Plag 2003: 37). From a constructionist point of view, these are instances of constructions that originally have a non-complex FORM level (more precisely a PHONOLGICAL level that as a whole is linked to the MEANING of the construction: FORM ['ɛdɪtə] ⇔ MEANING 'someone who prepares the literary work of another person (...)'[25]. Due to formal and semantic similarities, however, these constructions can come to be associated with a set of constructions that have a complex FORM level (such as *writer* ['wɹaɪt-ə]). Once this happens, corresponding 'input' constructions can be created via analogy to the other members of this constructional network as indicated in (3.87).

In contrast to backformations, which at least to some degree rely on the identification of form-meaning subunits of constructions, clippings and blends

---

[25] Source: www.oed.com/view/Entry/59553 [last accessed 02 January 2021].

clearly involve the omission of non-meaningful elements. The difference between the two latter types of shortenings is that in clippings a single word is shortened (*advertisement* ➔ *ad* (3.84a)), while in blends two existing words are combined into a single one by either shortening the first (*paramilitary* + *troops* ➔ *paratroops*), the second (*boat* + *hotel* ➔ *boatel*) or both words (*breakfast* + *lunch* ➔ *brunch* (3.86a); Plag 2003: 124–5). In both cases, however, it is important to adopt an output-based perspective to understand how these shortening processes work. Regardless of the parts that are truncated, the results of clipping and blending are always words that follow the phonotactic patterns of English. Phonotactics deals with syntagmatic phonological constraints of a language. In Modern English, for example, no word starts with the sound sequence [kn-] (cf. words like *knight*, which is pronounced with an initial [n-] by English speakers, while German speakers pronounce their corresponding cognate word *Knecht* with an initial [kn-]). Licit phonotactic patterns are thus phonological syntagmatic co-occurrence constraints that emerge as generalizations over the entire word constructions of a language.[26] Phonotactics is part of the larger field of prosody, which deals with all suprasegmental phenomena (including stress, rhythm and pitch). Since suprasegmental phenomena play a crucial role in explaining clipping and blending, the two types of shortening are sometimes called prosodic morphological processes (Plag 2003: 115–26).

The basic suprasegmental unit in prosody is the syllable (σ). Syllables are non-meaningful generalizations of sound chunks that all native speakers of a language can intuitively identify. Thus, if I ask you to tell me how many syllables there are in *ask, hotel, artistic* and *deliberate* you would probably all say one (*ask*), two (*ho, tel*), three (*ar, tis, tic*) and four (*de, li, be, rate*), respectively. Concerning the structure of syllables, they all obligatorily contain at least one central element, the so-called nucleus, which is usually realized by a vowel. This vowel can be preceded (the so-called onset) or followed (the so-called coda) by one or more consonants. This is illustrated in (3.88) by providing the syllable structure of the word *boat*:

(3.88)

a.

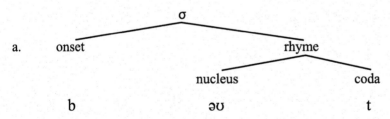

---

[26] Note that these generalizations are not static. Sound changes, for example, can affect the range of possible sound sequences. The Old English word for knight, *cniht*, for example, was pronounced with [kn-]. It was only during the Middle English period that this initial consonant cluster was reduced to [n-].

As you can see, the diphthong [əʊ] fills the nucleus position, while the consonant [b] is in onset and [t] in coda position. Moreover, (3.88) shows that nucleus and coda are combined into a unit called rhyme (which is on the same level as the onset). The name rhyme already gives you a clue as to why syllables are split up this way. From language play to high literary art, we know that almost all speakers can spontaneously rhyme words. Thus, people will rhyme *boat* with, for example, *goat*, *rote* or *vote*. A closer look at these examples shows that what we do when we rhyme is to vary the onset, while we keep nucleus and coda constant (which is why we consider them clustered together into an extra level called rhyme).

From a Construction Grammar perspective, it is important to note that such purely formal and meaningless generalizations are also part of a speaker's mental knowledge of language (though rhyming does, at least, have a function in language play and high literature, as pointed out above). In blending and clipping, however, we can see how the meaningless syllable structure determines the shape of the meaningful outcomes of these shortening processes. Take the blending of *smoke* and *fog* (3.86c): as (3.89) illustrates, the blend *smog* consists of the onset of *smoke* (indicated by underlining) and the rhyme of *fog* (indicated by grey shading):

(3.89)   Syllable structure of *smoke* and *fog*

a.   *smoke*   *fog*

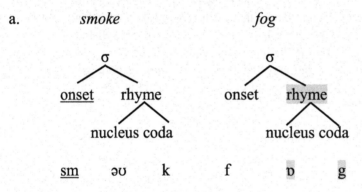

b.   Syllable structure of *smog*

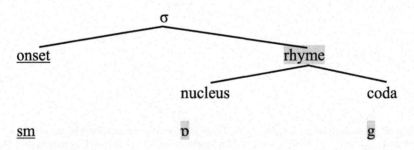

Thus, what happens in blends is the blending of the syllable structure of two words. Plag (2003: 124) gives a detailed overview of the various ways in which the syllable elements of two words can be blended. These include taking the onset of the first word and the coda of the second word (as in *smog* above), but also, *inter alia*, combining a full syllable (*boat*) with the final rhyme of a bisyllabic word (*hotel*; yielding *boatel*). For a full analysis of the constructional template of blends we would, of course, have to specify the various usage patterns that license these different types of prosodic blends. For our purposes, however, we can also resort to Plag's (2003: 123) schematic summary of all these processes: W X + Y Z → W Z. What Plag means by this is that blending always takes a prosodic element from the start of the first word (W X) and from the end of the second one (Y Z). Using this simplified representation (and being fully aware that a more detailed account would have to specify the various ways of combining the onset, nucleus and coda of the two input constructions), we can provide the following constructional template for noun–noun blends (which make up the majority of blends in English; Plag 2003: 123):

(3.90)

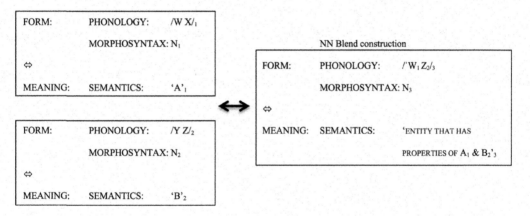

Blends denote entities that have properties of the referents of both elements (Plag 2003: 122), which is why we give the meaning of the NN Blend construction as specified in (3.96). Moreover, on the formal level, we indicate that they comprise the initial part of the first word (W_1) and the final part of the second word (Z_2).

Clippings function in a similar way, the only difference being that only a single word is truncated. In most cases, the final part of a word is omitted (cf. ~~advertisement~~ (3.84a), ~~examination~~ (3.84b)), though occasionally it is the front part that is clipped off if the final part is a stressed syllable (cf. ~~airplane~~ (3.84c); Plag 2003: 121). Again, we leave the precise prosodic constraints aside for now and give a constructional analysis of back clippings in (3.91):

(3.91)

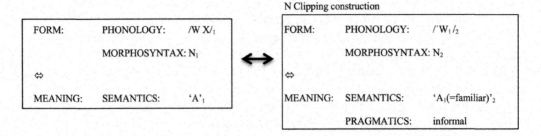

The original word (*advertisement*) and the clipped word (*ad*) have almost the same meaning since they denote the same concept. However, in the N Clipping construction I added the information 'familiar' to indicate that clippings are usually used to 'express familiarity with the denotation of the derivative' (Plag 2003: 121). On top of that, clippings are often used in less formal registers than the corresponding full words (in the BNC, *exam* has a frequency of about 33 tokens per one million words in spoken texts and only 4–5 tokens in academic texts, while *examination* occurs 12–13 times in one million words of spoken texts and 110–111 times in academic texts[27]). In light of this, the constructional template of the N Clipping construction also carries the pragmatic constraint that it is favoured in more informal text types.

3.3.5   Alphabetism and Acronym Constructions

So far, we have only looked at shortenings that seem to arise primarily in spoken language. Sometimes, however, we find clear examples in which words are orthographically shortened:

(3.92) Alphabetisms
   a.   Central Intelligence Agency ➜ CIA
   b.   Oxford English Dictionary ➜ OED
   c.   United States of America ➜ USA

(3.93) Acronyms
   a.   Oil Producing and Exporting Countries ➜ OPEC
   b.   Lightwave Amplification by Stimulated Emission of Radiation ➜ laser
   c.   radio detecting and ranging ➜ radar

In (3.92) and (3.93), the derived, shortened words are created by taking the initial letters of the component words[28]. When the letters of the output of this process are pronounced like individual letters as in (3.92), the words are called alphabetisms or initialisms. When the output is pronounced according to the phonotactic rules of English (3.93), we speak of acronyms.

---

[27] Corpus used: http://corpus.byu.edu/bnc/ [last accessed 02 January 2021].
[28] In *radar* (3.99c), the first two letters of radio are used. See Plag (2003: 126–9) for various other deviations from the general pattern of only taking initial letters.

Alphabetisms and acronyms are, obviously, also non-morphemic word formation patterns. (3.94) illustrates what a constructional template for alphabetisms might look like:

(3.94)

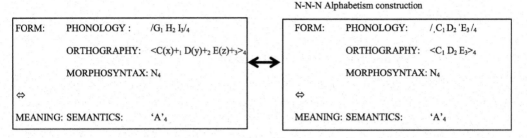

In (3.94), the most important element is, of course, the orthographic level, which plays a crucial role in these abbreviations. The orthographic representation on the left-hand side gives a variable for the capital letters ('C', 'D' and 'E') which are followed by an unspecified number of lower case letters (read the plus sign in '(x)+', '(y)+', '(z)+' as 'one or more lower case letters'). On the ORTHOGRAPHY level of the N-N-N Alphabetism construction, only the capital letters of the input words survive. On the PHONOLOGICAL level, I have repeated these capital letters, which is a shorthand notation for saying that each letter on the ORTHOGRAPHY level should be pronounced like a letter of the alphabet. Besides, I also included the standard stress pattern (with secondary stress on the first letter and primary stress on the final letter).

Acronyms receive a similar constructional analysis:

(3.95)

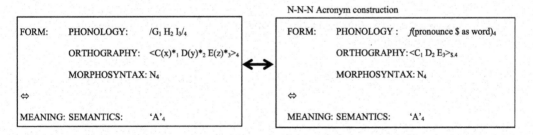

Concerning the various levels, (3.95) is identical to the construction in (3.94), except for the index '$'. This index is referenced on the PHONOLOGY level by a function f (a feature adopted from Head-Driven Phrase Structure Grammar; Pollard and Sag 1994), which simply states that the orthographic representation must receive a pronunciation like a normal English word. Admittedly, this is nothing more than hand waving and ignores the specific details of how speakers turn initial letters into regularly pronounced words. The specifics of this are well beyond the current exposition. However, by now it should have become apparent that formal and semantic similarities to existing words as well as phonotactic generalizations over the full construction network will play a crucial role in this process. Finally, whether the acronym differs in meaning from its input words is hard to say, though Plag suggests that 'within certain groups of speakers, the use of an abbreviation can be taken as a marker of social identity: speakers and listener(s), but not outsiders, know what the speaker is talking about' (2003: 128–9).

3.3.6   Eponymy and Neologism Constructions

For the sake of completeness, I also want to quickly discuss two minor types of word-formation processes: eponymy and neologisms. Eponyms are proper nouns from which a common noun is derived:

(3.96) a.   Sir James Watt ➜ Watt (derived unit of power)
     b.   Kleenex (brand name)➜ Kleenex (all types of tissue)
     c.   Hoover (brand name) ➜ Hoover (all types of vacuum cleaner)

The derived unit of power watt is named after the Scottish inventor James Watt (3.96a). Kleenex and Hoover started out as proper nouns for products from specific companies, but developed a generic meaning when people also used them to refer to all types of tissues (3.96b) and vacuum cleaners (3.96c), respectively. Cognitively, these formations draw on the domain-general principle of metonymy, which identifies an existing temporal, locational or causal connection between two contiguous phenomena and uses one to refer to the other (so you can, for example, say *I've read Shakespeare* since there is a causal connection between the author Shakespeare and the body of works he created). Metonymy also underlies the eponyms in (3.96). Since the various instances of this word-formation process are so distinct in form and character, however, it makes no sense to postulate a constructional template for eponyms. Instead, we will have to explain each instance on a one-by-one basis as created by the general cognitive process metonymy.

In a similar vein, we cannot give a constructional template for neologisms. These are newly coined words such as *Kodak*, *smurf* and *Xerox*, all of which were created without any overt model. In many cases, neologisms are created by companies to name new products, since these new inventions cannot be confused with the names of competing products (and due to their arbitrary form-meaning pair can become trademarked more easily; Butters 2008: 238–9). The only formal constraint on neologisms is that they 'sound English'; that is, they obey the emergent phonotactic constraints of the English constructicon.

3.4   Summary

In this chapter, we first introduced the classical definition of morphemes as the smallest form-meaning pairings. As we saw, a morpheme-based approach requires us to adopt a view of word-formation and inflection in which bound and free morphemes are combined in an additive fashion. Yet, throughout this chapter we came across a great number of morphological phenomena that could not easily be explained by such an input-based rule account. Instead, I advocated an output-based constructionist approach that takes bidirectional morphological correspondences between constructional schemas as the basis of word-formation and inflection. As predicted by usage-based approaches, more abstract constructions emerge gradually due to a great type frequency in the input. The resulting inheritance links between micro- and meso-constructions thus model how creative schemas can arise on top of specific, substantive micro-constructions. At the same time, bidirectional, horizontal correspondence rules account for the recursive potential of morphological patterns as well as instances where the alleged output of a process existed before the alleged input (as, for example, in the case of backformations).

We then moved on to discuss the various constructions needed to model the English inflectional system. In addition to a great number of irregular constructions that we pointed out are considered to be stored by all linguistic theories, we also postulated a considerable number of regular constructional templates (the V-Infinitive, V-3PS.SG.Present Tense, V-Past Tense, V-Present Participle, V-Past Participle, N-Plural, N-Genitive, as well as the analytic and synthetic adjective comparative and superlative constructions). For many of these inflectional constructions we also identified allomorphic subschemas and discussed the kind of evidence that would require us to assume a superordinate macro-construction that dominates the various allomorphy constructions. Finally, in line with the lexicon-syntax cline advocated by Construction Grammar, we saw that the different inflectional constructions ranged from more syntagmatic and syntactic (the V-3PS.SG.Present Tense construction) to more paradigmatic and lexical in nature (the N-Plural construction).

In the final section, I then moved on to present a constructional analysis of the major types of English word-formation: derivation, compounding, conversion, clipping, backformation, blending, alphabetism, acronyms, eponyms and neologisms. While morphological rule-based approaches could only offer alternative analyses for some of these processes, our constructionist approach enabled us to analyse all of these word-formation processes by morphological correspondence links between constructional schemas.

Exercises

3.1 Construction Grammar analyses do not rely on morphemes to account for word-formation and inflection phenomena. Discuss the difference between morpheme-based and output-based approaches to word-formation and inflection. Which phenomena seem to indicate that an output-based approach is empirically superior to a morpheme-based one?

3.2 Describe the allomorphic distribution of the genitive ending in (ia–c). Do you think that these three constructions give rise to an even more schematic superordinate construction? How do the different orthographic conventions for singular (*the cat's lasagne*) and plural nouns (*the cats' lasagne*) affect your answer?

   (i) a. John's birthday cake.
      b. Jack's birthday cake.
      c. Jess's birthday cake.

3.3 Give the construction correspondence set for the irregular adjective *good-better-best*.

3.4 As mentioned above, not all English compounds are endocentric. Take a look at the following set of compounds. For each set, first of all, identify the meaning of these compounds. (If you are not sure about some of them, you can check Plag 2003 or the free online English-language Wiktionary https://en.wiktionary.org/.) Then, provide a constructional analysis of the two types of non-endocentric compounds (for further information on these word-formation patterns; cf. Plag 2003: 145–8).

   (i) Appositional compounds
      a. actor-director
      b. poet-translator
      c. singer-songwriter
   (ii) Copulative compounds
      a. bittersweet
      b. sleepwalk
      c. twenty-one

4   Word, Phrasal and Idiom Constructions

We have just seen how constructional templates can be used to license new words. But what actually is a word? I know that this might seem like a very trivial question, yet as we will see, this is one of those issues that the more you think about, the less straightforward the answer becomes. In this chapter, we will therefore take a closer look at word constructions as well as the larger compositional constructions that they can occur in (phrasal constructions). On top of that, we will also focus on constructions that appear to consist of more than one word and yet have a single non-compositional MEANING that clearly goes beyond the meaning of all its elements – idioms. In fact, since the very first Construction Grammar publications dealt with the analytic problems that idioms posed for the dominant syntactic theories of the time, this will also enable us to trace the historical development 'from idioms to construction grammar' (Croft and Cruse 2004: 225).

4.1   Words, Words, Words?

As you will remember from Chapter 1, virtually all linguists agree that language is fundamentally a symbolic communication system and that the basic units of that system are words. Now when you compare words from different languages, say *heart* and its corresponding German word *Herz* or its Hungarian equivalent *szív*, you can see that these have the same underlying meaning 'heart', but different associated conventional forms ([hɛʁts] and [siːv]). Thus, they are arbitrary and conventional pairings of FORM and MEANING – what we have called constructions.

In line with what we have learnt so far, we can thus preliminarily speak of **word constructions** and as a next step should take a closer look at their place in the constructicon as well as potential schematic generalizations emerging from the input of word constructs. Before we do that, however, we have to overcome a seemingly trivial problem: what is a word construction and how can we find it? This should hardly be difficult, right? Everyone seems to know what words are, so it should be easy to identify word constructions. But think about it, how would you actually define 'words'? Words are pairings of form and meaning, of course, but as I argue throughout this book, so are all other types of constructions.

And they are not even the smallest pairings of form and meaning, because, as we have just seen (cf. Chapter 3), it is morphemes (such as *un-*X or Y-*able*) that are generally considered to be the smallest meaningful elements of a language.

With your new Construction Grammar background, however, you might now speculate that morpheme and word constructions differ with respect to their schematicity: as we saw in Chapter 3, morpheme constructions are partly substantive and partly schematic (cf. the phonologically-specified string [ʌn-] and the X slot in (3.4), respectively). In contrast to this, word constructions such as *heart*, *Herz* or *szív* are completely substantive (i.e., they contain no schematic slot in their FORM pole). We will see later in this chapter that such a view is also not without problems, but let us preliminarily define word constructions as the smallest fully substantive constructions of a language.

Yet, even if we agree for now on this constructionist definition of words, there are still some additional issues that we have to address. Take, for example, the word *kick* in (4.1):

(4.1)   But strikers are there to get **kicked** just as defenders are there **to kick** them.
          (BNC CH3 W_newsp_tabloid)

I think most of us would agree that (4.1) contains two instances (aka constructs) of the word *kick*. Both *kicked* and *to kick* here have the meaning 'strike or propel forcibly with the foot' (FrameNet[1]). In Chapter 3, we followed the standard linguistic convention and identified *kicked* and *to kick* as instances of two inflectional constructions (the V-Past Participle and V-Infinitive construction, respectively) that are linked by a bidirectional horizontal link in the constructicon. There we focused more on the entrenchment of these abstract inflectional constructions and their correspondence links due to their high type frequency (cf., e.g., other instances of the V-Past Participle construction such as *used, called, based, required, expected*[2] and their corresponding V-Infinitive constructions *to use, to call, to base, to require, to expect*). On top of that, however, due to their shared FORM and MEANING, the various inflectional constructs of *kick* (*to kick, kick, kicks, kicked* (past tense), *kicked* (past participle), *kicking* (present participle)) will also be associated in the constructicon via horizontal correspondence links. In addition to this, the various inflectional constructs could be argued to lead to the generalization of an abstract superordinate construction – a KICK Lexeme construction:

---

[1] Source: https://framenet2.icsi.berkeley.edu/fnReports/data/lu/lu2271.xml?mode=lexentry [last accessed 02 January 2021].

[2] These are the five most frequent regular past participle forms in the BNC (Source: http://corpus .byu.edu/bnc/ Query: [v?n*] [last accessed 12 July 2016]). Note that I am only using these for expository purposes, though. *Called*, for example, has 24,280 hits in the BNC, but a closer look at the individual tokens shows that not all of these are instances of the same word. The past participle tokens of *call* include, for example, both 'The film is based on the real life of a woman called Monica Jay.' (BNC CH1W_newsp_tabloid), in which *called* means something like 'named' and 'his wife had called the police' (BNC CH2 W_newsp_tabloid), in which it has the meaning of 'had made a phone call to'. Despite their similarity in FORM, their radically different MEANING poles thus preclude the possibility of seeing these as constructs of a single CALL word construction.

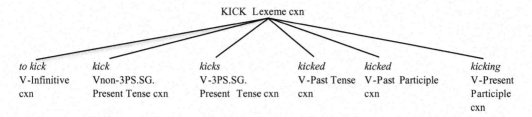

Figure 4.1 *The KICK Lexeme construction network*

Lexeme constructions are thus generalizations of various word constructs that exhibit a common symbolic FORM-MEANING pairing. In line with linguistic convention, in order to distinguish between abstract lexemes and their concrete realisations, we capitalize the former (e.g., KICK) and use italics for the latter (e.g., *to kick*).

What kind of information does a lexeme construction contain? If we look at the various inflectional constructs in Figure 4.1, we see that in the case of a regular verb such as KICK, all the concrete realisations share a common FORM element [kɪk] as well as the MEANING 'strike or propel forcibly with the foot'. On top of that, as the FrameNet[3] lexical entry for KICK reveals, this lexeme evokes the underlying CAUSE_HARM frame. The Core Frame Elements of this frame are given in bold in the definition in (4.2):

(4.2)   CAUSE_HARM frame
        The words in this frame describe situations in which an **Agent** or a **Cause** injures a **Victim**. The **Body_part** of the **Victim** which is most directly affected may also be mentioned in the place of the **Victim.** In such cases, the **Victim** is often indicated as a genitive modifier of the **Body_part**, in which case the **Victim** FE is indicated on a second FE layer.[4]

The SEMANTICS of the MEANING pole of the KICK Lexeme construction thus needs to specify that it draws on the CAUSE_HARM frame and that it is an AGENT[5] that strikes or propels forcibly with the foot at the BODY_PART of a VICTIM. Note that (4.1) shows that Core Frame Elements do not always have to be overtly expressed: while the second instance of KICK gives both the AGENT (*defenders*) as well as the VICTIM (*them*), the part with the first construct *kicked*

---

[3] Source: https://framenet2.icsi.berkeley.edu/fnReports/data/lu/lu2271.xml?mode=lexentry [last accessed 02 January 2021].
[4] Source: https://framenet2.icsi.berkeley.edu/fnReports/data/frameIndex.xml?frame=Cause_harm&banner= [last accessed 02 January 2021].
[5] The lexical entry of *kick* does not include CAUSE as a Core Frame Element, probably because kicking actions are normally assumed to be carried out intentionally by animate beings and CAUSES are defined as a 'non-intentional, typically non-human, force'. Source: https://framenet2 .icsi.berkeley.edu/fnReports/data/frameIndex.xml?frame=Cause_harm&banner= [last accessed 02 January 2021].

only mentions the VICTIM (*strikers*). Nevertheless, even though the AGENT is not overtly given in *strikers are there to get kicked*, we know that kicking obligatorily requires someone to perform this action. As we will see later in this and the next chapter, the reason for this has to do with the specific schematic constructions that lexemes are inserted into: while lexeme constructions evoke frames together with their respective Core Frame Elements, the larger schematic constructions constitute specific construals of a situation that might lead to the omission or suppression of Core Frame Elements. These phenomena are known as Null Instantiation in the Construction Grammar literature (cf. Croft 2001: 275–80; Lambrecht and Lemoine 2005; Ruppenhofer and Michaelis 2010) and, as I said, we look at them in more detail later. In contrast to this, Nonnull Instantiation constructions (Croft 2001: 277) require all Core Frame Elements to be overtly realised. For KICK, the following transitive sentences illustrate such cases of Nonnull Instantiation:

(4.3) a.   **The dancers**$_{AGENT}$ KICKED **him**$_{VICTIM}$ and trod on him
             until he got to his knees and crawled away.
      b.   **The French girl**$_{AGENT}$ came up behind him and KICKED **his**$_{VICTIM}$
             backside$_{BODY\_PART}$
             (Source: FrameNet[6])

An overt AGENT (*the dancers*) and a VICTIM (*him*) are represented in (4.3a), while (4.3b) is an example of the pattern that, on top of an AGENT (*the French girl*) provides the VICTIM as a genitive modifier of the BODY_PART.

Trying to summarize the above properties, we can arrive at the following lexeme construction:

(4.4)   KICK Lexeme construction
          FORM: PHONOLOGY: /kɪk/$_4$
                       MORPHOSYNTAX: V$_4$

          ⇔

          MEANING: SEMANTICS: Frame: CAUSE_HARM
                                      'AGENT$_1$ strikes or propels forcibly
                                      with the foot at BODY_PART$_2$ of
                                      VICTIM$_3$'$_4$

The construction in (4.4) identifies KICK as a verb (on the MORPHOSYNTAX level), which has a substantive PHONOLOGY pole. On the MEANING level, the evoked frame (CAUSE_HARM) is mentioned and the Core Frame Elements are the semantic roles included in the verbal definition provided under SEMANTICS.

Note that (4.4) only carries the information on the lexeme's MORPHOSYNTAX level that it is a verb V. Other constructionist approaches

---

[6] Source: https://framenet2.icsi.berkeley.edu/fnReports/data/lu/lu2271.xml?mode=lexentry [last accessed 02 January 2021].

would mention additional information on this level. As pointed out above, in this book we adopt the view that the syntactic realisation of Core Frame Elements is determined by the larger schematic construction that a lexeme construction is inserted into. Consequently, there is no need, for example, to specify an abstract syntactic frame that is linked to the Core Frame Elements in a lexeme construction, which specifies the syntactic valency of KICK (i.e., that it requires a subject and an object). After all, from a usage-based, bottom-up perspective it is far from clear what single syntactic generalization should emerge from the various Null and Nonnull Instantiations. The four KICK constructs in (4.1) and (4.3), for example, already include three different Nonnull Instantiation realisation patterns: VICTIM (cf. *strikers are there to get kicked* (4.1)), AGENT and VICTIM (4.3a) and AGENT, VICTIM and BODY_PART (4.3b). At the same time, however, the Frame Semantic definition in (4.2) does seem to imply that a kicking scene is prototypically construed as involving two participants (either AGENT and VICTIM (4.3a) or AGENT and VICTIM'S BODY_PART (4.3b)). In this respect, KICK is similar to other verbs such as KISS (which requires an AGENT and an ENTITY;[7] cf. *She*$_{AGENT}$ *kissed him*$_{ENTITY}$.) or WATCH (which evokes a PERCEIVER_AGENTIVE and a PHENOMENON;[8] cf. *Big Brother*$_{PERCEIVER\_AGENTIVE}$ is watching *you*$_{PHENOMENON}$.). Yet, even though these two lexemes evoke completely different frames (the MANIPULATION[9] and the PERCEPTION_ACTIVE[10] frame, respectively) and have different semantic core features, they also appear in the same Null Instantiation constructions (the Passive construction, which we will take a closer look at in Chapter 5):

(4.5)   **He**$_{ENTITY}$ was kissed. (Null Instantiation of AGENT)

(4.6)   **You**$_{PHENOMENON}$ were watched. (Null Instantiation of PERCEIVER_AGENTIVE)

One way of capturing these similarities would be to assume that every lexeme construction also contains syntactic information about the number and types of syntactic arguments that realize the Core Frame Elements. Some constructionist approaches (e.g., Sign-Based Construction Grammar; cf., for example, Michaelis 2013; Sag 2012; Section 7.2) use a so-called ARGUMENT-STRUCTURE (ARG-STR) attribute on a separate SYNTAX level to do this. A slightly simplified representation of a KICK Lexeme construction that includes this information is given in (4.7):

---

[7] Source: https://framenet2.icsi.berkeley.edu/fnReports/data/lu/lu11004.xml?mode=lexentry [last accessed 02 January 2021].

[8] Source: https://framenet2.icsi.berkeley.edu/fnReports/data/lu/lu1320.xml?mode=lexentry [last accessed 02 January 2021].

[9] Source: https://framenet2.icsi.berkeley.edu/fnReports/data/frameIndex.xml?frame=Manipulation [last accessed 02 January 2021].

[10] Source: https://framenet2.icsi.berkeley.edu/fnReports/data/frameIndex.xml?frame=Perception_active [last accessed 02 January 2021].

(4.7)   FORM: PHONOLOGY: $[kik]_4$
                         MORPHOSYNTAX: V_4
                         SYNTAX: ARG-STR: $<NP_1, NP_3>$
                                        or $<NP_1, [NP_{GEN3} \; NP_2]>$

        $\Leftrightarrow$

        MEANING: SEMANTICS: Frame: CAUSE_HARM
                                        'AGENT$_1$ strikes or propels forcibly
                                        with the foot at BODY_PART$_2$ of
                                        VICTIM$_3$'$_4$

As you can see, the only difference between (4.7) and (4.4) is the ARG-STR attribute with its value. The pointed brackets '$<\;>$' under this attribute signal a list of syntactic arguments with indexes linking them to the semantic Core Frame Elements. Thus, in (4.7) NP_1 is linked to the AGENT$_1$ participant, NP_2 to the Body_part$_2$ and NP_3 to the VICTIM$_3$. Besides, since there seem to be two syntactic frames (4.3a) and (4.3b), the ARG-STR contains two lists $<NP_1, NP_3>$ and $<NP_1, [NP_{GEN3} \; NP_2]>$ (with '**or**' indicating that either of the two lists has to be realised).

Similarly, KISS and WATCH would also have an ARG-STR list that contains a two-element list $<NP_1, NP_3>$ (the only difference being that the indexed numbers would link to the specific Core Frame Elements of the MANIPULATION and the PERCEPTION_ACTIVE frame, respectively). The Null Instantiation constructions in (4.1) and (4.5, 4.6) could then all easily be modelled by a mechanism that simply suppresses the first NP_1 ARG-STR element. Yet, while this is indeed a seemingly elegant generalization, it also runs into problems. Take, for example, the following:

(4.8)   One racing bike weighs 10 kg. (BNC FEH W_misc)

WEIGH evokes the DIMENSION frame[11] and has two Core Frame Elements, an OBJECT$_1$ (*one racing bike* in (4.8)) and a MEASUREMENT$_2$ (*10 kg* in (4.8)). If we were to link these to an ARG-STR list, we would again be able to encode this via $<NP_1, NP_2>$. This time, however, we cannot insert the lexeme into the Null Instantiation Passive construction (cf. Croft 2001: 35):

(4.9)   *10 kg was weighed.

So, our neat generalization that this construction merely suppresses the first element of the ARG-STR list does not hold. The reason for this is something that you probably already guessed: the Passive construction does indeed demote a Core Frame Element of a lexeme, but only one that is construed as taking an agentive role in the event (cf. (4.1) and (4.5) where an AGENT participant and (4.6) where an agentive PERCEIVER are not instantiated). The Passive construction thus does not blindly look at an abstract syntactic frame of a lexeme, but

---

[11] Source: https://framenet2.icsi.berkeley.edu/fnReports/data/frameIndex.xml?frame=Dimension [last accessed 02 January 2021].

more importantly only allows for lexemes to be inserted that exhibit the right kind of semantic participants (see also Section 5.1.3). However, if it is the semantics of lexeme constructions that decides their eligibility for insertion into Null and Nonnull constructions, then it seems we do not need an ARG-STR attribute for lexeme constructions. It is for this reason that we do not employ an ARG-STR attribute in the rest of the book.

Continuing with our investigation of what a word is, we should note that (4.4) gives the representation of a regular verb lexeme. In Chapter 3, however, we also came across various English irregular lexemes, the most irregular Present-day one being the verb BE:

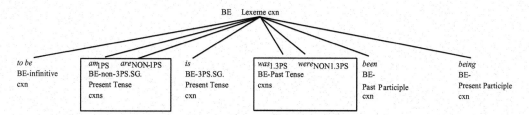

Figure 4.2 *The BE Lexeme construction network*

Figure 4.2 summarizes the various forms of BE, which we encountered in the last chapter. Unlike KICK, the inflectional realizations of an irregular lexeme such as BE cannot be predicted by the various productive schematic inflectional constructions. Instead, each of the inflected forms has to be learnt and stored individually. In addition to that, unlike KICK, the various realizations of BE are so different that no single phonological generalization can emerge. Instead, we simply give the lexeme label BE under its PHONOLOGY (without phonetic brackets in order to indicate that this is just a schematic label). In fact, this is one of these constructions where it is not quite sure whether speakers actually entrench a superordinate lexeme construction such as (4.10) or whether this is just a way by which we can capture the horizontal morphological links between the various inflection constructions in Figure 4.2.

(4.10)   BE Lexeme construction
           FORM: PHONOLOGY: BE_3
                        MORPHOSYNTAX: V_3
           ⇔
           MEANING: SEMANTICS: Frame: STATE[12]
                                         'An ENTITY$_1$ persists in a stable
                                         situation called a STATE$_2$'$_3$

At the time of writing, there is no entry for BE in FrameNet. For purposes of exposition, I have therefore chosen the most schematic frame that captures most of the verb's meaning, the STATE frame. If one allows for a wide definition of

---

[12] Source: https://framenet2.icsi.berkeley.edu/fnReports/data/frameIndex.xml?frame=Assessing [last accessed 02 January 2021].

STATE, then this captures diverse uses of BE such as *Tom is happy.* (STATE = feeling), *Tom is in London.* (STATE = location) or *Tom is a teacher.* (STATE = occupation). What (4.10) does not cover are uses of BE in grammatical constructions such as *was* in (4.5) or *were* in (4.6). These do, of course, follow the inflectional paradigm in Figure 4.2, but their meaning (as well as their distribution) is determined by the grammatical constructions (such as the Passive construction; see Section 5.1.3), which they are a part of.

What are the repercussions of the above discussion for our constructionist definition of words? We noted above that it seems reasonable to assume that *to be*, *is* or *were* all realize the same underlying 'word'. At the same time, we might justifiably say that these are three different words. In order to solve this issue, we must first of all remember the difference between constructs and constructions: constructs are individual tokens of usage; that is, each individual instance of *to be*, *is* or *were* that you say, hear, read or write. Constructions, on the other hand, are stored, mental form-meaning pairings that emerge from the exposure to constructs. In this case, speakers of English will have entrenched a *To Be* construction, an *Is* construction and a *Were* construction (as well as constructions for all other forms of the verb), since these are arbitrary and conventional symbolic pairings of FORM and MEANING and there is no other way the *to be*, *is* or *were* constructs could be licensed. It is these fully substantive (i.e., phonologically fully specified) constructions that we are going to call word constructions. On top of that, however, speakers will also identify the similarities in FORM, MEANING and distribution of these word constructions and form horizontal links in the constructicon. These similarities might then give rise to an abstract superordinate generalization, a BE Lexeme construction. Lexeme constructions thus capture the intuition that the various word constructions realize the same 'word'. Similarly, exposure to *to kick*, *kicks* and *kicked* constructs will also lead to the entrenchment of a *To Kick* construction, a *Kicks* construction and a *Kicked* construction. In addition to that, since this is a regular verb, these forms also increase the type frequency of the various inflectional constructions that are instantiated by them (namely, the V-Infinitive construction, the V-3PS.SG. Present Tense and the V-Past Tense construction, respectively; cf. Section 3.2.1). Finally, the strong FORM-MEANING correspondences of the various KICK constructions will also lead to the entrenchment of an abstract lexeme construction. Note that the only difference between regular lexemes such as KICK and irregular ones like BE concerns the status of their word constructions: the various word constructions realizing BE are so arbitrary that you will definitely have to store all of them in order to produce the correct English constructs with them. For a regular lexeme like KICK, you could also produce the various constructs simply by a combination of the abstract KICK Lexeme construction together with the abstract Inflectional construction (e.g., the V-Infinitive construction, the V-3PS.SG. Present Tense and the V-Past Tense construction; cf. Section 3.2.1). In other words, in order to produce *to kick*, *kicks* or *kicked* constructs you do not necessarily need stored *To Kick*, *Kicks* and *Kicked* word constructions. Nevertheless, from a usage-based perspective it is not important that you can model constructs in the most economical or storage-efficient way. As I pointed out in the previous chapters, even in cases where fewer abstract constructions would computationally suffice to produce constructs, input frequency is much more important than computational efficiency. Thus, provided that they are encountered with sufficient input frequency, the word constructions as well as the lexeme constructions (such as KICK, KISS or WATCH) can both be stored in a speaker's constructicon.

So far, we have thus encountered the following constructs: (1) those that lead to the entrenchment of word constructions (and perhaps also to the generalization of a lexeme construction; cf., e.g., *to be, is, were*) as well as those constructs that result in the storage of lexeme constructions (and, depending on input frequency, also word constructions; cf., for example, the various forms of KICK, KISS and WATCH). In addition to these, however, there are also word constructs for which, at least in written English, we only seem to have a single word construction: English has many words such as *and, in* or *the* that do not inflect and are always realized by the same orthographic constructs (cf. *I saw her **and** John **in the** garden.* with ***The** old mayor **and** his wife were **in** London.* – for the precise phonological realisation of these words see Section 4.2 below). Consequently, these constructs do not lead to the entrenchment of any inflectional constructions but might simply result in the storage of an *And* Word construction, an *In* Word construction and a *The* Word construction. Yet, once we take a closer look at these constructions things again become slightly more difficult: remember that we preliminarily defined word constructions above as the smallest fully substantive constructions of a language. This definition, however, does not quite work with *and, in* and *the*. *And* is a word that combines two (or more) elements (cf. *husband and wife / life and death / you and me / Tom, Dick and Harry / . . .*), so its FORM pole will have to include schematic slots for these variable elements (e.g., FORM: (X,) Y *and* Z). Similarly, *the* and *in* alone do not seem complete, but, for example, beg the question *the what?* and *in where?*, indicating that these also have schematic slots that need to be filled.

I would not be surprised if you are a bit confused by all of this – as I warned you at the start of the chapter, words are a much more complex issue than non-linguists might think. What we need to do now in order to see the big picture in all of this is to take a closer look at the various types of word constructions.

4.2   Word Classes and Basic Phrasal Constructions

In Section 3.2, we saw that we can identify four English word classes that differ with respect to the inflectional constructions that words combine with: nouns (Ns), verbs (Vs), adjectives (ADJs) and adverbs (ADVs). Yet, inflectional constructions are not the only criterion for word classes. As we shall see, and very much in line with the constructionist approach to language, similarities in FORM as well as MEANING properties also give rise to constructional word class generalizations.

Taking into account the MEANING of words to define word classes is not uncontroversial in modern linguistics (cf., e.g., Müller 2019: 17–19; Quirk et al. 1985: 74–5). Let's look at semantic definitions of nouns and verbs to illustrate some of the problems that are usually mentioned in linguistic textbooks, and how we can resolve these issues: in traditional school grammars and dictionaries, nouns are frequently defined as 'naming words' that refer 'to a person, place or thing', while verbs are defined as 'doing words' that express 'an action, process or event' (cf. Eppler and Ozón 2013: 20, 25; Müller 2019: 18; Taylor 2002: 208). This definition works well for TEACHER (a person), SCHOOL (a place) and PEN (a thing), three lexemes that can also appear in the inflectional N-Plural construction (3.52) introduced in Section 3.2.2. (cf. *teachers*, *schools*, *pens*) and thus clearly can be identified as nouns. Similarly, WALK, COOK and DISAPPEAR combine with the V-Past Tense construction (Figure 3.1) and denote an action, process and event meaning, respectively, in *He walked around the kitchen. / The pork cooked for four hours. / The cook suddenly disappeared.*

Other examples, however, are more problematic: a MONTH, e.g., is neither a person, place nor thing, but a time span (that can range from 28 to 31 days) – and yet, as the N-Plural construction shows, it acts like a noun (cf. *months* 'plural (month)'). Similarly, you can attend a single *conference* or multiple *conferences*, but a CONFERENCE seems to denote a range of combined activities, processes and events (people arriving, registering, going to and delivering talks, etc.) rather than a person, place or thing. In the same vein, BE, BELONG or RESEMBLE are clearly verbs since they combine with the set of verbal inflectional constructions (e.g., the V-Past Tense construction: *She was happy.*, *It belonged to me.*, *She resembled the Queen.*), but describe states rather than actions, processes or events.

The semantic definitions above are clearly not perfect. However, as we shall see shortly, the same applies to all other criteria that are used to identify word classes (cf. Herbst and Schüller 2008: 33–64). In fact, it is probably best to think of word classes as prototypical categories with gradient membership that have many semantic and formal properties. But what exactly is the prototypical meaning of nouns and verbs? A good way of approaching this question is to look at the difference in meaning between two related lexemes such as DESTROY and DESTRUCTION. According to FrameNet, both evoke the DESTROYING frame:

(4.11)   DESTROYING frame:
           A **Destroyer** (a conscious entity) or **Cause** (an event, or an entity involved
           in such an event) affects the **Patient** negatively so that the Patient no longer
           exists.[13]

The DESTROYING frame clearly describes an activity with two Core Frame Elements, a DESTROYER/CAUSE and a PATIENT. As (4.12) and (4.13) illustrate, both DESTROY and DESTRUCTION share this scene as part of their meaning:

---

[13] Source: https://framenet2.icsi.berkeley.edu/fnReports/data/frameIndex.xml?frame=Destroying
     [last accessed 02 January 2021].

(4.12)   [The bomb disposal unit]_{Destroyer} **destroyed** [the bomb]_{PATIENT} with a controlled explosion.

(4.13)   [The bomb disposal unit's]_{Destroyer} **destruction** of [the bomb]_{PATIENT} with a controlled explosion.

Both, the verb DESTROY as well as the noun DESTRUCTION thus denote the same type of activity – an action in which a DESTROYER destroys a PATIENT. How can I then still maintain that semantic information is part of the definition of word classes? The important thing to remember here is that the semantics we are talking about is not truth-conditional, but is cognitive in nature. What I mean by this is that (4.12) and (4.13) could, of course, be used to describe the same real-world event. But at the same time both lexemes are also slightly different construals of this situation. In (4.12), the situation is framed as a temporal event that unfolds in time, while in (4.13) it is construed as one atemporal entity – it is essentially treated like a thing. This is also reflected in the FrameNet definitions of the two lexemes: while DESTROY is defined as an action that can unfold over time ('to exert force so as to cause something to cease to exist'[14]), DESTRUCTION is defined as an atemporal thing ('an event of destroying'[15]).

The most sophisticated cognitive analysis of the semantic basis of word classes has been put forward by Cognitive Grammar approaches (cf., e.g., Broccias 2013: 197–9; Langacker 1987; Taylor 2002: 216 – for a similar approach informed by typological research; cf. Croft 2001: 86–107). While the details of this analysis are beyond the scope of the present book, we will nevertheless draw on the insights of Cognitive Grammar and will treat their semantic definitions as the prototypical meanings of word classes. In Cognitive Grammar, the prototypical meaning of nouns is a 'thing', that is the product of a cognitive grouping and reification of an entity as an atemporal unit (cf. Broccias 2013: 198). Applying this definition to DESTRUCTION, we can say that the DESTROYER/CAUSE and PATIENT as well as the action in which they are involved in the DESTROYING frame are grouped together and treated as one atemporal entity (one holistic stative thing). The meaning of verbs, on the other hand, is defined as a processual, that is a dynamic and temporal relationship (cf. Broccias 2013: 198). Consequently, DESTROY also evokes the DESTROYING frame but in a way that treats the relationship of DESTROYER/CAUSE and PATIENT as unfolding over time (which also explains why verbs can combine with temporal constructions such as the V-Past Tense construction).

This cognitive definition of the semantic basis of word classes can easily accommodate nouns denoting fictitious persons, places and things such as *Dumbeldore*, *Hogwarts* and *wands*, since it is not important whether these exist in the 'real world', but only that people can conceive of these as 'things' in the

---

[14] Source: https://framenet2.icsi.berkeley.edu/fnReports/data/lu/lu7622.xml?mode=lexentry [last accessed 02 January 2021].
[15] Source: https://framenet2.icsi.berkeley.edu/fnReports/data/lu/lu7625.xml?mode=lexentry [last accessed 02 January 2021].

technical sense (i.e., as cognitive atemporal entities). Moreover, this approach can also capture the meaning of abstract nouns such as LOVE, HATRED or DISLIKE and their corresponding verbs LOVE, HATE and DISLIKE: while all these words describe 'an Experiencer's emotions with respect to some Content',[16] the verbs emphasize the dynamic relationship between EXPERIENCE and CONTENT and focus on these emotions as they unfold over time. In contrast to this, the nouns present these emotions as holistic, atemporal entities. Again, the difference between nouns and verbs is not truth-conditional in nature (they do not necessarily refer to different situations in the real world), but one of construal (they are different cognitive perspectives on a situation).

4.2.1   Nouns and Noun Phrase Constructions

Now that we have identified the prototypical MEANING of nouns, we can move on to their FORM properties. In Chapter 3, we already used the FORM: MORPHOSYNTAX: N feature to mark words as nouns. This was helpful since it also allowed us to make explicit the internal morphological structure of complex nouns. In (3.77), we, for example, gave FORM: MORPHOSYNTAX: $[N_1+N_2]_{3=2}$ as the morphological pole of endocentric NN compounds (such as *armchair*, *steamboat* or *taxi driver*). In this notation, we used brackets and index numbers to indicate the word class of the whole compound (3=2, which meant that the second N determined the word class of the complex word).

Let us look at another noun to revise our MORPHOSYNTAX representation. Take the noun TEACHER, which is related to TEACH via a morphological correspondence link. More precisely, it is licensed, on the one hand, by the V-to-N Action Noun construction (3.87) and, on the other hand, it is obviously so frequent a construct of this superordinate construction that virtually all speakers of English will also have entrenched a specific TEACHER Lexeme construction. The constructional representation of this TEACHER Lexeme construction is given in (4.14), adding the prototypical word class meaning 'THING':

(4.14)   TEACHER Lexeme construction
          FORM: PHONOLOGY: $/\text{'ti:t}\int_1\text{-ə}_2/_3$
                      MORPHOSYNTAX: $[V_1 + \text{-ER}_2]_{N3}$

          ⇔

          MEANING: SEMANTICS: Frame: EDUCATION_TEACHING[17]
                                      THING: '[a] person who teaches in
                                      an educational establishment'$_3$[18]

---

[16] Source: https://framenet2.icsi.berkeley.edu/fnReports/data/frameIndex.xml?frame=Experiencer_focused_emotion [last accessed 28 June 2021].

[17] Source: https://framenet2.icsi.berkeley.edu/fnReports/data/frameIndex.xml?frame=Education_teaching [last accessed 02 January 2021].

[18] Source: https://framenet2.icsi.berkeley.edu/fnReports/data/lu/lu2247.xml?mode=lexentry [last accessed 02 January 2021]. The compositional semantics derived by the V-to-N Action Noun construction would only yield 'someone who does(teach$_1$)'. Yet, teacher is not only a very frequent term denoting anyone that teaches, but is normally limited to people who teach at a

Thus (4.14) is largely determined by the V-to-N Action Noun construction (3.93): on the morphological level, TEACHER is identified as a complex morpheme that comprises a verb V_1 and a -ER_2 suffix and as a whole is classified as a noun (as indicated by the index '$_{N3}$'). Note that it is thus the label at the edge of the MORPHOSYNTAX bracket encompassing the entire construction (here '$_{N3}$') that encodes in which larger syntactic context it can be inserted (i.e., in all places where nouns can go). Finally, (4.14) also adds the prototypical semantic information of nouns – that TEACHER is cognitively categorized as a 'THING'.

In addition to their prototypical semantic meaning, we already noted that nouns can also be identified by the inflectional constructions that they appear in (such as the N-Plural construction (3.46)). Alternatively, we can now say that the N slot in this inflectional construction is simply a shorthand for lexemes that have the features FORM: MORPHOSYNTAX: N and MEANING: SEMANTICS: THING. Again, however, there are also important exceptions to this generalization: the words *butter*, *music* and *dismay* are conceptualized as 'THINGS', yet you cannot, for example, use them in the N-Plural construction (cf. **butters*, **musics* and **dismays* with the meanings PLURAL(BUTTER), PLURAL(MUSIC), PLURAL(DISMAY), respectively). The reason for this is that we conceptualize these THINGS as unindividuated 'substances' (Taylor 2002: 367–8): they are internally homogeneous, meaning that even just a portion of them is still the same substance (a bit of butter is still butter) and getting more of them is also just going to give us the same substance (more butter is still just butter). Due to this construal and the resulting inflectional behaviour, words such as *butter*, *music* and *dismay* are usually labelled 'noncount nouns', 'uncount nouns' or 'mass nouns' (Herbst and Schüller 2008: 46; Quirk et al. 1985: 245–7). In contrast to this, TEACHER, SCHOOL and PEN are conceptualized as 'individuated objects' (Taylor 2002: 367–8): entities that have an inherent boundary, meaning that you cannot break them down into identical parts (a part of a teacher might be her head, arm or feet, but these alone do not qualify as a whole teacher) and a multiplication of them yields a group of individuals (two teachers are one teacher and another teacher). Consequently, nouns that are thus construed are 'count nouns'.

BUTTER, MUSIC and DISMAY thus seem to be less prototypical members of the N word class than count nouns such as TEACHER, SCHOOL and PEN. At the same time, noncount and count nouns also share important similarities concerning their constructional distribution. Prototypically, for example, nouns are used in so-called referential constructions (Croft 2001: 86–9), constructions that signal to the hearer which particular entity we are talking about:

Count nouns, as I have just argued, are cognitively construed as individuated THINGS. Yet, when we communicate, we normally do not just utter single count

---

school or university, which is why (4.14) gives this specific meaning that overrides the default meaning of the V-to-N Action Noun construction.

nouns to evoke their abstract semantic construal in the hearer. If I, for example, just say *man* then you will very likely ask me what exactly I mean by that – do I want to say something about men in general (their XY chromosomes, their dress code in different cultures, stereotypes about men...) or is there one specific man I would like to talk about. In order to make clear what exactly I am referring to – which entity in the real world (or fictional world) I want you to construe as a 'MAN-THING' (the so-called 'referent'), I need to put *man* into a referential construction.

Let me use the following joke to illustrate some of the most important English referential constructions for count nouns. The joke itself is not very funny (probably because it follows a well-known template and has a very predictable punch line), but it is a nice example to introduce referential constructions. There are quite a few of these in (4.15), but for purposes of exposition let us focus on the ones in boldface only:

(4.15) a.   **A man** walks into a bar and sits down next to **a dog**. 'Does **your dog** bite?' **he** asks **the barmaid**.
       b.   'No,' **she** replies. A few seconds later, **the dog** takes a massive bite
       c.   out of **his leg**. 'I thought **you** said **your dog** doesn't bite!' **the man** yells.
       d.   'That's not **my dog**,' **she** answers.[19]

The first thing to note about (4.15) is that, even though this is a fictitious story, it is clear that the speaker who tells the joke does not want to talk about men, women or dogs in general. Instead, the joke has three specific main protagonists: one man, one woman and one dog. Now in (4.15), I have highlighted all referential constructions that allow the hearer/reader of the joke to pick out these three entities. In (4.15a) you see that when *man* and *dog* are introduced for the first time, they both are preceded by *a*. The Singular Indefinite [*a* N] construction is used by speakers in English when they want to refer to one entity that they have construed as a count noun THING that they think the hearer is not yet able to identify. In other words, the *a* (or its allomorph *an*, which is used before nouns that start with a vowel, cf., for example, *a man*, *a dog*, *a woman*, but *an uncle*, *an eel*, *an aunt*) here basically signals to the hearer: 'I want to talk about one man and one dog, both of which I know you probably don't know.' Once speakers have thus introduced the entities they want to talk about, they can later draw on the Definite [*the* N] construction to refer to them again: in (4.15b), for example, you get *the dog* and in (4.15c) *the man*. The Definite [*the* N] construction thus allows speakers to signal: 'This is a noun THING and I think you know which one I am talking about.' Note that due to their complementary functions, you have to use the Singular Indefinite [*a* N] construction before the Definite [*the* N] construction when referring to the same entity. If you started this joke with the sentence **The man** *walks into a bar and sits down next to **the dog***... your hearers

[19] Source: www.dailymail.co.uk/home/article-1004201/ [last accessed 02 January 2021].

would immediately wonder which man and which dog you are talking about. Similarly, once you have introduced the dog in (4.15a), it would be very odd to continue in (4.15b) with *A few seconds later, **a dog** takes a massive bite*..., since hearers will wonder whether that is supposed to be a new dog now (because you signal to them that you don't think they know which dog you mean – even though you just introduced this referent a second earlier). Using *a **man** yells* in (4.15c) would be just as confusing (is there a second man yelling?). Note, however, that you do not always have to introduce nouns with the Indefinite [*a* N] construction. At the end of (4.15a), for example, the female protagonist is introduced by *the barmaid* and not *a barmaid*. The reason for this is that speakers give hearers a bit of credit and assume that they also take into account all relevant contextual and encyclopaedic information when trying to identify referents. In (4.15a), for example, the place of the story is introduced, as expected, by the Singular Indefinite [*a* N] construction *a bar*. Now, since we know from experience that bars have male and female bartenders, the speaker can introduce the female protagonist by the Definite [*the* N] construction in (4.15b). This is so because upon encountering *the barmaid*, hearers are expected to (unconsciously) think something like: 'I should be able to identify the referent of this – so what do I know so far? The story takes place in a bar and a bar has (at least) one male or female bartender. So, in this story, there is female bartender and the guy who just entered the bar addresses her.'

Both the Singular Indefinite [*a* N] construction and the Definite [*the* N] construction are complex constructions: on their FORM pole, they consist of (at least) two words, *a(n)* and *the* (which are traditionally labelled 'articles' or 'determiners' (DETs)) and a schematic N slot. The precise phonological realization of the two DET elements in these constructions depends on the following phonological context:

- if the next word has an initial vowel (such as *uncle*, *eel* or *aunt*), *an* [ən] is used in the Singular Indefinite construction (cf. *an* [ən] *uncle*, *an* [ən] *eel*, *an* [ən] *aunt*) and *the* is realised as [ði] in the Definite construction (cf. *the* [ði] *uncle*, *the* [ði] *eel*, *the* [ði] *aunt*);

- alternatively, if the next word starts with a consonant (such as *teacher*, *school* or *pen*), *a* [ə] is used in the Singular Indefinite construction (cf. *a* [ə] *teacher*, *a* [ə] *school*, *a* [ə] *pen*) and *the* is realized as [ðə] in the Definite construction (cf. *the* [ðə] *teacher*, *the* [ðə] *school*, *the* [ðə] *pen*);

- finally, the above variants of *a(n)* and *the* can be considered their default pronunciation. Since these are all normally unstressed, they are also called 'weak forms'. Both words, however, also have so-called 'strong forms', stressed variants that are used in special contexts: cf. *I said A* [ˈeɪ] *man entered a bar, not **THE** [ˈðiː] man!* In this example, the speaker uses contrastive stress on *a* and *the* (indicated by capitalization and boldface) to point out that she introduced an indefinite referent, and **not** a definite one. The strong forms of *a*, *an* and *the* are ['eɪ], ['æn] and ['ðiː], respectively. While these specific forms have to be stored for *a(n)* and *the*, we will see that English has several other words that also have a weak and a strong form with a similar distribution in use. These words are collectively known as function words or closed class words for reasons that will become apparent soon.

Unlike the morphologically complex words that we came across in the last chapter, the Singular Indefinite [*a* N] and the Definite [*the* N] construction do not create new words with a new MEANING. Instead, these multi-word constructions act as a single syntactic unit and are known as 'phrases'. Semantically, the noun contributes most of the content of this phrase, while the determiner only adds information on the definiteness of the noun. Since the determiner, thus, is semantically more dependent on the noun than vice versa, the noun is considered the head of the phrase. There are also at least three other reasons why the noun seems to be the head of these phrases, all of which are evidence that the noun and not the determiner affects the syntactic distribution of the construction (cf. Payne and Huddleston 2002: 357–8; for an alternative view that treats determiners as heads of their own phrases; see Radford 2004):

(1)   it is the grammatical NUMBER feature of the noun that agrees with the verb in subject–verb agreement: cf., for example, *the dog*$_{\text{3PS.SG}}$ *loves*$_{\text{3PS.SG}}$ *meat* vs *the dogs*$_{\text{3PS.PL}}$ *love*$_{\text{NON-3PS.SG}}$ *meat* (see also Section 3.2.1);

(2)   verbs can have restrictions on the nouns of referential constructions but do not place similar constraints on the determiner: e.g., *assassinate* evokes the KILLING frame,[20] which has a Core Frame Element VICTIM 'The living entity that dies as a result of the killing.' Due to this, a Definite [*the* N] construction with an animate noun such as *man* sounds much more natural than one with the inanimate noun *table*: cf. *They assassinated the man.* vs *They assassinated the table.*;

(3)   there are many more referential constructions that comprise only a noun (e.g., plural count nouns can be used in this way: *Dogs love meat.*) than ones that consist of a determiner only (e.g., **The love meat*; more on this below).

In light of all these facts, we treat the noun in the Singular Indefinite [*a* N] and the Definite [*the* N] construction as the semantic and syntactic head of the phrase and consequently call the phrases 'noun phrases (NPs)' (and employ the subscript $_{\text{NP}}$ to indicate this; cf. [*a* N]$_{\text{NP}}$ and [*the* N]$_{\text{NP}}$).

---

[20] Source: https://framenet2.icsi.berkeley.edu/fnReports/data/frameIndex.xml?frame=Killing [last accessed 02 January 2021].

So far, we only looked at two NPs that function as referential constructions. English, like most other languages, however, exhibits a far greater range of Indefinite and Definite constructions. Let us start with NP constructions that we can insert into the structure [ ]$_{NP}$ *just sat there.* and that have a definite reading (i.e., the hearer is expected to know their referent). In the joke (4.15), we already saw that the single count nouns *barmaid* (4.15a), *dog* (4.15b) and *man* (4.15c) can appear in the Definite NP construction, so these obviously can be inserted without problem into our test structure:

(4.16)   [*the* N$_{COUNT.SG}$]$_{NP}$
    a.   **The barmaid** just sat there.
    b.   **The dog** just sat there.
    c.   **The man** just sat there.

As can be seen in (4.17), plural count nouns can also occur in the Definite NP construction:

(4.17)   [*the* N$_{COUNT.PL}$]$_{NP}$
    a.   **The barmaids** just sat there.
    b.   **The dogs** just sat there.
    c.   **The men** just sat there.

Example (4.15) also showed that personal pronouns function like Definite NPs and can stand in for NPs such as (4.16) and (4.17): cf. *I* in (4.15c), which refers to the speaker, here the man; *you* in (4.15c), which is the addressee, here the barmaid; or *he* (4.15a) and *she* (4.15b,d), which refer to the man and the barmaid, respectively.

(4.18)   [Pronoun$_{PERSONAL}$]$_{NP}$
    a.   1PS.SG: **I** just sat there.
    b.   2PS.SG: **You** just sat there.
    c.   3PS.SG.MASC: **He** just sat there.
    d.   3PS.SG.FEM: **She** just sat there.
    e.   3PS.SG.NEUT: **It** just sat there.
    f.   1PS.PL: **We** just sat there.
    g.   2PS.PL: **You** just sat there.
    h.   3PS.PL: **They** just sat there.

Personal pronouns are thus Definite NP Referential constructions that do not just replace single nouns, but rather full NPs. (The name 'personal pro-noun-phrase' would thus be more appropriate for them – if it wasn't so cumbersome.) While we briefly came across personal pronouns in our discussion of subject–verb agreement in the last chapter, this is now the place to talk more about their MEANING. As referential constructions, personal pronouns pick out referents and they do this by combining semantic as well as pragmatic properties. Semantically, personal pronouns actually have a fairly limited meaning: their context-independent meaning is more or less identical with their grammatical properties. *I* means '1ST PERSON SINGULAR = speaker', *you* can be rendered as

'2ND PERSON (SINGULAR OR PLURAL) = addressee' and *she* as 'FEMALE 3RD PERSON SINGULAR = neither speaker nor hearer', etc. Who the speaker and addressee (as well as the other non-speaker, non-addressee participants) are – i.e., the precise referent of pronouns – is always context- and speaker-dependent and, consequently, part of their pragmatic meaning. From a pragmatic point of view, pronouns are deictic elements that refer in an indexical fashion: what this means is that, like an arrow, pronouns 'point' to their referents. Metaphorically speaking, whoever is saying *I* is holding an arrow that points towards themselves, while someone who utters *you* is pointing an arrow at their addressee. In order to correctly interpret such deictic elements it is thus crucial to know who uttered them, when and to whom. In more technical parlance, you need to know the deictic centre (also called 'origo'), i.e., the speaker as well as the contextual coordinates of an utterance; that is, time and place (cf., e.g., Saeed 2003: 182–9). For most of what you read here, for example, you unconsciously identified the deictic centre as the textbook in front of you and whenever *I* appears you thus (again metaphorically speaking) see an arrow pointing towards the author of the present text (= Thomas Hoffmann). Yet, when you read the joke in (4.15) you automatically knew that the *I* in (4.15c) did not point towards Thomas Hoffmann, but instead to the man that was mentioned in the joke. You did this because you had shifted the deictic centre of the direct quote from the textbook to the little story in the joke (and the direct quote containing the *I* was qualified as *the man yells*, which told you who the speaker of this sentence was).

Pronouns are also interesting syntactically because they have a different FORM for subject SBJ (see 4.18) and object OBJ position (4.20). For example, (4.19) shows that singular and plural count NPs have the same FORM in OBJ position as in SBJ position (4.16/4.17):

(4.19)   [*the* N$_{COUNT}$]$_{NP}$ in OBJ position
   a.   The woman saw **the barmaid / the barmaids**.
   b.   The woman saw **the dog / the dogs.**
   c.   The woman saw **the man / the men**.

Personal pronouns, on the other hand, with the exception of *you* and *it*, have distinct OBJ FORMs that must be stored in the constructional network:

(4.20)   [Pronoun$_{PERSONAL.OBJ}$]$_{NP}$ in OBJ position
   a.   1PS.SG.OBJ: The woman saw **me**.
   b.   2PS.SG.OBJ: The woman saw **you**.
   c.   3PS.SG.MASC.OBJ: The woman saw **him**.
   d.   3PS.SG.FEM.OBJ: The woman saw **her**.
   e.   3PS.SG.NEUT.OBJ: The woman saw **it**.
   f.   1PS.PL.OBJ: The woman saw **us**.
   g.   2PS.PL.OBJ: The woman saw **you**.
   h.   3PS.PL.OBJ: The woman saw **them**.

Demonstrative pronouns are similar to personal pronouns in that they are also deictic referring expressions whose interpretation depends on the specific discourse context. In contrast to the latter, however, demonstrative pronouns do not differentiate different persons. Instead, they just point to something that is either perceived by the speaker as being close to them ('proximal') or distant from them ('distal'):

(4.21)   [Pronoun$_{DEMONSTRATIVE.SG}$]$_{NP}$
  a.   SG: I want **this**$_{PROXIMAL}$ / **that**$_{DISTAL}$.
  b.   SG: **This**$_{PROXIMAL}$ / **That**$_{DISTAL}$ is what I want!

In (4.21a) and (4.21b) it is illustrated that, unlike personal pronouns, demonstrative pronouns have the same FORM in SBJ and OBJ position. The choice for reference to singular referents (say a beer) here is only between proximal *this* (if the beer is perceived as being close to the speaker) and distal *that* (if the beer is seen as distant). Similarly, for plural referents (say chips), you can choose between proximal *these* and distal *those*:

(4.22)   [Pronoun$_{DEMONSTRATIVE.PL}$]$_{NP}$
  a.   SG: I want **these**$_{PROXIMAL}$ / **those**$_{DISTAL}$.
  b.   SG: **These**$_{PROXIMAL}$ / **Those**$_{DISTAL}$ are what I want!

Neither Personal Pronoun nor Demonstrative Pronoun Reference constructions thus have a noun slot. In addition to that, English, like most languages, has another Definite Reference construction without an N slot and this is reserved for THINGS that are construed as individuated, but which are normally seen as non-countable: proper nouns. Proper nouns, such as the names of individuals, e.g., *Graeme*, *Alexander* and *Edgar*, or of places such as *Birmingham* or *Paris*, are normally considered labels that make unique, stable reference to one identifiable referent only, which explains why proper nouns normally cannot be pluralized (cf. ?*Graemes*, ?*Alexanders*, ?*Edgars*) and cannot be determined by *a* or *the* (?*a Graeme*, ?*an Alexander*, ?*the Edgar* ?). Besides, unlike personal pronouns and demonstrative pronouns this reference is almost always context-independent. In light of all these properties, it is not surprising that proper nouns alone can be used as Reference constructions:

(4.23)   [N$_{PROPER}$]$_{NP}$
  a.   **Graeme (Trousdale)** just sat there.
  b.   **Alexander (Bergs)** just sat there.
  c.   **Edgar (Schneider)** just sat there.

Now I just claimed that proper nouns normally have the above properties. While reading this, you might have already constructed a scenario where this is not the case. Sometimes we come across two individuals with the same name. There is, for example, **an** Edgar Schneider who used to be a German footballer,[21] as well as **an** Edgar Schneider that is a linguist.[22] In such cases, proper nouns are treated

---

[21] Source: https://en.wikipedia.org/wiki/Edgar_Schneider [last accessed 02 January 2021].
[22] Source: www.uni-regensburg.de/language-literature-culture/english-linguistics/staff/schneider/ [last accessed 02 January 2021].

like count nouns and can appear with a determiner (as in this sentence) or be pluralized (as in the hypothetical football chant *Two Edgar Schneiders, there are only two Edgar Schneiders!*).

Finally, English also has referential constructions with an N slot in which the head noun is determined by a preceding possessive pronoun (4.24), demonstrative pronoun (4.25/4.26), or possessive NP (including possessive proper nouns; 4.27):

(4.24)   [Pronoun$_{POSS}$ N]$_{NP}$
  a.   1PS.SG.POSS: **My dog** (4.15c) just sat there.
  b.   2PS.SG.POSS: **Your dog** (4.15c) just sat there.
  c.   3PS.SG.MASC.POSS: **His dog** (4.15a) just sat there.
  d.   3PS.SG.FEM.POSS: **Her dog** (4.15b, d) just sat there.
  e.   3PS.SG.NEUT.POSS: **Its dog** just sat there.
  f.   1PS.PL.POSS: **Our dog** just sat there.
  g.   2PS.PL.POSS: **Your dog** just sat there.
  h.   3PS.PL.POSS: **Their dog** just sat there.

(4.25)   [Pronoun$_{DEMONSTRATIVE.SG}$ N$_{COUNT.SG}$]$_{NP}$
  a.   **This/That barmaid** just sat there.
  b.   **This/That dog** just sat there.
  c.   **This/That man** just sat there.

(4.26)   [Pronoun$_{DEMONSTRATIVE.PL}$ N$_{COUNT.PL}$]$_{NP}$
  a.   **These/Those barmaids** just sat there.
  b.   **These/Those dogs** just sat there.
  c.   **These/Those men** just sat there.

(4.27)   [NP$_{GEN}$ N$_{COUNT.SG}$]$_{NP}$
  a.   **[The pub's] barmaid** just sat there.
  b.   **[Her husband's] friend** just sat there.
  c.   **[Alexander's] dog** just sat there.

The possessive pronouns (4.24) as well as the demonstrative ones (4.25/4.26) are in complementary distribution with the determiner *the*: cf. **the my dog*, **the this/ that barmaid* or **the these/those barmaids*. Now from a usage-based point of view, speakers will, of course, first of all, entrench specific constructions such as *my dog*, *my home*, *my castle*, etc., which due to their type frequency result in a [*my* N]$_{NP}$ Definite constructional template. This in turn, together with other templates arising from variations on (4.24b–h) such as [*your* N]$_{NP}$, [*his* N]$_{NP}$, etc., can give rise to an even more abstract [Pronoun$_{POSS}$ N]$_{NP}$ construction. Finally, similar templates will arise for the demonstrative pronoun + N patterns. Due to their shared MEANING of definite reference, similar FORM patterns and complementary distribution of the pre-N elements, these structures together with the [*the* N]$_{NP}$ construction can give rise to the following abstract Definite DET+N-NP construction:

(4.28)   Definite DET+N-NP
            construction (preliminary version)

FORM: PHONOLOGY: $/X_1\ Y_2/_3$
               MORPHOSYNTAX: $[DET_1\ N_2]_{NP3}$

$\Leftrightarrow$

MEANING: SEMANTICS: $\text{'DEFINITE}_1(N_2)\text{'}_3$
               PRAGMATICS: A_2 previously known by hearer

Thus (4.28) is labelled 'preliminary' since NPs can also contain other elements (such as the adjective *old* in *the old man*), which we will discuss in Section 4.2.1.3. The template, however, already gives the central properties of this construction: on the PHONOLOGY level, we need two elements X_1 and Y_2, which on the MORPHOSYNTAX level are identified as a determiner (DET_1) and a noun (N_2). The SEMANTICS level adds the constraint that the determiner must have a $DEFINITE_1$ reading and its PRAGMATICS requires that the noun A_2 is assumed to be known (i.e., identifiable) by the hearer.

As we will see, the NP construction network of English is pretty complex. If you do not want to delve any further into this topic, you can skip the next two sections and jump straight to Section 4.2.1.3, where I talk about optional modifiers (such as *the old man*). If you want to explore the full complexity of the English NP network, then continue with Section 4.2.1.1.

4.2.1.1   Definite NP Construction Network

Now, (4.28) only has a single DET slot, but (4.27a,b) each exhibit a structure where the determining element is not just a single word but an NP: *the pub's* and *her husband's* are both definite NPs with their own determining elements (*the* and *her*, respectively). How do we know that *the* and *her* here are determiners within a genitive NP and not just determiners of *barmaid* and *friend*? Well, first of all for (4.27b) only this reading seems to be available (you know that there is her husband, but from the sentence you cannot tell whether the friend is also her friend or just her husband's). Moreover, a look at the alternative PP_{OF}-Possessive constructions (Section 3.2.2) supports this view:

(4.29) a.   A barmaid of **the pub** just sat there.
       b.   ?The barmaid of **a pub** just sat there. (as an alternative to (4.27a))

(4.30) a.   A friend of **her husband** just sat there.
       b.   *Her friend of **a/the husband** just sat there.

In (4.29a) we see that the PP_{OF}-Possessive construction expresses the same meaning as (4.27a), as long as *pub* remains determined by *the* (and *barmaid* then can even be indefinitely determined by *a*). In contrast to this (4.29b) does not mean the same as (4.27a). Similarly, (4.30a) is equivalent to (4.27b), while (4.30) is not (thus the scope of *her* has to be over *husband* and not *friend* in (4.27b)). These examples thus indicate that the head nouns in (4.27) are not just determined by a single noun (in the N-Possessive construction), but by an NP with an N-Possessive head (cf. *the pub's* in (4.27a), *her husband's* in (4.27b) and the genitive proper noun NP *Alexander's* in (4.27c)). For the sake of simplicity, we encode this information ('an NP with an N-Possessive head') by the label 'NP$_{GEN}$'. The constructional template of this structure thus can be summarized as follows:

(4.31)   Definite NP$_{POSS}$+N-NP construction (preliminary version)
           FORM: PHONOLOGY: /X$_1$ Y$_2$/$_3$
                        MORPHOSYNTAX: [NP$_{GEN1}$ N$_2$]$_{NP3}$

           ⇔

           MEANING: SEMANTICS: 'DEFINITE$_1$(N$_2$) **and** RELATIONSHIP(A$_1$, B$_2$)'$_3$
                        PRAGMATICS: B$_2$ previously known by hearer

In (4.31), the first element X$_1$ is identified as an NP with an N-Possessive head (NP$_{GEN1}$) that has a definite meaning (DEFINITE$_1$) and the whole construction has the expected definite PRAGMATICS reading (similar to (4.28)). One thing, however, will probably strike you as odd: why did I just put down the semantic relationship between A$_1$ (genitive determiner NP) and B$_2$ (head noun) as 'RELATIONSHIP'? Isn't the relationship between them always one of POSSESSION (see also Chapter 3)? As Payne and Huddleston (2002: 475–8) argue, this is not the case: instead, they point out that there is a great range of possible relationships between the genitive NP and the head. They list more than twenty different relationships (which they claim is not even an exhaustive list), of which I would like to use the following five for a discussion of this ominous RELATIONSHIP:

(4.32) a.   Mary's green eyes ≈ Mary has green eyes.
       b.   Mary's husband ≈ Mary has a husband.
       c.   Mary's book ≈ Mary writes a book.
       d.   Mary's obituary ≈ Mary is the topic of an obituary.
       e.   Mary's surgery ≈ Mary undergoes surgery.
             (examples from Payne and Huddleston 2002: 474)

Examples of predicate structures which contain both head and determiner and which express a similar semantic relationship to the one of the definite NPs are also found in (4.32). As you can see, the relationship between *Mary* and *green eyes* in (4.32a) can be seen as a simple one of POSSESSION. We would, however, not claim that Mary possesses a husband in (4.32b). Rather, the relationship is better translated as Mary is in the kinship relation MARRIAGE with her husband. Similarly, (4.32c) has a reading in which Mary is the Author (and not just the Possessor) of the book in question. Moreover, in (4.32d) Mary just has the topic role of the obituary and the PATIENT role of the surgery in (4.32e). Besides, note that the same range of relationships can be expressed by possessive pronouns in the Definite PRON$_{POSS}$+N-NP construction:

(4.33) a.   My green eyes ≈ I have green eyes.
       b.   My husband ≈ I have a husband.
       c.   My book ≈ I write a book.
       d.   My obituary ≈ I am the topic of an obituary.
       e.   My surgery ≈ I undergo surgery.

But is this relationship between Genitive NP / possessive pronoun and head noun in these Definite constructions really just an arbitrary one to which we can find no generalization? Well, from a usage-based perspective, we would not be surprised to find that this relationship is actually a prototypical one with more or less central members. Take, for example, a look at the top twenty nouns that directly follow *my* in the COCA (Table 4.1):

Table 4.1. *Top 20 collocate nouns directly following* my *in the COCA corpus*[23]

Rank	N	Number of hits
1	LIFE	82,388
2	MOTHER	65,393
3	FATHER	63,239
4	WIFE	37,955
5	HEAD	35,564
6	HUSBAND	34,641
7	MIND	34,417
8	DAD	31,079
9	FAMILY	30,956
10	MOM	29,821
11	NAME	29,342
12	SON	28,784
13	FRIEND	28,706
14	HEART	28,526
15	PARENTS	26,144
16	FRIENDS	23,924
17	DAUGHTER	23,551
18	EYES	23,531
19	BROTHER	23,343
20	WAY	21,761

As you can see, eleven out of these twenty nouns express a KINSHIP frame[24] relation (*mother, father, wife, husband, dad, family, mom, son, parents, daughter, brother*), four denote a relationship of the BODY_PARTS frame[25] (*head, mind, heart, eyes*), while the remaining five describe 'a section of time in a person's lifetime'[26] (*life, way*), 'a particular linguistic form ... to refer to an

---

[23] Source: www.english-corpora.org/coca/. Query 'my *.[nn*]' [11 December 2020].
[24] Source: https://framenet2.icsi.berkeley.edu/fnReports/data/frameIndex.xml?frame=Kinship [last accessed 02 January 2021].
[25] Source: https://framenet2.icsi.berkeley.edu/fnReports/data/frameIndex.xml?frame=Body_parts [last accessed 02 January 2021].
[26] Source: https://framenet2.icsi.berkeley.edu/fnReports/data/lu/lu16371.xml?mode=lexentry [last accessed 02 January 2021].

ENTITY'[27] (*name*), and a relationship of mutual affection that is 'typically one exclusive of sexual or family relations'[28] (*friend, friends*).

In FrameNet, the BODY_PARTS frame definition explicitly mentions that the words evoking this frame are seen as 'belonging to a POSSESSOR'. This captures the intuition that clear cases of POSSESSION (*my money*) can be paraphrased similarly to ones with a BODY_PART relationship (*my hand*): cf. *I have money* and *I have a hand*. The reason for this lies in the construal of BODY_PART relationships, which are usually seen as cases of inalienable possession (e.g., unlike other possessions, you cannot forget taking a body part with you). One prototypical meaning expressed by genitive NPs and possessive pronouns is therefore (alienable and inalienable) POSSESSION. For the other type of proto-typical relationship, kinship, we argued above that a POSSESSION frame reading is not quite correct. Yet, *my Mum*, of course, also has an *I have a Mum* paraphrase, which indicates that in some sense kinship genitives are similar to the other two prototypical readings. As a solution to this problem, Langacker (2008: 83–5, 505–8) offers the following explanation: from specific genitive and possessive pronoun relationships a more schematic relationship emerges as a generalization – a so-called reference point relationship. This relationship is based on cognitive processing operations and is supposed to work as follows: what speakers do when they hear NPs such as *my money*, *my hand* or *my Mum* is to first of all identify the first entity (here *my*) as the reference point for a mental scanning operation. In other words, they construe the meaning of *my* and treat this as the anchor or starting point for the ensuing identification of the second entity (the target, here *money*, *hand* and *Mum*). This scanning operation is successful, since the reference point has various associated cognitive domains (we know, for example, that individuals have possessions of all sorts, have body parts and have various kinship family ties) that can be seen as the search space that we comb through to find a correct target. As we saw above, from a usage-based perspective, basic, highly frequent domain properties (such as the POS-SESSION, BODY-PARTS and KINSHIP frames) constitute prototypical relation-ships encoded by genitive NPs and possessive pronouns and are consequently the primary search domains for the mental scanning for a target. Similarly, however, all other semantic relationships expressed in, for example, (4.32) and (4.33) can also be explained by the schematic and abstract reference point relationship. Furthermore, as Langacker (2008: 84) points out, the reference point relationship is asymmetric in that 'conceiving of one entity makes possible to mentally access another', but not the other way round. Boys, for example, wear shoes and it is thus possible to access the target shoes via scanning the

[27] Source: https://framenet2.icsi.berkeley.edu/fnReports/data/frameIndex.xml?frame=Referring_by_name [last accessed 02 January 2021].

[28] Source: https://framenet2.icsi.berkeley.edu/fnReports/data/lu/lu2177.xml?mode=lexentry [last accessed 02 January 2021].

domain of boys (cf. *boys' shoes*). Conversely, shoes are not a reference point for boys (cf. **the shoe's boys*).

In light of the above, we can now modify the SEMANTICS of the Definite NP$_{POSS}$+N-NP construction, giving the vague label RELATIONSHIP (4.31) a cognitively more adequate description as 'REFERENCE-POINT-RELATIONSHIP(REFERENCE POINT$_1$, TARGET$_2$)':

(4.34)   Definite NP$_{POSS}$+N-NP construction (revised version)
           FORM: PHONOLOGY: /X$_1$ Y$_2$/$_3$
                        MORPHOSYNTAX: [NP$_{GEN1}$ N$_2$]$_{NP3}$
           ⇔
           MEANING: SEMANTICS: 'DEFINITE$_1$(N$_2$) **and**
                                 REFERENCE-POINT-RELATIONSHIP
                                     (REFERENCE POINT$_1$, TARGET$_2$)'$_3$
                        PRAGMATICS: A$_2$ previously known by hearer

The abstract Definite Pron$_{Poss}$+N-NP construction will, obviously, also include the REFERENCE-POINT-RELATIONSHIP(REFERENCE POINT$_1$, TARGET$_2$) in its SEMANTICS. Figure 4.3 illustrates how this MEANING is an emergent generalization over the more specific semantic relationships expressed by the Possessive Pronouns + N constructions:

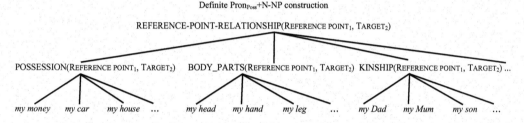

Definite Pron$_{Poss}$+N-NP construction

REFERENCE-POINT-RELATIONSHIP(REFERENCE POINT$_1$, TARGET$_2$)

POSSESSION(REFERENCE POINT$_1$, TARGET$_2$)   BODY_PARTS(REFERENCE POINT$_1$, TARGET$_2$)   KINSHIP(REFERENCE POINT$_1$, TARGET$_2$) ...

my money   my car   my house   ...   my head   my hand   my leg   ...   my Dad   my Mum   my son   ...

Figure 4.3 *Partial construction network of Definite Pron$_{Poss}$+N-NP construction*

So far, our discussion of NP constructions has predominantly focused on Definite N constructions that had a singular N$_{COUNT}$ head. A quick look at Table 4.2 reveals, however, that N$_{NONCOUNT}$ and plural N$_{COUNT}$ heads also can appear in most of these constructions, which is further evidence that speakers might entrench all three types of nouns as members of one N word class category.

Table 4.2 shows that for most Definite NP constructions we do not have to place any further restrictions on the subtype of N (that is, N$_{NONCOUNT}$, N$_{COUNT.SG}$ as well as N$_{COUNT.PL}$ can be inserted into the head N slot). Only the demonstratives *this/that* and *these/those* exhibit selectional restrictions: *these/those* require a N$_{COUNT.PL}$ head (*these/those pens*), while *this/that* can only occur with N$_{COUNT.SG}$ (*this/that pen*) and N$_{NONCOUNT}$ (*this/that milk*) heads. *This/that* therefore co-occur not just with N$_{COUNT.SG}$ but also with N$_{NONCOUNT}$ heads, and it, consequently, seems more appropriate to classify them as non-plural

Table 4.2. *Distribution of N types across Definite NP constructions*

	$N_{NONCOUNT}$ (*milk*)	$N_{COUNT.PL}$ (*pens*)	$N_{COUNT.SG}$ (*pen*)
Definite DET+N-NP cxns:			
[DET N]$_{NP}$	*the milk*	*the pens*	*the pen*
[Pron$_{Poss}$+N]$_{NP}$	*my/your/his milk*	*my/your/his pens*	*my/your/his pen*
[Pronoun$_{DEMONSTRATIVE.SG}$ N]$_{NP}$	*this/that milk*	**this/that pens*	*this/that pen*
[Pronoun$_{DEMONSTRATIVE.PL}$ N]$_{NP}$	**these/*those milk*	*these/those pens*	**these/*those pen*
Definite NP$_{POSS}$+N-NP cxns:			
[NP$_{GEN}$ N]$_{NP}$	[*the man's*] *milk*	[*the man's*] *pens*	[*the man's*] *pen*
[N$_{PROPER·GEN}$ N]$_{NP}$	[*Graeme's*] *milk*	[*Graeme's*] *pens*	[*Graeme's*] *pen*

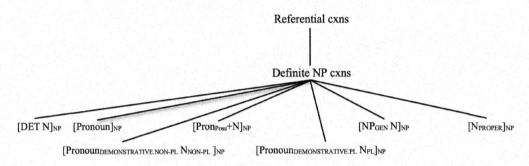

Figure 4.4 *A partial representation of the Definite NP construction network*

demonstrative pronouns (Pronoun$_{DEMONSTRATIVE.NON-PL}$). Definite DET+N-NPs with a demonstrative pronoun in their DET slot thus have the two subtypes Definite Pronoun$_{DEMONSTRATIVE.NON-PL}$+N-NP and Definite Pronoun$_{DEMONSTRATIVE.PL}$+N-NP with the FORM: SYNTAX constraints [Pronoun$_{DEMONSTRATIVE.NON-PL}$ N$_{NON-PL}$[29]]$_{NP}$ and [Pronoun$_{DEMONSTRATIVE.PL}$ N$_{PL}$]$_{NP}$, respectively.

Before we move on with Indefinite Referential constructions, it is probably a good idea to give a brief overview of the Definite NP constructions we have introduced so far. Figure 4.4 provides the Definite NP construction network that we have just uncovered.

4.2.1.2   Indefinite NP Construction Network

In the joke (4.15), we saw that in addition to Definite NP constructions speakers also need Indefinite NP constructions to introduce referents that they assume the hearer cannot identify yet at that point of the conversation. The

---

[29] The feature N_{NON-PL} 'translates' into [$N_{NON.COUNT}$ or $N_{COUNT.SG}$].

first type of Indefinite NP constructions that we came across in the joke is also the most frequent one in English, the Singular Indefinite NP construction with the determiner *a(n)* (cf. *a man, a dog*, and *a woman* in (4.15)). Historically, the Present-day indefinite article *a(n)* derives from the Old English (OE) word for 'one' (OE: *ane man* 'one man'). Sometime during the OE period, the MEANING of *ane* changed from 'one(x)' to 'indefinite(one(x))', acquiring the indefinite reading that is obligatory in Present-day English. As the name of its Present-day NP construction (cf. **Singular** Indefinite $[a \text{ N}]_{NP}$) indicates, in addition to indefiniteness, *a(n)* still has this meaning of picking out a single element today. It is therefore not surprising that it can co-occur with singular count nouns (4.35a), but not with plural count nouns (4.35b) (which denote a number of Ns bigger than one) and also not with noncount nouns (4.35c) (which cannot be counted since they cannot be construed as one individuated instance):

(4.35) $[a \text{ N}_{\text{COUNT.SG}}]_{NP}$
    a.   I have **a pen**.
    b.   *I have **a pens**.
    c.   *I have **a milk**.

The Singular Indefinite NP construction thus will have the restriction (as indicated in (4.35)) that the head noun has to be of the type $N_{\text{COUNT.SG}}$:

(4.36)   Singular Indefinite N_{COUNT}-NP construction (preliminary version)
           FORM: PHONOLOGY: $/ə_1 \text{ X}_{\text{initial.consonant2}}/_3$ **or** $/ən_1 \text{ X}_{\text{initial.vowel2}}/_3$
                        MORPHOSYNTAX: $[\text{DET}_1 \text{ N}_{\text{Count.SG2}}]_{NP3}$
           ⇔
           MEANING: SEMANTICS: 'INDEFINITE$_1$(ONE$_1$(N$_2$))'$_3$
                        PRAGMATICS: A$_2$ previously unknown by hearer

As before, I am trying to give constructions a maximally specific name so that you can easily identify them. Therefore (4.36) is called the 'Singular Indefinite N_{COUNT}-NP construction'. The PHONOLOGY of the construction has two mutually exclusive options (as indicated by '**or**'), which models the determiner's pronunciation depending on the following sound; see above. The MORPHOSYNTAX level then adds the constraint that only singular count nouns can fill the head slot ($N_{\text{COUNT.SG}}$) and the SEMANTICS level contains the information that the NP has an indefinite reading of one individuated noun ('INDEFINITE$_1$(ONE$_1$(N$_2$))'$_3$).

We have now seen the basic way of marking a singular count noun as indefinite in Present-day English. But what about plural count nouns and noncount nouns – how can we signal to a hearer that these should receive an indefinite reading? As it turns out, these nouns can simply occur without any determiner to indicate indefiniteness:

(4.37) $[\text{N}]_{NP}$
    a.   *I have **pen**.
    b.   I have **pens**.
    c.   I have **milk**.

This strategy does not work for singular count nouns (4.37a) – but that is not surprising since we already have a default Indefinite construction (4.36) for these types of nouns. For plural count and noncount nouns we thus need a separate Referential NP construction:

(4.38)   Non-Singular Indefinite $N_{COUNT/NONCOUNT}$-NP construction
           FORM: PHONOLOGY: $/X_2/_3$
                     MORPHOSYNTAX: $[N_{NONCOUNT2}$ **or** $N_{COUNT.PL2}]_{NP3}$
           ⇔
           MEANING: SEMANTICS: 'INDEFINITE$_1$(N$_2$)'$_3$
                     PRAGMATICS: A$_2$ previously unknown by hearer

The Non-Singular Indefinite $N_{COUNT/NONCOUNT}$-NP construction in (4.39) has no determiner slot. Now some approaches (e.g., generative theories such as Radford 2004 or even descriptive analyses such as Quirk et al. 1985) sometimes postulate a zero determiner ∅ for structures such as (4.37b,c). This phonologic-ally empty determiner is motivated in these approaches since it makes it possible to uniformly describe referential NPs as having a determiner slot that paradig-matically can be filled by, for example, either ∅ or *the* (cf. ∅ *pens* and *the pens*). Besides, the indefinite and definite meaning of the NPs can then be ascribed compositionally to the determiner alone (with ∅ carrying the indefinite and *the* contributing the definite meaning). In our constructionist approach, however, we do not have to postulate a phonologically invisible ∅ determiner that competes with the other overt determiners. From a Construction Grammar point of view, referential constructions are holistic units that carry the definite/indefinite mean-ing and that are, therefore, in paradigmatic opposition. This is in line with the surface orientation of the framework that in general eschews the postulation of invisible ∅ elements, whenever possible.

Moving on, we said above that the Singular Indefinite N_{COUNT}-NP construc-tion (4.36) also carries information concerning the quantity of the head noun (i.e., that we construe only one individuated entity after hearing *a man*). In contrast to this, the Non-Singular Indefinite $N_{COUNT/NONCOUNT}$-NP construction (4.38) gives us no such information. So how can we encode quantity information with these noun types? In order to specify, for example, an indefinite quantity, we have to add so-called quantifiers such as *some* /səm/:

(4.39) a.   *I have **some a pen**.
       b.   I have **some pens**.
       c.   I have **some milk**.

In (4.39b,c), adding *some* to the Non-Singular Indefinite $N_{COUNT/NONCOUNT}$-NP construction allows us to provide the information that we have some indefinite number of pens or some indefinite quantity of milk. In contrast to this, the use of an additional quantifier such as *some* in (4.39a) is blocked since the Singular Indefinite N_{COUNT}-NP construction already explicitly refers to a quantity of one, which clashes with the indefinite quantity meaning expressed by the quantifier.

Our Non-Singular Indefinite $N_{COUNT/NONCOUNT}$-NP construction (4.38) description will thus also need an initial slot for an optional *some* quantifier. Interestingly, *some* can also co-occur with bare singular count nouns, but in these cases it has a slightly different meaning (Quirk et al. 1985: 384):

(4.40)   **Some man** came round, and James phoned me afterwards, told me what he'd said.
          (BNC CKB W_fict_prose)

In (4.40), *some man* refers to a single individual, so *some* here does not specify an indefinite quantity. Instead, *some man* in (4.40) is roughly synonymous with *a man* and could be replaced by it (cf. *A man came round* ...). I say 'roughly synonymous' because *some man* clearly does not just mean a single indefinite man. In fact, it has the added meaning of 'a certain man' or 'some man or other' (Quirk et al. 1985: 384). Besides, while the indefinite quantifier of the Non-Singular Indefinite $N_{COUNT/NONCOUNT}$-NP construction is normally unstressed (/səm/), the *some* appearing with bare singular count nouns is stressed and pronounced as /'sʌm/ (Quirk et al. 1985: 257 [a]). Consequently, we cannot cover the examples in (4.39b,c) and (4.40) by a single *some* quantifier construction, which is part of both the Singular Indefinite $N_{COUNT/NONCOUNT}$-NP construction and the Singular Indefinite N_{COUNT}-NP construction. Instead, due to the phonological as well as semantic idiosyncrasies of the *some* + singular N_{COUNT} structures, we will need a specific constructional template to license these patterns:

(4.41)   *Some* Singular Indefinite N_{COUNT}-NP construction
          FORM: PHONOLOGY: /'sʌm$_1$ X$_2$/$_3$
                      MORPHOSYNTAX: [DET$_1$ N$_{Count.SG2}$]$_{NP3}$

          ⇔

          MEANING: SEMANTICS: 'a certain (ONE$_1$(N$_2$))'$_3$
                      PRAGMATICS: A$_2$ previously unknown by hearer

Thus, (4.41) is a specific Singular Indefinite N_{COUNT}-NP construction that paradigmatically competes with the prototypical Singular Indefinite N_{COUNT}-NP construction (4.37). In other words, speakers have a choice to say either *a man* or *some man* in (4.40), with each choice leading to a particular construal of the scene. While the Singular Indefinite N_{COUNT}-NP construction (4.36) just signals that the speaker introduces an indefinite single referent that she assumes the hearer cannot identify yet. The *Some* Singular Indefinite N_{COUNT}-NP construction has the added undertone that this is a certain individual for which the speaker does not consider it necessary to (or simply cannot) identify the referent.

The topic of quantifiers in NPs is a very complex one, which is why we will only be able to scratch the surface of it in this book. For further reading, I therefore strongly encourage you to look at descriptive grammars (such as Payne and Huddlestone 2002: 358–67; Quirk et al. 1985), but also specific research papers (such as Davidse 2004 and Declerck 1991). In the following paragraphs, we will limit ourselves to some of the most important English quantifiers, namely *any*, *no* and *all* (*every*, *many* and *much* are the topic of Exercise 4.2 at the end of this chapter)

Any [ɛni] is an interesting quantifier because it basically behaves like *some* – with the notable difference that it appears in negative contexts:

(4.42) a. *I don't have **any a pen**.
      b. I don't have **any pens**.
      c. I don't have **any milk**.

Like *some*, *any* cannot co-occur with *a* because of their incompatible meanings (4.42a). In negative contexts, however, *any* appears with plural count nouns (4.42b) as well as noncount nouns (4.42c). Both *some* and *any* thus refer to an unspecified quantity of the head noun. They differ, however, in whether the speaker can be sure whether the referent of the NP really exists: while *some* indicates that the speaker asserts that there is a positive quantity of the thing talked about (i.e., that there are some pens or some milk), *any* signals that the speaker is not sure whether a quantity of the thing she mentions really exists (i.e., whether there are any pens or any milk). This also explains why you will normally use *any*, and not *some*, in a question with which you ask for something that you cannot be certain actually exits: cf. *Have you got any milk?* vs *Have you got some milk?* (if you use the former question, then you indicate that you don't know whether the addressee has milk, while in the latter, you know they have it, you're just asking them politely instead of ordering them to give you some).

Moreover, just like *some* in (4.40), when used with a bare singular count noun, *any* is stressed ['ɛni] and has a special meaning:

(4.43)   Based on horror stories of recent years, maybe you've decided you're lucky to get a job, **any job**, at any salary. (COCA MAG 2015)

Any job in (4.43) refers to a single, indefinite occupation, with the added meaning 'it doesn't matter which job' (cf. Quirk et al. 1985: 391). Due to this idiosyncrasy, speakers of English will also have to store the following construction:

(4.44)   *Any* Singular Indefinite N_{COUNT}-NP construction
      FORM: PHONOLOGY: $/'\varepsilon ni_1 \ X_2/_3$
                      MORPHOSYNTAX: $[DET_1 \ N_{Count.SG2}]_{NP3}$

      ⇔

      MEANING: SEMANTICS: 'a certain $(INDEFINITE_1(ONE_1(N_2)))$
                                 but it doesn't matter which N_2'$_3$
                      PRAGMATICS: A_2 previously unknown by hearer

Another, special indefinite determiner is *no*, which basically denies the existence of any instantiation of the noun THING (Davidse 2004; Declerck 1991):

(4.45)   *I have **no a pen**. /

(4.46) a.   I have **no pen**.
    b.   I have **no pens**.
    c.   I have **no milk**.

With count singular nouns such as *pen*, *no* means something like 'not even one', which explains why it is incompatible with *a* (which means 'one'; (4.45)). The easiest way to model this is to assume that *no* [nəʊ] competes with *a(n)* for the DET_1 slot of the Singular Indefinite N_{COUNT}-NP construction (4.36) (and simply changes the SEMANTICS to 'INDEFINITE$_1$(NOT-ONE$_1$(N$_2$)'$_3$). Similarly, the Non-Singular Indefinite $N_{COUNT/NONCOUNT}$-NP construction can either appear without any quantifier (4.38; cf. *I have pens. / I have milk.*) or an optional DET_1 *some, any* or *no*, each of which contribute their specific indefinite quantifier reading to the construction (cf. *I have some/no pens. / I have some/no milk.* and *I don't have any pens. / I don't have any milk.*).

The last quantifier that we will look at is *all*:

(4.47) a.   *I like **all a teacher**.
    b.   *I like **all teacher**. / I waited **all day**.
    c.   I like **all music**.
    d.   I like **all teachers**.

The meaning of *all* is something like 'the whole quantity' (FrameNet s.v. *all. a*[30]) and thus implies the existence of more than one noun THING, which explains why it is incompatible with the Singular Indefinite N_{COUNT}-NP construction that singles out one particular single element only (4.47a). For the same reason, *all* can normally not co-occur with single count nouns (cf. **all* teacher* in 4.47b). The only exception is count nouns such as, for example, *day*, which can clearly be counted (*a day, one day, five days*, etc.), but which can also receive a noncount-like interpretation (in that they are construed as an internally homogeneous mass of time; cf. *all day* in 4.47b). For these special cases, we will therefore have to add a special *All* Singular Indefinite N_{COUNT}-NP construction (more on this below). In all other cases, *all*, like *some, any* and *no*, can be used to quantify indefinite plural (4.47d) as well as noncount nouns (4.47c). Since *all* is mutually exclusive with these other quantifiers in these contexts, we can again just add it as another DET option in the Singular Indefinite N_{COUNT}-NP construction and Non-Singular Indefinite $N_{COUNT/NONCOUNT}$-NP construction. Including all these quantifier constructions, Figure 4.5 shows that the basic inventory of indefinite NPs in English is slightly simpler than the one for definite NPs in Figure 4.4:

---

[30] Source: https://framenet2.icsi.berkeley.edu/fnReports/data/lu/lu13747.xml?mode=lexentry [last accessed 02 January 2021].

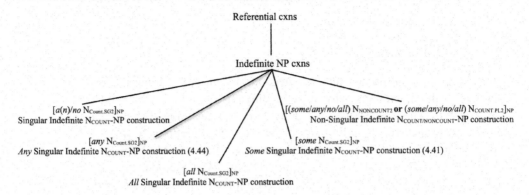

Figure 4.5 *A partial representation of the Indefinite NP construction network*

Now, it seems that Figure 4.5 could greatly be simplified by combining the *Any*, *Some* and *All* Indefinite N_{COUNT}-NP constructions with their corresponding Non-Singular Indefinite $N_{COUNT/NONCOUNT}$-NP constructions. Yet, you have to remember that *Some* and *Any* Indefinite N_{COUNT}-NP constructions have a special meaning that *Some* and *Any* Non-Singular Indefinite $N_{COUNT/NONCOUNT}$-NP constructions do not have (with the former two implying 'a certain indefinite one THING' and 'a certain indefinite one THING but it doesn't matter which', respectively). Similarly, the *All* Indefinite N_{COUNT}-NP construction superficially resembles the *All* Non-Singular Indefinite $N_{COUNT/NONCOUNT}$-NP construction. Yet, while the latter can host all sorts of noncount and plural count nouns, only a special subset of singular count nouns can co-occur with *all* (see above). When we look at the ten most frequent *all* + N combinations in the COCA corpus, we see that some types of the *All* Indefinite N_{COUNT}-NP construction, nevertheless, have a pretty high token frequency:

Table 4.3. *Ten most frequent* all + *NOUN sequences in COCA*[31]

Rank	ALL N	FREQ	N TYPE
1	ALL DAY	24,556	$N_{COUNT.SG}$
2	ALL KINDS	16,682	$N_{COUNT.PL}$
3	ALL THINGS	15,163	$N_{COUNT.PL}$
4	ALL NIGHT	14,536	$N_{COUNT.SG}$
5	ALL SORTS	11,316	$N_{COUNT.PL}$
6	ALL TIME	7,942	$N_{NONCOUNT*}$ / $N_{COUNT.SG*}$
7	ALL PEOPLE	7,305	$N_{COUNT.PL}$
8	ALL TIMES	6,496	$N_{COUNT.PL}$
9	ALL STUDENTS	5,952	$N_{COUNT.PL}$
10	ALL AGES	4,882	$N_{COUNT.PL}$

[31] Source: www.english-corpora.org/coca/. Query 'all *.[nn*]' [11 December 2020].

Table 4.3 contains seven plural count nouns (including *people*, which carries no plural inflectional construction, but is clearly construed as a plural noun; cf. *the people are.*$_{PL}$ *happy*). The list also includes two singular nouns, *day* and *night*, which in this construction receive the above-mentioned mass construal. At the same time, due to their high frequency, these types can be said to act as prototypes for the *All* Indefinite N$_{COUNT}$-NP construction (i.e., we can predict that other temporal count nouns could follow the model of these prototypical types). Finally, *time* has a noncount/mass reading (cf. *Much time had passed.*) as well as a count meaning (cf. *We met four times.*) but here, it is probably best analysed as a stored chunk (i.e., an idiom, see the discussion below) with the meaning 'always' (cf. *I will love you for all time.*[32]).

Interestingly, unlike indefinite *some* and *any*, the universal quantifier *all* also occurs in definite NPs, where it is not in complementary distribution with the definite article *the*:

(4.48) a.   *I like **all the teacher**.
       b.   I met **all the family**.
       c.   I like **all the teachers/all the families**.
       d.   I like **all the music**.

While (4.48a) is again ungrammatical due to the conflicting semantics of *all* (which implies more than one entity) and the singular count noun *teacher*, (4.48b) is acceptable since a family can also be construed as an internally homogeneous mass (i.e., we can either treat a family as a single, countable THING that contrasts with other family units, or as a mass THING in which individuals are seen as instances of a family). In contrast to this, *all* can co-occur with a wide range of plural (4.48c) and noncount (4.48d) definite NPs. Consequently, as in the Indefinite NP construction network (Figure 4.5), we would also need to subdivide the various constructions in the Definite NP network (Figure 4.4) into those that can always optionally co-occur with an *all* quantifier (those with a plural count noun or noncount head), and those for which this is only possible for certain construals (i.e., for singular count nouns that can receive a mass/noncount construal).

Let us leave this issue aside (for another publication) and turn to a more important generalization: from a classic, non-constructionist point of view, we might expect that the major factor determining the distribution of nouns in NPs is their word class characteristics. Thus, we would expect singular and plural forms of count nouns to behave more similarly than noncount nouns. Yet, as we have seen, that is not the case: it is plural count nouns and noncount nouns that show a more similar distribution across NPs than singular and plural count nouns (Taylor 2002: 372–3). From a cognitive perspective, we can therefore say that lexeme constructions are important (we, for example, expect plural *teachers* to prime singular *teacher*, and vice versa), but for the English referential constructions it is more important whether a noun THING is construed as a single,

---

[32] Source: https://dictionary.cambridge.org/dictionary/english/time [last accessed 02 January 2021].

individuated entity (single count noun) or a group (either of individuated entities (plural count nouns) or a homogeneous mass (noncount nouns)).

This concludes our discussion of the obligatory properties of English Referential NP constructions. Yet, the constructions that we have postulated so far can obviously not account for the full range of English NP constructions. As we will see in the next section, on top of all the obligatory information necessary to identify its discourse referent, NPs often also comprise optional, additional information.

4.2.1.3   Modifiers in NP Constructions

Take a look at the NPs in (4.49):

(4.49) a.   We were excited by [all the [**really good**]PREM reviews [**of this pub**]POM] and tried to visit - but couldn't park![33]

     b.   We were excited by [all the reviews [**of this pub**]POM] ...

     c.   We were excited by [all the [**really good**]PREM reviews] ...

     d.   We were excited by [all the reviews] ...

The 'simple' phrasal construct in (4.49d) should normally suffice for a hearer to establish the referent of the NP. Yet, (4.49a–c) shows that NPs also have optional slots preceding the head noun (*really good*) as well as following it (*of this pub*). Following traditional grammatical terminology, we shall call the former the PREMODIFIER (PREM) slot and the latter the POSTMODIFIER (POM) slot. These optional slots are part of all NP constructions (except for [Pronoun PERSONAL]NP-constructions; cf. *I saw* [**really good him*]):

(4.50) a.   ... he can be [a [**really good**]PREM player [**for us**]POM].[34]

     b.   ... he can be [a player [**for us**]POM].

     c.   ... he can be [a [**really good**]PREM player.

     d.   ... he can be [a player].

(4.51)   Fantastic local pub with ...

     a.   [[**really good**]PREM beer [**from its own micro brewery**]POM] ...[35]

     b.   [beer [**from its own micro brewery**]POM] ...

     c.   [[**really good**]PREM beer] ...

     d.   [beer] ...

As the examples above show, optional PREM and POM slots are part of, for example, Singular Indefinite NCOUNT-NP constructions (4.50) as well as Non-Singular Indefinite NCOUNT/NONCOUNT-NP constructions (4.51).

In contrast to the DET slot, however, an NP can contain more than one PREM and/or POM (see example (4.52)). These slots are therefore called 'iterative':

[33] Source: www.tripadvisor.co.uk/Restaurant_Review-g1471645-d5570871-Reviews-The_Cross_ Oak-Blackwood_Caerphilly_County_South_Wales_Wales.html   [last   accessed   04 December 2017].

[34] Source: www.independent.co.uk/sport/football/premier-league/shola-ameobi-s-younger-brother-line-be-best-8303747.html [last accessed 28 June 2021].

[35] Source: www.tripadvisor.co.uk/Attraction_Review-g2137553-d7368653-Reviews-Cerddin_ Brewery-Maesteg_Vale_of_Glamorgan_South_Wales_Wales.html   [last   accessed   04 December 2017].

(4.52) a.   ... he can be

  [a [nice]$_{PREM}$ [new]$_{PREM}$ [fast]$_{PREM}$ player [in midfield]$_{POM}$ [for us]$_{POM}$].

Later in this chapter, I will provide an overview of the various elements that can function as PREM or POM in English NPs. Right now, however, you might wonder whether we cannot just summarize all the above information in a single, maximally abstract construction. So, what is the most schematic representation of the English NP construction that we can formulate? Well, it should look something like (4.53):

(4.53)   Prototypical NP macro-construction
          FORM: PHONOLOGY: /X$_1$ (V$_3$)* Y$_2$ (W$_4$)*/$_5$
                      MORPHOSYNTAX: [DET$_1$ (PREM$_3$)* N$_2$ (POM$_4$)*]$_{NP5}$

          ⇔

          MEANING: SEMANTICS: 'DEFINITENESS$_1$(THING$_2$
                      (with PROPERTY$_3$)* (with PROPERTY$_4$)*)'$_5$
                      PRAGMATICS: REFERENCE$_1$(A$_2$ (with B$_3$)* (with C$_4$)*)

Example (4.53) is the most prototypical constructional template for English NPs. I call it 'prototypical' because it captures most NP constructs, but not all of them (N$_{PROPER}$-NP constructs such *Alex*, *Thomas* or *Graeme* and Pronoun-NP constructs such as *I*, *you* or *they* only consist of only one element, see above Section 4.2.1). Yet, if it does not apply to all NP constructs would we postulate that speakers actually have entrenched a construction such as (4.53)? It is not easy to answer this question empirically, since all the NP constructs we have come across could also be licensed by the various definite and indefinite NP constructions we have encountered in this chapter. From a cognitive perspective, however, categories are always prototypical, so it might be very likely that a form-meaning generalization such as (4.53) can also arise in a speaker's mind (due to the large type and token frequency of the various definite and indefinite NP constructions supporting it). Even if it turns out not to be psychologically real, however, (4.53) is at least a convenient generalization to capture the main properties of English NPs:

- First of all, English NPs contain a nominal head (MORPHOSYNTAX level: N$_2$) that linearly appears after an optional premodifier and before an optional postmodifier (PHONOLOGY: (V$_3$)* Y$_2$ (W$_4$)*). Semantically, it denotes a THING$_2$ that can be definite or indefinite, and thus is underspecified with respect to its reference.
- The reference of the NP is identified by the other obligatory element in English NPs, the determinative slot (MORPHOSYNTAX: DET$_1$). Determiners normally appear in initial position (PHONOLOGY: X$_1$) and provide information as to whether the NP is definite or indefinite (SEMANTICS: DEFINITENESS$_1$), thus also indicating the referent status of the NP (PRAGMATICS: REFERENCE$_1$).
- Finally, there are the optional pre- and post-modifiers that appear before and after the head noun, respectively (PHONOLOGY: (V$_3$)* Y$_2$ (W$_4$)*, MORPHOSYNTAX: (PREM$_3$)* N$_2$ (POM$_4$)*). These elements denote

optional properties that the head noun has and that are therefore put in parentheses and added by a boldface 'with' (SEMANTICS: (with PROPERTY$_3$)* (with PROPERTY$_4$)*, PRAGMATICS: (with B$_3$)* (with C$_4$)*). Since these positions are iterative, we use a Kleene star * to indicate that this slot can be empty or filled by one or more elements that function as PREMs and POMs in NPs (n.b., the Kleene star thus has a different meaning than the asterisk we use to signal the ungrammaticality of structures).

Thus, (4.53) is a helpful template for capturing most English NP constructs (even if we cannot be sure whether speakers really possess such an abstract NP construction). Next, let us look at the most prototypical PREM filler types: adjectives and adjective phrases.

4.2.2   Adjectives and Adverbs/Adjective Phrase and Adverb Phrase Constructions

In *all the **really good** reviews* (4.49a), *a **really good** player* (4.50a) and ***really good** beer* (4.51a), the PREM slot of the NP is filled with the string *really good*. Of the two words, *really* and *good*, we can see that the latter is the more important, obligatory one, while the former is optional:

(4.54) a.   We were excited by [all the [**good**]$_{\text{PREM}}$ reviews].
      b.   He can be [a [**good**]$_{\text{PREM}}$ player].
      c.   I like [[**good**]$_{\text{PREM}}$ beer]!

(4.55) a.   *We were excited by [all the [**really**]$_{\text{PREM}}$ reviews].
      b.   *He can be [a [**really**]$_{\text{PREM}}$ player].
      c.   *I like [[**really**]$_{\text{PREM}}$ beer]!

Now, *good* can obviously be graded. It has a comparative form *better* (*a better player*) and a superlative form *best* (*the best player*). In line with the discussion above, we can, thus, say that the GOOD Lexeme construction is linked to *Good* Absolute, *Better* Comparative and *Best* Superlative Word constructions. In Section 3.2.3, I already mentioned that only adjectives and adverbs in English have comparative and superlative forms, so what is GOOD, an adjective or an adverb? Prototypically, both adjectives and adverbs denote 'simplex non-processual relationships' (Broccias 2013: 199). In other words, they are construed as atemporal (unlike verbs) and relational (unlike nouns). The difference between the two is that adjectives are prototypically in a non-processual relation with a noun, while adverbs are in a non-processual relation with another category (either a with an adjective, a preposition, a verb or another adverb). In other words, prototypically, adjectives denote a PROPERTY that is ascribed to a THING, while adverbs denote a PROPERTY that is ascribed to an ACTION or another PROPERTY.

Now, in (4.54) *good* is clearly a PROPERTY ascribed to the head noun (*reviews*, *player* and *beer*, respectively) – it, therefore, is an adjective.

Actually, in English, the PREM slot of NPs is one of two constructions in which adjectives can, frequently, appear (4.56; this use is also called 'attributive'). The other is a predicative structure in which it follows a form of BE (4.57):

(4.56)   [A [**good**]_{PREM} player]_{NP}

(4.57)   The player is [**good**].

In both of the examples above, *good* is a PROPERTY that is ascribed to *player*, but in (4.56) it fills the PREM slot of an NP, while in (4.57) it fills a slot of the Predicative BE construction (see Sections 4.2.3 and 5.1.1). As just mentioned, most adjectives can appear in both of these constructions:

(4.58)   [A [bad/friendly/nice/new/quick/...] _{PREM} player]_{NP}

(4.59)   The player is [bad/friendly/nice/new/quick/...].

As with all prototypical properties, there are, however, some exceptions (see Aarts and Aarts 1988: 30). Some adjectives, for example, only appear attributively:

(4.60) a.   [This [**utter**]_{PREM} fool]_{NP}
       b.   [A [**mere**]_{PREM} girl]_{NP}
       c.   [His [**sole**]_{PREM} argument]_{NP}

(4.61) a.   *A fool is [**utter**].
       b.   *A girl is [**mere**].
       c.   *His argument is [**sole**].

Others can only be used predicatively:

(4.62) a.   *[This [**asleep**]_{PREM} fool]_{NP}
       b.   *[An [**alive**]_{PREM} girl]_{NP}
       c.   *[His [**alone**]_{PREM} father]_{NP}

(4.63) a.   This fool is [**asleep**].
       b.   A girl is [**alive**].
       c.   His father is [**alone**].

From a Construction Grammar perspective, part of the mental knowledge of speakers is, therefore, that prototypical adjectives can appear in both NP as well as Predicative BE constructions. For the adjectives in (4.60) and (4.63), however, only one positional variant will be entrenched. Nevertheless, all of the adjectives above have the expected relational meaning of denoting the PROPERTY of a THING.

Now, as many of the examples above show (see, e.g., (4.49a), (4.50a) and (4.51a)), the PREM slot of NPs does not just contain a single word. Instead, it hosts a combination of words, aka a phrase. As (4.54) and (4.55) show, of the two words in that phrase, it is the adjective *good* that is the more important one (since it is obligatory and is a PROPERTY that modifies the head noun of the NP). Consequently, we call this phrase an 'Adjective Phrase' (ADJP) construction and the NP construct *a really good player* has the following structure (4.64):

(4.64)   *A really good player* NP construct
           FORM: PHONOLOGY: /ə$_1$ [ˈɹɪəli ˈgʊd]$_3$ ˈpleɪə$_2$/$_5$
                          MORPHOSYNTAX: [DET$_1$ PREM:ADJP$_3$ N$_2$]$_{NP5}$

           ⇔

           MEANING: SEMANTICS: 'INDEFINITE$_1$(
                                   THING: player$_2$ **with** PROPERTY:
                                   really-good$_3$)'$_5$
                          PRAGMATICS: REFERENCE$_1$(A$_2$ **with** B$_3$)

As you can see, the ADJP$_3$ fills the PREM slot on the MORPHOSYNTAX pole
and is, for example, linked to the PROPERTY element on the
SEMANTICS pole.

But what about the internal structure of the ADJP *really good*? We already
established that *really* is only an optional element in this construction. In addition
to this, it modifies an adjective, that is it ascribes a PROPERTY to another
PROPERTY (it tells us something about the adjective *good*, namely that it is 'really',
i.e., particularly good). In line with our semantic prototype definition above, this
means that *really* is an adverb. Adverbs can, thus, function as an optional PREM
element in ADJPs (4.65). In addition to this, they can also modify other adverbs (see
quite in (4.66), *very* in (4.68)) or verbal ACTIONs (see *well* in (4.67)):

(4.65)   He is an [exceptionally good] player

(4.66)   He is a [[quite exceptionally] good] player

(4.67)   He played [well].

(4.68)   He played [[very] well].

As you can see in (4.66) and (4.68), the slots occupied by *exceptionally* in (4.65)
and *well* in (4.67) can be enriched by an optional adverb. Consequently, these
slots do not just host simple word constructions, but are actually slots for phrasal
constructions. Thus (4.69) shows what the ADJP construct for (4.66) looks like:

(4.69)   *quite exceptionally good* construct
           FORM: PHONOLOGY: /[kwaɪt ɪkˈsepʃənəli]$_1$ ˈgʊd$_2$/$_4$
                          MORPHOSYNTAX: [PREM:ADVP$_1$ ADJ$_2$]$_{PREM\_NP3:ADJP4}$

           ⇔

           MEANING: SEMANTICS: 'THING$_3$ **with** PROPERTY$_4$(PROPERTY$_2$
                          with PROPERTY$_1$)'$_4$

In (4.69), the ADVP$_1$ *quite exceptionally* fills the PREM slot on the MORPHO
SYNTAX pole of the ADJP construct. Moreover, in line with the prototypical
meaning of adjectives, the entire ADJP is in a non-processual relation with a
THING$_3$ that syntactically must be realised by an N$_3$. This N$_3$ obviously lies
outside of the construct in (4.69), but there are good reasons to include it in the
description above (as information that still needs to be added in order to fully know
who or what is *quite exceptionally good*). First of all, we will be able to indicate the
semantic difference between ADJPs and ADVPs, since these profile different

types of non-processual relationships. Second, as we will see, a great many types of modifiers can appear in all sorts of phrasal and clausal constructions where they are optional elements and where more than one modifier can appear in a slot (cf., e.g., the PREM and POM slot of NPs). At the same time, the modifiers themselves are quite restrictive with respect to the constructions they can appear in (see, e.g., the restrictions on certain types of ADJP in (4.60)–(4.63)). In other words, it seems as if the modifiers select and restrict the types of phrases that they are embedded into. For these reasons, it seems likely that speakers have stored this type of information in the constructional entries of modifiers. In formal approaches, this is encoded by, for example, introducing a feature called MOD (MODIFIED) to the MORPHOYSYNTAX that specifies that ADJPs, for example, can modify nouns [MOD N] or that ADVPs modify adjectives [MOD ADJ] or adverbs [MOD ADV] (see, e.g., Levine 2017: 87–8; Müller 2008: 73–8). In Chapter 7, we will take a closer look at formal approaches. As I said at the start of this book, however, the goal of the present introduction is not to provide you with a fully formal constructional model of English. My aim is to provide you with a usage-based constructional representation that constantly reminds you that for any constructional analysis we always have to take into account PHONOLOGY, MORPHOSYNTAX and SEMANTICS (as well as PRAGMATICS, where applicable). Beyond these labels, however, I will not introduce any subfeatures under these three attributes. Still, as you will see in Chapter 7, once you understand a representation such as (4.69), it will allow you to access all types of constructional works, from completely informal, usage-based descriptions to fully formal models. At the same time, the description remains maximally compatible with traditional approaches to English grammar (such as Aarts and Aarts 1988 or Quirk et al. 1985). So, what does all of this mean for the issue of modifiers? Well, as you can see in (4.69), I have simply added 'PREM_NP' (highlighted by light grey shading) at the edge of the MORPHOSYNTAX pole and by this, I indicate that the ADJP as a whole must function as a PREM to an N_3 (which is linked to a $THING_3$ element on the SEMANTICS pole).

Note, however, that our semantic description of PREMs in (4.69) is fairly simplistic. The meaning of the whole phrase is a complex $PROPERTY_4$ that combines the semantics of the premodifier $ADVP_1$ and the head ADJ_2. The meaning of *quite exceptionally* is, obviously, not just the combination of the meaning of $PROPERTY_1$:*quite* **with** $PROPERTY_2$:*exceptionally*. Instead, it would probably be better to give $PROPERTY_1$ scope over $PROPERTY_2$ (in predicate logic terms by, for example, treating $PROPERTY_1$ as a predicate which takes $PROPERTY_2$ as its argument; $PROPERTY_1(PROPERTY_2(x))$; e.g., quite'(exceptionally'(x))). In the following, however, again for the sake of simplicity, we will keep our simplified notation of linking optional MORPHOSYNTAX:PREM elements to optional **'with'** SEMANTIC: PROPERTY elements. Finally, (4.69) does not provide any PRAGMATICS information because the ADJP construct does not seem to have any discourse context-dependent properties.

Abstracting from the construct in (4.69), we can give the following preliminary characterization of ADJP constructions in English:

(4.70)   ADJP construction (preliminary version)
            FORM: PHONOLOGY: $/(X_1)\ Y_2/_4$
                         MORPHOSYNTAX: $[(PREM{:}ADVP)_1\ ADJ_2]_{PREM\_N3{:}ADJP4}$

            $\Leftrightarrow$

            MEANING: SEMANTICS: 'THING$_3$ **with** PROPERTY$_4$(PROPERTY$_2$
                         with PROPERTY$_1$)'$_4$

As with the NP construction (4.53), this Phrasal construction contains an optional slot (X_1) on the PHONOLOGY pole that is linked to an optional PREM element on the MORPHOSYNTAX level that in English always has to be of the type ADVP (and normally does not iterate, thus the absence of a '*' here) and which is linked to a PROPERTY$_1$ that modifies the PROPERTY$_2$ of the adjective. Furthermore, for the reasons just discussed, it specifies that whole ADJP$_4$ functions as a PREM_N$_3$ (which is linked to a corresponding THING$_3$ meaning on the SEMANTICS pole).

Similar to (4.70), we can then also provide a first representation of the ADVP construction:

(4.71)   ADVP construction (preliminary version)
            FORM: PHONOLOGY: $/(X_1)\ Y_2/_4$
                         MORPHOSYNTAX:
                         $[(PREM{:}ADVP_1)\ ADV_2]_{PREM\_ADV3}$ **or** $_{PREM\_ADJ3{:}ADVP4}$

            $\Leftrightarrow$

            MEANING: SEMANTICS: 'PROPERTY$_3$ **with** PROPERTY$_4$
                         (PROPERTY$_2$ **with** PROPERTY$_1$)'$_4$

The ADVP construction has an optional PREM slot that is filled by other ADVP$_1$s. As with the ADJP construction in (4.70), (4.71) also includes information as to the phrase-external PROPERTY$_3$ that is modified by the ADVP$_4$ (and which is indicated by the PREM$_3$ subscript, which specifies that ADVPs can function as premodifiers of ADVs 'PREM_ADV$_3$' (4.66) or ADJs 'PREM_ADJ$_3$' (4.65)).

We will refine the constructional templates for ADJPs and ADVP in the exercises section. Now that we have encountered NPs, ADJPs and ADVPs, it is time to look at arguably the most important word construction, namely verbs.

4.2.3   Verbs and Verb Phrase Constructions

4.2.3.1   Lexical Aspect / 'Aktionsart'

At the beginning of Section 4.2, I argued that verbs are constructions that prototypically construe an event as processual, that is a dynamic and temporal relationship. In other words, in addition to semantic roles, verbs also profile how an event is qualitatively unfolding over time. Now, each verb, of course, is one specific lexicalization (aka constructional-encoding) of a particular type of event. At the same time, guided by our perceptual system, we as humans seem to be prone to picking up on certain similarities across events. In particular, we seem to categorize verbs depending on the type of dynamic relationship they track over time, their 'lexical aspect' (or '*Aktionsart*'; Croft 2012: 31–69; Saeed 2003: 118–24).

The three parameters that are usually used to classify verbs according to their lexical aspect type are (Croft 2012: 33–7):

(1)   whether a situation is construed as changing over time ('dynamic') or not ('stative');
(2)   whether they extend in time ('durative') or not ('punctual'); and
(3)   whether they have a natural endpoint ('telic'/'bounded') or not ('atelic'/'unbounded').

To illustrate these properties, let us look at the examples in (4.72), for which I also provide the conventional lexical aspect labels (also known as 'Vendler classes'):

(4.72) a.   stative, durative, unbounded = State verbs:
            I know the answer.
       b.   dynamic, durative, unbounded = Activity:
            They danced.
       c.   dynamic, durative, bounded = Accomplishment:
            He painted a picture.
       d.   dynamic, punctual, bounded = Achievement:
            He reached the mountain top.
       e.   dynamic, punctual, unbounded = Semelfactive:
            She coughed.

State verbs such as the KNOW construction (or DESIRE, WANT, LOVE, etc.; Saeed 2003: 113) express events that are perceived as stative (not changing over time), durative (extending over time) and unbounded (not having any particular endpoint). In contrast to this, Activity verbs such as DANCE (or RUN, WALK, SWIM, etc.; Saeed 2003: 113) are also durative and unbounded, but dynamic; that is, they denote events where we can perceive some kind of qualitative change (such as couples moving across a dance floor, people moving with their feet and/or arms moving). Accomplishment verbs such as PAINT (or GROW UP, DRAW A CIRCLE, etc. Saeed 2003: 113) and Achievement verbs such as REACH (or RECOGNIZE, SPOT SOMEONE, etc.; Saeed 2003: 113) are both dynamic and bounded (there is a change of state when you have finally finished painting a picture or reached a mountain top). The difference between the two is that Accomplishments are durative (you spend some time painting a picture before it is finished), while Achievements are punctual (from one moment to another you suddenly recognize something or suddenly will have reached a mountain top). Finally, Semelfactives such as COUGH (or KNOCK or

SNEEZE; Saeed 2003: 113), like Achievements are dynamic and punctual, but unlike the latter do not lead to a qualitatively different state (after coughing or knocking everything is, more or less, the same as before the event).

As we shall see, the lexical aspect of a verb construction is a prototypical (and not a categorical) construal and interacts in interesting ways with other tense and aspect constructions (for an in-depth constructional analysis of this topic read Croft 2012). In Section 5.2, I will provide you with a comprehensive overview of the latter type of constructions. For now, it is just important that you understand the difference between tense and aspect: tense constructions are construals that express the temporal location of events relative to the deictic centre of the speaker (whether something, for example, happened in the past, that is, the time before speaking, or might happen in the future). Aspect, on the other hand, refers to the fact that speakers can construe one and the same event that happens at a specific point in time in different qualitative ways.

Let me illustrate the difference between tense and aspect by looking at how an accomplishment verb such as *bake* receives a slightly different construal in the Simple Present construction (4.73) and the Present Progressive construction (4.74):

(4.73)   Simple Present construction (preliminary version)
          FORM: MORPHOSYNTAX: $V_{1\text{SIMPLE PRESENT2}}$
          ⇔
          MEANING: SEMANTICS: 'PRESENT(STATE(V_1))'$_2$

(4.74)   Present Progressive construction (preliminary version)
          FORM: MORPHOSYNTAX [BE$_{\text{SIMPLE PRESENT2}}$ $V_{\text{PRESENT PARTICIPLE1}}$]$_3$
          ⇔
          MEANING: SEMANTICS: 'PRESENT$_2$(ONGOING(V_1))'$_3$

The constructions in (4.73) and (4.74) both locate an event as happening in the present, the time of speaking (hence the feature PRESENT on the SEMANTICS level). The difference is only that the Simple Present construction construes the event as a stable state (STATE in (4.73)), while the Present Progressive construction construes it as ONGOING (4.74). Besides, on the FORM level, the Simple Present construction requires a verb form that is marked as PRESENT (which includes the Present Tense 3PS.SG (e.g., *bakes*) as well as Present Tense non-3PS.SG constructions (e.g., *bake*). In contrast to this, the Present Progressive construction needs a present tense word form of BE (i.e., *am*, *are* or *is*) plus the present participle form of a verb (e.g., *baking*; for details of the various inflectional constructions; see Section 3.2.1).

Drawing on the two constructions in (4.73) and (4.74), we get the following two different present tense construals for a baking event:

(4.75)   He bakes muffins.

(4.76)   He is baking muffins.

Prototypically, *bake* evokes the COOKING_CREATION frame,[36] in which a COOK engages in an action that results in PRODUCED_FOOD. The Present Progressive construction locates this action in the present (tense) and construes it as 'the state of being "in the middle"' (Croft 2012: 155). However, since (4.76) focuses on the ongoing process of baking, the result (PRODUCED_FOOD) gets back-grounded. Thus, it is possible to say things like 'He is baking muffins – but he'll never get them done', if you think he will never produce muffins in the end. In contrast to this, the Simple Present construction condenses the whole process into an event that profiles a stable qualitative state (Croft 2012: 151–2). As such, the result (PRODUCED_FOOD) is also part of this construal, and 'He bakes muffins – but he'll never get them done', consequently, sounds odd. In fact, verbs that denote events that can occur regularly, such as *bake* often receive a habitual reading in the Simple Present construction (see Croft 2012: 150–1 for further details). Thus, upon hearing (4.75), we infer that he is habitually baking muffins.

Depending on their prototypical lexical aspect, different verbs more or less naturally combine with either of the two present tense constructions:

(4.77)   State verbs
    a.   Simple Present construction: I know the answer.
    b.   Present Progressive construction: ? I am knowing the answer.

(4.78)   Activity
    a.   Simple Present construction: They dance.
    b.   Present Progressive construction: They are dancing.

(4.79)   Accomplishment
    a.   Simple Present construction: He paints pictures.
    b.   Present Progressive construction: He is painting pictures.

(4.80)   Achievement
    a.   Simple Present construction: He reaches the mountain top.
    b.   Present Progressive construction: He is reaching the mountain top.

(4.81)   Semelfactive
    a.   Simple Present construction: She coughs.
    b.   Present Progressive construction: She is coughing.

Remember that state verbs are non-dynamic, durative and unbounded and, thus, by default denote a stable qualitative state. As a result, they can easily combine with the Simple Present construction (4.77a). It is more difficult to see what their meaning in the Present Progressive construction (4.77b) should be. After all, being in the middle of a stable state-of-knowing is no different to knowing things. (However, sometimes state verbs can receive an emphatic or emotional

---

[36] Source: https://framenet2.icsi.berkeley.edu/fnReports/data/lu/lu4896.xml?mode=lexentry [last accessed 02 January 2021].

meaning as in *I'm loving this!*, which highlights how much the speaker loves something 'right here and now').

Activities and accomplishments, on the other hand, are dynamic and durative, so the Present Progressive construction can easily focus on being in the middle of one of these events (4.78b, 4.79b). Now, unlike activities, accomplishments are bounded; that is, they are normally expected to culminate in some kind of end-point. Yet, when construed as ongoing in the Present Progressive construction, this endpoint is backgrounded and it is thus possible to say things like *He is painting pictures, but he'll never finish any of them.* The Simple Present construction, on the other hand, again construes activities and accomplishments holistically, which gives them a habitual interpretation (dancing in (4.78a) and painting in (4.79a) are construed as events that the subjects regularly participate in).

In contrast to the other event types, Achievements and Semelfactives are both punctual, so the holistic construal of these events as a currently stable qualitative state in the Simple Present construction is straightforward ((4.80a) and (4.81a), respectively). Yet, what happens to punctual events when they are combined with the Simple Progressive construction? Well, Achievements are bounded, so they normally have a single climax or culmination point. When combined with the Simple Progressive construction, this leads to a construal that focusses on being-in-the-middle of reaching this culmination point ((4.80b), for example, could be uttered just as they are in the middle of reaching the top of the mountain). In contrast to this, since Semelfactives have no natural endpoint, these receive an iterative meaning: (4.81b) means that someone is in the middle of coughing over and over again.

In addition to the prototypical event type (lexical aspect), another generalization across verbs concerns the number of profiled (i.e., obligatorily expressed) prototypical participants. The different lexical aspect types, for example, sometimes profile only one participant (the (a) examples in (4.82)–(4.86)), they are 'monovalent'. (Note that the ADJ *happy* in (4.82) is not treated as a second participant, but as part of a complex predicate BE *happy*.[37]) Other lexical items of the various lexical aspect types profile two participants (they are 'bivalent' or 'divalent'):

(4.82)   State verbs
    a.   monovalent: He_1 is happy.
    b.   divalent: She_1 adores $them_2$.

(4.83)   Activity
    a.   monovalent: She_1 swims.
    b.   divalent: He_1 plays the $trumpet_2$.

---

[37] There are several reasons for this: first of all, as we have seen above, ADJs such as *happy* can appear in premodifier position (cf. *a happy man*), where they only require one element (the head noun *man*) that they modify. Furthermore, many varieties of English, including African American English do not need the BE lexeme in these present tense predicative uses at all: cf. *He happy* 'He is happy'.

(4.84)   Accomplishment
     a.   monovalent: The ship$_1$ sinks.
     b.   divalent: She$_1$ bakes a cake$_2$.

(4.85)   Achievement
     a.   monovalent: He$_1$ dies.
     b.   divalent: She$_1$ won the race$_2$.

(4.86)   Semelfactive
     a.   monovalent: She$_1$ sneezed.
     b.   divalent: He$_1$ hit the lamp post$_2$.

In addition to this, trivalent patterns are found for some state verbs (cf. I_1 consider him$_2$ an idiot$_3$.) and Accomplishments (cf. I_1 gave him$_2$ a present$_3$.). Finally, so-called weather verbs such as *rain* or *snow* obligatorily require a subject in English (cf. *It rains.* or *It snows.* vs **Rains.* or **Snows.*) that does not correspond to any participant. These special types of activity verbs are therefore often considered 'avalent' or 'zerovalent'.[38]

As we will see in the next chapter, the uses in (4.82)–(4.86) should only be seen as the prototypical participant profiling patterns of verbs. Once verbs combine with various argument structure constructions, many more construals of the events they denote can be found. For our analysis of the Verb Phrase (VP), however, we need to take a closer look at verbs that prototypically encode two-participant events (divalent verbs) and that express a FORCE-DYNAMIC relation (Croft 2012: 198–219): in (4.82b)–(4.86b), the first participant is the 'INITIATOR' of a physical or abstract force that is directed at the second participant, the 'ENDPOINT'. In (4.86b), for example, the first participant clearly exerts physical force on the lamp post. In (4.82b), the force is only a mental feeling, but clearly an asymmetric one that goes from INITIATOR to ENDPOINT (just because she adores them, you cannot assume that they also adore her). How is this relevant for our discussion of VP constructions? Well, all of the examples so far were in the active voice, in which the INITIATOR is mapped onto the subject and the ENDPOINT becomes the object (remember that subjects can, inter alia, be identified by subject–verb agreement (see Section 3.2.1) and by the fact that personal pronouns that fill that slot appear in the subject case form, e.g., *he* or *she*; cf. Section 4.2). In the passive voice, however, the INITIATOR is back-grounded and becomes part of an optional *by*-phrase. Instead, the ENDPOINT now becomes the subject (Croft 2012: 252–63):

(4.87)   Passive of divalent state verb
           They$_{ENDPOINT}$ are adored (by her$_{INSTIGATOR}$).

---

[38] Though, as FrameNet points out, these verbs are part of the Precipitation frame, which does not profile any participant carrying out an action, but has profiled Core Frame Elements for Place and Time (as well as Precipitation, but the latter is often incorporated into the verb): https://framenet2 .icsi.berkeley.edu/fnReports/data/frameIndex.xml?frame=Precipitation&banner= [last accessed 06 April 2020].

(4.88)   Passive of divalent activity verb
           The trumpet$_{\text{ENDPOINT}}$ is played (by him$_{\text{INSTIGATOR}}$).

(4.89)   Passive of divalent accomplishment verb
           The cake$_{\text{ENDPOINT}}$ is baked (by him$_{\text{INSTIGATOR}}$).

(4.90)   Passive of divalent achievement verb
           The race$_{\text{ENDPOINT}}$ is won (by her$_{\text{INSTIGATOR}}$).

(4.91)   Passive of divalent semelfactive
           The lamp post$_{\text{ENDPOINT}}$ is hit (by him$_{\text{INSTIGATOR}}$).

Note that not all divalent verbs have a FORCE-DYNAMIC meaning. Spatial verbs, for example, encode causally undirected relations of a FIGURE (the entity that is being located or that is moving) and a GROUND (the entity that serves as the reference point for the location/motion; Croft 2012: 226–33):

(4.92)   The phone$_{\text{FIGURE}}$ is on the book$_{\text{GROUND}}$.

(4.93)   The book$_{\text{FIGURE}}$ is under the phone$_{\text{GROUND}}$.

In (4.92) and (4.93) there is no force exertion from one participant onto another. Instead, it depends on our construal of whether we see *the phone* or *the book* as the FIGURE (the thing that we want to foreground; this, for example, depends on whether someone is looking for the phone or the book). FIGURE-GROUND verbs, however, do normally not appear in the passive construction (cf. *The book is been on (by the phone)* or *The phone is been under (by the book)*). A FORCE-DYNAMIC interpretation thus seems to be an important prerequisite for verbs to enter the Passive construction (see also Exercise 4.5).

   We will have a closer look at the form, meaning and function of the Passive construction in Section 5.1.3. For our discussion of the VP, however, it is important that it not only requires a different order of INITATOR and ENDPOINT, but that it obligatorily consists of a BE Lexeme construction (e.g., *are* or *is* in (4.87)–(4.91)) plus a V-Past Participle construction (cf. Section 3.2.1).

4.2.3.2   Modality, Tense and Aspect

As the above shows, Verb Phrases (VPs) in English contain more than simple verbs. In addition to voice, tense and aspect, 'modality' is another grammatical category that is marked in VPs: the so-called modal verbs (*can, could, may, might, must, shall, should, will* and *would*; Herbst and Schüller 2008: 42) can also appear in VPs, and if they do, they precede all other verbal elements:

(4.94) a.   He **bakes** a cake.
       b.   He **may bake** a cake.
       c.   A cake **may be baked** (by him).

(4.95) a.   He **is baking** a cake.
       b.   He **may be baking** a cake.
       c.   A cake **may be being baked**.

Out of context, modal verbs have two potential meanings: they can express a deontic meaning; that is, they express a speaker's permission (or some sort of obligation). Thus, (4.94b) can be paraphrased as 'I (the speaker) allow him to bake a cake.' Alternatively, they can denote a speaker's assessment of the likelihood of an event. Then, (4.94b) would mean something like 'I (the speaker) think there's a probability that he bakes a cake.' Different modal verbs, obviously, differ to the degree of deontic or epistemic meaning that they express – just replace *may* with *must* in (4.94b) and (4.95b) above to see how different the sentences sound (for current constructionist research on English modal verbs; cf. Cappelle, Depraetere and Lesuisse 2019; Hilpert and Flach 2020).

What (4.94c) and (4.95c) show is that the aspect, modality, tense and voice information are layered in the English VP. Let us take a closer look at (4.95c):

(4.96)   A cake

      [may be_1]   = MODALITY (& TENSE) + V_{base}

      [be_1 $being_2$] = BE + V-ing = PROGRESSIVE

      [$being_2$ baked]   = BE + V-ed = PASSIVE

In (4.95c), be_1 and $being_2$ only appear once, but as (4.96) shows they each fulfil two functions in the construct: be_1 fills the second verb slot of the Modality construction (which has to be in the infinitive base form without *to*) as well as the initial slot of the Progressive construction (which requires an instance of a BE lexeme). *Being*$_2$, on the other hand, acts as the filler for the BE lexeme slot of the Passive construction as well as the second element of the Progressive construction (which specifies that it must be in a V-*ing* present participle).

As we will see in Section 5.2, tense and aspect constructions in English are not that easily separated. Nevertheless, if the VP is finite then it is always the first verbal element that shows tense and agreement:

(4.97) a.   He [bakes_{3PS.PRESENT TENSE}] a cake.

     b.   He [is_{3PS.PRESENT TENSE} baking] a cake.

     c.   He [was_{3PS.PAST TENSE} baking] a cake.

     d.   A cake [was_{3PS.PAST TENSE} being baked].

The reason we do not see any traces of this in (4.96) is that modal verbs are all finite, but have an invariant form for all grammatical persons (cf. *I may bake a cake.* vs *He may bake a cake.*). So, the order of our grammatical constructions in the VP seems to be MODALITY&TENSE > ASPECT > VOICE.

Finally, there is one more important grammatical meaning that is also encoded in the VP, namely negation:

(4.98) a.   He [is_{3PS.PRESENT TENSE} **not** baking] a cake.

     b.   He [was_{3PS.PAST TENSE} **not** baking] a cake.

     c.   A cake [was_{3PS.PAST TENSE} **not** being baked].

     d.   A cake [may_{PRESENT TENSE} **not** be being baked].

As (4.98a–d) show, negation is expressed by a *not* that follows the first tensed form of BE or a modal verb. The same also applies to the so-called

Present Perfect construction (FORM: HAVE + V-*ed* ↔ MEANING: 'an event in the past has present relevance'; Croft 2012: 162–4; for details, see Section 5.2):

(4.99) a. He [has$_{3PS.PRESENT TENSE}$ **baked**] a cake.
     b. He [has$_{3PS.PRESENT TENSE}$ **not baked**] a cake.

Other verbs, however, cannot simply be negated in this way (4.100a), for these the DO-Lexeme has to be added (4.100b):

(4.100) a. *He [bakes$_{3PS.PRESENT TENSE}$ **not**] a cake.
      b. He [does$_{3PS.PRESENT TENSE}$ **not** bake] a cake.

The relationship between positive and negated verbs is thus part of our constructional network:

	Positive		Negative
(4.101)	BE	↔	BE **not**
(4.102)	HAVE	↔	HAVE **not**
(4.103)	MODAL	↔	MODAL **not**
(4.104)	DO	↔	DO **not**
(4.105)	V$_{other}$	↔	DO **not** V$_{other}$

BE, HAVE, MODALs as well as DO have a horizontal link in the mental constructicon between their positive and negative form, in which the latter simply has a NOT after them (4.101)–(4.104). For all other verbs, their corresponding negative form has an additional DO (4.105).

Now, negation is not the only property that distinguishes BE, HAVE, DO and the MODAL verbs from all other lexical verbs (such as *bake*, *sink*, etc.), which is why the former are often classified as a single category called 'auxiliary verbs' (AUX). In English, AUX verbs are said to have the so-called NICE properties, which is an acronym for NEGATION (4.101)–(4.104), INVERSION (4.106), CODE (4.107) and EMPHASIS (4.108):

(4.106) a. **Is**$_{AUX}$ **he**$_{SBJ}$ baking a cake?
      b. **Has**$_{AUX}$ **he**$_{SBJ}$ baked a cake?
      c. **May**$_{AUX}$ **he**$_{SBJ}$ bake a cake?
      d. **Does**$_{AUX}$ **he**$_{SBJ}$ bake a cake?
      e. *****Bakes he**$_{SBJ}$ a cake?

(4.107) a. He is baking a cake, **is he**? (= 'is he baking a cake?')
      b. He has baked a cake, **has he**? (= 'has he baked a cake?')
      c. He may bake a cake, **may he**? (= 'may he bake a cake?')
      d. He does bake a cake, **does he**? (= 'does he bake a cake?')
      e. *He bakes a cake, **bakes he**? (= '*bakes he a cake?')

(4.108) a. He **is**$_{FOCUS}$ baking a cake!
      b. He **has**$_{FOCUS}$ baked a cake!

  c. He **may**$_{FOCUS}$ bake a cake!

  d. He **does**$_{FOCUS}$ bake a cake!

  e. #He **bakes**$_{FOCUS}$ a cake![39]

So, in contrast to other verbs (4.106e), BE, HAVE, MODALS and DO can appear initially in yes-/no-questions (4.106a–d), a construction that requires the AUX verb to precede the subject (the two are said to be 'inverted', hence the 'I' in the acronym NICE). Moreover, they can appear in tag questions (4.107a–d) (that are a shorthand 'code' for the full verb phrase, thus 'C' is for 'code'). Finally, AUX verbs can carry 'emphasis' (or contrastive focus) – thus (4.108a–d) can be used when someone has claimed the opposite and you want to emphatically stress that he is baking/has baked/may bake a cake! For all of these NICE functions, lexical verbs again need DO-support (4.104, 4.106d, 4.107d, 4.108d).

 Ok, so now that we have established everything that AUX verbs can do, what is the largest combination of auxilliary verbs you can get in English? Descriptive grammars say that the combination of MODAL + PERFECT ASPECT + PROGRESSIVE + PASSIVE yields the largest construct: *may have been being examined* (Quirk et al. 1985: 151). Yet, such constructs are relatively rare and might therefore not sound that good to you. In the 2020 version of COCA, which comprises more than one billion words, I only found six examples, including (4.109) – none of which are negated:[40]

(4.109) And now it turns out that

     the mud **should have been being thrown** at the Democrats by

      the Republicans.

     (COCA SPOK: YOUR WORLD WITH NEIL CAVUTO, 2017 (171027))

Summing up, in addition to a lexical verb, the English VP can also contain a combination of modality, tense, and aspect constructions, as well as negation constructions.

4.2.3.3 Other elements in the VP

 By now you might be wondering whether VPs only consist of (auxiliary and lexical) verbs, because I really only have been talking about these so far. Some descriptive grammars (such as Quirk et al. 1985) take this perspective. Most theories, however, reserve the term VP for structures that are larger than this (and which Quirk et al. 1985 call 'predicates'):

(4.110) He   [had eaten a full meal (ten minutes earlier)]

     and [(then) was swimming (in the lake) (for an hour)]!

---

[39] As an anonymous reviewer points out, (4.108e) is grammatical, but focuses on the lexical content of *bake*.

[40] The queries used were '_vm* have been being _v*' (6 hits) and 'vm* not have been being _v* (0 hits). Source: www.english-corpora.org/coca/ [last accessed 17 April 2020].

(4.111)   She   [may have baked muffins (at home)]
                 but   [did not bring any muffins (to work)]!

In (4.110) and (4.111), we find a single NP (*he* and *she*, respectively) that functions as the subject of two coordinated phrases. These phrases contain auxiliary and lexical verbs (*had eaten* as well as *was swimming* in (4.110) and *may have baked* as well as *did not bring* in (4.111)). On top of that, they also contain the non-subject obligatory Core Frame Elements of the verbs (aka 'complements'; *a full meal* in (4.110), *muffins* and *any muffins* in (4.111)) as well as all additional, optional time and place frame elements (which are often called 'adjuncts', and due to their optional nature are placed in parentheses in (4.110) and (4.111) above: *ten minutes earlier*, *then*, *in the lake*, *for an hour* and *at home*, *to work*).

Data such as (4.110) and (4.111) suggest that there is a form-meaning unit that comprises auxiliary and lexical verbs, non-subject Core Frame Elements as well as optional non-Core Frame Elements (Quirk et al. 1985: 78–9). In line with many other syntactic approaches, we call this unit V(erb) P(hrase). While the position of Core Frame Elements in VPs is fairly fixed and can be considered a stored property of the VP constructions, the placement of non-core adjuncts is extremely variable (4.112):

(4.112) a.   The book must have been placed on the shelf.
        b.   **By then** the book must have been placed on the shelf.
        c.   The book **by then** must have been placed on the shelf.
        d.   The book must **by then** have been placed on the shelf.
        e.   The book must have **by then** been placed on the shelf.
        f.   The book must have been **by then** placed on the shelf.
        g.   The book must have been placed **by then** on the shelf.
        h.   The book by then must have been placed on the shelf **by then**.
             (examples 4.113 b–h from Quirk et al. 1985: 490)

As (4.112a) shows, the phrase *by then* is optional, yet when it is present it can appear fairly freely inside as well as outside of the VP (though each position of the adjunct leads to a slightly different meaning of the entire construct). Adjuncts are thus like the modifiers of phrases, since they only add additional, optional information. At the same time, they differ from the PREM and POM modifiers we have seen in the NP, ADJP and ADVP, since for these latter phrases the positions of the modifiers are fixed (and can thus be said to be optional slots of the various phrasal constructions). In the next section, we will see that the distinction between core/complements and non-core adjuncts is not as clear-cut as it may seem right now, but that semantic, syntactic as well as frequency effects suggest that there is a gradient cline between them. For now, we can simplify our analysis of VP constructions by ignoring the presence of adjunct phrases (and assuming that the adjunct phrases will have to specify in which larger context they can occur – an approach taken by many formal constructional approaches, which assign a [MOD VP] feature to VP adjuncts).

Ignoring adjuncts for now, what do VPs such as *had eaten a full meal* and *was swimming* (4.110) or *may have baked muffins* and *did not bring any muffins*

(4.111) have in common and what is their semantic meaning? Well, as the examples in (4.110) and (4.111) show, finite VPs all miss one more obligatory element to count as a full sentence, namely a subject (*he* and *she* in (4.110) and (4.111)). From a semantic perspective, the subject is often considered the topic of the sentence; that is, what the sentence is 'about'. Conversely, VPs can be said to express something about a subject: 'the predicate is that which is asserted about the subject' (Quirk et al. 1985: 79; see also Croft 2012: 183). The Finite VP construction could thus be captured by the following template:

(4.113)   Finite VP construction
            FORM: PHONOLOGY: $/X_1 (V_2)*/_3$
                         MORPHOSYNTAX: $SUBJECT_4 [[V_1 (COMPL_2)*]_{VP3}$

            $\Leftrightarrow$

            MEANING: SEMANTICS: 'PREDICATION(ABOUT-TOPIC$_4$)'$_3$

The MORPHOSYNTAX level of (4.113) specifies that the construction contains at least the V slot (a combination of modality, tense, aspect and lexical verb constructions; see Section 4.2.3.2) plus all non-subject COMPLements. Since there can be zero (*He swam.*) to two complements (*He baked her a cake.*), depending on the chosen verb and the argument structure construction, we mark this slot by '(COMPL$_2$)*'. In addition to that, the MORPHOSYNTAX level also has a SUBJECT$_4$ slot **outside** of the VP construction, that on the SEMANTICS level is identified as the topic about which the VP says something ('ABOUT-TOPIC$_4$'). This means that this is a slot that is expected by the VP construction, but is not part of its phonological structure (and thus does not have a slot for the subject on the PHONOLOGY level). Finally, the meaning of the VP construction is prototypically identified as 'PREDICATION' (i.e., that quality of asserting something about the subject).

So far, we have discussed NPs, VPs, ADJPs and ADVPs, but what about phrases such as *for an hour* (4.110) or *at home* (4.111)? In the above examples, they were identified as functioning as adjuncts on the VP level and internally they clearly contain NPs (*an hour* and *home*, respectively). Yet, they also contain short little words such as *in, at, for* or *over* – so-called prepositions.

4.2.4   Prepositions and Preposition Phrase Constructions

Prepositions such as *in, on* or *at* are word constructions that prototypically locate THINGS in space. They are therefore relational and involve two elements: a FIGURE (sometimes also called a trajector) and a GROUND (also called a landmark; Broccias 2013: 199; Ungerer and Schmid 2006: 166):

(4.114) a.   The table$_{FIGURE}$ is **in the garden**$_{GROUND}$.
        b.   A book$_{FIGURE}$ is **on the table**$_{GROUND}$.

In these relationships, the FIGURE is the focal element that in the case of spatial prepositions is located with respect to the GROUND. So, in (4.114a) *the table* is the FIGURE and its location is given by the complement of the preposition *in*;

that is, *the garden*. Similarly, in (4.114b) *the book* is the FIGURE and *the table* is the GROUND. The notions of FIGURE and GROUND go back to principles of object recognition as proposed by Gestalt theory (see Eysenck and Keane 2015: 85–9): in our visual field, we tend to focus on something (the FIGURE) and perceive it as having a distinct form, while the GROUND is backgrounded. Which factors influence whether we identify something as a FIGURE (and, consequently, treat the rest of our visual field as the GROUND)? Psychological research has shown that the prototypical FIGUREs that humans tend to zoom in on are objects that are small, surrounded, symmetrical, have uniform visual properties (such as colour, texture and lightness) and are convex in shape (curving outwards; Eysenck and Keane 2015: 86–7). As Ungerer and Schmid (2006: 163–6) point out, our perceptual systems thus somewhat guide our choice of FIGURE and GROUND in language: in (4.114a), the table is not only smaller but also much more uniform in its visual properties. In contrast to this, the garden is a wider space with visual stimuli of different colour and texture. Thus, (4.114a) seems to us a perfectly acceptable sentence, while *The garden is around the table.* sounds odd, since we choose the less prototypical concept as the FIGURE of our utterance. The same applies to (4.114b): normal books are smaller, lighter and have more uniform visual properties than normal tables; thus, *the book* is selected as the FIGURE and *the table* becomes the GROUND. At the same time, since a table has uniform visual properties, the reversal of FIGURE and GROUND is much more acceptable in this case:

(4.115)   The table$_{FIGURE}$ is under the book$_{GROUND}$.

Now picture a scene in which a massive tome of a book is resting on a ridiculously small side table and read (4.115) again. I hope you will agree that it suddenly sounds a lot better. The point here is that our perception guides our verbal encoding of FIGURE and GROUND. At the same time, a central tenet of Cognitive Linguistics is that the meaning in our minds is always construed, which means that we often have the choice of a different perspective. Thus, even for the scene with the big book on the small table, a speaker can choose either (4.114b) or (4.115).

Spatial prepositions provide the location of a FIGURE by identifying a GROUND against which the former can be identified. Prototypically, as we have seen in the examples above, both FIGURE and GROUND are construed as NPs (*the garden, the table, the book*, etc.). Taking together all these pieces of information, we arrive at the preliminary PP template in (4.116):

(4.116)   Spatial PP construction (preliminary version)
            FORM: PHONOLOGY: / $Y_2 Z_3$ /$_4$
                         MORPHOSYNTAX: [[P_2 NP$_3$]$_{A\_VP:PP4\ or\ POM\_NP:PP4}$]

            ⇔

            MEANING: SEMANTICS:
                      'SPACIAL-RELATIONSHIP$_2$(FIGURE$_1$, GROUND$_3$)'$_4$

The meaning of the construction is the location of a FIGURE$_1$ against a GROUND$_3$, so both elements must be part of the SEMANTICS of the construction. On the FORM pole, however, there is no slot for the FIGURE. This makes sense since you can just use the PP *in the garden* independently as a short answer to the question *Where is the table?* Moreover, the PP can be embedded as a postmodifier in an NP (*the table in the garden*) just as well as an adverbial in the VP (*In the garden, he saw a table.*). Similarly to our solution for PREM and POM modifiers, the FIGURE is therefore again only encoded at the edge of the MORPHOSYNTAX pole as the function that the PP has in the larger syntactic context: A_VP:PP4 **or** POM_NP:PP4, which signals that the whole PP can either function as an 'A(djunct)' (sometimes also called 'A(dverbial)') in a VP 'A_VP' or a postmodifier in an NP 'POM_NP'). On the PHONOLOGY pole, we don't have a slot for the FIGURE. This has to do with the fact that in English the formal relationship of a PP and its surrounding context is actually fairly complicated. In fact, PPs differ as to how specific they are with respect to the PHONOLOGY as well as MORPHOSYNTAX characteristics of their FIGURE. Before I address this issue, however, I want to point out that the second major class of prepositions are ones that describe temporal relationships: and as it turns out, these are cognitively derived from spatial PPs:

(4.117)   The first World Cup$_{FIGURE}$ was in 1930$_{GROUND}$ ...[41]

(4.118)   Prince William$_{FIGURE}$ was born on June 21, 1982 $_{GROUND}$ ...[42]

As you can see, the PPs in (4.117) and (4.118) again relate a FIGURE to a GROUND, the only difference being that here the relationship is a temporal one (and not a spatial one). The constructional template for temporal PPs will therefore be similar to (4.116) – the only difference being that their SEMANTICS will be rendered as 'TEMPORAL-RELATIONSHIP$_2$(FIGURE$_1$, GROUND$_3$)'. Now, this is not a coincidence. While we directly interact in and with space, time is a more abstract category. Cognitive linguists have argued that our concept of time is derived metaphorically from our embodied concept of space (see, e.g., Lakoff and Johnson 1980: 467–9; Núñez and Cooperrider 2013; von Sobbe et al. 2019): imagine, for example, returning home after a short walk and just being a couple of yards away from your house. As you approach it, you get closer and closer until you arrive at your doorstep. During the approach you know that you are not (yet) home, but you can already see it. Your physical goal is ahead of you, and from experience you know that you will get there in the foreseeable future. This embodied experience of time as movement in space allows you to think about time in terms of spatial metaphors: *your future is **ahead** of you*, while *your past is **behind*** you. It is therefore not surprising to find that locative prepositions are used in most languages of the world to express temporal meaning (Haspelmath 1997). Usage from the COCA provides further support for this claim (Table 4.4):

---

[41] Source: https://prepress.co.uk/index.php/world-cup-come-england [last accessed 29 May 2020].
[42] Source: www.express.co.uk/news/royal/1142526/prince-william-birthday-how-old-is-prince-william-age-kate-middleton-age-difference [last accessed 03 June 2020].

Table 4.4. *Ten most frequent* in the N *patterns in COCA*[43]

Rank	String	Frequency
1	IN THE WORLD	86,763
2	IN THE UNITED	63,808
3	IN THE MIDDLE	49,873
4	IN THE MORNING	36,447
5	IN THE PAST	36,017
6	IN THE END	30,242
7	IN THE COUNTRY	29,021
8	IN THE FUTURE	28,460
9	IN THE US	28,041
10	IN THE HOUSE	26,420

Out of the ten top collocations, five contain spatial Ns (*world, United (States), country, US* and *house* (which includes hits for the House of Representatives as well as ordinary houses)), while four are temporal Ns (*morning, past, end* and *future*). The third ranked collocating N, *middle*, can be used spatially (*Even when my son is throwing a temper tantrum in the middle of the grocery store (last night), I still love him*; COCA 2012, BLOG, A Series of Events – Korea Adoption) as well as temporally (*At one point two men are running alongside a riverbank in the middle of the day.*; COCA 2012, BLOG, Would Real Wolves Act Like the Wolves of 'The Grey'? – News Watch).

4.2.4.1   Obligatory PPs

Before we explore other PPs than locational and temporal ones, let us revisit the issue of adjuncts/adverbials and complements. For as we will see, there are many PPs that are not easily classified in either of these two categories. In the preceding section on VPs (Section 4.2.3), we noted that adjuncts/adverbials are optional and fairly mobile within a sentence. Prototypical complements, on the other hand, are obligatory frame elements (cf. Huddleston 2002: 221). Applying this criterion, the following PPs must be 'complements':

(4.119) a. He relied on his mother.
         b. *He relied.

(4.120) a. Doughnuts consist of sugar.
         b. *Doughnuts consist.

(4.121) a. He slept with Sarah. ('had sex with')
         b. *He slept. ('had sex')

---

[43] Source: www.english-corpora.org/coca/. Query: 'in the _n*' [last accessed 08 June 2020].

(4.122) a.   He lived in the 16th century.
     b.   *He lived.

(4.123) a.   I was in Rome.
     b.   *I was.

(4.124) a.   I gave the book to John.
     b.   *I gave the book.

(4.125) a.   He put the book on the table.
     b.   *He put the book.[44]

Yet, even though all the PPs in (4.119)–(4.125) are obligatory, they obviously differ with regard to their subcategorization status: whereas copular verbs like LIVE and BE simply require some sort of complement (cf. *He lived vs He lived happily ever after/alone/with his girlfriend/on the moon/in the 16th century), RELY and CONSIST only license PPs with on and of, respectively (*It consists with sugar and water; cf. Huddleston 2002: 220). Furthermore, he slept would be perfectly grammatical if simply having its basic stative meaning (i.e., 'sleeping'). However, if it is supposed to refer to sexual intercourse, as in (4.121), SLEEP obligatorily needs to be constructed with a with-PP. As (4.121a) shows, in non-compositional V-PP combinations such as sleep with sbdy, the PP can be considered an obligatory complement, since its omission would lead to 'an unsystematic change in ... meaning' (Huddleston 2002: 220).

Due to their mandatory subcategorization relationship, V-P combinations such as rely on or sleep with 'have sex with' are often considered complex lexical items, so-called prepositional verbs. Yet, as Quirk et al. point out (cf. 1985: 1163), prepositional verbs exhibit several syntactic characteristics that seem to indicate that in contrast to so-called phrasal verbs (V-PART; e.g., turn on), they are not complex lexical V heads, but V-PP constructions. Phrasal verbs contain an element (a PARTicle) that looks like an obligatory preposition (cf. *He turned the lights.). Yet, as it turns out, phrasal verbs and prepositional verbs have completely complementary syntactic properties:

(4.126) a.   He turned$_V$ on$_{PART}$ the lights.
     b.   H turned$_V$ the lights on$_{PART}$.

(4.127) a.   He relied$_V$ on$_P$ his mother.
     b.   *He relied$_V$ his mother on$_P$.

As (4.126) shows, phrasal verbs such as turn on allow for an alternative syntactic word order in which the object (the lights) intervenes between verb and particle (4.126b). This is not possible with prepositional verbs (4.127b). Moreover, while the verb receives primary stress and the particle gets secondary stress in phrasal

---

[44] Contextual information obviously sometimes allows ellipsis of contextually retrievable arguments, so that the answer to the question *How much money did you give to charity?* can be *I gave five dollars* (cf. McKercher 1996: 97–8). Nevertheless, as the examples show, without context the goal PP is obligatory. Moreover, there does not seem to be a context that would license sentences like *He relied.*

verbs ('*turn* ˌ*on*), only the verb carries primary stress in prepositional verbs ('*rely on*, cf. Aarts and Aarts 1988: 43). The differences do not end there:

(4.128) a.   **On whom** did he rely?
      b.   *****On what** did he turn?

(4.129) a.   John **relied [heavily]**$_{\text{A:ADVP}}$ **on** his wealthy father-in-law.
      b.   *John turned **[quickly]**$_{\text{A:ADVP}}$ on the lights.

(4.130) a.   A: Who did he rely on? B: **On** his mother.
      b.   A: What did he turn on? B: *****On** the lights.

Examples (4.128)–(4.130) show that the *on* in *rely on* clearly forms a prepositional phrase with its complement, while the particle *on* in *turn on* seems more closely connected to the verb: in questions such as (4.128a), a preposition can appear at the start of the clause together with its WH-complement (since the WH-element seems to drag along the preposition like the pied-piper dragged along the rats in the famous fairy tale, this is sometimes called 'pied-piping'). Particles of phrasal verbs cannot be pied-piped (4.128b). In addition to this, an adverbial (A:ADVP) can be placed between a verb and its preposition (4.129a), but not between a verb and its particle (4.129b). Finally, when the complement of a prepositional verb is questioned, the answer can include the preposition (4.130a), while a particle cannot appear in a corresponding answer (4.130b).

    These differences show that we need different constructional templates for prepositional verbs and phrasal verbs.

(4.131)   *Turn on* Phrasal Verb construction
        FORM: PHONOLOGY: /'tɜːn$_2$ ˌɒn$_2$ Y$_3$/ **or** /'tɜːn$_2$ Y$_3$ ˌɒn$_2$ /$_4$
                         MORPHOSYNTAX: [V$_2$ PART$_2$ NP$_3$]$_{\text{VP4}}$
                         or [V$_2$ NP$_3$ PART$_2$]$_{\text{VP4}}$

        ⇔

        MEANING: SEMANTICS:
                         'CHANGE_OPERATIONAL_STATE$_2$(AGENT$_1$, Device$_5$)'$_4$ [45]

Thus (4.131) treats phrasal verbs as VPs that still need to combine with a SUBJECT (that realizes the AGENT$_1$, role). Moroever, the MORPHOSYNTAX level shows that verb and the particle together form a unit that receives a single meaning (indexed by '2' and identified as the 'CHANGE_OPERATIONAL_STATE' frame on the SEMANTICS level). On the PHONOLOGY level, the particle receives secondary stress and we indicate that it can be placed either in front (ˌɒn$_2$ Y$_3$) of or behind the element realising the object NP (Y$_3$ ˌɒn$_2$). (For more details on a constructional account of phrasal verbs; see Cappelle 2006.)

    In contrast to this, there is only one word order on the PHONOLOGY level of prepositional verbs and the preposition is unstressed:

---

[45] Source: https://framenet2.icsi.berkeley.edu/fnReports/data/frameIndex.xml?frame=Change_oper ational_state&banner= [last accessed 04 June 2020].

(4.132)   *Rely on* Prepositional Verb construction
          FORM: PHONOLOGY: /ɪɪˈlaɪ₂ ɒn₃ Y₄/₈
                      MORPHOSYNTAX: $[V_{2\_5} [P_{3\_5} NP_6]_{PP7}]_{VP8}$

          ⇔

          MEANING: SEMANTICS: 'RELIANCE₅(PROTAGONIST₁, MEANS₂)'₈[46]

So, (4.132) treats the construction as a VP₈ that still needs a subject (which will function as PROTAGONIST₁). On the MORPHOSYNTAX level, the preposition and its NP form a PP constituent (PP₇), but at the SEMANTICS level *rely on* together have a single meaning. ('RELIANCE₅'). This captures the fact that semantically *rely* and *on* have a single meaning, but syntactically are somewhat independent of each other.

Finally, as the examples in (4.124) and (4.125) illustrate, the class of trivalent verbs which realize one of their complements as a PP can also be divided into those which exclusively subcategorize for a particular preposition (the goal PP of the verb *give* is always headed by *to*; cf. (4.124)), and those which only require the PP to qualify as a goal (cf. *he put the book on the table/under the bed/in the oven*). For both of these, it seems possible to identify an independent meaning for verb and preposition and the difference between them is simply going to be that on the PHONOLOGY level, *give* specifies how the P has to be realized: /ˈgɪv₂ Y₅ tə₃ Z₅/, while *put* has an open P slot /ˈpʊt₂ Y₅ P₃ Z₅/. (Though more will be said about the difference between *He gave her the book* and *He gave the book to her* in Section 5.1.)

4.2.4.2   Optional PPs

As pointed out earlier, obligatoriness cannot be considered a sufficient criterion for the identification of complements (cf. *he read [the report]*). Therefore, it becomes necessary to take a closer look at the heterogeneous class of optional PPs:

(4.133) a.   John talked to Bill about Bob.
        b.   They worked at the job.

(4.134) a.   John died/sneezed/wept/apologised/laughed [in Rome].
                  (adapted from Radford 1988: 235)
        b.   Bill killed the cat/left his family/was drunk [on Saturday].

(4.135)   The murderer kills his victims [quickly/in a cruel way].

Even though the omission of the PPs in (4.133) does not result in an unsystematic change in the verb meaning (cf. *he worked/talked*), the main verbs can nevertheless be said to subcategorize for the given prepositions: in *work at the job* (4.133b), for example, the PP introduced by *at* does not specify the location of the action, but rather provides a theme-like object. Verbs like *talk*, on the other

---

[46] Source: https://framenet2.icsi.berkeley.edu/fnReports/data/frameIndex.xml?frame=Reliance&
        banner= [last accessed 04 June 2020].

hand, usually realize their theme as an *about*-PP (cf. (4.133a); also *he spoke about/thought about/dreamt about sth.*). Consequently, verbs licensing an optional PP theme argument must also specify in their lexicon entry which theme-preposition they can co-occur with (cf. the theme PPs **he worked about the job* vs **he talked at Bob*). Furthermore, (4.133a) does not mean that John talked **at** Bill, but **with** him: the PP *to John* does not simply denote the goal of the event, but refers to John as also taking an active role in the communication. Therefore, the verbs in (4.133) play an important role for the identification of the semantic roles of the prepositional complements: '[t]he choice of the preposition is not arbitrary, but nor is its content sufficient to identify the role by itself.' (Huddleston 2002: 228). As a result, these predicates must contain an optional PP slot in their lexical entry whose P-head must be specified for the required theme preposition.

As (4.134) shows, the most prototypical adjunct PPs are optional locative and temporal expressions that can appear with virtually any verb (see the constructional schema in (4.116)), while always maintaining a constant, independent meaning (cf. Radford 1988: 235). These PPs do not add core frame arguments to a predicate, but instead 'localise' events on a time-location scale (cf. Ernst 2002: 328; in Quirk et al.'s terminology being 'sentence adjuncts'; cf. 1985: 511–2). One way to illustrate the relative independence of such PPs is the *this happened*-test (cf. Brown and Miller 1991: 90): assuming that events can be paraphrased by *this happened*, any PP in the original sentence that can combine with the paraphrase will have to be analysed as modifying the entire event:

(4.136) a. John talked. *This happened to John/about Bill.
      b. They worked. *This happened at the job.

(4.137) a. John died/sneezed/wept/apologised/laughed.
         This happened in Rome.
      b. Bill killed the cat/left his family/was drunk.
         This happened on Saturday.

(4.138)   The murderer killed his victims.
         This happened quickly/in a cruel way.

According to the results in (4.136)–(4.138), not only the locative and temporal PPs in (4.137) but also the manner adverbials in (4.138) modify entire events. This agrees with Ernst's claim that manner adverbials compare events 'to other possible events of V-ing' (cf. 2002: 59). Therefore, the adverbials in (4.138) indicate that in comparison to other killings, the murders referred to are carried out comparatively fast or brutally. Furthermore, just as with locative and temporal adjuncts, the meaning of manner PPs in (4.138) appears to be independent from the event's predicate. In other words, the semantic role of the prepositional complement is exclusively determined by the preposition.

Interestingly, there is a 'mixed' group of PPs (cf. Trotta 2000) for which the semantic role of the prepositional complement also seems to depend solely on the preposition:

(4.139) a. He slept in a bed.
     b. He slept. *This happened in a bed.

(4.140) a. He ran to the church.
     b. He ran. *This happened to the church.

(4.141) a. He committed the crime with John.
     b. He committed the crime. *This happened with John.

(4.142) a. He killed the cat with a knife.
     b. He killed the cat. *This happened with a knife.

Even without context, the (prototypical)[47] meaning of the PPs in (4.139)–(4.142) can be established: *in the bed* and *to the church* are locational PPs, *with John* expresses accompaniment and *with a knife* refers to an instrument. Nevertheless, the *this happened*-test indicates that the 'mixed' PPs do not modify events. The mixed status of these PPs derives from the fact that, similar to the locational and temporal adjunct PPs, the semantic role of the prepositional complement is determined by the preposition, but that the entire PP also establishes a thematic relationship with the predicate, just like the complement PPs in (4.133). *In a bed* (4.139a), for example, does not merely specify a location but also an object affected by the 'sleeping' event. Therefore, the 'mixed' adjuncts (Quirk *et al.*'s 'predication adjuncts'; cf. 1985: 510–1) can be said to 'add participants to an event beyond the arguments of the predicate (which are also participants in the event)' (Ernst 2002: 131). Concerning their syntactic behaviour, the 'mixed' PP group presents the greatest challenge to any binary complement-adjunct classification.

Remember that in Section 4.2.3 we defined the domain of the VP construction (4.113) as including all complements, but excluding all adjuncts. One syntactic test that seems to support this distinction is the *do so* pro-form test (cf. Huddleston 2002: 223). *Do so* is supposed to replace a verb and all its internal complements (i.e., VPs). Consequently, combining this pro-form with an overt complement should produce an ungrammatical result, since all complements are already included in the pro-form (cf. Huddleston 2002: 223):

(4.143) a. *Jill keeps her car in the garage but Pam does so in the road.
     b. Jill washes her car in the garage but Pam does so in the road.
       (taken from Huddleston 2002: 223)

Since (4.143a) is ungrammatical, it follows that *in the road* is a complement of *keep* already covertly included in the pro-form. In contrast to this, since the locative PP can combine with *do so* in the second example, it would be classified as an adjunct in (4.143b).

---

[47] As always with semantic roles, the notion of 'prototypes' has to be stressed. It is, of course, conceivable that there is a context in which *with John* is used as an instrument (if, e.g., in a fairy tale, a giant throws a person at another protagonist and kills him; cf. Fillmore 1977: 66). This, however, is definitely not the prototypical reading of *with John*.

(4.144)   ?Jill walked on the grass
            but/and Pam did so on the pavement.

(4.145)   *Jill ran to the church but Pam did so to the house.

(4.146)   Jill killed a cat with Jack and Pam did so with Bob.

(4.147)   He killed the bats with a knife and Pam did so with a gun.

Now, Trotta claims that affected locative PPs can be combined with a *do so* pro-form, and thus, with regard to this particular test, should be classified as adjuncts (cf. 2000: 184). Contra Trotta, however, it must be argued that sentences like (4.144) do not seem to be fully grammatical, which would support an analysis of affected locative PPs as more 'complement-like'. With respect to the *do-so*-test, goal/source PPs also seem to behave like complements (4.146). The remaining two 'mixed' PPs; that is, those expressing accompaniment or referring to instruments, on the other hand, are identified as adjuncts by this test (cf. 4.146, 4.147).

Since the *do so* pro-form replaces VPs, we can consider it to be indicative of the insertion site of optional PPs: since the test yields ungrammatical results for affected locative PPs (4.144) and goal/source PPs (4.145), these prepositional phrases must be inserted VP-internally. Accompaniment and instrument PPs, however, would, according to the *do so*-test, have to be attached VP-externally. Note that the *do so*-test also identifies locative (4.148), temporal (4.149) and manner (4.150) sentence-adjunct PPs as VP-external elements:

(4.148)   John laughed in London and Bill did so in Rome.

(4.149)   Oscar left his wife on Monday and Felix did so on Saturday.

(4.150)   Bill greeted her in a friendly manner
            and Ted did so in a professional manner.

Thus, the constructional template of affected locative and goal/source PPs will state that these phrases have to be inserted VP-internally ([[ ]$_V$ [ ]$_{PP}$]$_{VP}$), while sentence-adjunct PPs (i.e., locative, temporal and manner PPs) and accompaniment and instrument PPs will specify that they combine with VPs ([ ]$_{VP}$ [ ]$_{PP}$).

Thus, while the *do so*-test reveals the actual syntactic attachment of PPs, the *this happened*-test discussed above differentiates PPs only with respect to their semantic relationship with the event they modify. This explains why the two tests seem to yield contradicting results: according to the *do so*-test accompaniment and instrument PPs appear more adjunct-like, while the *this happened*-test classifies them among VP-internal PPs such as affected locative and goal/source PPs. Once the *do so*-test is acknowledged as providing information on the syntactic configuration, while the *this happened*-test indicates whether a PP adds a participant frame role to the event, the apparent contradiction is resolved. This interpretation of the two tests is supported by the fact that *do so* is a VP-pro form, while *this happened* replaces core events (including the subject argument).

Summarising the above discussion, Figure 4.6 gives an overview of the various types of optional PPs that have been identified (please note, the optionality of optional 'complement' PPs is marked by parentheses):

Finally, from a usage-based perspective, it is, of course, possible that any verb and PP combination can become entrenched as a pattern of usage. Some evidence for this comes from the selectional restrictions on the various V/VPs that the 'mixed' and 'sentence adjuncts' co-occur with:

1.   Affected location PP, e.g., are limited to a small number of verbs (e.g., *sit, sleep, stand, walk*) which are responsible for the interpretation of the prepositional complements changing from mere locations into affected objects (in Figure 4.6 this restriction is indicated by the subscript V_ACTION). The range of possible P heads for these PPs, however, is clearly restricted (mostly to *in* and *on*).

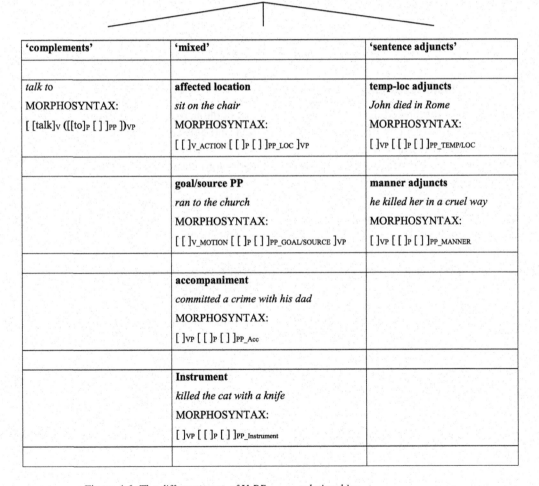

optional PPs

'complements'	'mixed'	'sentence adjuncts'
talk to MORPHOSYNTAX: [[talk]$_V$ ([[to]$_P$ [ ]]$_{PP}$])$_{VP}$	**affected location** *sit on the chair* MORPHOSYNTAX: [[ ]$_{V\_ACTION}$ [[ ]$_P$ [ ]]$_{PP\_LOC}$]$_{VP}$	**temp-loc adjuncts** *John died in Rome* MORPHOSYNTAX: [ ]$_{VP}$ [[ ]$_P$ [ ]]$_{PP\_TEMP/LOC}$
	goal/source PP *ran to the church* MORPHOSYNTAX: [[ ]$_{V\_MOTION}$ [[ ]$_P$ [ ]]$_{PP\_GOAL/SOURCE}$]$_{VP}$	**manner adjuncts** *he killed her in a cruel way* MORPHOSYNTAX: [ ]$_{VP}$ [[ ]$_P$ [ ]]$_{PP\_MANNER}$
	accompaniment *committed a crime with his dad* MORPHOSYNTAX: [ ]$_{VP}$ [[ ]$_P$ [ ]]$_{PP\_Acc}$	
	Instrument *killed the cat with a knife* MORPHOSYNTAX: [ ]$_{VP}$ [[ ]$_P$ [ ]]$_{PP\_Instrument}$	

Figure 4.6 *The different types of V-PP$_{optional}$ relationships*

2.   Goal/source PPs, on the other hand, are only licensed by 'motion verbs' (e.g., *travel, go, fly, walk, run, roll*). Yet, these verbs do not appear to impose subcategorization restrictions on the prepositions (cf. *he ran into/towards/to/for the house*).

3.   With both accompaniment and instrument PPs, the semantic role of the prepositional complement is mainly determined by the preposition. Yet, whereas the former can co-occur with a great range of verbs (e.g., *he laughed/ate/arrived/stood on the hill/killed the cat with his children*), the latter PP group appears to be restricted to actions implying or at least allowing for instruments *(he ate the apple/killed the cat/cut the bread with a knife* vs **he laughed with a knife).*

The above selectional restrictions on the types of V/VP are obviously semantic in nature (cf. the fact that goal/source PPs are only feasible with motion verbs or that instrument PPs require appropriate action events). From a usage-based perspective, this will lead to increased co-occurrence in language use and, consequently, entrenchment. Again, as with NPs and VPs, Chapter 5 will explore in more detail abstract phrasal constructions that obligatorily require certain types of PPs.

4.2.5   Main Word Classes and Beyond

In the preceding four sections, we have come across the five major word class constructions of English, whose FORM and MEANING properties are summarized in Table 4.5:

I consider Ns, Vs, ADJs, ADVs and Ps to be major word classes because these clearly build larger phrasal structures. They obviously also differ amongst each other with respect to crucial aspects. Ns, Vs, ADJs, ADVs, for example, are often classified as 'open class' items, since it is easy to introduce a new word to any of these categories (take, e.g., *Google* or *ungucci*, see Section 3.3). On the other hand, English speakers normally do not coin new prepositions (which is why they are classified as 'closed class' items). In the preceding sections, we also came across other closed class words which appeared in particular positions of the various phrasal constructions: personal pronouns such as *he* or *she* function as full NPs, while possessive pronouns fill the determiner slot of NPs (*her idea, his book*) and help to identify the referent of the head noun of NPs (similarly to articles such as *the* or *a(n)*, quantifiers such as *all* and *some*, or numerals such as *one* or *fourty-two*). Another word type that we came across in passing were conjunctions such as *and, but* and *or*:

(4.151) a.   It is the duty of every [man$_N$], [woman$_N$] and [child$_N$] to leave this world with more than what it had when we arrived.
          (COCA WEB 2012 Edge Magazine Online)
       b.   I was [really excited]$_{ADJP}$ but [really nervous]$_{ADJP}$.
          (COCA ACD 2010 Emergency Nurse)

Table 4.5 *Prototypical features of the major English word class categories*

	Nouns	Verbs	Adjectives	Adverbs	Prepositions
FORM: MORPHOSYNTAX:	N	V	ADJ	ADV	P
MEANING: SEMANTICS:	'THING'	'PROCESSUAL RELATIONSHIP'	'NON-PROCESSUAL RELATIONSHIP' STATIVE	'NON-PROCESSUAL RELATIONSHIP' DYNAMIC	'RELATIONSHIP OF FIGURE AND GROUND'
Constructional context	Referential cxns *the* N *a* N	Predication cxn	Modification cxn (PREM_N) or Predicative-BE construction	Modification cxn (MOD ADJ **or** ADV **or** V)	Ranging from complements over modifiers to adjuncts

165

c.   If you wanted to know if you were burning enough calories to stay fit, you [looked in the mirror]$_{VP}$ or [stepped on a scale]$_{VP}$. (COCA BLOG 2012 Apple Begins Selling the Nike+ FuelBand in Stores and Online)

As you can see in (4.151), the conjunctions *and*, *but* and *or* combine two (or more) constructions in a way that both seem equally important. Without the conjunction, either of the two constructions can also appear in the same syntactic context on their own (see 4.152):

(4.152) a.   It is the duty of every [man] …
      a.' It is the duty of every [woman] …
      a.'' It is the duty of every [child] …
      b. I was [really excited].
      b.' I was [really nervous].
      c. You [looked in the mirror].
      c.' You [stepped on a scale].

Because of this, *and*, *but* and *or* are known as coordinating conjunctions. Furthermore, as the examples in (4.151) show, normally coordinating conjunctions combine syntactic elements that have the same status: in (4.151a) three nouns are coordinated, in (4.151b) two adjective phrases, and in (4.151c) two VPs. Consequently, we can give the following constructional representation for the *And* Coordination construction (4.153; for an advanced discussion of coordination; see Müller 2019: 648–52):

(4.153)   *And* Coordination construction
       FORM: PHONOLOGY: $/X_1$+ and_2 $Y_{3/4}$
                  MORPHOSYNTAX: [CATEGORY$_1$+
                  and_2 CATEGORY$_3$]$_{\text{CATEGORY4=1=3}}$

      ⇔

       MEANING: SEMANTICS: '$\text{AND}_2(A_1$*, $B_3)$'$_4$

In (4.153), we specify that there are two (or more; hence the '+' after CATEGORY$_1$, meaning 'one or more') elements that are combined by the *And* Coordination construction. On the MORPHOSYNTAX level, we additionally specify that the CATEGORY of the concatenated elements has to be identical: if the first element is an N, all others have to be Ns as well, and the entire construct will also function as an N ($_{\text{CATEGORY4=1=3}}$).[48]

From a usage-based perspective, we obviously expect some conjoined constructs to become entrenched. Table 4.6 gives an overview of the ten most frequent N, N *and* N constructs in COCA, all of which can probably be considered entrenched constructions of American English:

---

[48] The identity constraint on the syntactic category of the coordinated elements is somewhat too strong: cf., e.g., *Our house is* [old$_{ADJP}$ *and in an older neighborhood*$_{PP}$]. (COCA 2013 NEWS: Denver Post.) What seems more important is that you coordinate elements that can fill the identical slot in the particular syntactic context. But this issue is beyond the scope of present book.

Table 4.6. *Top 10 N, N and N constructs in COCA*[49]

Rank	Constructs	hits
1	MEN, WOMEN AND CHILDREN	581
2	ALCOHOL, TOBACCO AND FIREARMS	245
3	MAN, WOMAN AND CHILD	210
4	BREAKFAST, LUNCH AND DINNER	193
5	BLOOD, SWEAT AND TEARS	113
6	NAME, ADDRESS AND PHONE	105
7	HEALTH, EDUCATION AND WELFARE	103
8	HOOK, LINE AND SINKER	94
9	BAR, RESERVATIONS AND CREDIT	91
10	TOBACCO, FIREARMS AND EXPLOSIVES	91

Another type of conjunctions are the so-called subordinators:

(4.154) a. **He is ill**. (COCA 2012 FIC: Texas Freedom!)
     b. Can't you see **that he is ill**?
       (COCA 2012 ACAD: Review of Contemporary Fiction)
     c. You are not obligated to become his nurse simply **because he is ill**, ...
       (COCA 2016 MAG: Slate Magazine)

As (4.154a) shows, *he is ill* can appear as an independent sentence, yet subordinators such as, for example, *that* (4.154b) or *because* (4.154c) can embed them in other sentences (as the object of *see* in (4.154b) or an adjunct of the sentence in (4.154c). Other English subordinators include *before*, *if*, *since* or *while* (for more details see Quirk et al. 1985: 997–1007). Now, the constituent introduced by subordinators is no longer an independent sentence, but bigger than any of the phrases we have looked at in this section. These constituents are often called clauses and their constructional analysis is the topic of the following chapter (Section 5.3).

Finally, we find words that express a speaker's emotional state and can be added to virtually any sentence: so-called interjections such as *oh*, *wow* or *gosh* (Aarts and Aarts 1988: 59):

(4.155) I say this having a lot of English friends who ... say things like '**oh** I really enjoyed my visit in America' (COCA B 2012 separated by a common language: saying 'please' in restaurants)

(4.156) And she's adorable. She has the best qualities of each of us. **Wow**. It sounds like you still like this guy (COCA 1995 Hazardous to Your Health episode: Hazardous to Your Health)

[49] Source: www.english-corpora.org/coca/. Query: _nn* _y* _nn* and _nn* [27 July 2020].

(4.157)   **Gosh** they're so fake! (COCA 2012 BLOG Lady Gaga's ^Born This Way^ - The Illuminati Manifesto | The Vigilant)

Interjections can thus be analysed as constructions that have a substantive PHONOLOGY level and a SEMANTICS/PRAGMATICS meaning that expresses strong subjective speaker emotions. Whether some of them have MORPHOSYNTACTIC restrictions; that is, whether they only appear in certain syntactic contexts, is a topic for future constructional research.

4.3   Idioms as Constructions

In the preceding sections, we looked at individual words and the phrasal constructions they appear in. Now in many traditional syntax textbooks, we would now move on to purely abstract syntactic rules. The reason for this is that traditionally the dominant view was that of a strict separation of the lexicon as the repository of conventional meaningful words and syntax as the domain of regular, purely structural operations. Starting in the 1980s, however, the first constructionist publications appeared that questioned this strict lexicon–syntax dichotomy (the most important ones, arguably, being Fillmore 1985, 1988; Fillmore, Kay and O'Connor 1988; Lakoff 1987 or Wierzbicka 1988). On the one hand, these authors showed that there is a class of linguistic expressions that clearly exhibits characteristics of both lexical idiosyncrasy as well as syntactic creativity that cannot be adequately accounted for by classical 'items and rules' analyses, namely idioms. On the other hand, they argued that many syntactic configurations possessed construction-specific properties that could not be explained by independent syntactic rules, but required speakers to store these phrasal structures as form-meaning pairs. In other words, the lexicon had to include much more syntactic information, and syntax exhibited much more idiosyncratic lexical behaviour than previously assumed.

Concerning idioms, '[i]t is not an exaggeration to say that construction grammar grew out of a concern to find a place for idiomatic expressions in the speaker's knowledge of a grammar of a language' (Croft and Cruse 2004: 225). Now, on closer inspection, idioms turn out to be a fairly complicated and heterogenous phenomenon. Consequently, for the purposes of the present book, we will only be able to offer a simplified analysis. Nevertheless, I will also try to point out some of the issues that a more fully-fledged analysis would have to account for.

The central property of all idioms is that they have a non-conventional meaning (Nunberg, Sag and Wasow 1994: 492–3) that requires speakers to store them in their mental lexicon. The meaning of idioms like *kick the bucket* 'to die' or *spill the beans* 'to divulge the information', for example, cannot be computed using the conventional, literal meanings of *kick* and *the bucket* or *spill* and *the beans* and must therefore be stored in the lexicon (cf. Croft and Cruse 2004:

248–53; Jackendoff 2002: 167–8). In addition to this, once idioms are inserted in a sentence any compositional, conventional reading (that would result in something like 'kick (with a foot)' 'a physical container' and 'spill' 'a certain type of food') must be precluded. It might seem at first that the best way to achieve this is to treat idioms as frozen, inflexible chunks that cannot be modified internally once they are passed on into the syntax. Such analyses have been advocated within Mainstream Generative Grammar (cf., e.g., Chomsky 1981: 146, n. 94; cit. in Jackendoff 2002: 168), and they do indeed work for so-called inflexible 'idiomatic phrases' such as *kick the bucket*, which are syntactically treated as single chunks (Nunberg, Sag and Wasow 1994: 497). As Nunberg, Sag and Wasow (1994: 496–7) point out, however, the majority of idioms are 'idiomatically combining expressions', which are not frozen units but which show some degree of syntactic flexibility:

(4.158) a.   There... **the beans** are **spilled!** (BNC EVN W_biography)
     b.   For three years, the government wrestled with **the beans** Boesky had **spilled**, trying to come up with airtight felony counts.
        (COCA 1991 MAG NatlReview)

In (4.158a) the idiom *spill the beans* appears in a passive sentence with *the beans* in subject position and in (4.158b) *the beans* is a clause-external antecedent to a relative clause (cf. *the beans that/which Boesky had spilled*). These structures cannot be explained by assuming that *spill the beans* is merely a single frozen idiom chunk. Instead, Nunberg, Sag and Wasow (1994: 496) point out that the parts of idiomatically combining expressions have non-conventional meanings that allow for the compositional computation of the (non-conventional) semantics of these idioms. In *spill the beans*, for example, *spill* means 'divulge' and *the beans* essentially denotes 'the information'. Since *the beans* is thus an NP with an independent meaning in this idiomatically combining expression, it can syntactically be separated from *spill* in passives (4.158a) or relative clause constructions (4.158b) without the idiom losing its non-conventional reading (so (4.159a) means 'The information was divulged!' and (4.158b) can be rendered as 'The information Boesky had spilled').

Due to their non-conventional meaning, idioms such as *spill the beans* definitely have to be learnt by speakers. Yet, they cannot be analysed as completely frozen chunks, since they 'have grammatical structure, structure of the kind that we ordinarily interpret by appealing to the operation of the general grammatical rules' (Fillmore, Kay and O'Connor 1988: 504). *The beans*, e.g., in (4.158) clearly functions like a normal NP, which means that phrasal information, something that would be reserved for the syntactic domain in items-and-rules approaches, has to be part of the lexical entry of *spill the beans*. Instead of maintaining a strict lexicon-syntax division, a logical conclusion is to treat idioms as complex constructions; that is, FORM-MEANING pairings that can also contain phrasal and syntactic information:

(4.159)   KICK *the bucket* Idiom construction
        FORM: PHONOLOGY: /KICK$_1$ [ðə 'bʌkɪt]$_2$/$_3$
                        MORPHOSYNTAX: [V$_1$ NP$_2$]$_{VP3}$

        ⇔

        MEANING: SEMANTICS: 'die (A$_4$)'$_3$

(4.160)   SPILL *the beans* Idiom construction
        FORM: PHONOLOGY: /SPILL$_1$ [ðə biːnz]$_2$] /$_3$
                        MORPHOSYNTAX: [V$_1$ NP$_2$]$_{VP3}$

        ⇔

        MEANING: SEMANTICS: 'divulge$_1$(A$_4$,the-information$_2$)'$_3$

        (modelled on Croft and Cruse 2004: 252)

Thus (4.159) and (4.160) provide constructional accounts of the idiomatic phrase *kick the bucket* and the idiomatically combining expression *spill the beans*, respectively. On MORPHOSYNTAX level, both idioms are analysed as VP constructions, which explains why they can freely co-occur with adverbials (cf. *when old Karl **finally** kicks the bucket* ... COCA 1992 FIC BjSF: QuantumLeap or *You **almost** spilled the beans to Boom-Boom*. COCA 1994 TV BoyMeetsWorld). The subject argument of both of these idioms is semantically selected for (A$_4$ = 'the person who dies' and 'the person who divulges the information'), and does not have to be part of the MORPHOSYNTAX description (because it can freely be added to the VP idiom, as long as the resulting construct meets the constraints of other constructions such as the subject–verb agreement construction). An important difference between (4.159) and (4.160) is the semantics of the VP-internal NP: while *spill* SPILL$_1$ and *the beans* [ðə biːnz]$_{NP2}$ are each linked to an independent meaning ('divulge$_1$' and 'the-information$_2$', respectively), the string *kick the bucket* [KICK ðə 'bʌkɪt]$_3$ as a whole receives a single interpretation as the predicate 'die( )$_3$' on the SEMANTICS level. This explains why we can easily form a passive version of SPILL *the beans* (4.158), but not KICK *the bucket* (*The bucket was kicked* ≠ 'Someone died').

As I mentioned at the start of this section, constructional templates such as (4.159) and (4.160) must be seen as simplifications. How can we, for example, account for utterances such as *until that final day when they kick the **proverbial** bucket* (COCA 2005 FIC BkJuv:WorldsStarTrek)? In this sentence, the [ðə 'bʌkɪt]$_2$, which we identified as single string in (4.159) has been broken up. If we were to formalize this, we would have to come up with a fairly complicated algorithm to account for this.[50] From a cognitive perspective, however, it is clear that analogy plays a role here: on the MORPHOSYNTAX level, *the bucket* is identified as an NP. This can lead to the activation of a 'normal' NP construction, which allows for optional modification (cf. *the ball* vs

---

[50] I am grateful to an anonymous reviewer for pointing this out to me.

the red ball; Section 4.2.1.3). This then enables speakers to create a construct such as *the proverbial bucket*, which can then be blended with the idiom construction in (4.159). Note that this blending process is a selective, domain-general cognitive process and not a computational algorithm. I discuss this in a bit more detail in Section 8.3. For now, it is enough to remember that we have already encountered a blending process that can easily combine the fixed phonological strings of two words (cf. *motor* + *hotel* > *motel*; Section 3.3.4). As I mentioned above, however, a more detailed analysis of idioms and all their creative uses is unfortunately beyond the scope of the present book.

Now, it might be objected that idioms are only a peripheral area of linguistic knowledge. Yet, as Fillmore, Kay and O'Connor note, idioms do not only make up a large part of a speaker's knowledge, they also 'interact in important ways with the rest of the grammar' (1988: 504). Moreover, idioms themselves are not, as we have just seen, a single homogeneous group of linguistic expressions. In addition to the question of internal compositionality, idioms can also be distinguished based on whether they are lexically filled (substantive) or lexically open (formal/schematic; Fillmore, Kay and O'Connor 1988: 505–6):

(4.161) a.   The jig is up. 'the game is up; it is all over'
             (adapted from Jackendoff 2002: 169; semantic definition from the
             Oxford English Dictionary Online s.v. *jig* 5. www.oed.com
             [last accessed 30 January 2016])
        b.   It was almost like the last spiteful act of a man who knew the jig was up.
             (OED: 1923, E. Wallace *Missing Million* xii. 100)

(4.162) a.   It takes one to know one.
             'only a person with a given personality, characteristic, etc.,
             is able to identify that quality in someone else'
        b.   *It took one to know one.
             (from Croft and Cruse 2004: 233; semantic definition from the Oxford
             English Dictionary Online s.v. *take* P7c. www.oed.com
             [last accessed 30 January 2016])

The idioms *the jig is up* (4.161a) and *it takes one to know one* (4.162a) are both completely lexically filled; that is, substantive. Yet, while the former at least licenses different tense forms (4.161b), the latter is even more tightly constrained in that the verb *take* always has to be realized in its third person singular indicative present tense form. Again, a constructionist approach is able to provide a straightforward analysis of this subtle difference:

(4.163)   *The jig is up* Idiom construction
           FORM: PHONOLOGY: /[ðə dʒɪg]$_1$ BE$_2$ ʌp$_{3/4}$
                     MORPHOSYNTAX: [NP$_1$ [V$_2$ ADV$_3$]$_{VP}$]$_{CLAUSE4}$

           ⇔

           MEANING: SEMANTICS: 'the-game$_1$ be$_2$ up$_3$'$_4$

(4.164)   *It takes one to know one* Idiom construction
        FORM: PHONOLOGY: $/ɪt_1$ teɪks$_2$ wʌn$_3$ tə$_4$ nəʊ$_4$ wʌn$_5/_6$
                    MORPHOSYNTAX: $[NP_1 \, [V_2 \, NP_3$
                              $[to_4 \, V_4 \, NP_5]_{VP}] \,]_{VP}]_{CLAUSE6}$

        ⇔

        MEANING: SEMANTICS: 'only$_2$ a-person-with-a-given-
                            personality$_3$ is-able$_2$ to-identify$_4$ that-quality-in-someone-
                            else$_5$'$_6$

The PHONOLOGY pole of (4.163) indicates that the verb position has to be filled with a tensed word form of the lexeme BE (thus, e.g., also licensing strings such as *the jig will be up*). In (4.164), however, the verb position is filled by a specific word form (*takes*) that allows for no other tensed realization of TAKE. Moreover, the internal structure of these two idioms is fairly fixed and they are treated as clauses on the MORPHOSYNTAX level. (Though again, via the blending of adjunct constructions we can add, for example, a VP-internal adverbial: *the jig was **really** up* ... COCA 2012 WEB fcir.org.). Finally, since their meaning is non-compositional and non-conventional, we do not render their SEMANTICS level in predicate logic notation (which is more useful when a construction has slots), but provide a paraphrase of their idiosyncratic meaning.

    Arguably of greater theoretical importance are formal/schematic idioms, which exhibit syntax-like creativity. English, for example, has a number of idioms that not only have an open subject slot but also contain VP-internal slots (Jackendoff 2002: 168):

(4.165)   NP TAKE NP *to task*
    a.   I am certainly going to take **you** to task for leaving my party so early. (BNC HGV W_fict_prose)
    b.   [...] the Dutch, after nearly fifty years, still take **the Germans** to task, albeit jokingly, for having confiscated thousands of bicycles during the occupation. (BNC EBW W_pop_lore)

(4.166)   NP SHOW NP *the door*
    a.   I had both the girls taught, but they were idle, and
        I showed **the teacher** the door in the end. (BNC CD2 W_fict_prose)
    b.   West Ham never showed **me** the door. (BNC CH7 W_newsp_tabloid)

(4.167)   NP GIVE NP *the boot*
    a.   I thought I told you I gave **her** the boot. (BNC G07 W_fict_prose)
    b.   And next day Mayor John Hughes gave **Mr Rees** the boot. (BNC CH2 W_newsp_tabloid)

(4.168)   NP PUT NP$_i$ *in pro$_i$'s place*
    a.   Some of the boys who had just left school used to be mischieful [sic!] when they brought the farm-horses in, but the smith had a few tricks to put **them** in **their** place. (BNC G09 W_non_ac_soc_science)

    b.   It was six o'clock in the evening, four hours since the Deputy Public Prosecutor had summoned Zen to his office in the law courts. When he arrived he had been told to wait, and he had been waiting ever since. **He was being put in his place**, softened up for what was to come.
        (BNC HTT W_fict_prose)

(4.169)   NP$_e$ GIVE NP *a piece of* pro$_e$'s *mind*
    a.   Boy, am **I** going to give **him** a piece of **my** mind when I see him.
        (BNC JY6 W_fict_prose)
    b.   The Full Moon in your own sign on the 10th
        urges **you** to give **others** a piece of **your** mind. (BNC CB8 W_pop_lore)

The examples in (4.165)–(4.169) illustrate that the phrasal slot in these idioms can be filled by various NPs (*you* (4.165a), *the Germans* (4.165b), *the teacher* (4.166a), *me* (4.166b), *her* (4.167a), *Mrs Rees* (4.167b)). The idioms in (4.168) and (4.169) interact with syntactic principles in an even more complicated way: the idiom NP PUT NP$_i$ *in* pro$_i$'s *place* (4.168) not only has a VP-internal NP-slot, but an additional requirement is that this NP must be co-referential with a following pronoun that functions as the determiner in a noun phrase headed by *place*, which itself is embedded in a prepositional phrase headed by *in* (co-referentiality in (4.168) is signalled by the index $_i$; cf. *them* and *their* in (4.168a) and *he* and *his* in (4.168b)). As (4.168b) shows, these idioms again exhibit syntactic flexibility and the schematic NP can, for example, also be realized as the subject in a passive sentence. In contrast to this, the expression X$_e$ GIVE NP *a piece of* pro$_e$'s *mind* (4.169) also has an NP and a determinative pronoun slot pro$_e$, but in this case the pronoun must be co-referential with the subject of an active clause (as signalled by the index e; cf. *I* and *my* in (4.169a) and *you* and *your* in (4.169b)).

    For the sake of illustration, (4.170) shows how we can model an idiom such as (4.169):

(4.170)   GIVE NP *a piece of* pro$_e$'s *mind* Idiom construction
        FORM: PHONOLOGY: /GIVE$_2$ Y$_3$ ə$_4$ piːs$_4$ əv$_5$ Z$_6$ maɪnd$_{7/8}$
                     MORPHOSYNTAX:
                     [V$_2$ NP$_3$ [a$_4$ piece$_4$ [P$_5$ [pron$_{6\_e1}$ N$_7$]$_{PP}$]$_{NP4}$]$_{VP8}$

        ⇔

        MEANING: SEMANTICS:
                     'give$_2$(A$_{e1}$,B$_3$, A's candid-uncomplimentary-opinion$_4$)'$_8$
        (modelled on Croft and Cruse 2004: 252)

The idiom expresses a meaning of 'to express one's candid (and uncomplimentary) opinion of someone else's conduct'[51]. In (4.170), the PHONOLOGY level

---

[51] Adapted from: OED online s.v. *bit* n.2 4.a https://oed.com/view/Entry/19517 [last accessed 27 July 2020].

has fixed, substantive parts (the lexeme construction GIVE$_2$ as well as large parts of the final NP [ə piːs əv ... maɪnd]). The person expressing this opinion is encoded on the SEMANTICS level and can freely be added on the MORPHOSYNTAX level (with the only requirement that this subject must be co-referential $_e$ with the pron$_6$ slot; cf. *I* and *my* in (4.169a) and *you* and *your* in (4.169b)).

In addition to the above parameters, Fillmore, Kay and O'Connor (1988: 505) mention another distinction relevant for idioms: while all of the above idioms follow the general syntactic rules of English (and can therefore be labelled 'grammatical idioms'), there are also a considerable number of idioms that deviate from the standard syntactic structure in significant ways (Jackendoff 2002:169):

(4.171) a.   *all of a sudden*
             Mm. I'm not worn no make-up for ages, 'cos me eyes seem to be like, itching **all of a sudden**. (BNC KB1 S_conv)
        b.   *by and large*
             By and large, there is general agreement as to what counts as doing economics or pharmacy. (BNC G0R W_ac_polit_law_edu)

(4.172)   *Far be it from* NP *to* VP. (usually NP is me)
        a.   Far be it from **us to condone tax evasion** (BNC CFT W_advert)
        b.   Far be it from **me to speak ill of the dead** (BNC FR9 W_fict_prose)

(4.173)   *How dare* NP VP!
        a.   Now, how dare **you say that**! (BNC: KB1 S_conv)
        b.   and one comment was how dare **these men gang up against us**. (BNC HUXS_interview_oral_history)

The substantive idioms *all of a sudden* (4.171a) and *by and large* (4.171b) function as adverbials/adjuncts despite the fact that nothing in their internal syntactic structure is adverbial (Jackendoff 2002: 169). Etymologically it is, of course, possible to explain these structures, but synchronically they constitute syntactic anomalies. As the idioms (4.172) and (4.173) prove, however, it is not even possible to claim that all extra-grammatical idioms enter the syntax as frozen chunks. Both *Far be it from* NP *to* VP and *How dare* NP VP! have phrasal NP and VP slots that can be filled creatively by various lexical items (*us* and *condone tax evasion* (4.172a), *me* and *speak ill of the dead* (4.172b) and *you* and *say that* (4.173a) and *these men* and *gang up against us* (4.173b), respectively).

Finally, Fillmore, Kay and O'Connor (1988: 506) note that some expressions (like *all of a sudden*) are idioms without special pragmatic constraints (idioms without pragmatic point), while others require specific pragmatic contexts to be used felicitously (e.g., greetings such as *Good morning* or the opening formula for fairy tales *Once upon a time* ...; these are called idioms with pragmatic point).

Idioms – non-conventional form-meaning pairings that undoubtedly have to be learnt and stored by speakers – combine lexical as well as syntactic properties and vary along several important parameters (idiomatic phrases vs idiomatically combining expressions, substantive vs formal, grammatical vs extra-grammatical, with and without pragmatic point). Since a constructional approach can capture the numerous and varied types of idioms, the next logical step is then to ask whether the (arguably much fewer) regular syntactic rules of a language could also be accounted for by constructions (Fillmore 1985; Fillmore and Kay 1993, 1995):

> It appears to us that the machinery needed for describing the so-called minor or peripheral constructions of the sort which has occupied us here will have to be powerful enough to be generalized to more familiar structures, in particular those represented by individual phrase structure rules. (Fillmore, Kay and O'Connor 1988: 534)

In the next chapter, we will explore this line of avenue further, seeing how even fully syntactic phenomena can be captured by a Construction Grammar approach.

4.4 Summary

In this chapter, we looked at word constructions and saw how a constructionist analysis can account for lexemes in terms of taxonomic constructional networks. Then we explored the semantic basis of the various word class constructions (particularly Ns, Vs, ADJs, ADVs, and Ps) as well as the larger phrasal constructions that they appear in. Finally, we saw how complex and diverse the group of idioms is. As I illustrated, Construction Grammar allows us to go beyond a simple lexicon–syntax dichotomy and capture all of these as form-meaning pairings. In the next chapter, we will continue our exploration of the lexicon-syntax cline.

Exercises

4.1 Show how speakers generalize from specific constructs to the [Pronoun$_{POSS}$ N]$_{NP}$ construction. Do this by drawing the taxonomic constructional network of [Pronoun$_{POSS}$ N]$_{NP}$.
4.2 Take a look at the following quantifier and noun combinations, only some of which are grammatical in English (Table 4.7):

Table 4.7. *Selected quantifier + N sequences*

Quantifier	+ N$_{NONCOUNT}$	+ N$_{COUNT.SG}$	+ N$_{COUNT.PL}$
every	*every milk …	every teacher …	*every teachers …
many	*many milk …	*many teacher …	many teachers …
much	much milk …	*much teacher …	*much teachers …

4.2.1 How does the meaning of the various quantifiers (the type of quantity they describe) explain why they can or cannot occur with a certain type of noun. (Hint: for those combinations that are grammatical, see whether they can be inserted into the sequence ... was_{SG} *there.* or ... $were_{PL}$ *there.* Can you see a difference in construal?)

4.2.2 Choose one of the quantifiers and give a representation of its constructional template.

4.3 Identify the phrases in (i–iv) that appear as postmodifiers in ADJPs (Aarts and Aarts 1988: 119–22):

   (i)   He was [afraid enough].

   (ii)   He was [afraid of the dark].

   (iii) He was [afraid to call her].

   (iv) He was [afraid that she wouldn't call].

4.4 Identify the phrases in (i–ii) that appear as postmodifiers in ADVPs (Aarts and Aarts 1988: 122–3):

   (i)   He did it [well enough].

   (ii)   He did it [better than they had expected].

4.5 Verbs and PPs: A FORCE-DYNAMIC interpretation seems to be an important prerequisite for verbs that enter the Passive construction (cf. *He kicked the ball. – The ball was kicked.* vs *It weighs 20 kg. – *20 kg was weighed.*). What do (i) and (ii) tell you about the relationship of the verb and the PP?

   (i)   He sleeps in this bed.

   (ii)   This bed has been slept in.

5   Complex Phrasal and Clausal Constructions

In the last chapter, we explored word constructions and the basic phrasal constructions that they appear in. In addition to that, we saw that English has a great number of schematic and substantive idioms that can best be described as constructions. In the present chapter, we continue this approach and investigate how syntactic phenomena such as argument structure (which tells us what happened) and its interaction with active and passive voice (which represent different vantage points from which to construe events) as well as tense and aspect (when and how something happened) can be analysed within Usage-based Construction Grammar. Moreover, we also look at abstract constructions for the various clause types (e.g., declaratives, interrogatives and imperatives, all of which basically express speakers' illocutions). Finally, we also look at how information structure constructions can be used to present information in a way that is most beneficial for a specific hearer in a discourse context.

5.1   Argument Structure Constructions

At the end of the last chapter, we came across a large number of idiom constructions that were partly schematic and partly substantive. In addition to these, however, there are also data that show that speakers possess completely schematic phrasal templates:

(5.1) a.   Could **he shriek himself unconscious** ...? (BNC W_fict_prose CJJ)
      b.   **Firefighters cut the man free** ... (BNC W_newsp_other_report K55)
      c.   **he had** often **drunk himself silly** (BNC W_fict_prose CDN)

SHRIEK is normally an Intransitive Verb Lexeme construction (one that does not require an object; cf. *Leila laughed and shrieked* BNC W_fict_prose AD9), yet in (5.1a) it has two obligatory post-verbal complements (*himself* and *unconscious*) that seem to depend on each other: while *he shrieked himself unconscious* is fine, neither **he shrieked himself* nor **he shrieked unconscious* alone would be grammatical. *Cut* and *drink*, on the other hand, can be used transitively; that is, with an object (cf. *I cut my fingernails all the time* BNC W_fict_drama FU6 or *he drank a large whisky* BNC W_fict_poetry FAS). Yet, the use of *cut* and *drink* in (5.1b,c) is clearly different from these transitive uses: while in *I cut my fingernails*, the fingernails are actually cut, the firefighters do not cut the man in (5.1b).

Similarly, you can drink a whisky, but not yourself (as in (5.1c)). On top of that, all the sentences in (5.1) also give the result that the shrieking, cutting and drinking action has on the object (it falls asleep, is set free or loose).

Many theoretical approaches (including Mainstream Generative Grammar as well as various types of dependency grammar-inspired theories) assume that it is the main verb that has the main function of selecting the number and types of obligatory and optional syntactic arguments in a clause. Yet, for the examples in (5.1) it seems implausible to assume that the verbs *shriek*, *cut* and *drunk* license the post-verbal arguments. Structures such as these led Goldberg (1995: 224) to argue that it is not the main verb alone that projects the syntax and semantics of a clause (Boas 2013: 236). Instead, she postulated a family of so-called argument structure constructions – abstract, completely schematic constructions that encode basic human event construals together with their obligatory arguments:

> The central senses of argument structure constructions have been argued to be associated with humanly relevant scenes: someone transferring something to someone, something causing something to move or to change state, someone experiencing something, something undergoing a change of state or location, and so on.   (Goldberg 1995: 224–5)

5.1.1   The Basic Argument Structure Constructions of English

Argument structure constructions thus express what Langacker has called 'conceptual archetypes' (Langacker 1991). The argument structure construction licensing the examples in (5.1) is, for example, known as the Resultative construction (Boas 2003, 2005a; Goldberg 1995, 2006; Goldberg and Jackendoff 2004):

(5.2)   Resultative construction
FORM: PHONOLOGY: $/A_1\ B_2\ C_3\ D_4\ /_5$
          MORPHOSYNTAX: $[SBJ_1\ [V_2\ OBJ_3\ OBL_4]_{VP}\ ]_5$

$\Leftrightarrow$

MEANING: SEMANTICS: 'CAUSE($EVENT_2(AGENT_1)$),
                         BECOME($PATIENT_3$, $RESULT\text{-}GOAL_4$))'$_5$
(adapted from Goldberg 1995: 189, 2006: 73; Müller 2008:111)

The construction in (5.2) is completely schematic; it only consists of syntactic slots for a subject (SBJ_1), verb (V_2), object (OBJ_3) and oblique (OBL_4, which includes adjective phrases like the ones in (5.1)). As we saw in Section 3.2.1, SBJs precede a finite, present tense verb with which they agree in number and person (cf. *He*3PS.SG *shrieks*3PS.SG *himself unconscious.*, *The Firefighters*3PS.SG *cuts*3PS.SG *the men free.*, *He*3PS.SG *drinks*3PS.SG *himself silly.*). OBJ slots, on the other hand, normally appear in the VP after the verb and prototypically encode a participant that is in some way affected by the FORCE-DYNAMIC action carried out by the SBJ participant (see also Section 5.1.3). All other obligatory elements in the VP that are not SBJ or OBJs are classified as OBL (and encode meanings such as, for example, states or locations). SBJ and OBJ slots are prototypically filled by NPs in English (5.1), but can also sometimes host finite clauses and non-finite clauses (though SBJ slots are much more permissible to these fillers; see Aarts and Aarts 1988: 147–58; Quirk et al. 1985: 1170–220):

(5.3) a.   [That his team won the tournament]$_{\text{CLAUSEfin:SBJ}}$ made him happy.
     b.   [Winning the tournament]$_{\text{CLAUSEnonfin:SBJ}}$ made him happy.
     c.   Liverpool FC got [what they wanted]$_{\text{CLAUSEfin:OBJ}}$ accomplished.
     d.   He got [Liverpool FC losing to Real Madrid]$_{\text{CLAUSEfin:OBJ}}$ [wiped from his memory].

The type of acceptable fillers for OBL slots depends on the semantics of the individual argument structure constructions (see Section 5.1.3), but includes ADJPs (5.4a), PPs (5.4b), NPs (5.4c) as well as nonfinite clauses (Quirk et al. 1985: 1170–220):

(5.4) a.   He wiped the table [very clean]$_{\text{ADJP:OBL}}$.
     b.   Pop music drives him [round the bend]$_{\text{PP:OBL}}$.
     c.   They elected him [president]$_{\text{NP:OBL}}$.
     d.   A judge ordered the recordings [to be made public]$_{\text{CLAUSEnonfin:OBL}}$.

What all the different fillers in (5.4) have in common is that they are interpreted as a state that results from the verbal action (RESULT-GOAL) in the Resultative construction.

Note also that most research in Construction Grammar gives the MORPHOSYNTAX of Resultative constructions (as well as all other argument structure constructions) as a flat structure where all slots appear on the same level ([SBJ$_1$ V$_2$ OBJ$_3$ OBL$_4$]). However, since coordination data show that argument structure constructions also have a subject-predicate structure (cf. *he [laughed himself silly]* and *[then shrieked himself unconscious]*), we group the non-subject elements into a VP (which corresponds to the predicate; cf. Section 4.2.3.3).

Turning to the representation of MEANING, we can see that, in (5.2), the non-verbal slots on the MORPHOYSYNTAX pole are identified, respectively, as the AGENT$_1$, EVENT$_2$, PATIENT$_3$ and RESULT-GOAL$_4$ participants of the resultative event on the SEMANTICS pole. Concerning the representation of the SEMANTICS pole, it is important to remember that we are using a predicate logic description here (as elsewhere in this book) only for purposes of exposition. Meaning in our minds is, of course, not truth-conditional in nature and we do not rely on features, but store meaning in a holistic and embodied fashion (Croft 2012: 13–19). As we will see, however, the notation used for the arguments structure constructions in this chapter will make it easier to compare the different notation systems employed by various constructionist approaches (Chapter 7). Besides, it allows us to quickly pinpoint the unique properties of argument structure constructions: as (5.2) shows, for example, the SEMANTICS pole of the Resultative construction also includes meaning elements ('CAUSE' and 'BECOME') that are not associated with any single element on the MORPHOSYNTAX level, and which, consequently, constitute a property of the construction. The shorthand 'CAUSE(EVENT$_2$(AGENT$_1$), BECOME(PATIENT$_3$, RESULT-GOAL$_4$))' can be translated as 'the AGENT$_1$ is participating in an Event$_2$ and by doing so CAUSES the PATIENT$_3$ to BECOME RESULT-GOAL$_4$'. The meaning of (5.1b), thus can be rendered as 'firefighers$_1$ are cutting$_2$ and by doing so CAUSE the man$_3$ to BECOME free$_4$'. Note that because of these SEMANTICS properties, the meaning of an argument structure construction can also extend the meaning of a verb lexeme construction: SHRIEK is normally a semelfactive verb (see Section 4.2.3). Yet, the scene in (5.1a) is construed as an achievement: by shrieking, the object (*himself*) ended up unconscious (a telic endpoint).

Argument structure constructions are completely schematic templates that need to be filled (or 'fused'; Goldberg 1995, 2006) with more substantive constructions. One central question of this process is how exactly a specific verb lexeme construction (such as SHRIEK, CUT and DRINK) with its specific semantic and syntactic argument selection requirements fuses with the slots of an argument structure construction. Goldberg (1995, 2006) addresses this issue by first of all distinguishing the semantic roles of argument structure constructions and verb constructions: while the semantic roles of argument structure constructions are referred to as 'argument roles', the ones of a specific verb are called 'participant roles' (Goldberg 1995: 43–66, 2006: 38–43). One major difference of these two types of semantic roles is that argument structure constructions encode cognitive generalizations of basic event types (e.g., 'something causing something to change location, [...], an instigator causing something to change state [...] or an instigator moving despite difficulty' Goldberg 1995: 39). As a result of this generality, the associated argument roles are also fairly general (cf. e.g., agent, cause, goal, instrument, path, patient, recipient, theme, etc.; Goldberg 2006: 39). In contrast to this, participant roles are rich frame semantic roles entailed by the meaning of a specific verb (Goldberg 2006: 39). The verbs in (5.1), for example, could be claimed to have the following participant roles:

(5.5) a.   SHRIEK <**shrieker**>
       b.   CUT <**cutter, cut.object**>
       c.   DRINK <**drinker**, liquid>

Frame Semantics (cf. Boas and Dux 2017; Croft 2012: 11–13; Croft and Cruse 2004: Chapter 2; Fillmore 1977, 1982, 1985; Petruck 1996) eschews truth-conditional definitions and instead considers the meaning of a word to comprise world and cultural knowledge, experiences and beliefs (Boas 2013: 237). Since verbal meaning is thus supposed to encode rich, encyclopaedic information, the frame semantic participant roles associated with verbs are also highly verb-specific: *shriek* entails someone who shrieks, a 'shrieker' (5.5a), *cut* implies a 'cutter' and a 'cut.object' (5.5b) and *drink* requires a 'drinker' and a 'liquid' that is drunk (5.5c). Concerning the roles of a verb, Goldberg distinguishes between profiled and nonprofiled participant roles. In contrast to the latter, profiled roles (indicated by bold type) are prominent, focal points of a scene that syntactically must be obligatorily expressed in all uses of the verb or, which, when not overtly expressed, are always contextually identifiable (a phenomenon known as definite null instantiation DNI; Boas 2013: 237; Croft 2012: 364; Goldberg 2006: 39).

To illustrate the difference between profiled and nonprofiled participant roles, compare the following examples:

(5.6) a.   For three hours **we worked and drank**, worked and ate, worked and packed.
            (BNC A6T W_misc)
      b.   He placed the dead rabbit carefully on the block then turned and looked at
            her [. . .]
            Now she waited as **he probed and cut** and then compared what had been
            exposed against the diagram spread across the double page.
            (BNC FRF W_fict_prose)

In both (5.6a) and (5.6b), the objects of *drink* and *cut* (the liquid and the cut. object) are not syntactically expressed. Yet, while in (5.6a) it is completely immaterial what was drunk, in (5.6b) it is obligatorily entailed that something was cut that is contextually retrievable (*the dead rabbit* in (5.6b)). This conclusion is supported by the fact that a rejoinder such as *I wonder what they drank* is fine for (5.6a), while *#I wonder what they cut* is strange for (5.6b) (which shows that the liquid role in (5.6a) is unspecified, while the cut.object role is already contextually specified; cf. Goldberg 2006: 41). The cut.object role is thus a profiled role that has a DNI in (5.6b), while liquid is a nonprofiled, optional role in (5.6a).

The participant roles of verb constructions can thus either be obligatory (profiled) or optional (nonprofiled). In contrast to this, constructional argument roles are always syntactically obligatory. Nevertheless, Goldberg also distinguishes profiled from nonprofiled constructional roles, but here the difference merely concerns the syntactic function associated with the argument role (Croft 2012: 366; Goldberg 2006: 40): those that are realized as core syntactic arguments (subject or object) are profiled argument roles; the ones that are realised as oblique arguments are nonprofiled argument roles. Thus, in the Resultative construction (5.2), all three argument roles are obligatory, but only the agent and patient are profiled (since they are realised as SBJ and OBJ, respectively), while the result-goal is a non-profiled role (realised as an OBL syntactic argument).

The most important issue then is, obviously, how the fusion of verbs and argument structure constructions actually works. For this, Goldberg (1995: 50, 2006: 39–40; cf. also Boas 2013: 237–8) postulates two principles that regulate this process: (1) The Semantic Coherence Principle specifies that the participant roles of verbs can only fuse with constructional argument roles that are semantically compatible. In addition to this, (2) the Correspondence Principle requires that lexically profiled and expressed participant roles must be fused with a profiled constructional argument role (i.e., a subject or object slot – the only exception being verb constructions with three profiled participant roles, in this case one of these can be fused with a nonprofiled argument role of a construction). In order to illustrate these principles, the examples from (5.1) are repeated in (5.7) together with participant and argument roles:

(5.7) a.　Could he$_{\text{SHRIEKER=AGENT}}$ shriek himself$_{\text{PATIENT}}$ unconscious$_{\text{RESULT-GOAL}}$ ...?
　　　　(BNC W_fict_prose CJJ)

　　b.　Firefighters$_{\text{CUTTER=AGENT}}$ cut the man$_{\text{CUT.OBJECT=PATIENT}}$ free$_{\text{RESULT-GOAL}}$ ...
　　　　(BNC W_newsp_other_report K55)

　　c.　He$_{\text{DRINKER=AGENT}}$ had often drunk himself$_{\text{PATIENT}}$ silly$_{\text{RESULT-GOAL}}$
　　　　(BNC W_fict_prose CDN)

In (5.7) all argument role slots of the Resultative construction (SBJ:AGENT, OBJ:PATIENT and OBL:RESULT-GOAL) are filled. In (5.7a) the SHRIEKER participant role of shriek can be considered to be semantically compatible with the agent argument role, and thus complies with the Semantic Coherence Principle. Since this is also the only profiled role of *shriek*, which, moreover, merges with a profiled constructional role (the subject slot associated with the agent role), the Correspondence Principle is also fulfilled. The fusion of the verb and argument structure construction is thus grammatical, with the more abstract construction supplying the slots for the PATIENT and RESULT-GOAL, which can be filled creatively independently of the verbal semantics. Similarly, (5.7b) and (5.7c) can be argued to obey the Semantic Coherence Principle (identifying the CUTTER and DRINKER participant roles as compatible with the agent and the CUT.OBJECT[1] as compatible with the patient slot) as well as the Correspondence Principle (with the profiled roles cutter and drinker as well as the CUT.OBJECT realized as core syntactic arguments, that is subjects and object, respectively).

In addition to the Resultative construction, a broad range of other abstract argument structure constructions have been identified in the constructional literature, the most prominent being the following ones (adapted, unless stated otherwise, from Goldberg 1995: 117, 142, 160, 208, 2006: 41, 73; Hoffmann 2017a).

One very basic construal, for example, involves a single event with just one participant:

(5.8) a.　state verb
　　　　I'm going to repeat that – the hashtag is #dontdoublemyrate.
　　　　Your voice matters.
　　　　(COCA 2012 WEB whitehouse.gov Blog Action Day: 'The Power of We' |
　　　　　The White House)

　　b.　activity verb
　　　　... and then **some of the younger people danced**
　　　　(COCA 2012 WEB ebooks38.com Verbs, All of Them Tiring –
　　　　Cold Mountain by Frazier, Charles)

---

[1] As mentioned above, however, this identification is less straightforward than in the other cases since *the man* in (5.7b) is clearly not the cut.object in this case but merely a patient affected by the action.

c.   accomplishment verb
      His ship sank in a storm (COCA 1990 ACAD NaturalHist Columbus, my
          enemy)
d.   achievement verb
      My goldfish died ... (COCA 2004 MAG BoysLife think & grin)
e.   semelfactive verb
      He coughed then reached for the sugar ...
      (COCA 2019 FIC The Maine Review Several States Away)

As (5.8a–e) illustrate, the Intransitive construction covers a wide range of lexical
aspect types. Consequently, its meaning is probably the most abstract of all
argument structure constructions. It basically just denotes events in which
something is happening to a single participant:

(5.9)   Intransitive construction
             FORM: PHONOLOGY: $/A_1\ B_2\ /_3$
                         MORPHOSYNTAX: $[\text{SBJ}_1\ [V_2]_{\text{VP}}\ ]_3$

             ⇔

             MEANING: SEMANTICS: '$\text{EVENT}_2(\text{PARTICIPANT}_1)$'$_3$

In (5.9), the Intransitive construction has a slot for a subject and a verb (where
V is obviously a shorthand notation for the combination of modality, tense and
aspect constructions; see Section 4.2.3.2) and its meaning is rendered as an event in
which a single participant is involved ('$\text{EVENT}_2(\text{PARTICIPANT}_1)$'). Note that
adjuncts of time and place can, of course, freely be added to any argument
structure construction. Thus, you could add a place adjunct like *there* to all of the
examples in (5.6). Remember that this is possible since adjuncts are modifiers that
select for an event (and it is not the event that selects for these adjuncts; see Section
4.2.3.3). In contrast to this, we will see that some argument structure constructions
select for time and place information – in these cases, however, the corresponding
phrases are not adjuncts, but realize obligatory constructional roles.

Let us move on to events with two participants, for this (5.10) is the most
prototypical constructional construal:

(5.10)   Transitive construction
             FORM: PHONOLOGY: $/A_1\ B_2\ C_2\ /_4$
                         MORPHOSYNTAX: $[\text{SBJ}_1\ [V_2\ \text{OBJ}_3]_{\text{VP}}]_4$

             ⇔

             MEANING: SEMANTICS: '$\text{TRANSFER-FORCE}(\text{EVENT}_2(\text{AGENT}_1),$
                                                          $\text{PATIENT}_3)$'$_4$

             Examples:
             She$_1$ kissed$_2$ him$_3$.
             He$_1$ sang$_2$ [a song]$_3$.
             They$_1$ smashed$_2$ [the wall]$_3$.

The SEMANTICS pole of the Transitive construction is rendered as 'TRANSFER-
$\text{FORCE}(\text{EVENT}_2(\text{AGENT}_1),\ \text{PATIENT}_3)$' in (5.10). This can be paraphrased as
'the AGENT$_1$ is V$_2$-ing and by doing so causes the Transfer-of-Force onto the

PATIENT$_3$'. Note, however, that the force that is transmitted need not always be physical or violent: as the examples in (5.10) show, the Transitive construction is used for a wide range of events, at the end of which the patient might physically be more or less the same (cf. *She kissed him*) or in a completely different state (cf. *They smashed the wall.*). Nevertheless, the prototypical meaning of the construction can be captured as the 'transmission of force [...] by an initiator with mental capacities exercising her/his control acting on a physical endpoint' (Croft 2012: 282). In *She$_1$ kissed$_2$ him$_3$*, 'TRANSFER-FORCE(KISSING-EVENT$_2$(she$_1$), him$_3$)', the agent uses minimal physical force to move their lips towards the patient and kisses him. In *They$_1$ smashed$_2$ [the wall]$_3$*, the SMASHING-EVENT encoded by the verb obviously leads to a more violent and lasting transfer of force. As you can see, while an argument structure construction provides the basic meaning of a scene, the verb still plays an important role in determining the precise details of how an event is construed.

Sometimes, particularly with mental events (Croft 2021: 182, 233), both participants have properties that allow for them to be encoded as AGENT or PATIENT:

(5.11) a.   Your answer pleases me (COCA 2000 MOV An Everlasting Piece)
       b.   I like your answer!
             (COCA 2012 WEB Is Now The Time To Move Away From Major U.S. Cities?)

In (5.11) *your answer* can be construed as the source of force transmission since it is a STIMULUS that changes the mental state of the first person speaker. At the same time, the EXPERIENCER of the event (*I/me*) uses force to direct their attention to the STIMULUS. In cases such as these, Croft (2012: 233) speaks of a '[b]idirectional transmission of force' (from STIMULUS to EXPERIENCER and vice versa), which allows for either participant to be construed as either agent or patient. At the same time, we can already see that the verb lexeme plays an important role: you cannot use the Transitive construction freely to create constructs such as **Your answer likes me.* or **I please your answer.* In these cases, specific verb lexemes seem to have encoded one of the two possible construals. The interaction of verb lexeme and argument structure constructions is one that we will therefore need to return to later in more detail.

Interestingly, English also has an argument structure construction for situations in which a FORCE-DYNAMIC action is attempted, but the final success of the action is backgrounded and only implied (Perek and Lemmens 2010):

(5.12)   Conative construction
          FORM: PHONOLOGY: /A$_1$ B$_2$ [ət C]$_3$ /$_4$
                     MORPHOSYNTAX: [SBJ$_1$ [V$_2$ OBL:*at*-PP$_3$]$_{VP}$]$_4$

          ⇔

          MEANING: SEMANTICS: 'ATTEMPT(TRANSFER-FORCE
                                (EVENT$_2$(AGENT$_1$), PATIENT$_3$))'$_4$

Examples:
She$_1$ kicked$_2$ [at the ball]$_3$.
He$_1$ clutched$_2$ [at the branch]$_3$.
They$_1$ shot$_2$ [at the sheriff]$_3$.
(adapted from Perek and Lemmens 2010)

The construction in (5.12) is what I would call a 'marginal argument structure construction' since the FORM level is mostly, but not completely schematic (the OBL$_2$ slot has to be realised by a PP headed by *at*). Moreover, the scene it encodes, one of attempted transmission of force ('ATTEMPT(TRANSFER-FORCE(...))'), is obviously quite a specific one. This does not mean that our perceptual system does not pick up on these scenes. However, future research is needed to see whether such constructions really are 'basic human scenes' (that surface in all human languages). (Besides, as Perek and Lemmens (2010) point out, there is also a related Conative construction with a slightly different meaning, which is associated with continuous actions; for ease of exposition, however, we cannot go into this right here.)

Returning to the Transitive construction, examples like (5.13) are sometimes claimed to be problematic instances for this constructional template:

(5.13)   Bob weighed 15 stone (Hilpert 2019: 51)

Example (5.13) has two participants (*Bob* and *15 stone*), but the event it describes clearly involves no transmission of force (Croft 2012: 205, 226). On the contrary, it expresses a fairly static meaning, namely that of Bob having a certain weight. So, the construct in (5.13) does not fit the semantics of the Transitive construction. Moreover, most Transitive constructs have a corresponding passive (cf. *He was kissed.*, *A song was sung.* and *The wall was smashed.*) that backgrounds the agent participant (see below for details on the Passive construction). Yet, there is no passive construct corresponding to (5.13) (**15 stone was weighed.*). Consequently, we are dealing with a different argument structure construction here, the Copulative Attribute construction:

(5.14)   Copulative Attribute construction
            FORM: PHONOLOGY: /A$_1$ B$_2$ C$_3$ /$_4$
                        MORPHOSYNTAX: [SBJ$_1$ [V$_2$ OBL$_3$]$_{VP}$]$_4$

            ⇔

            MEANING: SEMANTICS: 'POSSESS-EVENT$_2$(THEME$_1$,
                                                    ATTRIBUTE$_3$)'$_4$

            Examples:
            She$_1$ is$_2$ [in a good mood]$_3$.
            He$_1$ seems$_2$ [a happy man]$_3$.
            It$_1$ smelled$_2$ [very good]$_3$.

The Copulative Attribute construction (5.14) has a MORPHOSYNTAX pole that at first glance seems fairy similar to the one of Transitive construction, but actually differs in one crucial respect: the post-verbal element indexed '3' is not classified as an object, but as an OBL (in more traditional structuralist approaches it is sometimes labelled 'subject complement' (Quirk et al. 1985) or 'subject attribute' (Aarts and Aarts 1988)). The reason for this is that different types of phrasal constructions can appear in the post-verbal slot of the two constructions: while the PATIENT of the Transitive construction is prototypically realised by NPs, the attribute of the Copulative Attribute construction can be realised by PPs (*in a good mood*), NPs (*a happy man*) or the prototypical construction for expressing properties – Adjective Phrases (*very good*). On the SEMANTICS pole, we capture the meaning of the construction by specifying that the V slot hosts a verb with a static meaning of 'POSSESS-EVENT$_2$', which means that the intended construal is that the THEME$_1$ possesses the mentioned ATTRIBUTE$_3$. In contrast to the Transitive construction (5.10), where the verb thus added an independent contribution to the overall meaning (indicated by the EVENT$_2$), in Copulative constructions the verb must fit the POSSESS-semantics of the construction. As a result, there are far fewer verb lexemes that can merge with the latter construction.

Note that there are many subtypes of copular constructions (Mikkelsen 2011; Quirk et al. 1985: 1171–6), which might warrant independent constructional templates, but which we cannot discuss all in this introductory textbook (but see Exercise 5.2 below for one of these subtypes). Nevertheless, I want to point out that the template in (5.14) is also flexible enough to accommodate constructs in which a locational PP fills the OBL slot:

(5.15) a.   She is at home.
     b.   He is in London.
     c.   They were on a deserted island.

In (5.15), the subjects can be said to have the properties ascribed to them by the OBL PPs (*at home, in London, on a deserted island*). In addition to that, you will remember that locational PPs encode a FIGURE-GROUND relationship. So, the fact that the subject has the property of a FIGURE that is located in space is contributed by the Spatial PP construction (4.117).

In addition to statically locating referents, humans obviously also perceive that a great number of things are moving in space (FIGURES moving in/on/towards a GROUND). One construction that allows us to talk about such events is the Intransitive Motion construction (5.16):

(5.16)   Intransitive Motion construction
       FORM: PHONOLOGY: /A$_1$ B$_2$ C$_3$ /$_4$
                   MORPHOSYNTAX: [SBJ$_1$ [V$_2$ OBL$_3$]$_{VP}$]$_4$

       ⇔

       MEANING: SEMANTICS: 'MOVE(EVENT$_2$(THEME=FIGURE$_1$),
                             GOAL=GROUND$_{3\_PATH/LOCATION}$)'$_4$
       Examples:
       He$_1$ ran$_2$ [out of the house]$_3$.
       [The fly]$_1$ buzzed$_2$ [into the room]$_3$.
       [People]$_1$ strolled$_2$ [along the river]$_3$.

The Intransitive Motion construction is used for the construal of a THEME=FIGURE$_1$ (e.g., *he, the fly, people* in (5.16)) carrying out an EVENT$_2$ that causes (*ran, strolled*) or accompanies (*buzzed*) movement in space. The path or location of this movement (GOAL=GROUND$_{2\_PATH/LOCATION}$) is expressed by the OBL$_3$ slot on the MORPHOSYNTAX level.

Sometimes, however, we do not just perceive the movement of an element, we also feel that there is an agent that caused this movement. For this type of construal, we draw on the Caused Motion construction (5.17):

(5.17)   Caused Motion construction
         FORM: PHONOLOGY: /A$_1$ B$_2$ C$_3$ D$_4$/$_5$
                      MORPHOSYNTAX: [SBJ$_1$ [V$_2$ OBJ$_3$ OBL$_4$]$_{VP}$]$_5$

         $\Leftrightarrow$

         MEANING: SEMANTICS: 'CAUSE(EVENT$_2$(AGENT$_1$),
                                     MOVE(THEME= FIGURE$_3$,
                                     GOAL=GROUND$_{4\_PATH/LOCATION}$))'$_5$
         Examples:
         She$_1$ kissed$_2$ [her shoes]$_3$ [under the sofa]$_4$.
         He$_1$ sang$_2$ [them]$_3$ [out of the room]$_4$.
         They$_1$ laughed$_2$ [the actor]$_3$ [off the stage]$_4$.

In the Caused Motion construction, the AGENT$_1$ (*she$_1$, he$_1$, they$_1$*) is doing something (kissing, singing, laughing; cf. 'EVENT$_2$(AGENT$_1$)' on the SEMANTICS level) that causes the THEME=FIGURE$_3$ (expressed by the OBJ$_3$ slot; *her shoes$_2$, them$_2$, the actor$_2$*) to move along/towards a GOAL=GROUND$_4$ (the OBL$_4$ slot).

It is important to remember that arguments structure constructions are construals, mental viewpoints, and that sometimes one and the same event can be construed by several constructions, each of which focuses on a different aspect of a situation:

(5.18) a.   The workers$_1$ loaded books$_2$ [onto the truck]$_3$.
       b.   The workers$_1$ loaded [the truck]$_2$ [with books]$_3$.

Both (5.18a) and (5.18b) can be used to talk about the same loading event: workers are putting books (FIGURE) onto a truck (GROUND). Thus (5.18a) has the FIGURE *the books* as an OBJ, and the GROUND is expressed as a path OBL *onto the truck* (Croft 2012: 226–7). In (5.18b), however, the truck becomes the OBJ, while *the books* is part of an OBL *with*-PP. These differences in FORM also corresponds to a difference in MEANING: the Caused Motion construction focuses on how the event affects the books by coming to be located on the truck (5.18a). In contrast to this, the variant in (5.18b) highlights instead how the truck is affected by this event (Croft 2012: 310–11; Goldberg 2006), that is, ending up being filled with books. For this latter construal, speakers have to draw on the so-called Causative *with* construction (5.19):

(5.19)   Causative *with* construction
           FORM: PHONOLOGY: $/A_1 B_2 C_3$ [wɪð D]$_4/_5$
                        MORPHOSYNTAX: [SBJ$_1$ [V$_2$ OBJ$_3$ OBL:*with*-PP$_4$]$_{VP}$]$_5$

           ⇔

           MEANING: SEMANTICS: 'CAUSE(EVENT$_2$(AGENT$_1$),
                                             BE(PATIENT=GROUND$_3$,STATE$_2$)
                                             BY(MEANS=FIGURE$_4$))'$_5$
           Examples:
           She$_1$ loaded$_2$ [the truck]$_3$ [with books]$_4$.
           He$_1$ sprayed$_2$ [the walls]$_3$ [with paint]$_4$.
           They$_1$ heaped$_2$ [the plate]$_3$ [with mashed potatoes]$_4$.

In the Causative *with* construction, another marginal argument structure construction, the GROUND is interpreted as an affected PATIENT and linked to the OBJ$_3$ slot. Moreover, under this construal, the PATIENT ends up in the STATE$_2$ of being loaded and the FIGURE is only seen as the instrument with which this is achieved ('BY(MEANS=FIGURE$_4$)'). We will return to the competition between the Causative *with* construction and the Caused Motion construction soon. Before that, however, let me introduce another two argument structure constructions.

First of all, we look at another marginal argument structure construction expressing certain movement events that has attracted considerable attention in the constructionist literature (Goldberg 1995, 2006; Traugott and Trousdale 2013): the *Way* construction.

(5.20)   *Way* construction
           FORM: PHONOLOGY: $/A_1 B_2$ [C$_3$ weɪ$_4$]$_5$ D$_6/_7$
                        MORPHOSYNTAX:
                        [SBJ$_1$ [V$_2$ [PRON$_{3=1}$ *way*$_4$]$_{OBJ5}$ OBL: PP$_6$]$_{VP}$]$_7$

           ⇔

           MEANING: SEMANTICS: 'CREATE-MOVE(EVENT$_2$(THEME=FIGURE$_1$),
                                             GOAL=GROUND$_{6\_PATH/LOCATION}$)'$_7$
           Examples:
           She$_1$ worked$_2$ [her$_{3=1}$ way$_4$]$_5$ [to the top]$_6$.
           He$_1$ danced$_2$ [his$_{3=1}$ way$_4$]$_5$ [into the club]$_6$.
           They$_1$ belched$_2$ [their$_{3=1}$ way$_4$]$_5$ [out of the restaurant]$_6$.

The *Way* construction prototypically combines movement as well as path creation (sometimes the PP:OBL can also encode only manner as in *He joked his way into the meeting*. 'He went into the meeting while joking' Goldberg 1995: 202). It encodes a scene in which a THEME=FIGURE$_1$ carries out an action specified by the V$_2$ (EVENT$_2$(THEME=FIGURE$_1$)) and by doing this creates a path GOAL=GROUND$_{6\_PATH/LOCATION}$ along which he or she moves. The construction thus can be used for construals in which an action of a participant (working, dancing, belching) is interpreted as allowing them to move along a newly created path (*to the top, into the club, out of the restaurant*). The construction clearly encodes a very specific, and as I would argue marginal, scene and should therefore only be considered a marginal argument structure construction (although in Present-day English it is, of course, a fairly productive construction). On the MORPHOSYNTAX level, this marginal status is also indicated by the fact that the construction is not fully schematic. Instead, it has an OBJ_5 element that must be headed by the noun way_3 and include a possessive pronoun $PRON_{3=1}$ that must be coreferential with the SBJ_1 (cf. *She$_1$ worked$_2$ [her$_{3=1}$ way$_4$]$_5$ [to the top]$_6$.* vs. **She$_1$ worked$_2$ [his$_{3 \neq 1}$ way$_4$]$_5$ [to the top]$_6$.*).

In contrast to this, the final argument structure construction that I want to talk about is a fully schematic one and clearly describes a humanly relevant scene – the Ditransitive construction:

(5.21)   Ditransitive construction
           FORM: PHONOLOGY: /A$_1$ B$_2$ C$_3$ D$_4$/$_5$
                       MORPHOSYNTAX: [SBJ$_1$ [V$_2$ OBJ$_3$ OBJ$_4$]$_{VP}$]$_5$

           ⇔

           MEANING: SEMANTICS: 'CAUSE(EVENT$_2$(AGENT$_1$),
                                       RECEIVE(RECIPIENT$_3$, THEME$_4$))'$_5$
           Examples:
           She$_1$ sent$_2$ him$_3$ [an email]$_4$.
           Jack$_1$ passed$_2$ her$_3$ [the salt]$_4$.
           [The waiter]$_1$ served$_2$ them$_3$ [their dinner]$_4$.

The Ditransitive construction encodes scenes in which an AGENT$_1$ carries out an event (sending, passing, serving) that is construed as causing a RECIPIENT$_3$ (him$_3$, her$_3$, them$_3$) to receive a THEME$_4$ (an email$_4$, the salt$_4$, their dinner$_4$). On the MORPHOSYNTAX level, the construction has four slots for SBJ$_1$, V$_2$ and two objects (OBJ$_3$, OBJ$_4$).

5.1.2   Degrees of Schematicity: The Network of Argument Structure Constructions

After presenting the most prominent argument structure constructions, let us take a closer look at how verb lexeme constructions combine with argument structure constructions. As you probably already noted along the way, a single verb lexeme construction such as BREAK can appear in several different argument structure constructions (5.22):

(5.22)   a.   Transitive construction: Bill kicked the ball.
           b.   Conative construction: Bill kicked at the ball.
           c.   Cause Motion construction: Bill kicked the ball off the field.
           d.   Resultative construction: Bill kicked the man unconscious.
           e.   Ditransitive construction: Bill kicked Bo the ball.
           f.   *Way* construction: Bill kicked his way through the crowd.

(examples from Perek and Lemmens 2010)

Instead of assuming that speakers have six different KICK lexemes (with six different complementation patterns), Construction Grammar postulates one verb lexeme with the meaning 'strike or propel forcibly with the foot' that draws on the CAUSE_HARM Frame.[2] The various argument structure constructions in (5.22) then afford the speaker with various different construals of KICKING events (e.g., whether it was only attempted (5.22b), or whether it resulted in movement (5.22c) or change in state (5.22d) of the VICTIM of the event). (Remember Chapter 2, where we discussed how children gradually acquire the ability to use verb lexemes in more than one argument structure construction).

As Boas (2013: 238) points out, this constructionist approach to argument structure has been very successful and has not only inspired research into English argument structure constructions (for a most recent publication; see Perek 2015). There are also a considerable number of constructionist studies that have analysed argument structure constructions in, inter alia, Dutch, Finnish, French, German, Hindi, Iclandic, Japanese, Spanish, Swedish and Thai (see Boas 2013: 238; Hoffmann 2017a: 300–1).

Nevertheless, several assumptions of the above approach to argument structure constructions have also been questioned. Croft (2012: 364–74), drawing on work by Nemoto (1998), Boas (2003) and Iwata (2005), shows that Goldberg's definition of profiling is not without problems. In Frame Semantic and Cognitive Grammar approaches, where the term profiling originated, '[a] profiled concept is the part of a semantic frame that is denoted by a linguistic expression' (Croft 2012: 364). As pointed out above, however, unlike these purely semantic approaches, Goldberg has additional syntactic criteria for the profiling status of her roles – the syntactic obligatoriness of participant roles and the core argument status of argument roles (Croft 2012: 365). One problem of the criterion of syntactic obligatoriness is that it cannot be decided out of syntactic context, that is outside of the context of argument structure constructions. As Croft (2012: 364–74) shows, this approach runs into significant empirical problems. Take the verb *spray*, which can, for example, appear in the Caused Motion construction (5.17) as well as the Causative *with* construction (5.19):

(5.23)   Caused Motion construction
           Bob sprayed paint onto the wall. (From Iwata 2005: 387)

(5.24)   Causative *with* construction
           Bob sprayed the wall with paint. (From Iwata 2005: 387)

In (5.23) and (5.24) *spray* seems to imply the frame semantic participant roles SPRAYER (*Bob*), LIQUID (*paint*) and TARGET (*wall*). Yet, which of these

---

[2] Source: https://framenet2.icsi.berkeley.edu/fnReports/data/lu/lu2271.xml?mode=lexentry [last accessed 14 August 2020].

participant roles are profiled? According to Goldberg (1995:178; see also Croft 2012: 367), LIQUID and TARGET, but not SPRAYER are profiled participant roles of *spray*:

(5.25) a.   Water$_{LIQUID}$ sprayed onto the lawn$_{TARGET}$
     b.   The men$_{SPRAYER}$ sprayed the lawn$_{TARGET}$
        (adapted from Croft 2012: 368)

In (5.25b), only SPRAYER and TARGET are realised, but Goldberg (1995: 178) argues that the LIQUID role is still profiled since it is missing but contextually identifiable (i.e., a case of DNI; an analysis Croft 2012: 368 contests). In contrast to this, (5.25a) without the SPRAYER role is grammatical and has no DNI reading. Consequently, Goldberg offers the following participant role frame for *spray* (with square brackets for profiled roles that can be suppressed via DNI):

(5.26)   <SPRAYER, **TARGET, [LIQUID]**>   (adapted from Goldberg 1995: 178)

Yet, Croft (2012) showed that even the TARGET role can be omitted without giving rise to any DNI reading:

(5.27)   The broken fire hydrant$_{SPRAYER}$ sprayed water$_{LIQUID}$ all afternoon.
        (adapted from Croft 2012: 367)

This kind of reasoning thus leads to a lexical construction *spray* in which no participant role is profiled and obligatory (if (5.25b) does not necessarily give rise to a DNI reading, the participant frame for *spray* would end up as <SPRAYER, TARGET, [LIQUID]>; see Croft 2012: 367–8).

Even more problematic is the fact that Goldberg's approach cannot explain why some verb constructions are occasionally incompatible with certain argument structure constructions:

(5.28)   The lawn$_{SBJ:LOCATION}$ gleamed with dew$_{with-PP:LIQUID}$

(5.29)   *The lawn$_{SBJ:LOCATION}$ sprayed with water$_{with-PP:LIQUID}$

The argument structure construction underlying (5.28) and (5.29) has a subject slot that specifies a LOCATION and a *with*-PP slot for a LIQUID. According to the Semantic Coherence Principle (cf. Croft 2012: 368), the TARGET participant role of *spray* should be able to fuse with the LOCATION slot (as it does in the Caused Motion construction, cf. (5.17)) and the LIQUID participant role should perfectly match the constructional LIQUID argument role. (Additionally, if all participant roles are nonprofiled, as argued above, the Correspondence Principle does not apply.)

To explain the difference in grammaticality between (5.28) and (5.29), it is obviously not enough to just take into account the number and types of participant roles of a verb. In addition to this, the (dis)ability of verbs to fuse with certain argument structure constructions also depends on the verbal semantics; that is, the event type a verb describes (Croft 2012: 368). Iwata (2005: 387–90) uses the different licit grammatical contexts for *smear* and *spray* to illustrate this:

(5.30) a.   They smeared paint on the wall. (Caused Motion construction)
     b.   They smeared the wall with paint. (Causative *with* construction)

As (5.30) shows, *smear*, like *spray*, occurs in both the Caused Motion and Causative *with* construction. Furthermore, *smear* can also be argued to possess a similar set of participant roles (SMEARER, TARGET, LIQUID). Yet, as (5.31a) shows, while *spray* can also be used in the Intransitive Motion construction (5.16), *smear* cannot fuse with this argument structure construction (5.31b):

(5.31) a.   Paint$_{\text{LIQUID}}$ sprayed on the wall$_{\text{TARGET}}$. (Intransitive Motion construction)
     b.   *Paint$_{\text{LIQUID}}$ smeared on the wall$_{\text{TARGET}}$. (Intransitive Motion construction)

Iwata (2005: 388) points out that the reason for this does not lie in different participant role profiles, but instead is tied to the frame semantic scene encoded by a verb: verbs like *spray* (or *splash*) encode a scene in which the manner of movement of the liquid (going in a mist) is construed as a subevent that can be focused on independently of the initial action of the external causer (the sprayer). Consequently, *spray*-verbs can fuse with the Intransitive Motion construction, which encodes manner of movement of a theme to a location. In contrast to this, the manner of smearing is continuously construed as dependent on a co-occurring action of the external causer (e.g., manual movement). As a result, there is no independent subevent of *smear* (or *daub*, etc.) that could fuse with the Intransitive Caused Motion construction.

Phenomena such as (5.31) have led several Construction Grammarians (e.g., Boas 2005a, 2005b, 2013: 238; Croft 2012; Iwata 2008; Nemoto 2005) to argue for a greater prominence of the frame semantic meaning of verbs. On top of this, these researchers claim that abstract argument structure constructions such as the ones we have seen above often overgenerate and that speakers cognitively seem to have stored more verb-specific argument structure templates. Take, for example, the Ditransitive construction: while the template in (5.21) might seem to license all types of ditransitive structures, it turns out that, depending on certain verb classes, different types of meanings can be expressed (Croft 2012: 375–80; Goldberg 1995: 38; see there for various other subclasses of the construction):

(5.32) a.   Central Sense: agent successfully causes recipient to receive patient
          verbs that inherently signify acts of giving:
          give, pass, hand, serve, feed, ... [Modulation: actual]
          e.g., She passed him the salt.
     b.   Central Sense: agent successfully causes recipient to receive patient
          verbs of instantaneous causation of ballistic motion:
          throw, toss, slap, kick, poke, fling, shoot, ... [Modulation: actual]
          e.g., She threw him the ball.

c.   Agent causes recipient not to receive patient
     verbs of refusal:
     refuse, deny [Modulation: negative]
     e.g., She denied him the answer.

As (5.32) shows, the three verb classes lead to crucially different meanings:
while the verbs in (5.32a) and (5.32b) entail that the possessive relation of the
Ditransitive construction obtains, the verbs in (5.32c) entail a negative modulation (the recipient does not receive the theme). On top of that, verbs such as
throw, *toss*, *slap*, etc. (5.32b) lead to an instantaneous ballistic motion reading of
the Ditransitive construction that is absent from similar constructions with
verbs such as *give*, *pass* or *hand*, (5.32a). In order to address this issue,
Goldberg (1995: 38) advocates a polysemy account in which the construction
in (5.21) is enriched by various submeanings (such as whether the transfer of
possession is actual (5.32a,b) or negative (5.32c); see also Croft 2012: 376).
One problem with this approach is that it wrongly predicts that verbs from one
class should also be used freely with any of the other polysemous meanings.
Yet this is not the case: *pass* in the Ditransitive construction cannot mean
'X passes Y to receive Z by instantaneous ballistic motion' nor can *refuse* be
made to mean 'X refuses Y to receive Z (and Y successfully receives Z)' (Croft
2012: 377). Due to this, instead of postulating a single, maximally abstract,
polysemous Ditransitive construction, Croft (2012: 378) argues that a family of
related Verb-Class-Specific constructions have to be postulated. The following
three Verb-Class-Specific constructions could then be said to license the distribution in (5.32):

(5.33)   Verb-Class-Specific Ditransitive constructions (adapted from Croft 2012: 378)
    a.   FORM: PHONOLOGY: /A_1 B_2 C_3 D_4/$_5$
                      MORPHOSYNTAX: [SBJ$_1$ [GIVING.V$_2$ OBJ$_3$ OBJ$_4$]$_{VP}$]$_5$

         ⇔

         MEANING: SEMANTICS: 'CAUSE$_2$(EVENT$_2$(AGENT$_1$),
                                 RECEIVE$_2$(RECIPIENT$_3$, THEME$_4$))'$_5$
    b.   FORM: PHONOLOGY: /A_1 B_2 C_3 D_4/$_5$
                      MORPHOSYNTAX:
                      [SBJ$_1$ [BALL.MOT.V$_2$ OBJ$_3$ OBJ$_4$]$_{VP}$]$_5$

         ⇔

         MEANING: SEMANTICS: 'CAUSE(BALL.MOT.-EVENT$_2$(AGENT$_1$),
                                 RECEIVE(RECIPIENT$_3$, THEME$_4$))'$_5$
    c.   FORM: PHONOLOGY: /A_1 B_2 C_3 D_4/$_5$
                      MORPHOSYNTAX:
                      [SBJ$_1$ [REFUSE.V$_2$ OBJ$_3$ OBJ$_4$]$_{VP}$]$_5$

         ⇔

         MEANING: SEMANTICS: 'REFUSE$_2$(CAUSE(EVENT$_2$(AGENT$_1$),
                                 RECEIVE(RECIPIENT$_3$, THEME$_4$)))'$_5$

Croft (2012: 380) highlights that the three types of Verb-Class-Specific
Ditransitive constructions interact differently with the intuitive semantics of the

various verb classes: while the Ditransitive construction in (5.33a) adds no meaning to verbs such as *give, hand, serve*, etc., the one in (5.33b) adds a modulation of actual transfer of possession to verbs that themselves do not encode this meaning (cf. *He threw a stone.*, for example, implies no transfer of possession at all). In (5.33a), this is indicated by linking the GIVING.V_2 to all parts of the transfer meaning on the SEMANTICS level ($CAUSE_2(EVENT_2(\ldots)$, $RECEIVE_2(\ldots)))$. In contrast to this, this transfer meaning is part of the argument structure construction in (5.33b) and the verb just adds the ballistic motion of the event carried out by the agent ($BALL.MOT.\text{-}EVENT_2(AGENT_1)$). Finally, verbs such as *refuse* or *deny* already imply a negative modulation, but no transfer of possession (cf. *He refused to do it.* → *He did not do it.*), so that (5.33c) only adds the latter meaning component to the basic verbal semantics (indicated by $REFUSE_2(\ldots)$ having scope over the entire ditransitive meaning).

There is, however, evidence that suggests that even Verb-Class-Specific Ditransitive constructions overgenerate in some cases. Goldberg (1995: 130; see also Croft 2012: 378), for example, notes that not all refusal verbs can fuse with the (REFUSE.V-)Ditransitive construction (5.34):

(5.34)   She refused/denied/*prevented/*disallowed/*forbade him a kiss.

In addition to Verb-Class-Specific Ditransitive constructions, this appears to call for even more specific Verb-Specific constructions such as the following (adapted from Croft 2012: 379):

(5.35) a.   REFUSE-Verb-Specific Ditransitive construction
   FORM: PHONOLOGY: /A_1 REFUSE$_2$ C_3 D_4/$_5$
           MORPHOSYNTAX:
           [SBJ$_1$ [REFUSE.V$_2$ OBJ$_3$ OBJ$_4$]$_{VP}$]$_5$

   ⇔

   MEANING: SEMANTICS: 'REFUSE$_2$(CAUSE (EVENT$_2$(AGENT$_1$),
               RECEIVE(RECIPIENT$_3$, THEME$_4$)))'$_5$
  b. DENY-Verb-Specific Ditransitive construction
   FORM: PHONOLOGY: /A_1 DENY$_2$ C_3 D_4/$_5$
           MORPHOSYNTAX:
           [SBJ$_1$ [REFUSE.V$_2$ OBJ$_3$ OBJ$_4$]$_{VP}$]$_5$

   ⇔

   MEANING: SEMANTICS: 'REFUSE$_2$(CAUSE(EVENT$_2$(AGENT$_1$),
               RECEIVE(RECIPIENT$_3$, THEME$_4$)))'$_5$

Instead of a single Ditransitive construction, it thus seems more appropriate to talk of a network of Ditransitive constructions. Figure 5.1 gives a partial representation of what such a network could look like (using a slightly simplified FORM-MEANING notation employed by Hoffmann 2017b):

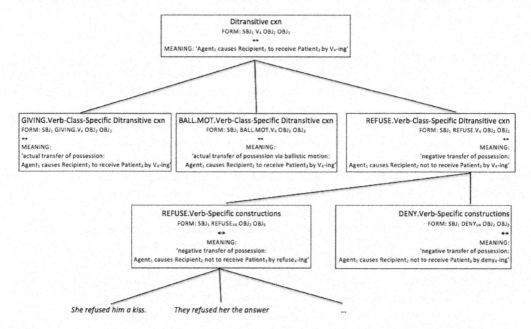

Figure 5.1 *Partial construction network for the Ditransitive construction (from Hoffmann 2017b: 314)*

At the bottom of Figure 5.1, we find specific utterances (so-called constructs) such as *She refused him a kiss* that form the basic input of construction learning. Constructional networks are similar to prototype taxonomies (Ungerer and Schmid 2006: 7–63) in that there are basic-level items such as *chair* (the Verb-Class-Specific Ditransitive constructions in Figure 5.1) that are situated between more general, superordinate terms such as *furniture* (the Ditransitive construction in Figure 5.1) and more specific subordinate ones, for example, *kitchen chair* (the REFUSE.Verb-Specific constructions in Figure 5.1). Just like prototype taxonomies, constructional networks exhibit 'default inheritance' effects (cf., e.g., Croft and Cruse 2004: 262–5; Ginzburg and Sag 2000: 5–8; Goldberg 2003: 222–3): normally (by default) a subordinate construction will inherit all properties from its superordinate construction, but a more specific construction can also override inherited properties. All subordinate constructions of the most schematic Ditransitive construction, for example, inherit its transfer of possession meaning, but the REFUSE.Verb-Class construction overrides the default modulation of actual transfer with its negative modulation. Cognitively, constructional taxonomies are also motivated by priming effects of constructions with a similar form and/or meaning (cf. e.g., Bock 1986a, 1986b; Bock and Griffin 2000; Hudson 2010: 75–6; though as Croft 2013: 218–23 points out, alternative visualizations such as geometric or network representations can also be used to capture these relationships between constructions).

How do speakers acquire networks such as Figure 5.1? From a usage-based perspective, the answer depends on the interaction of input frequency and mental entrenchment: high token frequency of a single, specific construct leads to the entrenchment of a phonologically filled construction (Chapter 2; Croft and Cruse 2004: 292–3; Langacker 1987: 59–60). Thus, even a construct such as *She refused him the kiss* can become entrenched if it is encountered often enough. High type frequency of a pattern, that is, different lexicalizations such as *She refused him the kiss*, *They refused her the answer* or *Leeds United have refused Sky TV entry into Elland Road . . .*,[3] due to the domain-general capacity of pattern detection and schematization (Bybee 2010), lead to the storage of a more abstract construction (such as the REFUSE.Verb-Specific Ditransitive construction). Under this view, constructional taxonomies emerge in a bottom-up fashion. The resulting levels of schematicitity are sometimes referred to using a classification first introduced by Traugott (2008a, 2008b): entrenched, substantive constructions, which appear at the bottom of the mental constructicon (such as *She refused him the kiss*), are called 'micro-constructions'. A high type frequency of micro-constructions can then lead to the generalization of more abstract 'meso-constructions' such as the REFUSE.Verb-Specific Ditransitive construction (or at an even more abstract level, the REFUSE.Verb-Class Ditransitive construction, since there can be more than one level of meso-constructions). Finally, the most schematic constructions such as the Ditransitive construction at the top of Figure 5.1 are labelled 'macro-constructions'. Since most constructs could also be generated by drawing on existing micro- and meso-constructions, for many phenomena the question of whether a macro-construction has to be postulated at all is an empirical one from a usage-based perspective. Barðdal (2008, 2011), for example, has shown that the productivity of abstract constructions can be seen as an inverse correlation of type frequency and semantic coherence, with highly abstract macro-constructions only arising if the underlying meso-constructions have a high type frequency and a high degree of variance in semantic distribution.

The right level of granularity of constructional schematicity remains a central issue in all Construction Grammars (and is a point that we will return to in Chapter 7). As previous research has shown, not all macro-level argument structure constructions exhibit the same degree of productivity: while the *Way* construction (5.20), for example, can fuse with a considerable number of different verbs (Goldberg 1995: 199–218), the Resultative construction (5.2) is lexically more constrained and thus much less productive (Boas 2005a, 2013: 237–8; Goldberg and Jackendoff 2004). An important insight of Construction Grammar research thus is that constructional generalizations can occur at varying degrees of schematicity (Hilpert 2013: 201–3) – even for a set of similar constructions such as the argument structure constructions.

What a usage-based perspective thus allows us to do is to ask new questions about what the coverage (Goldberg 2019) of a construction is: which exemplars of an argument structure construction are, for example, frequently attested. Which elements appear in the various FORM slots of a construction? We have already seen that the V slot of argument structure constructions seems much

---

[3] Source: www.leeds.vitalfootball.co.uk/lufc-sky-tv-refused-entry-to-elland-road/ [last accessed 25 June 2021].

Table 5.1. *Distributional properties of five Argument Structure constructions in the spoken part of the ICE/GB (data from: Perek and Lemmens 2010)*

Construction	Most frequent verb	Other frequent verbs (>1%)
Ditransitive (5.21)	*give* (50%)	*tell* (14%), *show* (8%), *offer* (5%), *send* (4%), *get* (3%), *ask, do* (2% each), *buy, teach* (1% each)
Caused Motion (5.17)	*put* (24%)	*give* (12%), *take* (9%), *get* (8%), *send* (6%), *bring* (4%), *leave* (3%), *place, throw* (2% each), *impose, add, hand, offer, pay, sit* (1% each)
Intransitive Motion (5.16)	*go* (32%)	*come* (24%), *get* (7%), *move, run* (3% each), *walk, return, arrive* (2% each), *fall, embark, head, fly* (1% each)
Resultative (5.2)	*make* (40%)	*put* (14%), *get, leave* (9%), *bring* (5%), *turn* (4%), *drive, take* (2% each), *elect, force, have, let, throw* (1% each)
Intransitive-Resultative (subtype of (5.2))	*become* (38%)	*get* (30%), *go* (8%), *come* (4%), *fall, end up* (3% each), *prove* (2%), *grow, evolve, form* (1%)

more constrained than the other slots (such as SBJ, OBJ or OBL). In Chapter 2, we came across language acquisition data that clearly showed prototype effects for argument structure constructions: in child–caretaker interaction, GIVE, for example, is the most frequent verb used by children and caretakers alike in the Ditransitive constructions. These results, together with the above findings, have led researchers to explore the productivity of the V slot in adult speech in more detail. Perek and Lemmens (2010), for example, show that in adult speech (from the ICE-GB corpus) there is also a single verb that appears far more frequently than any other verb in the V slot of five selected argument structure constructions (see Table 5.1).

Remember that corpus evidence alone does not guarantee that the above figures are reflective of the actual input frequencies that individual speakers of a language are exposed to (Schmid 2020). Nevertheless, since these results are corroborated from other corpus and language acquisition studies (see Chapter 2), we have at least good reason to assume that the GIVE.Verb-Specific Ditransitive construction is a prototypical member of the Ditransitive construction network, just as the MAKE.Verb-Specific Resultative construction is a central member of the Resultative construction network.

Mere frequencies, however, might be misleading since *get*, for example, appears in all five argument structure constructions in Table 5.1. Does that mean it is significantly associated with all these constructions? In order to answer this question, Stefanowitsch and Gries (2003) developed a statistical test that takes into account how often a word (W) appears in a particular construction (C) – but also how often other words (¬W) appear in that construction (C), how often the target word (W) shows up in other constructions (¬C) and finally, how often other words (¬W) occur in other constructions (¬C). By combining all of these four possibilities, this method, known as 'simple collexeme analysis', allows researchers to test statistically how strong a word and a particular construction are actually attracted or repelled (for details on the actual statistics; see Stefanowitsch 2013). Running such a test over the ditransitive constructs from the ICE-GB, Stefanowitsch (2013: 293), for example, found that the top five verb lexemes that were significantly attracted to the Ditransitive construction were GIVE, TELL, SEND, ASK and SHOW.

Simple collexeme analysis is only one type of a family of tests that Gries and Stefanowitsch put forward for identifying the association of slot fillers in constructions. In addition to their 'distinctive collexeme analysis' (which tests how strongly a word is attracted to or repelled by two semantically or functionally similar constructions such as the Particle-First v. Object-First Verb Particle construction), the 'co-varying collexeme analysis' tests the association of words across two slots of a single construction. A co-varying collexeme analysis of the V and OBJ$_2$ slot of the Ditransitive construction (Stefanowitsch 2013: 300), for example, revealed that combinations TELL ... *what*, ASK ... *question*, or TELL ... *that* turned out be significantly associated.

From a usage-based perspective, these lexically-specific filler combinations are part of the network of Verb-Class as well as Verb-Specific argument structure constructions. The slot fillers of Verb-Specific argument structure constructions have also been the focus of valency-based constructionist research: Herbst (2018) speaks of 'collostructions' – corpus evidence that is indicative of how the argument role slots of Verb-Specific argument structure constructions are frequently realized. Based on data from the BNC, Herbst (2018), identifies the following prominent SBJ and OBJ fillers in the CATCH-Verb-Specific Transitive construction (the log-likelihood is another statistical measure that shows the significance of the association of a word to a slot; values log-likelihood > 3.84 are considered significant, see http://ucrel.lancs.ac.uk/llwizard.html):

Table 5.2. *Collo-profile of the verb* CATCH *in the monotransitive construction (adapted from Herbst and Hoffmann 2018: 208)*

Monotransitive construction with *catch*					
CATCHER as AGENT		*CATCH*	THING CAUGHT as PATIENT		
he	675	4416.5976	eye	342	5686.8238
she	489	3550.6208	sight	293	5055.7113
I	560	2889.0927	glimpse	192	4149.4308
you	354	1622.6562	fire	156	2052.7937
they	274	1401.8892	breath	126	1959.8675
we	180	801.6969	him	210	1490.0314
it	137	165.0341	attention	93	1088.2738
wind	15	123.1111	train	69	851.6845
	frequency	log-likelihood		frequency	log-likelihood

As you can see in Table 5.2, pronouns (such as *he*, *she*, *I* and *you*) appear most frequently in the SBJ slot of the construction, while idiomatic uses (such as CATCH *s.o.'s eye* or CATCH *sight of s.th.*) are most significantly associated with the OBJ slot.

Usage-based approaches hold that a lot of our linguistic performance draws on constructions we have heard frequently and have consequently deeply entrenched. At the same time, we do not always just repeat what we have encountered before. Languages are complex symbolic systems that allow speakers to produce novel utterances that they have never heard before. In fact, linguistic creativity is considered to be one of the design features (Hockett 1960) of human language, or as Chomsky (1965) put it, 'an essential property of language' (see also Hoffmann 2018, 2020a; Section 8.3). In addition to lexically-specific constructions, the abstract argument structure constructions discussed in Section 5.1.1 are therefore also useful for speakers: these flexible templates allow them to creatively express novel meanings such as *Could he shriek himself unconscious …?* (5.1a) or *he had often drunk himself silly* (5.1c). The interaction of Verb-Specific, Verb-Class-Specific and abstract argument structure constructions therefore remains a hot topic for future constructionist research.

5.1.3   Argument Structure Constructions and Passive: Lexical versus Phrasal Construction

So far, we have provided phrasal analyses of argument structure constructions that all imply a fixed word order: the Resultative construction in (5.2), for example, has the $SBJ_1 \leftrightarrow AGENT_1$ slot preceding the verbal slot, while $OBL_4 \leftrightarrow RESULT\text{-}GOAL_4$ follows $OBJ_3 \leftrightarrow PATIENT_3$ in post-verbal position. Since English has a fairly fixed word order, this mapping of hierarchical structure into linear order is often unproblematic for most declarative clauses. However, as Müller (2006) points out, such phrasal constructions with a fixed order of argument roles nevertheless raise certain issues. These issues are best illustrated with data from another language: German, for example, is a language with a freer word order than English, and it exhibits many different orderings of the constituents of the Resultative construction:

(5.36) a.   Er   fischt   den Teich   schnell   leer.
             he   fishes   the pond   quickly   empty.
       b.   Den Teich   fischt   er   schnell   leer.
             the pond   fishes   he   quickly   empty.
       c.   Schnell   fischt   er   den Teich leer.
             quickly   fishes   he   the pond   empty
       d.   Leer   fischt   er   den Teich nicht.
             empty   fishes   he   the pond   not.

(examples a.–d. from Müller 2006: 853)

(5.37)   ... (weil)   er   den Teich   leer   fischt.
           ... (because)   he   the pond   empty   fishes.

The meaning of the main clause examples (5.36a–d) as well as the subordinate clause (5.37) all roughly translate into 'he quickly fishes the pond empty' in English (with (5.37d) being negated). Yet, while English has subject–verb order in main and subordinate clauses, German has verb-second order in main clauses (5.36) and verb-final order in subordinate clauses (5.37). One way to account for this is to assume two sets of Resultative constructions, a main clause variant with the verb slot in second position and a subordinate variant with verb in the final slot. Such an approach, however, would still have to explain that the verb order variation in (5.36) and (5.37) is not specific to Resultative constructions, but applies to all German argument structure constructions (and thus constitutes a structural generalization that speakers entrench fairly quickly). Alternatively, one could argue that constructional templates such as (5.2) only specify syntactic dominance but do not determine the linear order of constituents (see Müller 2006: 862). Then, the various structures in (5.36) could all be explained by the interaction of the Resultative construction, which would not specify the linear precedence information, and, for example, an information structure construction that would specify that the initial constituent preceding the verb in (5.36) receives a topic interpretation (see Section 5.4).

The latter explanation is feasible for the examples in (5.36), which do indeed differ with respect to their topic-comment structure (and which can therefore not be considered structural alternatives that are fully synonymous). More problematic, even for languages with a fixed word order such as English, however, are valency-changing constructions such as passives:

(5.38)   The man was cut free (by the firefighters).

In the passive sentence (5.38) the argument linking of argument roles and syntactic function is clearly different from the Resultative construction template in (5.2): in (5.38) the PATIENT is realized as subject, while the AGENT, as expected in a passive sentence, is demoted to an optional oblique position (the complement of the optional by-PP). All Construction Grammar approaches will, of course, assume a Passive construction. Examples such as (5.38), however, beg the question of whether it makes sense to first fuse verbs with an argument structure construction such as (5.2) and then to assume the Passive construction to change the valency as well as word order of this template (since this has a transformational flavour that is strongly eschewed in Construction Grammar approaches).

In essence, three alternative types of analysis for this problem have been advocated in the constructionist literature: first of all, early constructionist approaches (Fillmore and Kay 1995; Michaelis and Ruppenhofer 2001: 55–7) treated argument structure constructions as well as the Passive construction as linking constructions that simultaneously were to unify with lexical constructions (such as the *cut* Verb construction). These analyses, however, were technically flawed in that the valency lists of the various constructions were represented as sets. Since set unification could not be defined in a way that allowed for the automatic unification of the various input constructions, these analyses were soon abandoned (see Müller 2006: 863–6, 2019: 324–7 for a more detailed discussion).

The second approach emerged from formal syntactic theories such as Head-Driven Phrase Structure (HPSG) and Sign-Based Construction Grammar (SBCG, see Chapter 7). Researchers within these approaches (*inter alia*, Müller 2006; Sag 2012) argue for a lexical construction account. In their analysis, the Passive construction and various argument structure constructions such as the Resultative construction (as well as various other constructions) are unary lexical constructions that take a lexical verb construction as their daughter node and link it to a mother node with the appropriate argument structure. A simplified version of a Lexical Resultative construction is provided in (5.39) (based on Müller 2006: 873 and reinterpreted as a feature description following Meurers 2001; Müller 2019: 288):

(5.39)   Lexical Resultative construction. (simplified and adopted version of Müller 2006: 873)

$$
\left(
\begin{array}{c}
\text{(resultative) MTR} \\[4pt]
[\text{FORM}: V_2 \text{ SUBCAT } <NP_1, NP_3, ADJP_4> \\[4pt]
\leftrightarrow \text{MEANING}: \text{`CAUSE(EVENT}_2(\text{AGENT}_1), \text{BECOME (PATIENT}_3, \text{RESULT-GOAL}_4))\text{'}] \\[4pt]
| \\[4pt]
\text{(verbal) DTR} \\[4pt]
[\text{FORM}: V_2 \text{ SUBCAT } <NP_1> \leftrightarrow \text{MEANING}: V_2]
\end{array}
\right)
$$

Such analyses are the constructionist equivalent of lexical rules: an input lexical item (the verbal daughter node) is related to an output lexical item (the resultative mother node). Once the lexical construction in (5.39) has licensed a resultative verb (e.g., *cut* SUBCAT $<NP_1, NP_3, ADJP_4>$), this output construction can become the input of a Passive construction that yields the required passivized verb form (e.g., *cut*$_{passive}$ SUBCAT $<NP_3, ADJP_4, (PP_{by} NP_1)>$). Only once all lexical constructions are applied can syntactic constructions then create phrasal patterns.

Lexical constructionist analyses have the advantage of significantly reducing the number of postulated constructions and of directly capturing generalizations such as the passive formation across all types of argument structure constructions. At the same time, they re-introduce a lexicon–syntax dichotomy, a distinction that has been refuted by much Construction Grammar and

Cognitive Linguistic research. As a case in point, take the Ditransitive construction above (5.19): the data in (5.32) and (5.34) showed that a single abstract Ditransitive construction cannot capture the distribution of the various semantic subtypes. Similarly, one would need not only one but (at least) two separate unary lexical constructions for verbs of instantaneous causation of ballistic motion and negative transfer of possession, respectively. This, of course, can easily be done and is not a substantial argument against lexical accounts. More problematic, however, are idiosyncratic constraints on the interaction of argument structure constructions and the Passive construction:

(5.40)   He was given/passed/handed/served/fed the soup.

(5.41) a.   He was thrown the ball.
       b.   ?He was kicked the ball.

While a passive version of all verbs that inherently signify acts of giving (5.40) is perfectly acceptable, not all verbs of instantaneous causation of ballistic motion seem to be able to appear in passive ditransitive structures (cf. (5.41a) vs (5.41b)).[4] If the passive is a lexical construction independent of argument structure constructions, this type of restriction cannot be accounted for in a straightforward way. More generally speaking, a problem of lexical construction accounts is that they are too powerful and tend to overgenerate (Carpenter 1992; cf. also van Trijp 2014: 618–29).

Besides, unary lexical constructions of the type given in (5.39) require that a mother node (output) always has a lexical daughter node (input). Yet, there are some verbs that only appear in passive sentences that lack an active equivalent/ input (Hilpert 2019: 42):

(5.42) a.   Pat is reputed to be very rich.
       b.   Kim is said to be a manic depressive.
       c.   It is rumoured that there will be an election before the end of the year.
            (Examples from Hilpert 2019: 42)

Data such as (5.41) and (5.42) have led to a third approach (Croft 2001: 215, 2013: 215–16, 220; Goldberg 2006: 22, fn. 3; van Trijp 2014: 624), which postulates active as well as passive argument structure constructions as separate, albeit related constructions. Under this analysis, speakers are expected to possess a Passive Ditransitive construction that is horizontally connected to the Active Ditransitive construction (5.21) in the constructional network in the same way as morphological constructions such as *fair-unfair* are related (see Section 3.1):

---

[4] While a Google search for 'was thrown the ball' site:.uk yields 8,210 hits, the equivalent query 'was kicked the ball' site:.uk gives no single hit. Source: www.google.de [last accessed 14 February 2016].

(5.43)   Active Ditransitive   Passive Ditransitive construction
          construction
          a. She₁ gave₂ him₃ [a present]₄.   ↔   a.' He₃ was given₂ [a present]₄ (by her₁).
          b. He₁ sent₂ her₃ [a present]₄.   ↔   b.' She₃ was sent₂ [a present]₄ (by him₁).
          c. Jack₁ passed₂ her₃ [the salt]₄. ↔   c.' She₃ was passed₂ [the salt]₄ (by Jack₁).

What is the difference between (5.43a–c) and (5.43a'–c')? On the formal level, we see that the passive alternative has (1) the lexeme BE plus the past participle form of a full verb (*was given, was sent, was passed*) and (2) that the subject of the Active Ditransitive construction corresponds to an optional *by*-PP in the Passive Ditransitive construction. The second point is a clue as to the different meanings of active and passive sentences: both active and passive ditransitives denote the same event (an agent causing a recipient to receive a theme). Yet, actives and passives turn out to be different construals of the same scenes (see van Trijp 2014): active constructions take the agent to be the vantage point from which the event is construed by putting it into subject position. Passive constructions, on the other hand, background the agent (which becomes part of an optional *by*-PP adjunct) and construe the most affected, patient-like participant as the vantage point of the scene, by placing it into subject positions. The subject slot in English thus informs hearers which participant is the vantage point from which to view a scene.

Due to type frequency, data such as (5.43a'–c') will give rise to a Passive Ditransitive construction as shown in Figure 5.2 (for the purpose of exposition only the MORPHOSYNTAX and SEMANTICS level of the constructions are given):

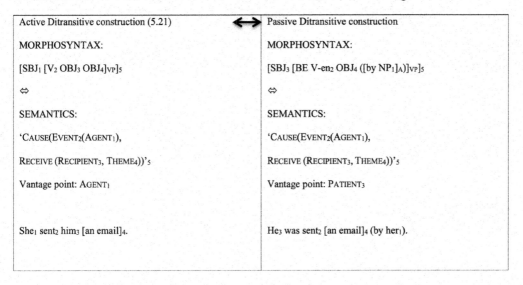

Active Ditransitive construction (5.21)	Passive Ditransitive construction
MORPHOSYNTAX:	MORPHOSYNTAX:
[SBJ₁ [V₂ OBJ₃ OBJ₄]ᵥₚ]ₛ	[SBJ₃ [BE V-en₂ OBJ₄ ([by NP₁]ₐ)]ᵥₚ]ₛ
⇔	⇔
SEMANTICS:	SEMANTICS:
'CAUSE(EVENT₂(AGENT₁),	'CAUSE(EVENT₂(AGENT₁),
RECEIVE (RECIPIENT₃, THEME₄))'ₛ	RECEIVE (RECIPIENT₃, THEME₄))'ₛ
Vantage point: AGENT₁	Vantage point: PATIENT₃
She₁ sent₂ him₃ [an email]₄.	He₃ was sent₂ [an email]₄ (by her₁).

Figure 5.2 *Active and Passive Ditransitive construction*

As you can see in Figure 5.2, both constructions have the same SEMANTICS ('CAUSE(EVENT₂(AGENT₁), RECEIVE(RECIPIENT₃, THEME₄))') since they describe the same scene. The only difference on the SEMANTICS level is that the Active Ditransitive has the agent as its vantage point, while the Passive Ditransitive makes the most patient-like participant (here the recipient) its vantage point. On the MORPHOSYNTAX level, this is reflected by the subject slot (which always is linked to the vantage point of a construction). Moreover, as pointed out above, the passive construction contains BE V-en$_4$ and the NP linked to the agent is part of an optional by-PP adjunct ([*by* NP$_1$]$_A$).

It is obviously not just ditransitive scenes that allow for this alternative construal. In fact, all of the argument structure constructions that have a FORCE-DYNAMIC meaning with an agent exerting (physical or mental) force onto a patient allow for either agent or patient to become the vantage point. Take, for example, simple transitive scenes:

(5.44)   Active Transitive construction   Passive Transitive construction
         a. She$_1$ kissed$_2$ him$_3$. $\leftrightarrow$ a.' He$_3$ was kissed$_2$ (by her$_1$).
         b. He$_1$ sang$_2$ [a song]$_3$. $\leftrightarrow$ b.' [A song]$_3$ was sung$_2$ (by him$_1$).
         c. They$_1$ smashed$_2$ [the wall]$_3$. $\leftrightarrow$ c.' [The wall]$_3$ was smashed$_2$ (by them$_1$).

Again, (5.44a–c) and (5.44a'–c') denote the same events, only from different vantage points: while the former construe the agent as their vantage point, the latter have the patient as their vantage point. As with the Passive Ditransitive construction, the Passive Transitive construction has the patient participant in subject position, and contains the string BE V-en$_2$ and the NP linked to the agent as part of an optional by-PP adjunct ([by NP$_1$]$_A$):

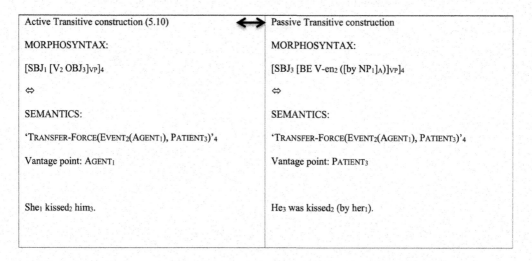

Active Transitive construction (5.10)	Passive Transitive construction
MORPHOSYNTAX:	MORPHOSYNTAX:
[SBJ$_1$ [V$_2$ OBJ$_3$]$_{VP}$]$_4$	[SBJ$_3$ [BE V-en$_2$ ([by NP$_1$]$_A$)]$_{VP}$]$_4$
$\Leftrightarrow$	$\Leftrightarrow$
SEMANTICS:	SEMANTICS:
'TRANSFER-FORCE(EVENT$_2$(AGENT$_1$), PATIENT$_3$)'$_4$	'TRANSFER-FORCE(EVENT$_2$(AGENT$_1$), PATIENT$_3$)'$_4$
Vantage point: AGENT$_1$	Vantage point: PATIENT$_3$
She$_1$ kissed$_2$ him$_3$.	He$_3$ was kissed$_2$ (by her$_1$).

Figure 5.3 *Active and Passive Transitive construction*

In Exercise 5.3, you will be asked to find the other argument structure constructions that have both active and passive versions. Beyond that, we will probably have to postulate additional, more specific passive constructions for the various verb-class and argument structure constructions that we saw in Section 5.1. What is clear, however, is that all these pairs of active and passive sentences will show the same systematic correspondences we have seen above: shared SEMANTICS with alternative vantage points (agent vs patient) and corresponding different subjects (as well as the passive marker BE V-en$_3$). Consequently, speakers will also be able to generalize this correspondence to abstract active and passive constructional templates:

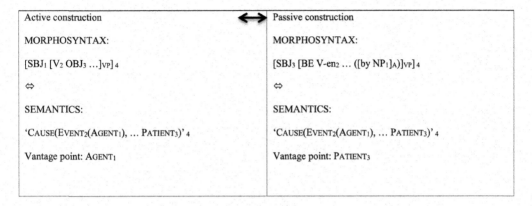

Active construction	Passive construction
MORPHOSYNTAX:	MORPHOSYNTAX:
[SBJ₁ [V₂ OBJ₃ ...]ᵥₚ] ₄	[SBJ₃ [BE V-en₂ ... ([by NP₁]ₐ)]ᵥₚ] ₄
⇔	⇔
SEMANTICS:	SEMANTICS:
'CAUSE(EVENT₂(AGENT₁), ... PATIENT₃)' ₄	'CAUSE(EVENT₂(AGENT₁), ... PATIENT₃)' ₄
Vantage point: AGENT₁	Vantage point: PATIENT₃

Figure 5.4 *Abstract Active and Passive construction*

On the SEMANTICS level, all the templates require that there is an event that can be construed as involving an agent doing something that affects a patient. Which of the two semantic roles is adopted as vantage point then influences the choice of subject (as well as all the other MORPHOSYNTACTIC properties we have already talked about).

Figure 5.4 has very abstract constructional templates for actives and passives. Note, however, that unlike lexical analyses, we do not take one structure (actives) to be the input and the other (passives) to be the output of a lexical rule. Instead, as with our morphological constructions, we interpret the relationship between active and passive sentences as a bidirectional link in the constructicon. One advantage of this phrasal approach over alternative lexical analyses is that, in addition to the many systematic correspondences between the two types of constructions, such an approach also allows active and passive versions of argument structure constructions to exhibit individual idiosyncratic properties and does not require one structure to be the input for the other (Hilpert 2019: 42). Structures such as (5.42) would, for example, be nodes in the passive taxonomic network that do not have corresponding alternatives in the active construction network (similarly to, e.g., *un-gucci*; see Section 3.1).

Finally, the requirement that corresponding Active-Passive constructions are alternative construals of FORCE-DYNAMIC events also explains the behaviour of so-called prepositional passives in English:

(5.45)   Active construction   Passive construction
   a. She₁ **worked₂** (on the plans)₃.   ↔   a.' (The plans)₃ have been **worked₂ on**
                                                                       (by her₁).

   b. She₁ **slept₂ (on** this sofa)₃.   ↔   b.' This sofa₃ has been **slept on₂** (by her₁).
   c. He₁ ran₂ [to the church]₃.   ↔   c.' *[The church]₃ has been run to₂ (by him₁).
   d. He₁ committed₂ [the crime]₃   ↔   d'. *[His father]₄ has been committed₂
       [with (his father)₄].   [the crime]₃ with
                                                                       (by him₁).

In (5.45a/a'), a female agent is exerting mental force onto the plans, which are clearly affected by her efforts. Consequently, the vantage point of this event can either be the agent (5.45a) or the patient (5.45a'), which in the case of a prepositional verb leads to the preposition *on* being stranded (left behind in the clause). Similarly, an optional PP (see Section 4.2.4.2) such as *on the sofa*, can also become the subject of a passive clause, since in this case the sofa can be seen as an affected patient (maybe it is still warm, there is some kind of indent, etc.). In contrast to this, in the Intransitive Motion construction (5.45c) it seems impossible to construe the church has being somehow affected by someone running to it – hence the fact that (5.45c') sounds odd. Finally, in (5.45d), *with his father* does not encode a patient, but an accompanying agent, which is why (5.45d') is not a possible passive construal of the scene.

5.2   Tense and Aspect Constructions

Argument structure constructions allow us to encode basic human scenes – what happened (e.g., whether something moved in space, someone exerted force onto a single object, or something possesses certain qualities). Now, the great thing about humans is that we cannot just talk about events that are happening right now. We can also describe scenes that occurred in the past or events that might happen in the future. The constructions that allow us to encode this systematically are the so-called Tense and Aspect constructions that we already touched upon in our discussion of the VP. There, we already investigated the difference in construal between the Simple Present construction and the Present Progressive construction (see Section 4.2.3). Example (5.46) illustrates the result of the KISS construction in the Transitive construction combining with the Simple Present construction, while (5.47) shows the combination with the Present Progressive construction (and with *I* and *him* filling the subject and object slot of the argument structure construction):

(5.46)   Transitive construction + KISS construction + Simple Present construction
+ *I* construction + *Him* construction:
I kiss him.

(5.47)   Transitive construction + KISS construction + Present Progressive
construction + *I* construction + *Him* construction:
I am kissing him.

KISS evokes the MANIPULATION frame and has as its Core Frame Elements an AGENT (a 'kisser') that touches an ENTITY (a 'kissee') with their lips 'as a sign of love, affection, or greeting'.[5] Now, let us take a closer look at how the

---

[5] Source: https://framenet2.icsi.berkeley.edu/fnReports/data/lu/lu11004.xml?mode=lexentry [last accessed 25 September 2020].

Transitive construction + KISS construction + Simple Present construction combine in (5.46) (ignoring *I* and *him* for now):

(5.48)   Transitive construction + KISS construction + Simple Present construction:
          FORM: PHONOLOGY: $/A_1$ $\underline{kis_2}$ C_3 $/_4$
                   MORPHOSYNTAX: $[\overline{SBJ}_1$ [$V_{2=}\underline{KISS}$ SIMPLE PRESENT2
                   $OBJ_3]_{VP}]_4$

          ⟺

          MEANING: SEMANTICS: 'PRESENT$_2$(STATE(
                                TRANSFER-FORCE($\underline{Kissing}$-EVENT$_2$
                                (AGENT=$\underline{Kisser}_1$), PATIENT=$\underline{Kissee}_3$)))'$_4$

As you can see, the Simple Present construction (highlighted by grey shading) adds the information that we view the event as a STATE that is true at the PRESENT moment. Moreover, it also adds requirements to the PHONOLOGY as well as the MORPHOSYNTAX level. The main FORCE-DYNAMIC meaning and PHONOLOGY/MORPHOSYNTAX slots are added by the Transitive construction, while the KISS verb specifies that the specific event was one of kissing (which entails a kisser and kissee, which are mapped onto the AGENT and PATIENT of the Transitive construction, respectively). (However, remember that from a usage-based perspective, depending on the input frequency of sentences such as (5.46), it is also possible that speakers do not have to combine all these constructions, but have already entrenched a KISS-Verb-Specific Transitive construction).

As we will see, like the Simple Present Tense construction, all of the other tense constructions in this section also have a progressive alternative. Because of this, we will postpone the analysis of the Progressive construction to the end of this section and focus on the non-progressive tense constructions first. In light of what we have learnt so far, we can start with the following, final representation of the Simple Present construction:

(5.49)   Simple Present construction (final version):
          FORM: MORPHOSYNTAX: $V_{1SIMPLE\ PRESENT2}$
          ⟺
          MEANING: SEMANTICS: 'PRESENT(STATE(V_1))'$_2$

The construction in (5.49) is identical to the template we formulated in the last chapter (4.73) and on the MORPHOSYNTAX level comprises only a verb in the simple present (which will have the precise PHONOLOGY form specified by the inflectional constructions in Section 3.2). The English Simple Present Tense construction prototypically construes a scene as a state that holds at the present moment, which includes inherent properties of an individual (*I am German.*), transitory states (*I feel ill.*) as well as habitual events (*I swim every day.*; cf. Croft 2012: 149–52). Particularly habitual readings illustrate the importance of distinguishing construal from real-world events: say you are swimming a couple of lanes in your local swimming pool and meet a friend who does not know that you are an avid swimmer. By telling her *I swim every day.* you construe your regular swimming activity as a state that is true at the present moment. In contrast to this, the progressive alternative *I am swimming.* focuses on the activity as ongoing. (If you are swimming right then, *I am swimming.* alone would probably be stating the obvious and thus perhaps be a strange thing to say. Instead, you might say something like *I am swimming two more lanes.*, meaning I am currently doing this, but implying not for very much longer, we can chat afterwards.)

Just as we can locate events as holding at the time of speaking, we can also talk about scenes that have occurred before the present moment:

(5.50)   I kissed him.

In (5.50) we use the Simple Past construction to express that the kissing event has happened before the time of speaking. The constructional template for this is similar to the one for the simple present (5.49):

(5.51)   Simple Past construction (final version):
FORM: MORPHOSYNTAX: $V_{1PAST\ TENSE2}$
⇔
MEANING: SEMANTICS: 'PAST(STATE(V_1))'$_2$

The Simple Past construction has the constraint that it only contains a past tense form of a verb on its MORPHOSYNTAX level. (Remember that depending on the verb lexeme we are going to find irregular forms, such as *I was ill.* as well as regular word forms such as *I kissed her* here; cf. Section 3.2.) The shorthand 'PAST (STATE( ))'$_2$ on the SEMANTICS level expresses the fact that the event denoted by the verb took place before the time of speaking and is construed as a state (cf. Croft 2012: 155–62). Again, this construal is but one way of viewing the same event: say you are a painter and finished a painting yesterday. By using the Simple Past construction, *I painted a picture.*, you focus on the whole event as a single point that holds for a time before your time of speaking. In contrast to this, by choosing a progressive construal, *I was painting a picture.*, you construe the scene as an ongoing activity before your time of speaking (one that extended over time and might not even have been completed successfully; cf. *I was painting a picture but wasn't able to finish it.*)

Just as we can talk about things happening before the present situation, we can also make predictions about the future:

(5.52)   I will kiss him.

(5.53)   I am going to kiss him.

The above examples show that we have two major future constructions, a *Will* Future construction (5.54) and a *Going to* Future construction (5.55):

(5.54)   *Will* Future construction (final version) :
FORM: MORPHOSYNTAX: [$WILL_2\ V_{1BASE}$]$_3$
⇔
MEANING: SEMANTICS: 'FUTURE$_2$(STATE(V_1))'$_3$

(5.55)   *Going to* Future construction (final version):
           FORM: MORPHOSYNTAX: [BE$_{\text{PRESENT TENSE2}}$ GOING$_2$ TO$_2$ V$_{\text{1BASE}}$]$_3$
           $\Leftrightarrow$
           MEANING: SEMANTICS: 'FUTURE$_2$(STATE(V$_1$))'$_3$

The MORPHOSYNTAX of the *Will* Future construction contains a verb in the base form (V$_{\text{BASE}}$) preceded only by *will* (or occasionally sometimes *shall* instead: *I shall kiss you.*; but note that this has a slightly different meaning; cf. Bergs 2010). In contrast to this, the *Going to* Future construction contains a present tense verb form of BE followed by the string GOING TO and then a V$_{\text{BASE}}$. The two constructions do not just differ in FORM, however: while both (5.54) and (5.55) simply give 'FUTURE$_2$(STATE( )'$_3$ as their SEMANTICS, the two constructions slightly differ in meaning: while the *Going to* Future construction is used for situations that are very likely to happen in the future, the *Will* Future construction is used when a speaker is much less certain that an event will actually take place (for an explanation of this, cf. the historical evolution of the two constructions in Section 6.2).

So far, we have looked at ways of relating events directly to the current speaking time by placing them either prior to (Simple Past construction), simultaneously with (Simple Present construction) or after (*Will* and *Going to* Future construction) the time of our utterance. Humans, however, have also developed more complicated ways of talking about events in time. Take, for example, the English Present Perfect construction:

(5.56)   I have kissed him.

In (5.56), the kissing event is clearly situated before our speaking time. How is (5.56) then different from the Simple Past construal *I kissed him.* (5.50)? More than seventy years ago, Reichenbach (1947: 287–98) pointed out that in addition to event time and speaking time, we sometimes also include another temporal point in our construal: the so-called reference time (also called 'orientation time'; Declerck 2006: 22–6). While the reference time of the Simple Past is identified as the event time, the Present Perfect construes the reference time as coinciding with the present speaking time. What this means is that the Present Perfect is used to talk about an event that happened in the past but has some kind of relevance for the present. Thus, when a speaker says *I kissed him.* (5.50) then she only wants to express that this was an event that happened in the past. In contrast to this, (5.56) construes that the event still has some consequence for the present (e.g., that the feelings associated with the kiss can still be felt or that the kiss had some other kind of consequence; Croft 2012: 162–4). Similarly, if you say *I did my homework.* that only places the event in the past, while *I have done my homework.* means that this has present relevance (you can show it to me or you can now do something else). Thus (5.57) tries to capture these properties of the English Present Perfect construction:

(5.57)   Present Perfect construction (final version):
           FORM: MORPHOSYNTAX: [HAVE$_{PRESENT\ TENSE2}$
                                        V$_{PASTPARTICIPLE1}$]$_3$
           $\Leftrightarrow$
           MEANING: SEMANTICS: 'PRESENT$_2$(PERFECT$_2$(STATE(V$_1$)))'$_3$

The MORPHOSYNTAX level of the Present Perfect construction requires a
present tense form of HAVE (i.e., *have* or *has*) followed by a past participle
form of the verb. On the meaning level, we try to capture the fact that it construes
an event as having taken place in the past (encoded by 'PERFECT$_2$(STATE( ))')
that has relevance for the present time of speaking ('PRESENT$_2$( )').
    There is also a related Past Perfect construction:

(5.58)   I had kissed him.

Past perfect (5.58) is used to describe an event in the past (event time) that
happened before another event (reference time). Thus, you could, for example,
put it into the following context: *I had kissed him before I left*. The time of the
leaving event (the reference time) took place before the time of speaking. Even
before the speaker left, however, he or she had previously carried out the kissing
action (event time). The past perfect can therefore be said to be a past-before-
past. Alternatively, in analogy to the present perfect, we can say that the event in
the past-before-past still had relevance at another time in the past. We thus only
need to slightly change the constructional template in (5.57) to capture the
meaning of the Past Perfect construction:

(5.59)   Past Perfect construction (final version):
           FORM: MORPHOSYNTAX: [HAD$_{PAST\ TENSE2}$ V$_{PASTPARTICIPLE1}$]$_3$
           $\Leftrightarrow$
           MEANING: SEMANTICS: 'PAST$_2$(PERFECT$_2$(STATE(V$_1$)))'$_3$

In (5.59), the MORPHOSYNTAX level contains a past tense form of HAVE
(i.e., *had*) and the first tense feature of the SEMANTICS level is specified as
'PAST( )'. Apart from that, the template is identical to (5.57).
    The difference between event time and reference time is not only relevant when
talking about past events. We also have a so-called Future Perfect construction:

(5.60)   I will have kissed him (by the time you arrive).

In (5.60) we specify an event in the future (your arrival) as a reference point by
which another event (me kissing him) will already have taken place. Again, we
thus have an event that will be completed, but with relevance for a later reference
point. The constructional template for this can again easily be built by adapting
our previous perfect constructions:

(5.61)   Future Perfect construction (final version):
           FORM: MORPHOSYNTAX: [WILL$_3$ HAVE$_2$ V$_{PASTPARTICIPLE1}$]$_4$
           $\Leftrightarrow$
           MEANING: SEMANTICS: 'FUTURE$_3$(PERFECT$_2$(STATE(V$_1$)))'$_4$

In (5.61), the invariant WILL on the MORPHOSYNTAX level is linked to the 'FUTURE$_3$( )' meaning on the SEMANTICS level, while the invariant form HAVE links to the 'PERFECT$_2$( )' meaning.

Remember that I said earlier that all the tenses we have just discussed also have a progressive alternative version – (5.62) illustrates this:

(5.62) a.   Present progressive: I am kissing him.
      b.   Past progressive: I was kissing him.
      c.   Future Progressive: I will be kissing him.
      d.   Present Perfect Progressive: I have been kissing him.
      e.   Past Perfect Progressive: I had been kissing him.
      f.   Future Perfect Progressive: I will have been kissing him.

While their non-progressive alternatives construe events as STATEs, the progressive constructions underlying (5.62) all view events as ONGOING. Moreover, all progressive constructions require a form of BE followed by the present participle of the verb (see also Section 4.2.3). It is thus pretty straightforward to come up with templates for all of the constructions in (5.62). Beyond that, we can also generalize all of the instances in (5.62) to a more abstract Progressive construction:

(5.63)   Progressive construction: (final)
      FORM: MORPHOSYNTAX: [... BE$_2$ V$_{\text{PRESENT PARTICIPLE1}}$]$_3$
      $\Leftrightarrow$
      MEANING: SEMANTICS: '... (ONGOING$_2$(V$_1$))'$_3$

All that (5.63) does is encode the fact that any progressive will have a form of BE followed by the present participle of the verb. Besides, on the SEMANTICs level, it specifies that the event that is talked about is construed as 'ONGOING$_2$( )'.

5.3   Core Clause Constructions

As we have just seen, once researchers extended their constructional view beyond idioms, they noted that many other syntactic phenomena such as argument structure and the active-passive alternation required a constructional analysis. On top of that, it turned out that even some of the apparently most regular and abstract syntactic patterns such as clause types exhibited a great number of idiosyncratic properties. In one of the earliest constructionist publications, Fillmore (1985) pointed out a complex type of WH-Interrogative construction that can be 'spiced up' by introducing interjections such as *the heck, the devil, in heaven's name,* etc.:

(5.64) a.   What **the heck** did you see?
      b.   *You saw what **the heck**?
         (Fillmore 1985: 81)

(5.65) a.   What **the devil** did you fix it with?
      b.   *With what **the devil** did you fix it?
          (Fillmore 1985: 81)

(5.66) a.   I can't imagine what **in heaven's name** she cooked?
      b.   *I couldn't eat what **in heaven's name** she cooked.
          (Fillmore 1985: 81)

(5.67) a.   What **the heck** did you choose?
      b.   Who **the heck**'s fault do you think it is?
      c.   Why **the heck** did you choose it?
      d.   *Which **the heck** did you choose?
          (Fillmore 1985: 82)

The examples from (5.64) to (5.67) illustrate the major idiosyncrasies of the construction: while WH-Initial Interrogatives (*What did you see?*) normally have a corresponding in-situ echo question (*You saw what?*), the complex Expletive-Phrase WH-Interrogative construction[6] (5.64a) does not have an equivalent echo question (5.64b). Moreover, the Interrogative construction in question only licenses a single WH-item in initial position (5.65a), all other phrasal material associated with the WH-item cannot be preposed (5.65b). Next, the expletive phrases are grammatical in (embedded) interrogative clauses (5.66a), but not in superficially similar embedded free relative clauses (5.66b). Finally, the construction is acceptable with a range of WH-items (5.67a,b,c), but explicitly bars *which* (5.67d).

All of these constraints cannot be captured by a general (phrase structure or transformational movement) rule. Instead, the phenomenon requires a constructional account:

(5.68) Expletive-Phrase WH-Interrogative construction
       FORM: PHONOLOGY: $/ A_1 B_2 C_3 /_4$
                              INTONATION: falling
                MORPHOSYNTAX: $[[X_{[+wh]\_1} Y_2 \ldots]_{XP[+wh]} [\ldots]_{CLAUSE\_3}]_4$
                                        $X \neq$ *which*
                                          Y = Expletive Phrase (*the heck, the hell, …*)
       ⇔
       MEANING: SEMANTICS: 'EMPHATIC$_2$(INTERROGATIVE)'$_4$
       (modelled on Fillmore 1985: 83)

The template in (5.68) is a highly schematic construction, which nevertheless has very specific constraints on its initial slots: as the MORPHOSYNTACTIC level indicates, the first element must be a WH-word ($X_{[+wh]}$), but not *which* ($X \neq$ *which*) and the phrases that can fill the Y slot must come from a limited number of expletive phrase constructions (Y = Expletive Phrase (*the heck, the*

---

[6] The label Expletive-Phrase WH-Interrogative construction is mine; Fillmore (1985) provides no special name for this construction.

hell, ...)). Due to its high degree of schematicity, its meaning is consequently fairly vague (specifying on the SEMANTICS level only that it is an interrogative that has an emphatic quality to it). If speakers must (and obviously do) learn such a schematic construction, then it is only a small step to claim that regular WH-Interrogatives can also be stored in a constructional template.

Let us now take a look at the various 'regular' (that is highly frequent) sentence types of English and see how these can be captured by constructional templates (see, e.g., Ginzburg and Sag 2000: 6–10; Hoffmann 2013: 313; Sag, Wasow and Bender 2003: 487):

(5.69)   Declarative clause:
     a.   Ben was tired.
     b.   Ben made more mistakes.

(5.70)   WH-Interrogative:
     a.   **What** was Ben?
     b.   **What** did he make?

(5.71)   Yes-/No-Interrogative:
     a.   **Was Ben** tired?
     b.   **Did he** make mistakes?

(5.72)   Imperative:
     a.   **Stay** awake!
     b.   **Don't make** mistakes!

(5.73)   WH-Exclamative:
     a.   **How** tired Ben was!
     b.   **What** a mistake he made!

(5.74)   WH-Relative Clause:
     A pilot shouldn't be tired, **which** Ben was.
     The mistakes **which** he made ...

The above sentences obviously differ with respect to their prototypical phonological and morphosyntactic form as well as semantic function (Herbst and Schüller 2008: 148–63; Hoffmann 2013: 309):

The declaratives in (5.69) usually have a falling intonation, have a subject (*Ben*) that precedes the verbs (*was tired*; *made*), they exhibit subject–verb agreement (see Section 3.2.1) and semantically often express a statement. After the verbs, we have an optional slot for the rest of the predicate ('REST-PREDICATE') that will be provided by various other constructions (cf. arguments of the argument structure construction as in **Ben** made **more mistakes.**, or adjunct constructions *Ben made more mistakes* **yesterday**.) The constructional template in (5.75) summarizes these properties:

(5.75)   Declarative clause construction
     FORM: PHONOLOGY: / A_1 B_2 (C_3) /$_4$
                           INTONATION: falling$_4$

MORPHOSYNTAX: $[SBJ_{AGR} [V_{finite\_AGR\_2}$

$(REST\text{-}PREDICATE_3)]_{VP}]_4$

$\Leftrightarrow$

MEANING: SEMANTICS: 'STATEMENT'$_4$

Again, we abbreviate the meaning of this template by simply saying it expresses a 'STATEMENT' (which is going to be specified by the various constructions filling the A, B and C slots). Subject–verb agreement is indicated by the identical subscript 'AGR' on the subject and the finite verb on the MORPHOSYNTAX level (see Section 3.2.1). Then the rest of the predicate, provided by other constructions (see Section 5.1), follows.

Concerning the subject slot, note that this normally is filled by an NP construction, but English also allows for other constructions to appear in this position:

(5.76) a.   [That he was tired] is a lie.
       b.   · [To know her] is to love her.
            (COCA 2012 SPOK: ABC_GMA, NEW ^@DANCING^@ CAST;
            CELEBRITIES REVEALED LIVE)
       c.   [After school]$_{PP}$ is when the home-schooling session begins.
            (COCA 2004 MAG: Ebony, Putting CHILDREN First in a JET-SET
               FAMILY)

In (5.76a) a finite *that*-clause fills the subject slot, while in (5.76b) a non-finite clause functions as the subject. Example (5.76c) has a PP in subject position. What all these examples have in common is that the default agreement pattern for these non-NP subjects requires a 3rd Person Singular verb form (*is* in (5.76)).

Examples (5.70) and (5.71) show the two major patterns for formulating questions in English: WH-Interrogatives ask for information on a constituent by placing a WH-question word (*who, whose, what, which, how, when, where, why*; Sag 2010: 491) in clause-initial position. Just like declaratives, WH-Interrogatives normally have a falling intonation. Depending on the syntactic function of the questioned constituent, we can then identify two subtypes: if the constituent that is asked for is the subject, the sentence has the same word order as the Declarative clause construction (cf. (5.70a) or *Who framed Roger Rabbit?*, *Who is that girl?*, *Whose trousers are these?*). Example (5.77) provides the constructional template for this sentence type:

(5.77)   WH-Subject Interrogative construction
           FORM: PHONOLOGY: $/ A_1 B_2 (C_3) /_4$
                                        INTONATION: falling$_4$
                       MORPHOSYNTAX: $[WH\text{-}SBJ_{AGR} [V_{finite\_AGR\_2}$
                                        $(REST\text{-}PREDICATE)_3]_{VP}]_4$

           $\Leftrightarrow$

           MEANING: SEMANTICS: 'QUESTION'$_4$
           (based on Herbst and Schüller 2008: 150)

Nonsubject WH-Interrogatives also have the questioned WH-constituent in the clause-initial position (5.70b), but they require a finite auxiliary to precede the subject of the clause (that is, this sentence type exhibits obligatory 'subject–verb inversion' (SAI)). If the verbs of the construct contain a finite auxiliary because of modality, tense and aspect constructions (as in *What is she playing?*, which has a BE lexeme contributed by the Present Progressive construction) or for other reasons (as in *What **has** he got?*, in which the primary verb HAVE is present as the verbal head), then this has to appear before the subject. All other remaining verbs have to follow the subject (*What is she **playing**?*, and *What has he **got**?*). If the modality-tense-aspect constructions do not provide an auxiliary and there is no primary verb, the DO-Lexeme construction has to be added (cf. *What **did** he say?*, *Where **did** they go?*, *Why **did** they buy this?*). Example (5.78) summarizes these facts in a constructional template:

(5.78)   WH-Nonsubject Interrogative construction
            FORM: PHONOLOGY: /A$_1$ B$_2$ (C$_3$)/$_4$
                                                 INTONATION: falling$_4$
                         MORPHOSYNTAX: [WH$_1$ AUX$_{finite\_AGR\_2}$ SBJ$_{AGR\_3}$
                                                 (REST-PREDICATE)$_3$ ...]$_4$

            ⇔

            MEANING: SEMANTICS: 'QUESTION'$_4$
            (based on Herbst and Schüller 2008: 151)

As we will see, SAI is a property of many English sentence types. Yes-/No-Interrogatives (5.71), which do not ask for a constituent of the sentence but question whether the sentence as a whole is true or not, also have obligatory SAI. In contrast to WH-Interrogatives, Yes-/No-Interrogatives have a rising intonation and can thus be captured by the template in (5.79):

(5.79)   Yes/No Interrogative construction
            FORM: PHONOLOGY: /A$_1$ B$_3$ (C$_3$)/$_4$
                                                 INTONATION: rising$_4$
                         MORPHOSYNTAX: [AUX$_{finite\_AGR\_1}$ SBJ$_{AGR\_2}$
                                                 (REST-PREDICATE)$_3$ ...]$_4$

            ⇔

            MEANING: SEMANTICS: 'QUESTION'$_4$
            (based on Herbst and Schüller 2008: 151)

In (5.77)–(5.79) only the most frequent interrogative constructions in English are provided. In fact, there are many other ways of asking questions in English (e.g., using the Declarative clause template in (5.75) but with a rising intonation such as *He is ill?* or so-called in-situ questions in which the WH-word remains clause-internally such as *He did what?*. For an in-depth discussion of English interrogative constructions see Ginzburg and Sag 2000).

Let us now turn to the imperative constructions exemplified by (5.72). Imperatives are usually directed at someone who is within earshot of the speaker. Imperatives have a falling intonation and often do not contain a subject, since it is this addressee that is supposed to fulfil the role of the subject. So, *Stay awake!* is interpreted as *You stay awake!* (with the latter illustrating that a subject can sometimes be present). Imperatives do not show overt agreement marking between this optional subject and the verb (cf. *Someone open this door!*; from Herbst and Schüller 2008: 154). For the constructional template in (5.80), we can therefore specify that all that is needed is the V-base form (infinitive without *to*; cf. Section 3.2.1) of the verb:

(5.80)   Imperative construction
            FORM: PHONOLOGY: $/(A_1) \; B_2 \; (C_3)/_4$
                                     INTONATION: falling$_4$
                         MORPHOSYNTAX: $[(SBJ)_1 \; V_{base\_2}$
                                     $(REST\text{-}PREDICATE)_3 \ldots]_4$

            $\Leftrightarrow$

            MEANING: SEMANTICS: 'DIRECTIVE'$_4$
            (based on Herbst and Schüller 2008: 151)

As Croft and Cruse (2004: 320–1) have shown, the simple template in (5.80) cannot capture all properties of English imperatives. As it turns out, imperatives have idiosyncratic properties when being negated that cannot be predicted by the general negation construction (Section 4.2.3.2):

(5.81) positive declarative
      a.   FORM: BE$_{AUX}$ + ADJ[7]   b.   FORM: VERB
                  He is happy.   *He sleeps.*

(5.82) negative declarative
      a.   FORM: BE$_{AUX}$ + NOT + ADJ   b.   FORM: DO + NOT + VERB
                  He isn't happy.   *He doesn't sleep.*

(5.83) positive imperative
      a.   FORM: *be*$_{AUX}$ + ADJ   b.   FORM: VERB
                  Be happy!   *Sleep!*

(5.84) negative imperative
      a.   ~~FORM: BE$_{AUX}$ + NOT + ADJ~~   b.   FORM: DO + NOT + VERB
            FORM: DO + NOT + BE + ADJ   *Don't sleep!*
                  Don't be happy!

As (5.81a) shows, adjectives require a form of the copula BE in English to create well-formed positive declarative clauses. Since the negative adverb NOT needs to attach to an auxiliary verb in English, negative declarative clauses with adjectives can then simply be formed by attaching NOT to BE (cf. 5.82a). In contrast to this, full verbs need additional *do*-support in negative predication

---

[7] For the purposes of illustration and in order to make the analysis comparable to that of Croft and Cruse (2004), I limit myself to sentences with just a single adjective or verb. A more precise constructional analysis will, however, have to take into account that the constructions actually have slots that accommodate full adjective phrases (*He is proud of his son*) and verb phrases (*He kissed the bride*; Müller, personal communication).

phrases (cf. 5.82b). Moving on to positive imperatives, (5.83) shows that these pattern with their declarative counterparts in that adjectives need to co-occur with *be* (5.83a), while full verbs can appear on their own (5.83b). Negative imperatives, however, differ from their positive alternatives: since NOT could attach to *be*, the construction that might be expected would be BE + NOT ADJ. Yet, as can be seen in (5.84a'), the construction instead exhibits *do*-support. Consequently, Croft and Cruse (2004) argue for the taxonomy shown in Figure 5.5 for English imperative predication phrases:

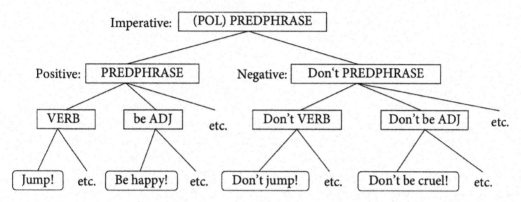

Figure 5.5 *The English Imperative construction network (Croft and Cruse 2004: 321)*

Croft and Cruse point out (2004: 320) that illocutionary force seems to be more important for the imperative taxonomy in English than differences in predicate type. In Figure 5.5, this is represented by verbal and adjectival predicates not being subnodes of an independent PREDICATION construction that then simply combines with independent negation and imperative constructions (since this would lead to the ungrammatical structure Be_{AUX} + NOT + ADJ in (5.84a)). Instead, negative commands in English form their own node in the imperative network and include the constraint that they have to be introduced by *Don't* – regardless of whether the predication phrase involves an adjective or verb.

From a usage-based perspective, the network in Figure 5.5 will, obviously, also be affected by the type and token frequency of the various constructions. Highly frequent imperative constructs such as *Don't worry!* or *Be happy!* (or even their combination as in the song 'Don't worry, be happy!') can become entrenched as micro-constructions in the mental constructicon. On the other hand, high type frequency, that is, patterns that are observed with many different items, can lead to the emergence of more abstract schematic superordinate constructions (such as the VERB!, *Don't* V! or Be ADJ! meso-constructions). In an earlier study, I investigated the distribution of Imperative constructs in the British component of the International Corpus of English (ICE-GB; (Hoffmann 2013: 316)). The results from this study are summarized in Table 5.3:

Table 5.3 *Imperative constructs in the ICE-GB corpus (Hoffmann 2013: 316)*

	Positive	Negative (*Don't ...*)	Sum
V!	1,430	87	1,517
BE + ADJ!	29	10	39
	1,459	97	1,556

If the ICE-GB data are taken to be representative of the input of Imperative constructions that British English speakers are exposed to, then Table 5.3 implies that positive full verb imperatives (V!) are by far the most frequent type and should therefore be far more strongly entrenched in the mental constructicon than the other meso-constructions. Moreover, a statistical test of the data revealed that there are far more negative adjective imperatives than expected by chance, making those few instances of the *Don't be* ADJ constructions more salient, which might also add to this structure being more deeply entrenched.

Moreover, as a collostructional analysis (see Section 5.1.2) of the verbal imperatives in the ICE-GB corpus showed (Stefanowitsch 2013; Stefanowitsch and Gries 2003), there also seem to be specific lexicalizations that are significantly associated with the imperative construction (and, consequently, more deeply entrenched): the five most strongly attracted verbs in Stefanowitsch and Gries's study were *let, see, look, listen, worry* (2003: 231–3), with *worry* exclusively appearing in negative imperatives (thus implying a more strongly entrenched *Don't worry* micro-construction). Besides the issue of which (more) substantive constructions are entrenched in the speakers' mental grammars, the constructionist analysis of their data also allowed Stefanowitsch and Gries to draw important conclusions about the semantic meaning and pragmatic force of Imperative constructions in English. Previous studies had emphasized that imperative sentences prototypically have a directive function of a speaker wanting the hearer to perform a requested action that is desirable to the speaker. In contrast to this, the most strongly attracted verbs in Stefanowitsch and Gries's study implied a meaning that could be seen as more beneficial to the hearer, with the speaker suggesting and advising rather than commanding. Moreover, the actions requested by these verbs seemed to be more directed at ensuring future cooperation and interaction between speaker and hearer than being purely for the benefit of the speaker (Stefanowitsch and Gries 2003: 233). As this illustrates, usage-based approaches also help us better understand the semantic pole of constructions that at first glance seem pretty simple and straightforward.

While imperatives are directed at a hearer, WH-Exclamatives such as *How tired Ben was!* (5.73a) or *What a mistake he made!* (5.73b) emphatically express the speaker's feeling. More specifically, this construction is used to indicate that a speaker considers someone or something exceptional compared to a prototypical instance of the phenomenon. So, if you hear someone say *How tired Ben was!* then he or she wants to express that Ben was extraordinarily tired.

Similarly, *What a mistake he made!* means that the mistake was an exceptionally noticeable one. WH-Exclamatives can only be introduced by *What* NP (*What a nice woman she is!*, *What mistakes he made!*, or *What luck they had!*) or *How* and *How* ADJP/ADVP (*How I love Construction Grammar!*, *How old he is!*, or *How quickly they scored!*). Moreover, as the examples above show, in contrast to WH-Interrogatives, WH-Exclamatives normally do not exhibit subject-auxiliary inversion (cf. *How old he is!* and not **How old is he!*). Summarizing these facts, (5.85) provides the constructional template for WH-Exclamative constructions:

(5.85)   WH-Exclamative construction
           FORM: PHONOLOGY: /A_1 B_2/$_3$
                                      INTONATION: falling$_3$
                        MORPHOSYNTAX: [WHAT-NP$_1$
                        or HOW (ADJP/ADVP)$_1$ REST-CLAUSE$_2$]$_3$
           ⇔
           MEANING: SEMANTICS: 'EXCLAMATION'$_3$
           (based on Herbst and Schüller 2008: 156)

On the MORPHOSYNTAX level, we specify that the initial phrase of a WH-Exclamative construction must be either a *What* NP or a *How* (ADJP/ADVP) sequence. This WH-phrase can have several syntactic functions (though WH-subjects are rare; cf. *What an enormous crowd came!*; Quirk et al. 1985: 833). Since WH-Exclamatives do not show SAI and the rest of the clause can be accounted for by other constructions (such as the subject–verb agreement; cf. Section 3.2.1), we can just code the remaining part of the clause as 'REST-CLAUSE'.

So far, the constructions that we have seen licensed independent sentences. In contrast to this, relative clauses (5.74) are always embedded in larger sentences:

(5.86) a.   Carl [...] turned on the projector, **which he had made from a shoe box**, **a magnifying glass, and his phone**. (COCA 2015 FIC: Paris Review The Throwback Special: Part 2)

       b.   Most people assumed she was a nurse, or maybe even a doctor, **which was not true**, ... (COCA 2015 FIC: All things tending towards the eternal)

In (5.86a) the relative clause functions as a postmodifier in the NP *the projector*, while in (5.86b) it is an adjunct in the main clause *Most people assumed she was a nurse, or maybe even a doctor*. Since the use of relative clauses as NP postmodifiers is much more frequent than the sentential use in (5.86b), we will focus on the former types in the following.

Semantically, we can distinguish so-called 'restrictive' relative clauses that are obligatory and help to identify the reference of the head noun (cf. *He has two projectors. I mean the projector which he made from a shoe box, a magnifying glass, and his phone.*) from non-restrictive ones, which only provide additional information to a noun whose referent is already identified (cf. *He has only one projector, which (by the way) he made from a shoe box, a magnifying glass, and his phone.*; Quirk et al 1985: 1239). On top of other factors (there often is a pause in speech before a non-restrictive relative clause, which is reflected in orthography by a comma), there is another difference between the two types of relative clauses: both types of relative clauses can be introduced by a clause-initial WH-element (namely, *who, whose, which, when, where, why*; Sag 2010: 491). In addition to that, restrictive relative clauses can also be introduced by *that* (5.87a) and some even have no relative word at the start of the clause at all (a so-called bare relative clause; 5.87b):

(5.87) a.   Carl [...] turned on a projector that he had made from a shoe box, a magnifying glass, and his phone.

       b.   Carl [...] turned on a projector he had made from a shoe box, a magnifying glass, and his phone.

Note that in Standard varieties of British and American English, bare relative clauses are only possible if a relative pronoun does not function as the subject of the clause:

(5.88) a.   It's mostly a quick scan through the emails **that arrived overnight**, to see if there are any matters requiring immediate attention or response. (COCA 2012 BLOG http://allvirtual.me/2012/09/13/ [last accessed 02 January 2021])

       b.   *It's mostly a quick scan through the emails **arrived overnight**, ...

In order to capture these differences, we thus need a Restrictive Relative Clause construction for Subject Relative Clauses:

(5.89)   WH-Subject Restrictive Relative Clause construction

         FORM: PHONOLOGY: $/A_1\ B_2/_3$

                                INTONATION: $falling_3$

               MORPHOSYNTAX: $[SBJ:WH\text{-}REL_1$

                                $REST\text{-}CLAUSE_2]\ ]_{POM\_NP:RC\ 3}$

            ⇔

         MEANING: SEMANTICS: 'RESTRICTIVE MODIFICATION'$_3$

The WH-Subject Restrictive Relative Clause construction has a subject WH-relative pronoun (*who, which, whose N*, and also including relative *that*; 'SBJ: WH-REL$_1$'). Its SEMANTICS is 'RESTRICTIVE MODIFICATION' and it functions as a postmodifier in an NP ('POM_NP').

     For all other finite restrictive relative clauses, we can draw on the following constructional template:

(5.90)   WH-Nonsubject Restrictive Relative Clause construction

         FORM: PHONOLOGY: $/(A_1)\ B_2/_3$

                                  INTONATION: $falling_3$

               MORPHOSYNTAX: $[(nonSBJ:WH\text{-}REL_1)$

                                $REST\text{-}CLAUSE_2]\ ]_{POM\_NP:RC\ 3}$

            ⇔

         MEANING: SEMANTICS: 'RESTRICTIVE MODIFICATION'$_3$

If the WH-REL does not function as the subject of the relative clause, it can either be realized by the above list of relative words or does not have to be present at all (hence the parentheses on the PHONOLOGY and MORPHOSYNTAX level). Now, if you fully want to analyse the relative clause constructions in English, you will need several additional constructions. The most detailed analysis of English relative clauses has been put forward by Sag (1997), who also provides constructional templates for non-finite restrictive relative clauses such as *the data on which to depend, the place to visit* or *the guy standing on my foot*. A detailed discussion of all these constructions is well beyond the scope of this book. Before moving on to information structure constructions, however, Figure 5.6 summarizes the network of the major English clause constructions:

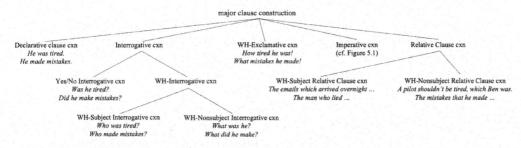

Figure 5.6 *The major clause constructions of English*

5.4   Information Structure

So far, we have come across a great number of constructions that allow speakers to express how they construe a scene. Take the following situation where, while celebrating a late winning goal, a football player (Christian Benteke) breaks his manager's glasses (here Jürgen Klopp's, as happened after Liverpool's 5–4 win over Norwich City in 2016). One way to frame this scene is either the Active Transitive construction (5.91) or the Passive Transitive construction (5.92):

(5.91)   Active Transitive construction:
          Christian Benteke broke Klopp's glasses …[8]

(5.92)   Passive Transitive construction:
          Klopp's glasses were broken by Christian Benteke …[9]

---

[8] Source: www.dailypost.co.uk/sport/football/football-news/10781034   [last   accessed   02 January 2021].
[9] Source: www.dailymail.co.uk/sport/football/article-4071468/ [last accessed 02 January 2021].

As we said above, the FORCE-DYNAMICe event that (5.91) and (5.92) describe is the same, the only difference is the vantage point from which you are looking at the scene. So far in our discussion, we thus focused on how speakers view events and how they then have various constructions at their disposal to express these different construals. However, we do not just use language to voice our own solipsistic point of view. Language is also a social phenomenon that we use to coordinate and cooperate with others – and as we all know, other people do not necessarily view the same event in the same way that we do. We are very much aware that other people know different things and might have different commu-nication intentions than us (we have what is called a 'theory of mind'; Tomasello 2003: 277). The fact that we can put ourselves in other people's shoes (or state of minds, if you like) is a crucial fundamental prerequisite for language. Remember that in Chapter 2 we saw that the first steps of acquiring a language required joint attention and intention-reading, both of which involve identifying what other people are focusing on and what they are probably thinking. Then, in Section 4.2.1, we saw that what we think another person knows influences how we introduce referents into the discourse (Lambrecht 1994; Leino 2013: 335; can you still recall the lame joke from (4.15)?): when we first mention a referent, we need to use an Indefinite NP construction (*A man* walks into *a bar* ...) because we expect the hearer not to be actively thinking about it (it is an 'inactive referent' in the hearer's mind). Then, once we have introduced it, we can take the referent to be 'active' in the mind of the hearer and we signal this by using a Definite NP (*the man*) or Personal Pronoun NP construction (*he*). In-between these two states, we have referents that are 'semi-active' or 'accessible'; that is, they have not been explicitly mentioned in the previous discourse, but we can expect the hearer to at least peripherally have activated them (in the bar joke, once you hear *a bar* you evoke the mental frame of a BAR and, consequently, are not surprised if the speaker continues with *The barman looked at him and said* ... because our BAR frame includes the fact that there is going to be bar staff working there).

The choice of these NPs thus has nothing to do with the scene that we want to talk about, but with 'information structure': 'the means by which the speaker intends the sentence to inform the hearer, in the context of previous discourse' (Jackendoff 2002: 408). Information structure is not only relevant when it comes to the introduction of referents. In any situation speakers must (unconsciously) assess which information a hearer knows at a certain point (the 'presupposition'; Jackendoff 2002: 409) and what constitutes newly supplied information to the hearer (known as 'focus' or 'rheme'; Jackendoff 2002: 409; see also Hilpert 2019: 106–12; Lambrecht 1994; Leino 2013).

The clearest indication that information is going to be new to a hearer is, of course, if they explicitly ask for it: let me illustrate this with the football example mentioned at the start of the section. Say a friend told you about the Liverpool–Norwich match and at one point uttered either (5.91) or (5.92). Now, maybe you are in a pub and because of all the background noise you did not hear the name of the player who broke the glasses, then you could ask the question in (5.93).

Alternatively, if you did not quite catch what Benteke broke, you could use the question in (5.94). In both cases, because you have been taking about football and this game in particular for some time, we can assume that you and your friend know and have activated the names of the player and the manager. Yet, depending on your question, your friend will now know which piece of information is going to be new to you (i.e., whether Benteke or Klopp's glasses are in focus), and will structure his/her answer accordingly:

(5.93) Who broke Klopp's glasses?
(5.93') Potential answers:

a. BENTEKE.
b. BENTEKE broke Klopp's glasses.
c. Klopp's glasses were broken by BENTEKE.
d. It was BENTEKE that broke Klopp's glasses.
e. It was BY BENTEKE that Klopp's glasses were broken.
f. * It was KLOPP'S GLASSES that Benteke broke.
g. * It was KLOPP'S GLASSES that were broken by Benteke.

(5.94) What did Benteke break?
(5.94') Potential answers:

a. KLOPP'S GLASSES.
b. Benteke broke KLOPP'S GLASSES.
c. KLOPP'S GLASSES were broken by Benteke.
d. * It was BENTEKE that broke Klopp's glasses.
e. * It was BY BENTEKE that Klopp's glasses were broken.
f. It was KLOPP'S GLASSES that Benteke broke.
g. It was KLOPP'S GLASSES that were broken by Benteke.

Examples (5.93'a) and (5.94'a) show that a simple NP can be a perfectly acceptable answer to such a question. In both of these cases, the NP receives a special focus intonation, marking it as new information: it has a high-fall accent; that is, a high tone on the stressed syllable of **BEN**teke and **KLOPP'S GLA**sses, respectively, that falls steeply on the following unstressed syllables to a low tone (in the following we are going to encode this as 'H*L'; see Wells 2006: 262[10]). In (5.93') and (5.94'), I have indicated this focus accent in all examples by simply putting the focused NP in capitals (i.e., BENTEKE and KLOPP'S GLASSES, respectively).

When you then look at (5.93' b,c) and (5.94' b,c), you see that you can also use this accent to mark the focus information in the Active Transitive construction (5.91) as well as the Passive Transitive construction (5.92). Simplifying somewhat, we can thus give (5.95) as the Focus NP construction that captures these properties:

(5.95)   Focus NP construction
          FORM: PHONOLOGY: INTONATION: PITCH: $H*L_1$
                      MORPHOSYNTAX: NP_1

          $\Leftrightarrow$

          MEANING: SEMANTICS: 'REFERENT'$_1$
                      PRAGMATICS: $FOCUS_1$

---

[10] This notation is based on the ToBI (Tones and Break Indices) system, which, however, also uses additional phrase and boundary tones that we ignore for easy of exposition (Wells 2006: 262).

The Focus NP construction (5.95) only specifies that an NP (MORPHOSYNTAX) is realized on the PHONOLOGY level with a high-fall H*L accent and links to a REFERENT on the SEMANTICS level that pragmatically is a FOCUS (i.e., new information for the hearer). Consequently, we can use it to indicate focus in all declarative clause and argument structure construction combinations (cf. *BENTEKE broke Klopp's glasses into pieces* or *KLOPP'S GLASSES were broken*).

Perhaps even more interesting are the examples in (5.93'd–g) and (5.94'd–g), since they exhibit a special construction that English speakers also possess to highlight focused information – *It* Cleft constructions. The first type of these constructions consists of an *it* subject, a form of BE, a focused element and then a dependent clause with the remaining predication (except for the focused element, so (5.93'b), for example, is equivalent to (5.93'd)). Note that (5.93'f,g) and (5.94'd,e) show that the element following the form of BE must be the new information (i.e., the focused element), or else the sentences sound off:

(5.96)   *It* Cleft construction (Type 1)
          FORM: PHONOLOGY: / it_1 BE_2 C_3 D_4 $/_5$
                                         INTONATION: PITCH: $H*L_3$
                       MORPHOSYNTAX: [SBJ_1 V_{BE2} OBL_3
                                         [*that* REST-CLAUSE]$_{dependent\ clause4}$]$_5$

          ⇔

          MEANING: SEMANTICS: 'STATEMENT'$_5$
                     PRAGMATICS: $FOCUS_3$ / $PRESUPPOSITION_4=ACTIVE_4$

Similarly to Declarative Clause constructions, *It* Cleft constructions express a statement. In contrast to the former, they, however, have an OBL_3 element that must be a $FOCUS_3$ and, consequently, carry a high-fall accent ($H*L_3$). The *that* dependent clause$_4$ might look like a relative clause,[11] but is not a postmodifier of the focused OBL_3 phrase and does not have the restrictive semantics associated with relative clauses: *It was [the player [that the fans liked]*RELATIVE CLAUSE] restricts the reference of the head noun *player* to only the one that the fans liked, whereas in the cleft clause *It was Benteke that broke Klopp's glasses* the *that* clause does not need to restrict the reference of the proper noun *Benteke*. Finally, as Lambrecht (2001a: 497; see Hilpert 2019: 116) points out, the dependent clause$_4$ has to be a presupposition: it must be activated in the hearer's short-term memory and is something which the hearer also considers 'a center of current interest and hence a potential locus of predication' (Lambrecht 2001a: 475–6; PRAGMATICS: $PRESUPPOSITION_4=ACTIVE_4$) – otherwise the use of an *It* Cleft construction will sound odd in context. Imagine if the sports commentators, instead of (5.91) or (5.92), had recounted the Benteke incident with *It was BENTEKE that broke Klopp's glasses* (5.93'd) without first making sure that

[11] Occasionally, *who* can replace *that* in the dependent clause (Aarts and Aarts 1988: 76).

the hearer had already activated the knowledge that Klopp's glasses were broken. Without the dependent clause being an active presupposition and Benteke being in focus, all of these would sound strange and unexpected (though see below for a second type of *It* Cleft).

A construction that is closely related to *It* Cleft Clauses are WH-Cleft constructions (also known as Pseudo-Cleft constructions; Aarts and Arts 1988: 98; Herbst and Schüller 2008: 156; Hilpert 2019: 113–18; Lambrecht 2001a):

(5.97) a.   (The one) who broke Klopp's glasses was BENTEKE.
     b.   (The one) by whom Klopp's glasses were broken was BENTEKE.

(5.98) a.   What Benteke broke was KLOPP'S GLASSES.
     b.   What was broken by Benteke was KLOPP'S GLASSES.

As you can see in (5.97) and (5.98), in WH-Cleft constructions, the focused element appears at the end of the sentence: the subject of this construction comprises the rest of the proposition in a *who* or *what* clause that precedes a form of BE, which functions as main verb. Pragmatically, WH-Clefts can be used interchangeably with *It* Clefts in many situations. From a processing perspective (Hilpert 2019: 115), however, WH-Clefts are often preferred if the focused element is fairly long and heavy (due to the principle of end weight; see Section 3.2). Thus, the WH-Cleft in (5.99b) would be preferred over the *It* Cleft in (5.99a) if the focused referent is a heavy NP such as *the player who was later sold to Crystal Palace because of this incident*:

(5.99) a.   It was [the player who was later sold to Crystal Palace because of this incident] that broke Klopp's glasses.
     b.   Who broke Klopp's glasses was [the player who was later sold to Crystal Palace because of this incident].

Moreover, WH-Clefts always require the WH-clause to express information that is presupposed, which means that it is activated in the hearer's short-term memory and is something which the hearer at the same time considers 'a center of current interest and hence a potential locus of predication' (Lambrecht 2001a: 475–6). In contrast to this, a second type of *It* Cleft exists that has presupposed information in the OBL slot and new focus information in the dependent clause (Delin and Oberlander 2006; Hilpert 2019: 116; Lambrecht 2001a: 484):

(5.100)   A: What is so special about Liverpool FC?

(5.101)   B: It was at Anfield that I watched my first live Premier League game.

(5.102)   B: #Where I watched my first live Premier League game was at Anfield.

Following the question in (5.100), the information that the speaker watched their first live Premier League game at Anfield is clearly new information. Yet, while the *It* Cleft construction in (5.101) is a perfectly acceptable answer, the WH-Cleft in (5.102) sounds odd in this context (indicated by '#'). The reason for this is that there exists a second type of *It* Cleft construction in which the dependent clause can express new information (and will therefore be highlighted by a high-fall accent H*L), while the OBL position can be considered presupposed (since talking about Liverpool FC activates the frame Premier League football club whose football stadium is at Anfield; Delin and Oberlander 1995, 2006; Prince 1978). The corresponding constructional pattern is given in (5.103):

(5.103)   *It* Cleft construction (Type 2)

        FORM: PHONOLOGY: $/ \text{It}_1 \text{ BE}_2 \text{ C}_3 \text{ D}_4 /_5$

                              INTONATION: PITCH: H*L_4

                              MORPHOSYNTAX: $[\text{SBJ}_1 \text{ V}_{\text{BE2}} \text{ OBL}_3$

                                          $[\textit{that} \text{ REST-CLAUSE}]_{\text{dependent clause4}}]_5$

          $\Leftrightarrow$

        MEANING: SEMANTICS: 'STATEMENT'$_5$

                       PRAGMATICS: FOCUS_4 / PRESUPPOSITION_3

In contrast to this, WH-Cleft constructions only work if the WH-clause with the presupposition contains a continuing topic from the previous discourse (which is why *What is so special about Liverpool FC is that I watched my first live Premier League game there.* sounds a lot better).

(5.104)   WH-Cleft construction

        FORM: PHONOLOGY: $/ \text{A}_1 \text{ BE}_2 \text{ C}_3 /_4$

                                        INTONATION: PITCH: H*L_3

                        MORPHOSYNTAX: $[\text{SBJ:}[\text{WH-element REST-}$

                                          $\text{CLAUSE}]_1 \text{ V}_{\text{BE2}} \text{ OBL}_3]_4$

                                          WH-element = *who, what*

          $\Leftrightarrow$

        MEANING: SEMANTICS: 'STATEMENT'$_4$

                       PRAGMATICS: FOCUS_3 / PRESUPPOSITION_1

                                  (with $\text{TOPIC}_{\text{continuing}}$**)**

In (5.104), the WH-subject clause$_1$ (which most frequently contains a clause-initial *who* or *what*; Hilpert 2019: 117) is marked as PRESUPPOSITION_1, while the OBL$_3$ is in FOCUS$_3$ and consequently normally gets the associated pitch accent (H*L_3).

Now, the main function of the three information constructions, the two *It* Clefts as well as the WH-Cleft construction, is to highlight the new, focused information. At the same time, they obviously also have a topic-comment structure. Remember that in Section 4.2.3.3, we introduced the term topic as often being defined as 'that which the sentence is about' (Lambrecht 1994: 118). In Declarative Clause constructions, we identified the subject slot as prototypically associated with the topic of a proposition. Topic-status is independent of whether information is new (focus) or not (presupposed). In both *It* Cleft constructions (5.96) and (5.103), we can say that the OBL slot indicates what the sentence is about. Thus, independently of whether it encodes new or presupposed information, the OBL is going to be the topic which the sentence is about, while the dependent clause provides a (new or presupposed) comment on it.

In WH-constructions (*What I want is zigazig-ah*), it is the WH-clause that provides the topic (= *What I want*), while the focused OBL slot provides the comment (= *zigazig-ah*).

In English, speakers also have several constructions at their disposal to change the topic or introduce a new one:

(5.105)   Benteke broke KLOPP'S GLASSES.
            These had been really expensive.

(5.106)   Benteke broke KLOPP'S GLASSES.
            As for Arjen Robben, he broke Klopp's heart.

(5.107)   Benteke broke KLOPP'S GLASSES.
            Regarding that scene, Klopp later said he hadn't seen Benteke running towards him.

The sentence in (5.105) shows how thematic progression often works: the focus (often also called 'rheme', here *Klopp's glasses*) of the first clause becomes the topic (often referred to as 'theme') of the following clause by filling the subject slot and being instantiated by an anaphoric pronoun (here *these*). In (5.106), the *As for* X construction is used (Hilpert 2019: 110) to introduce a new topic (*Arjen Robben*, who scored the winning goal against Klopp's side in the 2013 Champions League final). *Regarding* X, (like *About* X, or *Concerning* X,), has a similar function in (5.107) of shifting to a new topic (here making the whole event the topic of the next sentence). In contrast to focus, topic in English is phonologically marked by a rise on the accented syllable of the topic phrase (e.g., **THE**se, *As for Arjen* **RO***bben*, *Regarding that* **SCE***ne*). In the following, we will encode this by the notation 'L+H*').

In addition to the examples above, English also has three widely used constructions that speakers can use for topic management:

(5.108)   Topicalization: **Klopp's glasses,** Benteke broke.

(5.109)   Left-Dislocation: **Klopp's glasses,** Benteke broke **them**.

(5.110)   Right-Dislocation: Benteke broke **them, Klopp's glasses**.

The example in (5.108) is an instance of the Topicalization construction, which has the topic that a speaker wants to talk about in clause-initial position instead of appearing clause-internally (cf. the corresponding 'normal' declarative construct *Benteke broke* **Klopp's glasses**.). As you can see, the Left-Dislocation construction (5.109) looks similar, but on top of having the topic phrase in clause-initial position it also has a so-called resumptive pronoun (*them*) in the position where we would expect the topic phrase in a 'normal' declarative construct. Finally, the Right-Dislocation (5.110) again has a clause-initial pronoun that in this case functions cataphorically; that is, it points to a topic phrase that follows the main clause.

At this point you might wonder why English has two constructions that seem to have the same job of introducing topics. As you might remember, in

Section 3.2.2, we introduced the Principle of No Synonymy (Goldberg 1995: 67–8), which basically states that we do not expect languages to have two or more constructions that are perfectly synonymous. As it turns out, empirical studies have shown that there are indeed subtle differences with respect to the usage constraints of the three topic constructions above (Gregory and Michaelis 2001; Hilpert 2019: 119–20; Lambrecht 2001b): the topic phrase in the Topicalization constructions, for example, is very often already topical and therefore realized by a pronoun (e.g., *Klopp's glasses . . . **These**, Benteke broke.*). Besides, the topics of Topicalization constructions in general do not seem to persist for very much longer. In contrast to this, the Right-Dislocation construction continues or maintains an established topic that was already topical. Similarly, the Left-Dislocation construction also has a topic that persists longer in the following discourse, but in contrast to the other two constructions, is used to announce or establish a new topic.

In addition to these functional differences, there are also formal ones: while Left- and Right-Dislocation constructions mostly just exhibit NP topics, Topicalization constructions show a greater range of different types of topic phrases (Sag 2010: 513):

(5.111) a.   NP: The glasses, he broke.
        b.   PP: On the pitch, they fell.
        c.   ADJP: Unhappy, Klopp was.
        d.   ADVP: Carefully, he picked them up again

In light of this, we can summarize the constructional template for the Topicalization construction with a topicalized NP as follows:

(5.112)   Topicalization construction
           FORM: PHONOLOGY: $/A_1 \ B_2/_3$
                                          INTONATION: PITCH: $L+H*_1$
                        MORPHOSYNTAX: [[Topicalized Phrase$_1$] REST-
                                          CLAUSE$_2$]$_3$
                                          [Topicalized Phrase$_1$] = NP, PP,
                                          ADJP, ADVP

                        $\Leftrightarrow$

           MEANING: SEMANTICS: 'STATEMENT'$_3$
                       PRAGMATICS: (active/ending) TOPIC$_1$ / COMMENT$_2$

The Topicalization construction (5.112) has a TOPIC that is marked as continuing an active topic that is potentially ending soon. Moreover, on the MORPHOSYNTAX level, the topic is realized as an initial phrase$_1$ (NP, PP, ADJP or ADVP) that is marked by a rising intonation (PITCH: $L+H*_1$) on the PHONOLOGY level.

The Left-Dislocation construction (5.113) looks fairly similar to (5.112):

(5.113)   Left-Dislocation construction
           FORM: PHONOLOGY: $/A_1 \ B_2/_3$
                                          INTONATION: PITCH: $L+H*_1$

MORPHOSYNTAX: [[Topicalized Phrase$_1$]
                                    [REST-CLAUSE$_2$ PRON$_1$]]$_3$
                                    [Topicalized Phrase$_1$] = NP

⟺

MEANING: SEMANTICS: 'STATEMENT'$_3$
                     PRAGMATICS: (new/continuing) TOPIC$_1$ / COMMENT$_2$

The only difference is that the Left-Dislocation construction tends to announce a 'new and continuing TOPIC$_1$' and that it has a resumptive pronoun (PRON$_1$) in the REST-CLAUSE that is co-indexed with the initial topic phrase.

In contrast to this, the Right-Dislocation construction in (5.114) has an active TOPIC$_1$ that is continuing, and appears at the right edge of the construction on the FORM level:

(5.114)   Right-Dislocation construction
            FORM: PHONOLOGY: /B$_2$ A$_1$/$_3$
                                                     INTONATION: PITCH: L+H*$_1$
                         MORPHOSYNTAX: [[REST-CLAUSE$_2$ PRON$_1$]
                                                     Topicalized Phrase$_1$]$_3$
                                                     [Topicalized Phrase$_1$] = NP

⟺

MEANING: SEMANTICS: 'STATEMENT'$_3$
                     PRAGMATICS: (active/continuing) TOPIC$_1$ / COMMENT$_2$

In this section, we have seen that speakers have a great number of constructions at their disposal to formulate their messages in a way that is beneficial for the flow of information and, consequently, the understanding of the hearer. Following other authors, I have labelled these phenomena 'information structure constructions'. As Lambrecht (1994: 16–17; cit. in Leino 2013: 341) points out, however, this term is somewhat misleading. Any construction, whether it is an Active Declarative construction or an *It* Cleft or Topicalization construction must be pragmatically adequate in a specific situation and is thus carefully chosen to meet the cognitive demands of the hearer. In this sense, all clause-level constructions are 'information structure constructions'. The constructions discussed in this section just tend to receive more scientific attention, since they deviate in FORM and MEANING from the more frequent and thus in this sense 'more canonical' declarative constructions.

5.5   Filler-Gap Constructions

When you compare declarative clauses such as (5.115) with the clause constructions that contain an initial nonsubject WH-element (5.116a–c) or a topicalized phrase (5.116d), you can see that the latter share a property: the constructions in (5.116) all have a clause-initial phrase (sometimes referred to as a 'filler'; highlighted by boldface in (5.116a–d)) that in declaratives corresponds to an element that would be realized in the post-verbal position (*a few mistakes* in (5.115)).

(5.115)   Declarative: I have made **a few mistakes**.

(5.116) a.   WH-Interrogative: **What** did I make $\_i$?
     b.   WH-Exclamative: **What mistakes** I made $\_i$!
     c.   WH-Relative: The few mistakes [**which** I made $\_i$] cost me dearly.
     d.   Topicalization: **Mistakes**, I've made a few $\_i$ ...

Another construction that we have not covered yet, but which also displays this property is the so-called Comparative Correlative construction (5.117):

(5.117)   Comparative Correlative construct:
     [The more tired I was $\_i$,]Clause$_1$
     [**the more mistakes** I made $\_i$]Clause2

Like the constructions in (5.116), Comparative Correlative constructions have clause-initial phrases (*the more tired* and *the more mistakes*) that would appear clause-internally in Declarative constructions (*I was more tired. / I made more mistakes.*). In contrast to WH-Interrogatives and WH-Relative Clauses, Comparative Correlative constructons, however, consist of two clauses (C1: *the more tired I was* / C2: *the more mistakes I made*), each of which computes a semantic differential (the difference between how much more tired I was at a later time t_2 than at an earlier point in time t_1 and the difference between how many more mistakes I made at time t_2 than at an earlier point in time t_1; Hoffmann 2019a; Sag 2010: 525–6). In addition to this, the second clause C2 is interpreted as the 'apodosis'/result of the 'protasis'/cause specified by C1 (i.e., e.g., *the more tired I was* → *the more mistakes I made*). Moreover, while the two clause-initial *the*-s might look like articles, they are obviously not (in (5.117): *more tired* is an ADJP and ADJPs do not have a determiner slot). Instead, the two [ðə]s have a meaning of 'as ... so ...' (5.117), which can thus be paraphrased as 'as I was more tired, so I made more mistakes'. From a Construction Grammar perspective (Hoffmann 2019a), Comparative Correlative constructions can thus be seen as a template that consists of two clauses, each of which has to be introduced by fixed phonological material ([ðə ...]$_{C1}$ [ðə ...]$_{C2}$). The second position in each clause is then a schematic slot for the filler, which in this construction must be a comparative phrase (cf. *the **happier/sadder/older** I was*, C2: *the **more mistakes**/the **more cakes**/the **more presents** I made*). As in the other constructions, the filler is then followed by the REST-CLAUSE (cf. *the more she slept, the happier she felt*; *the richer a man is, the bigger his car is*).

Comparative Correlatives exhibit many additional idiosyncratic properties (see Hoffmann 2019a for a more detailed discussion). For our purposes, however, we can capture their main features using the constructional template in (5.118):

(5.118)   Comparative Correlative construction
          FORM: PHONOLOGY: /[ðə$_1$ A$_2$ B$_3$]$_{C1}$ [ðə$_4$ C$_5$ D$_6$]$_{C2}$/$_7$
                     MORPHOSYNTAX: [[*the*$_1$ [Comparative Phrase]$_2$
                                        REST-CLAUSE$_3$]$_{C1}$
                                        [*the*$_4$ [Comparative Phrase]$_5$
                                        REST-CLAUSE$_6$]$_{C2}$]$_7$
          ⇔
          MEANING: SEMANTICS:
                     '[As the degree of Comparative Phrase$_2$ increases/decreases
                        with respect to clause C1]$_{CAUSE}$
                     [so the degree of Comparative Phrase$_5$ increases/decreases
                        with respect to clause C2]$_{EFFECT}$'$_7$

For the sake of illustration, take a look at how the schema in (5.118) licenses a construct such as *The longer I think about it, the more interesting the topic gets*, in which *more* and *more interesting* fill the Comparative Phrase slots (subscripts $_2$ and $_5$) on the MORPHOSYNTAX level, while *I think about it* and *the topic gets* appear in the REST-CLAUSE slots (subscripts $_3$ and $_6$). Finally, its meaning can be rendered as 'As the degree of length increases with respect to me thinking, so the degree of being interesting increases about the topic.'

Now, as I said above, the constructions in (5.116a–d) and (5.117) all share the property of having a clause-initial filler phrase. In Mainstream Generative Grammar (Chomsky 1995, 2000), these structural similarities are explained by a single trans-formational operation (which has been called 'A-bar movement' or 'WH-movement'): the filler is supposed to originate in the position that *mistakes* occupies in (5.115) and then later moves to the clause-initial position, leaving behind a 'gap' (indicated by '_$_i$' in (5.116a–d) and (5.117)). Consequently, these structures in (5.116a–d) and (5.117) are sometimes collectively referred to as 'filler-gap' constructions.

Now, it would be quite impressive if we could explain all these different structures by a single constraint (such as movement). However, there are many pieces of evidence that argue against such a movement account: first of all, psycholinguistic studies have shown that gaps are not cognitively real (Pickering and Barry 1991). For this reason, a constructional account that assumes no movement transformations is to be preferred. Second, Sag (2010: 490–6) pro-vided an in-depth analysis that argued that Mainstream Generative Grammar analyses gloss over important differences between the various constructions:

- The filler in some of these constructions is a WH-element (such as, for example, WH-Interrogatives ***What** did I make?*), but in others it is not (cf. the NP *mistakes* in the Topicalization construction ***Mistakes**, I've made a few.*).
- Not all fillers are equally possible in all constructions (cf. the WH-Interrogative ***What book** did she read?* vs the WH-Exclamative ****What book** she read!*).
- Similarly, some constructions allow for an optional *that* to introduce the REST-CLAUSE (cf. the Comparative Correlative *The more*

> books (*that*) you read, the more interested you became.), while others do not (cf. the WH-Interrogative *What* (**that*) did you read?).

- Some constructions exhibit obligatory subject-auxiliary inversion (cf. *What **has she** read?* vs **What she has read?*); others have optional subject-auxiliary inversion (cf. *The more my head has ached, the more **have I** indulged in humour* or *The more my head has ached, the more **I have** indulged in humour*; from Culicover and Jackendoff 1999: 559). Other constructions obligatorily do not allow inversion at all (cf. the Relative construction **the mistakes which **did I make** vs *the mistakes which I made*).

- Not all constructions allow for nonfinite REST-CLAUSEs (cf. the Relative clause *the room **in which to meet*** vs a Topicalization clause such as **My bagels (for them) to like*).

- Finally, some of the constructions at hand function as independent clauses (e.g., WH-Interrogatives) while others need to be embedded (e.g., relative clauses). Only Comparative Correlative constructions obligatorily consist of two clauses.

All these divergent properties prove that it is not possible to simply explain all of these filler-gap constructions by a single constraint only. Instead, we need to encode the above features in the various constructional templates that we covered in Section 5.3. Note that we already included most of the properties, such as obligatory subject-auxiliary inversion or the type of filler phrase in our constructional templates. As you can see from the list above, for a more precise analysis of the constructional core clause network, there are, however, a couple of features that would still need to be added (such as whether the REST-CLAUSE has to be finite or not).

Yet, by now you might wonder why people considered analysing all the various filler-gap constructions by a single constraint in the first place? Well, in addition to the great number of differences discussed above, the constructions also exhibited some interesting similarities. For one, it seems possible to insert certain syntactic material between the filler phrase and the REST-CLAUSE in an almost unconstrained fashion (which is why filler-gap constructions are sometimes called 'unbounded', Sag 2010: 505):

(5.119) a.   WH-Interrogative: **What** [did John say [that Bill claimed [**that I made** $_i$]]]?
   b.   WH-Exclamative:
        What mistakes [John said [that Bill claimed [**that I made** $_i$]]]!
   c.   WH-Relative:
        The few mistakes [**which** [John said [that Bill claimed [**that I made** $_i$]]]] cost me dearly.
   d.   Topicalization:
        Mistakes, [John said [that Bill claimed [I've made a few $_i$ . . .]]].

If you wanted to, you could, of course, add even more reporting verbs (also referred to as 'bridge verbs') to (5.119) (e.g., *Sarah pointed out that Jennifer argued that Peter believed . . . that John said that Bill claimed that I made.*), though at a certain point you might lose track because your mind does not work like a computer.

At the same time, while filler-gap constructions seem to be unbounded with respect to the amount of intervening material, they were also argued to all exhibit 'island effects' (Sag 2010: 505). The idea here was that that there existed some purely syntactic structures in the REST-CLAUSE that acted as 'islands' from which it was impossible to move or extract fillers:

(5.120)   He read the report that was about my mistakes.

(5.121) a.   WH-Interrogative: *What did he read the report [that was about _i]]?
         b.   WH-Exclamative: ***What mistakes** he read the report [**that was about** _i]!
         c.   WH-Relative: *The few mistakes
                          [**which** he read the report [**that was about** _i] cost me dearly.
         d.   Topicalization: ***Mistakes**, he read the report [**that was about** _i].

Example (5.121) seems to show that it is impossible to move/extract a filler from a relative clause (*that was about X*) that modifies a noun (here *report*). Originally, this restriction was known as the Complex Noun Phrase constraint (Ross 1986; see Müller 2019: 462).

Now, evidence such as the unbounded nature of filler-gap constructions, together with the fact that all these constructions appeared to exhibit the same island constraints, led Generative Grammarians to argue that this must be innate, syntactic knowledge (part of Universal Grammar; see Section 2.1.1). As it turns out, however, things are slightly more complicated. For one, the Complex Noun Phrase constraint does not hold in all languages (Müller 2019: 462), and exceptions can even be found in English (Müller 2019: 465):

(5.122)   Then you look at what happens in languages you know and languages
           thati you have a friend [who knows _i].   (Charles Ferguson, lecture at
           university of Chicago, 1971; cit. in McCawley 1981: 108)

In (5.122), *that*[12] is the filler for a gap that is embedded in the relative clause *who knows*. Contrary to the Complex Noun Phrase constraint, however, (5.122) this is perfectly acceptable.

Moreover, in contrast to the predictions of Generative Grammar, even cases of extraction that do not involve complex NPs are not all equally acceptable:

(5.123)   Who did she think that he saw _i?

(5.124)   *Who did she mumble that he saw _i?

---

[12] Some Generative Grammarians would argue that the *that* in this sentence is a base-generated complementizer that has not moved. Instead, they would have to assume an underlying, phonologically empty pronoun that has moved. However, this does not affect the validity of the example here.

(5.125)   *Who did she realize that he saw _$_i$?   (Examples 5.123–5.125 from
           Ambridge and Goldberg 2008: 352)

In contrast to (5.123), which sounds perfectly acceptable, sentences seem to become unacceptable if the bridging structure contains a manner of speaking verb (*mumble*) or a factive verb (*realize*; Ambridge and Goldberg 2008: 352). Yet, if filler-gap constructions are to be constrained by purely syntactic constraints (as argued by Generative Grammar), then why does the semantics of the verb seem to play a role here?

Clearly, a purely syntactic account cannot explain all the above details. Instead, building on work by Erteschik-Shir and Lappin (1979), Ambridge and Goldberg (2008), we can put forward a cognitive, constructionist explanation of island effects. They argue that information structure plays a major role here. As they note, all the unacceptable structures seem to involve fillers that are 'extracted' from backgrounded/presupposed material (also Müller 2019: 464–5): *She saw the report that was about him.* presupposes that there was a report that was about him. We can illustrate this with the negation test: presuppositions remain constant under negation and the corresponding *She didn't see the report that was about him.* still assumes that there was this report. Consequently, **Who did she see the report that was about?* is not acceptable because some invisible syntactic constraint (such as the Complex NP Constraint) has been violated. It sounds odd because fillers seem to be focused, new information and thus cannot be 'extracted' or linked to presupposed information. Similarly, *She mumbled that he saw someone.* and *She realized that he saw someone.* both presuppose that he saw someone (cf. *She didn't mumble that he saw someone.* and *She didn't realize that he saw someone.*). This explains why (5.124) and (5.125) are unacceptable: 'Backgrounded constructions are islands' (Ambridge and Goldberg 2008: 358; see Müller 2019: 465 for a discussion of other processing-related phenomena that affect the acceptability of filler-gap structures).

Constructs that involve 'filler-gap' constructions cannot be explained by a simple, single movement operation. Instead, they constitute a family network of constructions with varying individual properties (concerning the phrase type of the filler, whether they are main or subordinate clauses, etc., see Section 5.3). Finally, as we have just seen, even the phenomena that originally were seen as their uniquely common syntactic properties, their unboundedness and the existence of island effects, turned out to be functionally motivated.

5.6   Summary

The present chapter investigated the most abstract and syntactic end of the lexicon-syntax cline. We explored how argument structure constructions interact with tense and aspect constructions, as well as with constructions of perspectivation (active and passive voice), which allow speakers to construe the same event from different vantage points. We also looked at the various clause type-constructions (e.g., Declarative, Interrogative and Imperative constructions) that enable speakers to express their illocutions. Next, we ventured into the realm of information structure and discussed several constructions that are important for the flow of information in discourse. Finally, we saw how information structure also affects filler-gap constructions. Thus, we were able to provide a cognitive, functional explanation for the phenomenon that was considered purely syntactic in nature by Generative Grammar.

Exercises

5.1 Hilpert (2019: 51) argues that (i) is a problematic construct that cannot easily be explained by the abstract Transitive construction (5.10).
   (i) Bob remembered his appointment?
   What do you think is the problem? Can you find any argument that could justify that we account for this example using the Transitive construction?

5.2 At first glance, the examples in (i–iii) might look like instances of the Copulative Attribute construction (5.14):
   (i)   She$_1$ grew$_2$ [tired]$_3$.
   (ii) He$_1$ became$_2$ [a happy man]$_3$.
   (iii) It$_1$ proved$_2$ [rather helpful]$_3$.
   Yet, their meaning is clearly incompatible with the Copulative Attribute construction. Specify in what way their meaning is different and write a constructional template for them (adapting the Copulative Attribute construction).

5.3 Which active argument structure constructions, other than the ones we discussed in Section 5.1.3, have a FORCE-DYNAMIC meaning that allows for an alternative passive construal? Try to provide the passive constructional template for as many as possible.

6 Constructional Variation and Change

In this chapter, we will explore constructionist approaches to language variation and change in English. As part of this, we will see how classic sociolinguistic studies can be accounted for by a usage-based constructionist perspective. Then, we will look at how Construction Grammar offers a cognitive explanation of the evolution of new first and second language varieties of English around the world. Finally, we will learn how Construction Grammar approaches analyse diachronic linguistic change.

6.1   Synchronic Variation

All languages are characterized by inherent variation (Hudson 1997, 2007a): there is regional variation (people in different places speak differently), social variation (different social groups in the same place speak differently) as well as functional variation (the same speaker in the same place will speak differently depending on the communicative situation, for example, talking to one's parents vs talking on the phone to one's boss). As more than sixty years of sociolinguistic research have shown, this variation is not random, but characterized by 'orderly heterogeneity' (Weinreich, Labov and Herzog 1968: 99–100): whenever speakers can choose between two or more alternatives, there are linguistic as well as social factors that systematically affect the choice of a particular variant. In sociolinguistic terms, the choice of a particular variant of a dependent variable is influenced by independent factors such as its linguistic context, the stylistic level of the discourse and social characteristics of the speaker (see for example Preston 1996). How is that possible? How is all this information stored in a speaker's mind?

Quantitative sociolinguistics emphasizes the relationship between actual linguistic performance and the linguistic system which underpins language use: who you speak to, how many different varieties you are exposed to and with which social groups you identify crucially affects the variation you are exposed to in your linguistic input. To this, Usage-based Construction Grammar offers a cognitive explanation of how speakers (unconsciously for the most part) acquire all this knowledge. As we saw in Section 2.1.3, usage-based approaches claim that based on specific tokens of usage, speakers store information such as

> [...] phonetic detail, including redundant and variable features, the lexical
> items and constructions used, the meaning, inferences made from this
> meaning and from the context, and properties of the social, physical and
> linguistic context.   (Bybee 2010: 14)

Usage-based Construction Grammar thus offers a cognitive framework for
sociolinguistics that can not only model synchronic variation but also provides
a principled explanation of the interaction of cognitive processes and the statistical and contextual factors affecting variation.

6.1.1   Cognitive Sociolinguistics

Let me illustrate how this works using Labov's (1972) classic sociolinguistic study on rhoticity in New York (see, e.g., Radford et al. 2009: 57–9):
before World War II, New Yorkers mostly did not pronounce the (r) in words
such as *bar* or *work* (i.e., at the end of words or before consonants). Then in the
1960s, Labov noticed that some people seemed to pronounce the (r) (their speech
was 'rhotic'), while others did not. Was that just a random phenomenon or was
there a pattern behind this? In order to investigate this, Labov went to three
different department stores: (1) an upper-middle class, expensive store (Saks), (2)
a lower-middle-class store (Macy's) and (3) an inexpensive, working-class store
(Klein). In each of these, he looked for as many shop assistants as he could find
and asked each of them where he could find a product that he knew was on the
fourth floor. The answer of the shop assistants consequently was *fourth floor*,
which is a phrase that contains two (r)s in different phonetic environments – in
one case the (r) appears before a consonant (*fourth*), in the other it occurs at the
end of the word (*floor*). Labov investigated several variables in this study, but in
the following I will only focus on the main sociolinguistic findings (for more
details see Radford et al. 2009: 57–9):

As Labov's statistical analysis showed, the social variable CLASS significantly influenced whether speakers pronounced their (r)s or not. While shop
assistants in the working-class shop (Klein) had the lowest percentage of (r)s, the
ones from the upper-middle class shop (Saks) exhibited the highest number of
(r)s in their speech (and the lower-middle class speakers from Macy's were right
in-between these two groups). From this, Labov concluded that social CLASS
crucially influences rhoticity in New York (see also Mather 2012 for a recent
real-time replication study). How can we explain such findings from a Usage-
based Construction Grammar point of view? Upper-middle-class speakers seem
to have picked up a rhotic pronunciation first and these are the customers that
frequent shops like Saks. The shop assistants there, like most staff, can be
expected to accommodate their speech to that of their customers. When their
customers ask about *skirts, shirts, sweaters* and so on, the shop assistants would
very often hear a rhotic pronunciation of these words. In line with the predictions
of usage-based approaches, these exemplars would thus be stored with the

phonetic detail that they are rhotic as well as the social information that an upper-middle class speaker produced it. In the long run, this will lead to the storage of these words that not only contains semantic meaning but also social meaning. Take, *skirt*, for example:

(6.1)   FORM: PHONOLOGY: /sk$_3$rt/$_1$
                      MORPHOSYNTAX: N$_1$

           ⇔

           MEANING: SEMANTICS: 'skirt (piece of clothing)'$_1$
                      PRAGMATICS: SOCIAL: upper-class$_1$

As (6.1) shows, speakers who hear the rhotic pronunciation often will store this word construction as one that is associated with upper-class speech. On the other hand, the non-rhotic pronunciation will be associated with the SOCIAL MEANING: working class. Once they have encountered enough rhotic word constructions of the type in (6.1), speakers might entrench a generalization that we can capture in the following constructional template:

(6.2)   FORM: PHONOLOGY: / r# /$_1$ **or** / rC /$_1$
           ⇔
           MEANING: SEMANTICS:
                      PRAGMATICS: SOCIAL: upper-class$_1$

This construction contains the information that an /r/ at the end of the word ('/ r#$_1$ /') **or** before a consonant ('/ rC$_1$ /') on the PHONOLOGY level is associated with an upper-class dialect on the MEANING level. What we should note here is that word-final /r/s are more salient, that is more auditorily prominent, than the ones occurring before a consonant. Consequently, we can expect the schema to be stronger entrenched for the word-final /r/s. This explains why Labov found that consistently and across all social classes the (r)s in word-final position were pronounced more often. Besides, we could ask again whether (6.2) is a generalization that is stored as a constructional template as in (6.2) or just as implicit knowledge that emerges from a cloud of specific rhotic constructions such as (6.1). Either way, we can see that the combined storage of FORM and MEANING allows us to provide a cognitive explanation for socially-driven, phonetic variation.

Now, the rise of the rhotic pronunciation in New York can be characterized as a 'change from above' the level of consciousness (Labov 2001). Speakers seemed to be aware of the two pronunciations. Moreover, when Labov used different elicitation methods in a follow-up study, New Yorkers from all classes produced more /r/s in more formal settings. When focusing on their pronunciation (as when they carefully read word pairs or word lists), they all exhibited more /r/s than in casual speech. So far, we have only illustrated how this type of variation can be captured by a Construction Grammar analysis. But what about changes that people do not notice consciously ('change from below' in Labov's terminology), can this also be explained by a Usage-based Construction Grammar approach?

An example of such a change was also discovered by Labov in the 1960s (see Aitchison 2013: 60–7): when he went to Martha's Vineyard, an island off the coast of Massachusetts, he noticed that some islanders showed signs of an older pronunciation of the vowels in words such as *house* and *life*. Whereas some people on the island had the modern Standard American English pronunciation [haʊs] and [laɪf], some had retained the older variants [həʊs] and [ləɪf]. Now, you might think that it was mostly older speakers that still kept the old pronunciation and that in a couple of generations all islanders would use the new forms. Yet, to Labov's surprise, he noticed that a group of younger speakers also pronounced *house* and *life* as [həʊs] and [ləɪf]. Once he started to investigate the phenomenon, it turned out that the older pronunciations were found particularly with young males that strongly identified with the island and had little regard for the many tourists from the mainland that swarmed the island over the summer months. Instead, they idolised a group of older, local fisherman, who for them represented the 'real Martha's Vineyard' (and who still had retained the older forms [əʊ] and [əɪ]). As a result, this group of younger men avoided speaking to the tourists, and instead spent time with the fishermen, where they were exposed to older pronunciations, which they associated with a positive social meaning of a 'local Martha's Vineyard identity'. From a usage-based perspective, it is obvious that they thus got more type and token frequency of the older variants than the other islanders who interacted more with the tourists. What we see here is that social meaning and emotional factors play a role. The older variants were entrenched by this network of younger males because of their emotional attachment with the island. Example (6.3) gives a constructional template that captures the mental knowledge underlying the behaviour of these speakers. Note that input frequency, obviously, plays a great role here: some individuals might only be loosely associated with the local fishermen network, and will only have entrenched some particular, highly frequent word constructions such as *house, boat, float* or *I, life, night*. Others will be more central members with high type and token frequency input that consequently show a linguistic behaviour that can be captured by (6.3).

(6.3)   FORM: PHONOLOGY: / $əʊ_1$ / **or** / $əɪ_1$ /
         ⇔
         MEANING: SEMANTICS:
                      PRAGMATICS: SOCIAL: positive local-identity$_1$

In the change from above in New York as well as the change from below on Martha's Vineyard, input frequency as well as accommodation to a (consciously or unconsciously) prestige variety seem to be crucial. From a cognitive perspective, it is important to point out, however, that accommodation is not simply someone perfectly copying another speaker. Instead, speakers accommodate to their perception of an interlocuter's speech, and the features that they pick up on will be mediated by their own existing constructional network, the (acoustic as well as social) salience of the phenomenon as well the degree of exposure (see Hollmann 2013: 503–5).

Now, the present chapter cannot offer an in-depth introduction to the field of sociolinguistics (for this, cf., e.g., Chambers 2008; Coulmas 2013; Meyerhoff 2019 – or one of the many other excellent sociolinguistics textbooks). Instead, we will look at a couple of selective phenomena that illustrate how sociolinguistics has evolved as a field over the years. For this, we will follow Eckert (2012), who distinguishes three waves of sociolinguistics.

The first wave of sociolinguistics was started by Labov's New York study (Eckert 2012: 88–91). This approach was characterized by quantitative studies that investigated the effect that major demographic variables (such as CLASS, AGE or GENDER) had on linguistic variation. Another classic example of first wave sociolinguistics was Trudgill's (1974) study on English in Norwich. One of the phenomena he looked at was the variable pronunciation of (ING) (see Chambers 2008: 122–3). Some speakers pronounced the final syllable of words such as *eating, going* or *sleeping* as [-ɪŋ], while others said [-ən] (*eatin', goin'* or *sleepin'*). Similar to rhoticity in New York, CLASS played an important role: working-class speakers almost exclusively used the [-ən] variant, while middle- class speakers almost only exhibited the Standard English variant [-ɪŋ]. Interestingly, however, Trudgill also detected an interaction with GENDER: across all groups, woman consistently used the standard variant more often than men (with the effect being most pronounced in the lower middle classes). Interestingly, the fact that men tend to use a higher frequency of nonstandard forms was something that was found repeatedly in twentieth-century sociolinguistic studies (Labov 1990: 205–6). Many potential reasons for this have been discussed in the literature (unequal power, status-consciousness, etc.; see Chambers 2008: 158). What is important to remember, though, as you are probably well aware, is that in contrast to the biological category sex, the social category GENDER is a dynamically constructed one, which means that the GENDER roles of women and men (as well as those of people identifying with a another, third option) are fluid and prone to change. So, how the effect of GENDER will affect linguistic variation in the twenty-first century is an open question. For the Norwich data from the 1970s, we can, however, note that the constructional template in (6.4), which captures the non-standard *in'* variant was not only marked as a local prestige variant ('positive local-identity') but also as particularly characteristic of male speech:

(6.4)   FORM: PHONOLOGY: / ən# /$_1$
         ⇔
         MEANING: SEMANTICS:
                    PRAGMATICS: SOCIAL: positive local-identity$_1$ I esp. male
                                                                    speech$_1$

First wave sociolinguistics significantly furthered our understanding of the relationship of language and society. From the 1980s, however, the second wave of sociolinguistics (Eckert 2012: 91–3) highlighted the fact that broad categories such as CLASS or GENDER sometimes fail to capture the complex nature of linguistic variation in local communities. As a consequence, drawing on ethnographic methods, the focus of second wave studies was on locally relevant social categories. A good example of such an approach is Eckert's study on teenage speech in suburban Detroit (Eckert 2004). As anyone who has ever been a teenager themselves knows, not all adolescents speak alike. In her study, Eckert identified two local subgroups of adolescents: the 'Jocks' (mostly middle class, school-oriented kids that aspired to white-collar jobs) and the 'Burnouts' (predominantly working-class kids that rejected the school culture and aspired to blue-collar jobs). Now, in the speech of both, Eckert observed standard negation patterns such as (6.5) as well as non-standard 'double negation' (6.6):

(6.5)   I did**n't** do **anything**.

(6.6)   I did**n't** do **nothing**.

As you can expect from their descriptions above, the Jocks used the standard form (6.5), which is also the prestige form taught at school, much more frequently than the Burnouts, who had many more instances of double negation. Yet, while Burnout boys and girls did not differ greatly with respect to this variable, the Jocks showed a GENDER effect: though the Jocks girls hardly exhibited double negation at all, the Jocks boys roughly used it in one out of five times. What this shows is that social categories do not exclusively predetermine your use of sociolinguistic variants. Since double negation was a feature that was characteristic of the Burnouts (who were seen as tough and street smart), Jocks boys occasionally also used it, probably to also appear tough and street smart. The SOCIAL MEANING of the construction can therefore be summarized as something like 'anti-school cool'. (6.7) provide the corresponding constructional template:

(6.7)   FORM: PHONOLOGY:
                       MORPHOSYNTAX: [... NOT ... NOTHING]$_1$
           ⇔
           MEANING: SEMANTICS:
                       PRAGMATICS: SOCIAL: positive local-identity$_1$ |
                                          'anti-school cool'$_1$

Despite their different approach to social categories, both first and second wave sociolinguistic studies were largely static in nature. They seemed to imply that once you can identify the right categories you could predict a speaker's linguistic behaviour. However, we have just seen in the Eckert's Detroit study, linguistic identities are not really static. The Jocks boys largely exhibited the expected standard negation form in their speech, but occasionally also produced the non-standard one. The current third wave of sociolinguistics (Eckert 2012: 93–7), therefore, focuses on the linguist behaviour as 'acts of identity':

> [T]he individual creates for himself the patterns of his linguistic behaviour so as to resemble those of the group or groups with which from time to time he wishes to be identified, or so as to be unlike those from whom he wishes to be distinguished.   (Le Page and Tabouret-Keller 1985: 181)

As Le Page and Tabouret-Keller point out, individuals can (consciously and unconsciously) change their linguistic performance in situations in order to dynamically express different sociolinguistic identities. A good example for this is Bell's (1984) study on intervocalic *t*-voicing in New Zealand English (*t*s that occur between two voiced sounds). Bell noted that in New Zealand English (as in many other varieties of English) speakers sometimes voice intervocalic *t*s, so *writer* [ˈraetə] is pronounced as [ˈraet̬ə] ([t̬] sounds a bit like a [d]; for more information on the vowel pronunciation in New Zealand English; cf. Bauer and Warren 2004). Now, as he noticed, even the same radio newscaster reading out the same news text showed variable pronunciations depending on the station that the news was broadcast on: if the station was geared towards an audience of higher-class status, the newscasters showed considerably fewer instances of *t*-voicing than if the station had an alleged lower-class status. It is pretty easy to provide a constructional template for the non-standard variant:

(6.8)   FORM: PHONOLOGY: / VOICED t̬ VOICED /₁
                         MORPHOSYNTAX:

             ⇔

             MEANING: SEMANTICS:
                         PRAGMATICS: SOCIAL: positive non-standard-identity₁

More important is the insight that speakers can have (6.8) as well as the more standard variants in their mental constructicon and that the choice between the two is not fully deterministic. In more formal contexts, the standard variant would, of course, be the unmarked choice. In informal settings, the voiced variant might be the more expected choice. In any situation, speakers can of course also choose to produce the non-expected alternative variant (Coulmas 2013). This choice, however, is potentially interpreted as meaningful – maybe the speaker even tries to make a point by using a non-standard variant in a formal context. In any case, the choice of sociolinguistic constructions is always indexical – your choices of these constructions always reflect which social group you identify with at any moment in time, whether you are consciously aware of this or not.

So far, a number of Construction Grammar studies have looked at sociolinguistic variation (cf., e.g., Colleman 2010; de Clerck and Colleman 2013; de Vogelaer 2010; Grondelaers, Speelman and Geeraerts 2007, 2008; Szmrecsanyi 2010; for an overview see Hollmann 2013). Most of these studies have taken a rather classical, first wave variationist approach in that they have looked at how static sociolinguistic parameters (such as text type, register or dialect) act as independent variables in their analyses. There are, however, also some recent studies (Hoffmann 2015; Hollmann and Siewierska 2007, 2011; Kristiansen 2008) that move away from static constraints and focus more on the active stylization of individuals by dynamic linguistic acts of identity. These third wave constructionist approaches promise some fascinating avenues for future cognitive sociolinguistic studies.

6.1.2   Post-Colonial Englishes

Today, English is no longer exclusively spoken in Britain and the United States. It is the main language of Australian and New Zealand TV broadcasting, the language in which Kenyan politicians address their parliament, as well as the first language spoken at home by almost one third of all Singaporean children (Schneider 2011: 159). Besides being used as the world-wide lingua franca, many of the varieties of English around the world historically arose in colonial settings, which is why they are called 'Post-colonial Englishes'. These include L1 varieties such as American English or Australian English as well as L2 varieties such as Kenyan English or Hong Kong English. In this section, we will briefly explore what a constructionist analysis of the rise and development of these Post-colonial Englishes looks like.

As Schneider (2003, 2007) argues in his Dynamic Model, the evolution of these 'post-colonial' varieties crucially depends on the social interaction of the colonizers (the 'settler (STL) strand') and the various indigenous people (the 'indigenous (IDG) strand'). In line with previous research on contact linguistics (Mufwene 2001; Thomason 2001; Winford 2003; cf. Schneider 2007: 21–2), the Dynamic Model assumes that stronger social contact between the STL and IDG groups leads to greater linguistic interaction. Greater interaction, obviously, entails increased type and token frequency and Usage-based Construction Grammar should thus be an ideal cognitive theoretical model for the sociolinguistic Dynamic Model. Let us look at the basic types of contact scenarios and explore how Construction Grammar can provide an explanation for the various varieties emerging in these situations (cf. Mufwene 2001, 2004; Schneider 2007: 24–5, 2011: 45–8; see Hoffmann 2021 for more details):

The earliest types of contact scenarios can be traced back to the late Middle Ages and happened in so-called trade colonies. British seafarers and merchants travelled, for example, to West Africa or Asia to trade in spices or other oriental goods (and, sadly, even other human beings that were enslaved). The contact between the (British) STLs and local IDG traders during the exchange of goods, commodities and slaves in these situations was only sporadic and short-lived. Moreover, no common lingua franca was available to the two parties, which often led to the spontaneous development of a simplified and reduced means of communication, so-called pidgins. Pidgins derive some of their properties from the superstrate STL language (mostly lexical items) and some from the substrate IDG languages (mostly phonological as well as syntactic features). On top of that, however, pidgins also exhibit several features that can neither be found in the super- nor the substrate input languages and that, therefore, must be the result of the specific language contact characterizing this type of situation or possibly universal contact characteristics (e.g., Lefebvre 2004: 23–8). One characteristic feature of pidgins, for example, is that show they a strong preference for analytic structures and only a smaller number of clausal patterns (Winford 2003: 276). Take the following examples from Cameroon Pidgin English (taken from Mesthrie et al. 2000: 271):

(6.9) a.   This small swine he **been go** for market
           'This little piggy **went** to the market'
       b.   This small swine he **been stay** for house
           'This little piggy **stayed** home'

The two lines in (6.9) are from the Cameroon Pidgin English version of the well-known 'This little piggy' nursery rhyme. As you can see, in contrast to the synthetic British English past tense verb *stayed* (which draws on the Simple Past construction (5.51)) and the irregular *Went* construction, Cameroon Pidgin English uses an analytic *been* + V_{base} pattern to express past tense:

(6.10)   Simple Past construction (Cameroon Pidgin English)
           FORM: PHONOLOGY: / bin_1 X_2 /$_3$
                        MORPHOSYNTAX: [$been_1$ V_{base2}]$_3$

           $\Leftrightarrow$

           MEANING: SEMANTICS: '$PAST_1(STATE(V_2))$'$_3$

As can be seen in the corresponding template (6.10), the construction has an analytic structure: the invariant element *been* marks the past tense reference, while the second slot specifies the event encoded by the verbal predicate. From a Construction Grammar perspective, the prevalence of analytic grammatical con-structions such as (6.10) in pidgins must be interpreted as a cognitive preference for pairings of one form-one meaning (for further support of this view, cf. Baker and Huber 2000: 853; Velupillai 2015). This view receives at least some support from language acquisition: as we saw in Chapter 2, during the earliest stages of language acquisition, children first employ holophrase constructions, that is linguistic symbols such as *Birdie!* or *Lemme-see!*, which they treat as unanalysed chunks to express their intentions with respect to a specific scenario (cf. Diessel 2013; Tomasello 2006: 23). Already in the next step, however, around the age of eighteen months, children start to tweak these utterance-level constructions by adding a single substantive construction or by inserting such a substantive form-meaning pairing into the former holophrase structure (Tomasello 2003: 308–9). The earliest stages of creative language use, thus, involve the use of analytic meso-constructions (e.g., verb-island constructions and item-based construc-tions) and it is therefore no surprise that these types of constructions are crucial during the birth of new languages during pidginization.

Moreover, domain-general cognitive processes (such as iconicity, metaphor or metonymy) play a great role in how these analytic constructions are used to express concepts for whom pidgin speakers have no available stored construction (examples (6.11), from Mesthrie et al. 2000: 282):

(6.11) a.   gras   bilong   hed
           grass   belong head
           'hair'
     b.   wara   bilong   skin
           water belong skin
           'sweat'
     c.   pinga bilong lek
           finger belong leg
           'toe'

In (6.11) is illustrated how an 'N belong N' construction is used to encode concepts such as *hair, sweat* and *toe*. Similar to what we find in L1 acquisition, the construction can be seen as a verb-island construction that has slots for two nouns:

(6.12)   N-*bilong*-N construction (Cameroon Pidgin English)
             FORM: PHONOLOGY: / X_1 bilɔŋ$_2$ Y_3 /$_4$
                            MORPHOSYNTAX: $[N_1$ *bilong*$_2$ $N_3]_4$

        ⇔

        MEANING: SEMANTICS: 'THING$_4$ with METONYMY RELATION$_2$ to
                                THING$_3$ and METAPHOR RELATION$_2$ to
                                THING$_1$'$_4$

As the template in (6.12) shows, the construction is intended to denote a THING$_4$ that is not explicitly mentioned. So how do people know what the speaker meant? Well, the second N_3 slot gives them an entity that is metonymically related to the concept they want to express (*head, skin, leg*) and the first slot N_1 provides a THING$_1$ that is metaphorically similar to it (*gras, water, finger*). Drawing on the construction in (6.12) and using domain-general cognitive processes, hearers can thus successfully infer the intended meaning ('finger belong leg' → toe).

In contrast to trade colonies, plantation colonies were founded in the Caribbean and the Americas between the seventeenth and nineteenth centuries and exhibited a different type of contact scenario: in addition to the English STLs, another non-IDG group was brought to these colonies: these included either slaves, which were relocated by force (mostly from Africa) or indentured labourers (from, for example, India). Plantation colonies, therefore, consisted of a considerable number of STL English speakers, an IDG group (which in some cases was marginalized or even exterminated as on most Caribbean islands; cf. Schneider 2007: 61) as well as a non-IDG group, which usually constituted the numerical majority and comprised the largest number of speakers from various language backgrounds. The multilingual situation of the slaves in these colonies 'typically lead to strong contact-induced restructuring and possibly to creolization' (Schneider 2007: 60). Creoles are also newly created languages that evolve in contact settings without an available lingua franca. In contrast to pidgins, however, creoles are used in a wider range of situations and often become the L1 of a second generation of speakers. As a result of being the major means of daily communication, creoles develop more complicated grammatical structures than pidgins. At the same time their grammatical structures also tend to be analytic rather than synthetic (Velupillai 2015). Take the following example from Jamaican Creole (data from Patrick 2008: 614):

(6.13)   Jamaican Creole
   a.   Mi run.   'I ran.'
   b.   Mi lov im   'I love him.'

(6.14) a.   Mi ben ron.   'I had run.'
     b.   Mi ben lov im   'I loved him.'

As (6.13) shows, in Jamaican Creole an unmarked stative verb such as *love* gets a present tense interpretation, while an activity verb such as *run* is interpreted as past tense. The structure *ben* + V is then used to express a PAST-BEFORE reading. Consequently, (6.14a) *ben ron* means 'had run' and (6.14b) *ben lov* means 'loved'.

(6.15)   Simple Past-before construction (Jamaican Creole)
           FORM: PHONOLOGY: / ben_1 X_2 $/_3$
                      MORPHOSYNTAX: $[ben_1$ $V_{base2}]_3$
           ⇔
           MEANING: SEMANTICS: 'PAST-BEFORE$_1$(STATE(V_2))'$_3$

Example (6.15) provides a template for this Simple Past-before construction. As you can see, similar to the Cameroon Pidgin English construction (6.10), (6.15) is analytic in that the PAST-BEFORE meaning is encoded by a single substantive element (ben_1). At the same time, we have already seen that the precise interpretation of (6.15) will depend on the verbal aspect of the predicate (something that the template glosses over). Moreover, creoles are also more complex since tense constructions interact with aspect constructions (data from Patrick 2008: 614):

(6.16)   Mi a ron.   'I am running.'

(6.17)   Mi ben a ron. 'I was running.'

The above examples illustrate that Jamaican Creole also has a progressive construction that is marked by a *a* + V_{base} sequence (with the tense marker *ben* preceding it in (6.17); in Exercise 6.2 below, you will be asked to provide a template for this construction). The constructional networks of grammatical constructions that we find in creole languages are, therefore, much more complicated than the ones exhibited by pidgin languages. At the same time, we again find a strong preference for analytic meso-constructions in which each element is assigned a single meaning only (in contrast to the many synthetic tense and aspect constructions we identified for Standard British and American English; see Section 5.2).

The final two types of colonies were characterized by a longer and more intense STL and IDG contact situation: on the one hand, exploitation colonies developed in the eighteenth and nineteenth centuries. In these cases, foreign countries came under the political and administrative control of European colonial powers, but only a limited number of STL administrators were actually deployed to these colonies. Instead, in line with the British policy of indirect rule (Lange 2004: 908), a small, local IDG elite was educated and trained to run the country. The members of these IDG elites were mainly introduced to a formal type of English through education that is often described as 'an elitist class marker, formal and influenced by written styles to the point of being "bookish"' (Schneider 2011: 46). It is this type of formal English that was the source of many Present-day African and Asian ESL varieties. On the other hand, settlement colonies were created by the large-scale migration and settlement of English-speaking STLs. Settlement colonies include, for example, the United States, Canada, Australia as well as New Zealand and linguistically are characterized by two processes (Schneider 2011: 47): first, the STL strand usually contained people from many different English dialect backgrounds. Due to extensive dialect contact and mutual accommodation in the colonies, the dialect differences between the various STL speakers tended to be minimized and a new common dialect arose via this process of *koinéization* (Trudgill 2004). Second, the IDG groups in these colonies were suddenly faced with a dominant superstrate English-speaking community, which often required 'them to become bilingual or even undergo language shift' (Schneider 2011: 27).

While trade, plantation, exploitation and settlement colonies clearly differed in the details of their contact scenario, Schneider (2003, 2007) argues that they are all characterized by five evolutionary phases that new post-colonial varieties could successively go through and that would be affected by distinct social, historical as well as political conditions.

Phase I ('Foundation') refers to the time when English is first transplanted to a new colony. At this point, communication between the STL and IDG strands is fairly limited, which only leads to the borrowing of a few salient lexical items such as place names into the local variety of English. In constructionist terms, the STL speakers thus add a limited number of fully substantive constructions to their mental constructicon that are highly salient in the local context ('anybody who is new to a region will ask for names of places and landmarks and accept them as [...] the names which these localities simply "have"'; Schneider 2007: 36). Consequently, these place names will also have a high token frequency, which will further facilitate their entrenchment. Finally, due to their referential meaning, these mappings of form and meaning are fairly easily learnt by the STL speakers.

While the STL strand then gradually adapts to its new home in Phase II ('Exonormative Stabilization'), its (socio-)linguistic identity still remains essentially British. During this stage, STL-IDG contact is still superficial but enough to result in 'numerous borrowings from indigenous languages [. . . which largely] designate the local fauna and flora, soon followed by words for cultural terms, customs and objects found to be peculiar to the indigenous community' (Schneider 2007: 39). The increased contact thus leads to the borrowing of a set of fully substantive, locally salient and very frequent micro-constructions. In contrast to the toponymic constructions of the foundation phase, these constructions are not referential in meaning but denote sets of objects (cf. Schneider 2007: 39). Nevertheless, these are still straightforward substantive pairings of form and meaning that can easily be added to the taxonomic constructional networks of the STL strand.

During Phase III ('Nativization'), mainly after the political independence of the former colonies, the settlers have to accept the colony as their new home. Contact and linguistic negotiation between the two strands then leads to 'structural nativization'; that is, large-scale linguistic effects, from lexical borrowing and the development of a local accent to morphological, grammatical and syntactic innovations (Schneider 2007: 71–112). These '[i]nnovations and distinctive structural properties of PCEs [Post-colonial Englishes] are frequently positioned **at the interface between lexis and grammar**, i.e., certain words but not others of the same word class prefer certain grammatical rules or patterns' (Schneider 2007: 83; my emphasis). Thus, Singapore English has *resemble to s.o.* instead of *resemble s.o.*; East African English has *pick s.o.* instead of *pick s.o. up*; and New Zealand English *has protest sth.* instead of *protest against sth* (Schneider 2007: 46–7). Thus, structural innovations in Post-colonial Englishes in Phase III do not involve the across-the-board introduction of new grammatical rules. Instead, on an item-by-item basis, certain words exhibit new patterns (meso-constructions such as Singapore English [SBJ *resemble to* OBJ] or New Zealand English [SBJ *protest* OBJ]), and it is these that serve as the model for lexical diffusion at a later stage when new and idiosyncratic innovations emerge. This is again in line with what we saw in Chapter 2, since item-specific generalizations (e.g., verb-islands) are also the first productive, schematic constructions we observed in the early stages of L1 acquisition. Note that this does not mean that PCEs will stop at this stage: as Van Rooy (2010: 15) rightly points out, adult learners (here of the IDG group) will be 'able to generalise rules on the basis of less evidence, because their cognitive abilities to notice patterns are more advanced'. Thus, due to their advanced cognitive skills, L2 learners might be able to generalize faster from meso- to more abstract macro-constructions (perhaps even 'too fast' in that they tend to overgeneralize schemas by ignoring exceptions of the L1 system, leading to more regular systems; cf. Szmrecsanyi and Kortmann 2009; Van Rooy 2010: 14; for a state-of-the-art summary of Construction Grammar research on L2 acquisition, cf. Ellis 2013). Nevertheless, despite the fact that L2 learners might arrive more quickly at taxonomic constructional networks with macro-constructions, it does not follow that they do not generalize to a meso-constructional level first. From a Usage-based Construction Grammar perspective, it is therefore not surprising that the **first** structural innovations of PCEs occur at the interface between lexis and grammar (see above), that is at the meso-constructional level even if, in a next step, more abstract macro-constructions might be added more quickly to the constructicon of L2 learners (than would be expected for L1 learners).

This stage is followed by Phase IV ('Endonormative Stabilization'), in which the novel linguistic norms are 'accepted as adequate also in formal usage' (Schneider 2003: 250) and the new variety of English is characterized by great linguistic homogeneity. From a Construction Grammar perspective, this can be interpreted as stabilization of the newly created taxonomic constructional networks via convention across large parts of population. The final stage of the Dynamic Model is Phase V ('Differentiation'), when the variety differentiates into new regional and social dialects. A constructionist interpretation of these developments is that these processes of dialect birth in Post-colonial Englishes involve the functional re-alignment and innovation of constructions as linguistic means of identity (Le Page and Tabouret-Keller 1985). The variation displayed by Phase V varieties can consequently be analysed using the Cognitive Sociolinguistics framework outlined in Section 6.1.1.

The above theoretical claims about the relationship of the Dynamic Model and Construction Grammar have also already received some empirical support: Mukherjee and Gries (2009), for example, tested the interaction of verbs and three types of constructional patterns (ditransitive, transitive and intransitive uses) in three Asian varieties (Phase III: Hong Kong, Phase III–IV: Indian and Phase IV: Singapore English) against British English data. They found that the phase of the varieties correlated positively with the number of innovative uses: the more advanced a variety was in the Dynamic Model, the more different were its uses of verbs in the various complementation patterns from British English. In addition to these distributional differences, Hoffmann (2014, 2019a, 2021) argued that the various phases of the Dynamic Model should correlate with an increasing slot productivity: similar to first language acquisition processes, the first patterns of a construction that are expected to arise are partly substantive, partly schematic meso-constructions during phase III. Focusing on the Comparative Correlative construction (see Section 5.5, e.g., *the more you eat the fatter you'll get*), Hoffmann found that Phase III varieties such as Philippine English rely more on several specific comparative word combinations such as *higher … lower* or *more … more* (Hoffmann 2014: 175). In contrast to this, more advanced varieties such as Jamaican English (Phase IV) only exhibited one significant comparative phrase combination (*more … greater*), and the variability of comparative phrases in the native variety British English was so high that no single combination of words turned out to be statistically significant (Hoffmann 2014: 175–6). The productivity of constructional slots of the Comparative Correlative construction, thus, does indeed seem to correlate with a variety's stage in Schneider's model (with more advanced varieties exhibiting greater slot productivity and relying less on specific, substantive fillers). Recently, a handful of studies have been carried out that seem to support this hypothesis (Brunner and Hoffmann 2020 on the *Way*-construction in Post-colonial Englishes; Laporte 2019 on *Make*-V constructions in Asian varieties of English; see Hoffmann 2021 for more details).

The present section explored how Construction Grammar offers a cognitive theoretical explanation for the evolution of 'New Englishes'. As we will see in the next section, the theory has also been successfully applied to the diachronic change from Old English to Present-day English.

6.2   Diachronic Change

While not all synchronic variation leads to diachronic change, it has been shown that there is no change without previous variation. In Section 6.1.1, we have already discussed several patterns of variation that led to local changes: in New York, for example, rhoticity has steadily been gaining ground in the last fifty years (Mather 2012) and on Martha's Vineyard, the local centring diphthongs have also increased in use (Pope, Meyerhoff and Ladd 2007). Modern sociolinguistics has contributed significantly to our understanding of the social dynamics that turn synchronic variation into change (e.g., that in Western societies of the twentieth century, upper-working and lower-class women often drove change-from-above towards new overt prestige variants, while working class men were often at the forefront of change-from-below towards a local variant with covert prestige; Aitchison 2013: 68–9; Labov 2001). But how does change arise in the first place? What happens in the mind of a single speaker so that existing constructions change, and new constructions arise? These are topics of diachronic Construction Grammar (cf., e.g., Barðdal et al. 2015; Hilpert 2013; Traugott and Trousdale 2013).

Let us go back to the future: in Section 5.2 we looked at two grammatical constructions that are used in Present-day English to express future reference, namely the *Will* Future construction (5.54) and *Going to* Future construction (5.55). As it turns out, neither of these two constructions existed in Old English (c.500–1000). Of the two, the *Going to* Future construction is the younger one. Even in Shakespeare's work (during the so-called Early Modern English period, c. 1500–1700), BE *going to* was used in its literal sense of 'movement in space' and, hence, similar in use to other movement verbs such as BE *journeying to* (examples below from Bybee 2006: 719):

(6.18)   Sir, the Germans desire to have three of your
           horses: the duke himself will be to-morrow at
           court, and they **are going to** meet him.   (Merry Wives of Windsor, IV.3)

(6.19)   Don Alphonso,
              With other gentlemen of good esteem,
              Are journeying to salute the emperor   (Two Gentlemen of Verona, I.3)

In both (6.18) and (6.19), a movement event is expressed (going and journeying) that
was carried out for a particular purpose (in order to meet the duke and to salute the
emperor, respectively). From a Construction Grammar perspective, these constructs
can thus be seen as a combination of a GO/JOURNEY Word construction and a
Purpose construction (a To-Infinitive clause with purpose meaning).

Now, from a Usage-based Construction Grammar perspective, language
'change is change in usage, and the locus of change is the construct, an instance
of use' (Traugott and Trousdale 2013: 2). What that means is that any change
that occurs must first happen during the processing of a construct that was
assembled using existing constructions. Moreover, as Traugott and Trousdale
(2013) point out, the domain-general processes that enable change have to be
distinguished from the actual mechanisms of change. Analogical thinking and
parsing are always available to humans, but do not always lead to change.
Traugott and Trousdale (2013), therefore, coined special terms for when these
processes are actually involved in the creation of new constructions. In these
cases, they speak of 'analogization' if analogical thinking gives rise to a new
construction and of 'reanalysis/neoanalysis' if parsing results in the entrenchment of a new construction. Take the *are going to* construct in (6.18): pragmatically, the Purpose construction 'entails intention of activity at a later time'
(Traugott 2015: 71; Bybee 2006: 719–21) – in other words the future realisation of the event denoted by the verb of this clause (meeting the duke).
Moreover, the movement verb means that the participants are already on their
way to carry out this intention, making it fairly likely that this future event will
actually happen. Thus, the construct in (6.18) has the pragmatic implications of
expressing a future intention. Example (6.20) illustrates the properties of this
construct:

(6.20)   *Going to* + Purpose Clause construct:
          FORM: MORPHOSYNTAX: [... BE$_{\text{PRESENT TENSE1}}$ GOING$_2$ [TO
                       V$_{\text{BASE\_3}}$ ...]$_{\text{PURPOSE CLAUSE}}$]$_4$
          ⇔
          MEANING: SEMANTICS: 'PRESENT$_1$(PRE-PROGRESSIVE[1]
                       (GO-EVENT$_2$)) & PURPOSE: EVENT$_3$'$_4$
                       PRAGMATICS: (FUTURE INTENTION)$_3$

As (6.20) shows, the BE *going* part of the construct still has the GO-movement
meaning and on the MORPHOSYNTAX level is separated from the TO Purpose

---

[1] This is marked as 'pre-progressive' since the Progressive construction itself was also evolving
during this time. We cannot go into details here, but cf. Petré (2017) for a constructional analysis
of the development of this construction.

Clause. As discussed above, the latter has the pragmatic inference of referring to a FUTURE INTENTION.

At one point then, neoanalysis must have taken place and this frequent pragmatic inference of future intention became re-analysed as a semantic property of a new BE *going to* construction. In this construction, the original meaning of movement was gradually lost, as Early Modern English data show:

(6.21)   Duke: Sir Valentine, whither away so fast?
          Val.   Please it your grace, there is a messenger
                  That stays in to bear my letters to my friends,
                  And I **am going to** deliver them.
          (Two Gentlemen of Verona, III.i.51; from Bybee 2006: 720)

As Bybee (2006: 720) points out, in (6.21) the Duke asks Valentine where he is going. The answer, however, does not mention any location. Instead, it just provides the future intention of the speaker, which indicates that this meaning is already becoming semanticized.

Finally, the MEANING pole re-analysed future from a pragmatic implication to a semantic property of the construction and the original movement meaning of GO was gradually lost. These changes also led to a change on the FORM pole (in which $[\ldots \text{BE}_{\text{PRESENT TENSE1}} \text{ GOING}_2 [\text{TO V}_{\text{BASE\_3}} \ldots]_{\text{PURPOSE}}$ is re-analysed as a $[\text{BE}_{\text{PRESENT TENSE2}} \text{ GOING}_2 \text{ TO}_2 \text{ V}_{\text{1BASE}}]$ constituent). This, then, resulted in the Present-day *Going to* Future construction (5.55), repeated here as (6.22)) that licenses constructs such as *It's going to rain.*, which clearly do not entail any motion and only have a purely future meaning.

(6.22)   *Going to* Future construction (final version) :
          FORM: MORPHOSYNTAX: $[\text{BE}_{\text{PRESENT TENSE2}} \text{ GOING}_2 \text{ TO}_2 \text{ V}_{\text{1BASE}}]_3$
          $\Leftrightarrow$
          MEANING: SEMANTICS: 'FUTURE$_2$(STATE(V$_1$))'$_3$

Now, future intention is, of course, a common inference for all types of constructs involving a movement verb plus Purpose construction, such as, for example, (6.19). However, as Bybee (2006) pointed out, in language use GO was by far the most frequent motion verb to appear in such constructs and thus was the prime target for this change. (Besides, GO also denotes the least specific type of movement, which is consequently easier to bleach and be replaced by the new future meaning than verbs that express a more specific type of motion such as *travel* or *journey*).

The second Present-day future construction we discussed in Section 5.2, the *Will* Future construction, emerged slightly earlier than the *Going to* Future construction. In Old English, the verb *willan* still meant 'to want' (i.e., a sense of VOLITION that can still be seen in nominal uses such as *This is my will.*, i.e., 'This is what I want'; Aitchison 2013: 117). Now, if you express that you want something, then you are aiming to get it in the future. So, again a potential pragmatic inference of *will*-constructs in Middle English (*c.*1000–1500) was that of FUTURE INTENTION. (Though note that from experience we know that the likelihood of actually succeeding in getting something is not as high as in the case of the *going to* cases above where participants did not just wish to achieve something but had already physically embarked on a journey to do it. This difference in likelihood is something that we shall return to below.)

In Middle English, we already find constructs that are compatible with the original VOLITION meaning ('I want …') as well as the modern FUTURE meaning ('I will …'):

(6.23)   I wyl nauther grete nor grone.
            'I want/will neither cry nor groan'   (Sir Gawain and the Green Knight,
            14c., from Aitchison 2013: 117)

Constructs such as (6.23) that allow for both the original as well as the new readings are sometimes called a 'bridge context' or 'critical context' (see Traugott and Trousdale 2013: 101). Even if the writer still intended (6.23) to express the original volition meaning, the FUTURE INTENTION reading would at least be present as a pragmatic inference:

(6.24)   *Will*-Volition construct:
            FORM: MOPRHOSYNTAX: $[SBJ_1 \ WILL_{PRESENT \ TENSE2}$
                                       $[V_{BASE\_3} \cdots]_{OBJ}]]_4$

            $\Leftrightarrow$

            MEANING: SEMANTICS: 'PRESENT$_1$(STATE
                                    (WANTING-VOLITION-EVENT$_2$(AGENT$_1$,THEME$_3$)))'$_4$
                         PRAGMATICS: (FUTURE INTENTION)$_3$

As you can see in (6.24), in the VOLITION reading, WILL is still the main verb of the construction and the thing that is desired is expressed as part of its object.

In contrast to this, if the writer was already using (6.23) in the future sense of 'I will …', then the construct has undergone neoanalysis with WILL now expressing the semanticized FUTURE meaning and acting as an auxiliary – which in the end leads to the Present-day *Will* Future construction (5.54), repeated here as (6.25):

(6.25)   *Will* Future construction:
            FORM: MOPRHOSYNTAX: $[WILL_2 \ V_{1BASE}]_3$
            $\Leftrightarrow$
            MEANING: SEMANTICS: 'FUTURE$_2$(STATE(V$_1$))'$_3$

As Traugott and Trousdale (2013) point out, the constructional changes involved in the grammaticalization of a construction are gradual. On the one hand, they involve processes of reduction: both future constructions exhibit (a) phonetic reduction (cf. *It's **gonna** rain. / It'**ll** rain.*), (b) semantic reduction (*It's going to rain.* no longer entails movement in space; *It will rain,* no longer entails volition) as well as (c) grammatical reduction (*going to* and *will* are auxiliary verbs and no longer full lexical verbs in the future constructions). On the other hand, there are signs of extension: after the change is complete, the new grammatical constructions are more productive and are able to collocate with elements that previously were semantically or syntactically impossible (cf. *It's gonna* **rain**. / *It'll* **rain**.; Himmelman 2004 calls this 'host class extension').

In contrast to other approaches to language change, diachronic Construction Grammar thus adopts a usage-based view of language change in which individual tokens of use (constructs) play a major role. Moreover, as Traugott and Trousdale highlight it is not just individual constructions that change, but the entire constructional network (2013: 50–76) that is affected and influences the direction of change. Take the *Going to* and *Will* Future constructions: several other constructions (e.g., Purpose clauses) and their pragmatic implications played a role in their emergence. Besides, the fact that a *Will* Future construction was already emerging when the *Going to* Future construction started to develop also affected the pathway of change. It would, of course, have been possible that in the end English only used one of the two constructions to express futurity. However, since both were emerging at roughly the same time and since they slightly differed in their pragmatic inferences (*going to* entails a much more likely future than *will*), the Principle of No Synonymy (Goldberg 1995: 67–8; Section 3.2.2) led to functional differentiation: as mentioned in Section 5.2, the *Going to* Future construction is used for situations that are very likely to happen in the future, while the *Will* Future construction is used when a speaker is much less certain that an event will actually take place. This shows that the original pragmatic inferences might still be part of the constructional knowledge of the two constructions (Bergs 2010; Hilpert 2008). Moreover, it proves that it is not individual constructions that change, but the network of related constructions.

Finally, note that the terms 'constructional change' and 'constructionalization' have a special meaning in diachronic Construction Grammar (Hilpert 2013; Traugott and Trousdale 2013): constructional change is the broader term that includes all types of changes to a construction, including those that affect only its FORM pole (e.g., that Middle English [nɪçt] turned into Present-day *night* [naɪt] without any change in meaning) or only its MEANING pole (e.g., when, without a change of pronunciation, *cool* started to mean '[a]ttractively shrewd or clever; sophisticated, stylish, classy; fashionable, up to date; sexually attractive' OED s.v. *cool* 8.). Constructionalization, on the other hand, is a term coined by Traugott and Trousdale (2013) when a new construction has emerged as a result of changes to both FORM and MEANING:

> Constructionalization is the creation of form$_{new}$-meaning$_{new}$ (combinations of) signs. It forms new type nodes, which have new syntax or morphology and new coded meaning, in the linguistic network of a population of speakers.   (Traugott and Trousdale 2013: 22)

In the above examples, we would thus speak of the *Going to* Future and the *Will Future* constructions as having constructionalized once we have evidence for new FORM properties (e.g., contraction, host class expansion) as well as new MEANING properties (e.g., the new future reference).

A short introduction to the principles of diachronic Construction Grammar such as the present section can, of course, not provide a full history of the English language. Instead, we have used the future tense constructions to illustrate how such approaches try to account for language change. Note that while there are many major research monographs on constructional approaches to language change (notably, Barðdal et al. 2015; Hilpert 2013; Traugott and Trousdale 2013), a constructionist textbook on the history of English is still missing and desperately needed to provide a fuller picture as to how Construction Grammar can fully explain the diachronic evolution of English from the Old English period to the present-day.

6.3   Summary

In this chapter, we looked at language variation and change. As I tried to show you, Construction Grammar is a framework that can successfully be applied to synchronic variation as well as diachronic change. Moreover, regardless of whether we looked at the social variation of pronunciation in New York, the evolution of Post-colonial Englishes around the world or the diachronic development of future constructions, language in use – the individual constructs encountered by speakers – played a major role. In addition to that, we saw how speakers use and extend their constructional networks drawing on domain-general processes. Finally, we learnt that social and pragmatic contextual constraints need to be part of our constructional representations if we wish to provide a full explanation of variation and change.

Exercises

6.1 What kind of Construction Grammar approach is best suited to explain sociolinguistic variation?

6.2 In Section 6.1.2, we saw that Jamaican Creole marks tense and aspect:
   (i)   Mi a ron.   'I am running.'
   (ii)   Mi ben ron.   'I had run.'
   (iii) Mi ben a ron.   'I was running.'
   Provide a constructional template for the Jamaican Creole Progressive construction.

6.3 Explain how the diachronic evolution of the *Going-to* Future and the *Will* Future construction explain their synchronic differences.

6.4 How does 'constructionalization' differ from 'constructional change'?

7 Constructional Approaches and Formalisms

As mentioned in Chapter 1, all Construction Grammar approaches consider constructions, that is form-meaning pairings, to be the central units of language. On top of that, virtually all approaches subscribe to Goldberg's (2013) four tenets of (i) the lexicon-syntax continuum, (ii) the taxonomic network of organization of the constructicon, (iii) surface structure-orientation and (iv) cross-linguistic variability and generalization. Nevertheless, the various Construction Grammar approaches also differ on a couple of crucial points that result in a wide range of representational formats. In this chapter, I will outline the major differences between non-usage-based (such as Berkeley Construction Grammar and Sign-Based Construction Grammar) and usage-based approaches (Parallel Architecture, Cognitive Construction Grammar, Embodied Construction Grammar, Fluid Construction Grammar and Radical Construction Grammar). Finally, the chapter will also address the question as to how the meaning pole of constructions is analysed in the various approaches – which ranges from semantic paraphrases (Cognitive Construction Grammar) over first-order predicate logic (Fluid Construction Grammar) to Frame-based approaches (Sign-Based Construction Grammar).

7.1   Construction Grammars

Despite the common core of assumptions outlined in Chapter 1, the various major constructionist approaches that have been developed over the past thirty years differ significantly with respect to their view on several non-trivial issues. It is these differences that explain why currently some people speak of Construction Grammars and not a single Construction Grammar theory. Currently, the major Construction Grammar approaches are the following:

- **Berkeley Construction Grammar** (BCG; Fillmore 1985, 1988; Fillmore, Kay and O'Connor 1988; Michaelis 1994; Michaelis and Lambrecht 1996);
- **Sign-Based Construction Grammar** (SBCG; Boas and Sag 2012; Michaelis 2010, 2013);
- **Parallel Architecture** model (PA; Booij 2013; Jackendoff 2002, 2013);
- **Fluid Construction Grammar** (FCG; Steels 2011, 2013; Van Trijp 2014);

- **Embodied Construction Grammar** (ECG; Bergen and Chang 2005, 2013);
- **Cognitive Construction Grammar** (CCG; Boas 2013; Goldberg 1995, 2006, 2019; Lakoff 1987);
- **Radical Construction Grammar** (RCG; Croft 2001, 2012, 2013).

These various approaches differ and agree with each other in a way that can best described by seeing Construction Grammar as a prototypical category with all of these approaches as exemplars that exhibit family resemblance effects. The main issues that distinguish these approaches from each other (or in some cases unite them) are (see also Croft and Cruse 2004: 265–90; Goldberg 2006: 213–26):

- **Constructional storage**: does a theory adopt a complete inheritance or usage-based position?
- **Formalization**: is the theory fully formalized or not?
- **Processing**: does the theory explicitly try to account for language production and processing?
- **Constructional types**: are all constructions necessarily seen as form-meaning pairings or are defective constructions (with form but without meaning and vice versa) also postulated?
- **Theory of meaning**: is the meaning pole of constructions represented in terms of truth-conditional, model theoretic terms or in a way that is compatible with cognitive semantic approaches such as, for example, embodiment simulation or frame semantics?

Arguably the most important issue is the first one: some researchers still defend the competence-based complete inheritance approach, which only postulates something as a construction if it has some idiosyncratic pairing of morphological, syntactic, lexical, semantic, pragmatic or discourse-functional properties. Kay, for example, argues that only those linguistic phenomena should be considered as constructions that a speaker needs to know to 'produce and understand all possible utterances of a language *and no more*' (2013: 32). In stark contrast to this, and in line with virtually all of the findings from the empirical studies on first and second language acquisition as well as psycho- and neurolinguistic evidence, Bybee (2006, 2010, 2013) advocates a usage-based Construction Grammar approach (see also Chapter 2). As she points out, the mental grammar of speakers is shaped by the repeated exposure to specific utterances and in which domain-general cognitive processes such as categorization and cross-modal association play a crucial role in the entrenchment of constructions. Consequently, specific phonological linguistic usage-events (exemplars) are stored together with rich semantic and pragmatic information first and any generalization is the result of an emergent, bottom-up categorization and generalization process.

The second issue concerns the question of formalization: some researchers aim to make all of their assumptions and postulated units formally explicit in order to allow for 'more precise empirical prediction, enhanced comparability of analyses across languages, and theoretical clarity' (Sag, Boas and Kay 2012: 3). In contrast to this, other Construction Grammarians argue that 'grammatical categories and roles are not general across constructions but are only defined with respect to particular constructions' (Goldberg 2006: 216), which precludes the use of construction-independent, general formalizations.

The remaining issues are: third, whether a Construction Grammar theory is explicitly designed to model language production as well as processing or whether it is developed as a processing-neutral model of linguistic knowledge. Fourth, whether cognitive generalization can also lead to defective constructions with only a form or meaning pole. Finally, the approaches differ greatly as to their semantic model adopted for the meaning pole.

A detailed introduction to the various Construction Grammar approaches is obviously beyond the scope of the present textbook (they would each require a textbook of their own). Hoffmann and Trousdale (2013), however, is still a good starting point if you want to explore any of the approaches in more detail. In the following, I will instead contrast the various Construction Grammars and focus particularly on the five central issues of controversy mentioned above. Moreover, using the Caused Motion construction (5.17; repeated below as 7.1), I will illustrate how our constructional template translates into the constructional representations employed by the various approaches:

(7.1)   Caused Motion construction
          FORM: PHONOLOGY: /A_1 B_2 C_2 $D_{3/4}$
                       MORPHOSYNTAX: $[SBJ_1\ [V_2\ OBJ_2\ OBL_3]_{VP}]_4$

          $\Leftrightarrow$

          MEANING: SEMANTICS:
                       'CAUSE(EVENT$_2$(AGENT$_1$),
                       MOVE(THEME=FIGURE$_3$,
                          GOAL=GROUND$_{4\_PATH/LOCATION}$))'$_4$

7.2   Complete Inheritance Approaches: BCG and SBC

Berkeley Construction Grammar (BCG) and Sign-Based Construction Grammar (SBCG) are the only constructionist approaches that currently still advocate a complete inheritance approach. Historically, BCG[1] is the oldest Construction Grammar with first publications of this framework surfacing in the late 1980s to early to mid-1990s (Fillmore 1985, 1988; Fillmore, Kay and O'Connor 1988; Michaelis 1994; Michaelis and Lambrecht 1996). The main initial motivation behind BCG was the goal to develop a grammatical framework that would analyse core as well as peripheral

[1] Originally, publications with the framework only referred to it as Construction Grammar. The attribute 'Berkeley' was added only recently to distinguish it from other constructionist approaches (Fillmore 2013; Sag, Boas and Kay 2012: 2).

grammatical patterns by the same mechanisms (Fillmore 2013). BCG is a formalized theory that uses 'boxes within boxes' representation and feature structures that are also known as attribute-value-matrixes (AVM). As indicated by their name, AVMs have attributes (e.g., 'cat' for CATEGORY) that can have various values (e.g., n(oun), v(erb), p(reposition), etc.). In BCG, for example, the AVM of a noun like *dog* has the feature structure [cat <n>], while a verb like *give* has the feature structure [cat <v>]. However, the formalism used to combine constructions in BCG (set unification) turned out to be computationally problematic (for details see Müller 2006: 863–6, 2019: 324–7; Sag, Boas and Kay 2012: 6). This was one of the reasons why Paul Kay later started to collaborate with Ivan Sag, Hans Boas and Laura A. Michaelis on an approach called Sign-Based Construction Grammar (SBCG). SBCG is also a formalized Construction Grammar theory that evolved out of ideas from BCG and construction-based Head-Driven Phrase-Structure Grammar (HPSG) (Ginzburg and Sag 2000; Pollard and Sag 1994; cf. Kim and Michaelis 2020; Michaelis 2013). Like BCG and HPSG, SBCG employs feature structures to model linguistic phenomena. Some parts of SBCG AVMs even look a bit similar to the ones used in BCG (*dog*, e.g., has the feature structure [CAT *noun*], and *give* the feature structure [CAT *verb*] in SBCG). However, unlike BCG, but similar to HPSG, the feature structures of SBCG are typed, that is, arranged in a hierarchical inheritance classification taxonomy (Carpenter 1992; see also Chapter 1). BCG and SBCG are processing-neutral approaches that make no predictions about the actual online parsing or production of constructions. Moreover, unlike usage-based approaches, both frameworks draw on meaningless phrasal constructions to license sentences and thus postulate the existence defective constructions. A case in point is subject–verb agreement in English (Section 3.2.1) as exhibited in $He_{3PS.SG}$ $loves_{3PS.SG}$ *you* vs $They_{3PS.PL}$ $love_{3PS.PL}$ *you*. In SBCG, this would be modelled by a purely syntactic constraint that has no associated meaning pole and would, for example, simply specify that the finite verb has to be marked as [AGR 3sing] '3rd person singular' if its subject argument also has the feature [AGR 3sing] (Sag, Wasow and Bender 2003: 107).

Turning to the meaning pole of constructions, early BCG work was already influenced by insights from Frame Semantics (Petruck 1996) and later by its technological implementation in the FrameNet database http://framenet.icsi .berkeley.edu/ (cf., e.g., Boas 2006, 2009; Fillmore, Johnson and Petruck 2003). Early HPSG Construction Grammar (Ginzburg and Sag 2000) and SBCG (Sag 2010) represented the meaning of constructions by model theoretic, truth-conditional semantic theories (such as Situation Semantics or Montague Possible Worlds Semantics). Recent SBCG approaches, however, also implemented Frame Semantics as their semantic model (Fillmore, Lee-Goldman and Rhodes 2012; Sag 2012: 87–8).

Now, let us look at how these two approaches model the Caused Motion construction (7.1). Since BCG has essentially been superseded by SBCG, in the following I will only use AVMs from the latter approach. The main theoretical points of the analysis are, however, not affected by this, since both approaches essentially offer a similar analysis: both BCG and SBCG adopt a lexicalist approach (see Section 5.1.3). Consequently, they postulate a derivational construction that includes a lexical verb construction as their input daughter ('DTR') node and link it to an output mother ('MTR') node with the appropriate argument structure (Figure 7.1):

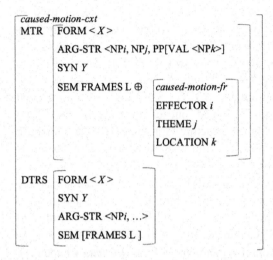

Figure 7.1 *SBCG representation of Caused Motion construction (adapted from Michaelis 2013: 149)*

At first glance, Figure 7.1 might look completely different to our representation of the Caused Motion construction (7.1). Once you take a closer look, however, you should be able to see that both templates encode the same information – only in slightly different ways. First look at the MTR node: its SEMantic pole includes the CAUSED_MOTION_FRAME with the roles EFFECTOR, THEME and LOCATION. These correspond to the semantic roles AGENT, THEME=FIGURE and GOAL=GROUND in (7.1), respectively. Also, these semantic roles carry indexes (SBCG uses lower case letters such as i, j and k) that are expressed by subscript numbers (1, 2 and 3) in (7.1). The MORPHOSYNTAX level of (7.1) is thus partly represented by the ARGUMENT-STRUCTURE (ARG-STR) feature in SBCG (see also Section 4.1 for details on the ARG-STR feature). As the indexes show, the first NPi, in the ARG-STR of the MTR is linked to the EFFECTORi role, while NPj is linked to the THEMEj and the NPk complement of the PP to the LOCATIONk. Let me illustrate this with an example. The construct *She sneezed the napkin off the table.* would consequently receive the following interpretation:

(7.2)   She$i$ sneezed   [the napkin$j$]   [off [the table$k$]].
           EFFECTORi THEMEj LOCATIONk

A major difference between Figure 7.1 and (7.1) concerns the syntactic FORM pole: the construction in (7.1) is an active phrasal construction (and, therefore, has functional labels for its schematic slots such as SBJ, OBJ or OBL). The MTR construction in Figure 7.1 is a lexical construction that still needs to be combined with active or passive constructions (and therefore only has labels such as NP*i* or NP*j* in its syntactic slots). In Section 5.1.3, we already discussed the differences between lexical and phrasal constructions and the different implications they have for the architecture of our grammar. For the interpretation of constructional templates such as Figure 7.1, it is only important that you remember that the DTRS feature encodes the input and the MTR node the output of this construction. Take, for example, an intransitive verb such as *sneeze*: if this is put into the DTRS structure in Figure 7.1, then the construction will copy its semantic Frame Sneezing (encoded by the variable 'L') and copy it to the output construction (as you can see the 'L' is still part of the SEM pole of the MTR). What the MTR part adds (indicated by the append symbol '$\oplus$') is simply the desired caused motion meaning. So, the event of the output is still a sneezing event, but one that has a caused motion meaning. Besides, the valency of the output construction has been extended by an NP*j* and a PP. In essence, the constructional template has created a new lexical *sneeze* construction that has the required syntactic and semantic information to license (7.2).

7.3   Models of Human Language Processing: PA, FCG and ECG

In contrast to BCG and SBCG, all other Construction Grammar approaches subscribe to a usage-based view. Out of these, Parallel Architecture (PA; Jackendoff 2002, 2013), Fluid Construction Grammar (FCG; Steels 2011, 2013) and Embodied Construction Grammar (ECG; Bergen and Chang 2005, 2013) are all explicitly designed to model language processing and production. On top of that, all three are formalized syntactic approaches (though only FCG and ECG use feature structures, while PA uses subscripts to link atomic constructional elements across the various constructional poles). Besides, in PA, phonology, syntax and semantics are described as independent generative components within a speaker's mental grammar. Constructional units (i.e., pairings of phonological, (morpho)syntactic, and semantic structures), which are called 'lexical items' in PA, then function as small-scale interface rules between the three generative components. In addition to normal form-meaning pairings, PA also postulates defective constructions, for example, abstract syntactic principles without meaning (such as the VP-construction [$_{VP}$V NP]) or semantic principles without syntactic form, such as *reference transfer* in *I have read Shakespeare* (Shakespeare = 'books/plays by the author Shakespeare'). Another example of such a defective construction is the PA Subject–Verb Agreement construction (7.3), which has no meaning pole but simply links the first grammatical function GF (i.e., the subject) with the tense-carrying verbal element (T) and via coindexation of subject and agr(eement) suffix ensures feature concord:

(7.3)   Subject–verb agreement in PA
          $[GF_i(> \dots)]_k \Leftrightarrow [_s \dots T + agr_i \dots]_k$
          (Culicover and Jackendoff 2005: 192)

Concerning the representation of the meaning pole of constructions, PA employs Jackendoff's Conceptual Semantics (2002: 267–421), a mentalistic, decompositional conceptual theory (that as we will see, uses similar features to the ones employed in our approach).

As (7.4) shows, the representation of the Caused Motion construction in PA is fairly similar to our template (7.1):

(7.4)   The PA Caused Motion construction
          Syntax: NP_1 V NP_2 PP_3
          Semantics: X_1 CAUSE [Y_2 GO $Path_3$]
          MEANS: [VERBAL SUBEVENT]
          (Jackendoff 2010: 290)

Like (7.1), (7.4) is a phrasal construction that uses subscript numbers to identify links across the FORM-MEANING poles. Like SBCG, however, (7.4) uses phrasal labels (NP_1, NP_2, PP_3) for the syntactic slots, instead of functional ones. The Semantics pole, on the other hand, can be seen as straightforward paraphrase of (7.1), since both approaches use semantic primitives such as CAUSE. *She sneezed the napkin off the table* would thus be analysed as in (7.5):

(7.5) She_1 sneezed [the napkin]$_2$ [off the table]$_3$
          Syntax: NP_1 V NP_2 PP_3
          Semantics: she_1 CAUSE [the-napkin$_2$ GO off-the-table$_3$]
          MEANS: [SNEEZING]

Next, FCG is a computational formalism that developed out of research into artificial intelligence and language evolution, which makes no claims about psychological validity (Steels 2011: 3). In contrast to this, ECG is explicitly designed as a computationally model of the cognitive and neural mechanisms that underlie human linguistic behaviour and draws on insights from cognitive linguistic research (Bergen and Chang 2005, 2013). These differences in objectives are also reflected in the semantic theory adopted by the two approaches: while FCG standardly employs truth-conditional first order predicate calculus,[2] ECG relies on cognitive models of mental simulation and embodied schemas. Moreover, while FCG allows for defective constructions, constructions in ECG are always form-meaning pairings (though purely form or meaning schemas are nevertheless considered to exist).

Subject–verb agreement in FCG, for example, can be captured by a purely formal constraint that requires matching number and person features of the subject NP (number?n) (person?p) and the verb (number?n) (person?p). Here

---

[2] Yet, since FCG is more of an approach than a dogmatic theory, it is not surprising that some FCG implementations also use, for example, Frame Semantics or other semantic theories (cf. Steels 2011: 79).

'number' and 'person' are attributes and '?n' and '?p' are values that are instantiated by variables. Token identity, the identical variable ?x on two elements,
ensures that these must be identical (see Steels and de Beule 2006: 220). In ECG,
subject–verb agreement would not be modelled by a defective construction.
Instead, argument structure constructions such as the Transitive or the
Intransitive construction would have an additional constraint that ensures
subject–verb agreement (e.g., 'verb.person ↔ agent.person' or 'verb.person ↔
theme.person'). (Since the FCG formalism is flexible, however, individual
researchers can also write FCG grammars www.fcg-net.org that would avoid
defective constructions and only include form-meaning pairings.)

Again, let me now illustrate the different approaches using the Caused Motion
construction. FCG uses LISP syntax to encode AVM, which means that when
reading FCG analyses, you need to keep in mind that the values of attributes are
put in parentheses; that is, 'attribute (value)' (in fact, parentheses play an
important role in organizing AVMs). Moreover, instead of index numbers as in
(7.1), variables are used to identify elements across different levels. All these
variables are preceded by a question mark ('?n', '?p', etc.; see above). Finally,
the FORM and MEANING pole are linked via a bidirectional arrow '<->'. Note
that in the following, the top part of the construction provides the MEANING
pole, while the lower half gives the FORM pole:

(7.6)   FCG Caused Motion construction (simplified from the Appendix[3] to van
           Trijp 2014)
           (def-construction caused-motion-cxn (:label cxn)
           . . .

           . . .

                   (meaning (== (caused-motion ?ev)
                       (causer ?ev ?x)
                       (transferrable-entity ?ev ?y)
                       (location ?ev ?z))

           . . .

               (?subject (args (?x)) (. . . (sem-role actor)))
               (?object (args (?y)) (. . . (sem-role undergoer)))
               (?oblique (args (?z)) (. . . (sem-role location[4])))
               ((J ?verb-phrase) . . .
               ((J ?caused-motion-clause)
                   ?the-meaning
                   (sem-subunits (?subject ?verb-phrase ?object ?oblique))
                   (sem-cat ((sem-function proposition)))))
           <->
           . . .

---

[3] Source: www.degruyter.com/supplemental/journals/cogl/26/4/article-p613.xml/cog-2014-0074ad
    .zip [last accessed 19 November 2020].
[4] Van Trijp 2014 labels this 'theme', but for the purpose of exposition it has been re-labelled
    'location'.

```
(?subject
    (syn-cat (==1 (phrase-type NP)
             (syn-role subject)))))
(?object
    (syn-cat (==1 (phrase-type NP)
             (syn-role object)))))
(?oblique
    (syn-cat (==1 (phrase-type PrepP)
             (syn-role locative)))))
((J ?verb-phrase) . . .
((J ?caused-motion-clause)
    (syn-subunits (?subject ?verb-phrase ?object ?oblique))
    (syn-cat ((clause-type caused-motion))))))
```

Again, at first glance the template in (7.6) can be overwhelming. But do not despair – remember all that it does is give a very detailed AVM of the FORM and MEANING pole of the construction. Now, start at the top with the MEANING pole: '(caused-motion ?ev)' just signals that this is a caused motion ev(ent). The causer of this event is identified by the variable ?x '(causer ?ev ?x)', ?y is the entity that is moved '(transferrable-entity ?ev ?y)' and ?z marks the path '(location ?ev ?z)'. In the next couple of lines, ?x, ?y and ?z are then identified as the semantic ?subject, ?object and ?oblique. If you then jump to the FORM part (below the <–>), the you can see that syntactically these semantic roles correspond to the syntactic roles ?subject, ?object and ?oblique and are realized by NP, NP and PrepP, respectively. As these pieces of information show, the template is a phrasal construction. Finally, the penultimate line 'syn-subunits (?subject ?verb-phrase ?object ? oblique)' specifies the same order of syntactic elements as does (7.1).

ECG also draws on AVMs to model constructions but uses a format that looks slightly different. Example (7.7) gives the ECG version of the Caused Motion construction:

(7.7)   ECG Caused Motion construction (adapted from Dodge and Petruck 2014: 43)[5]
          construction ActiveTransitveCausedMotion
          subcase of ActiveTransitive

              . . .

          constituents
          np1: NP
          v: Verb
          np2: NP
          pp: Path-PP

---

[5] For the sake of exposition, I have adapted the template in the following way: the subject NP has been added to this construction (similar to the format of argument structure constructions in Bergen and Chang 2005, 2013). Dodge and Petruck (2014) seem to postulate an independent construction that licenses the subject in these cases. Moreover, I have modelled the meaning pole on the format used by Bergen and Chang (2005, 2013). The precise details of the ECG analysis are, however, well beyond the scope of the present book.

form
    constraints
            np1.f **before** v.f
            v.f **before** np2.f
            np2.f **before** pp.f
    meaning: CausedMotion
        . . .
            CausedMotion.agent <−> np1.m
            CausedMotion.theme <−> np2.m
            CausedMotion.path <−> pp.m
  . . .

Attributes in ECG are highlighted by boldface. The first line tells us that the construction is labelled as 'ActiveTransitveCausedMotion' (since a different phrasal template is postulated for active and passive sentences; see also Section 5.1.3), which is a subcase of the more general ActiveTransitive construction. Example (7.7) is a phrasal construction, which like (7.1) has a **form** and **meaning** pole. Instead of using subscript indexes or variables, relationships between these two poles are expressed in ECG by naming the elements first: under **constituents**, (7.7) declares that the construction has three elements a Verb, an NP and a Path-PP, which will from then on be referred to as 'v', 'n' and 'pp', respectively (so 'v: Verb' can be translated as 'in the following "v" is used to talk about the properties of the Verb'). If you only want to provide information on the meaning or form level of an element you add the suffix '.m' or '.f', respectively. So 'np1.f' stands for form pole of the first NP and 'np1.m' for its meaning pole. Under **form**, the **constraints** attribute specifies the linear order of the phrasal constituents of the construction. The **before** relation is used to encode linear precedence (**meets** is used when two elements have to be directly adjacent; Bergen and Chang 2005: 156). So 'np1.f **before** v.f' means that the form pole of NP1 precedes the form pole of the verb (the following two constraints encode the order we also have in (7.1), with the verb preceding the second NP and the latter appearing before the path PP). As mentioned above, ECG is a cognitive theory that claims that mental meaning crucially involves mental simulation and embodied schemas. Consequently, the term 'CausedMotion' on the **meaning** pole of (7.7) is not an abstract semantic feature. Instead, it links to a cognitive schema that speakers have generalized over all the actual instances of caused motion that they have seen and experienced. The Caused Motion schema, therefore, for example, includes the information that it is a FORCE-DYNAMIC event (see Section 4.2.3) in which the agent is the source of energy, the theme is the target and as a result of which the latter is being moved along a path towards a goal (see Bergen and Chang 2005: 166 for a formalization of this schema). Now, (7.7) does not only reference the Caused Motion schema, it also details how the roles of the Caused Motion construction map onto meaning parts of this embodied schema: double arrows '<−>' in ECG express identification constraints (Bergen and Chang 2005: 152), so 'CausedMotion.agent <-> np1. m' means that the meaning pole of NP1 (np1.m) is identified with the agent of the CausedMotion schema. Similarly, 'CausedMotion.theme <-> np2.m' states that the meaning of NP2 is that of theme of the Caused Motion schema, while the PP is interpreted as the path ('CausedMotion.path <-> pp.m').

7.4   Non-Formalized Usage-Based Approaches: CCG and RCG

The remaining two approaches, Cognitive Construction Grammar (CCG; Boas 2013; Goldberg 1995, 2006; Lakoff 1987) and Radical Construction Grammar (RCG; Croft 2001, 2012, 2013) are both usage-based approaches that are not intended to directly model language production and processing and that eschew formalization (since grammatical categories and roles are considered to elude simple cross-constructional generalizations). Both CCG and RCG are influenced by previous research into Cognitive Grammar (CG; inter alia, Broccias 2013; Langacker 1987, 2000, 2008, 2009). Following CG, and like ECG, CCG and RCG take language to be grounded in embodied human experience and language-independent cognitive processes such as association, automatization, schematization and categorization. One major difference, however, is that CG sees constructions as pairings of a semantic pole with a phonological one, whereas CCG and RCG also postulate (morpho-)syntactic information in their form pole. Neither CCG nor RCG allow for defective constructions (nor does CG). Consequently, subject–verb agreement in these approaches is modelled similarly to ECG; that is, as a constraint/construction that is a subpart in the various relevant constructions (such as the Intransitive construction (INTRSBJ INTRV) or the Transitive construction (TRSBJ TRV TROBJ); cf. Croft 2013: 220; Croft and Cruse 2004: 288). With respect to the semantic model underlying their meaning pole, both CCG and RCG draw on cognitive theories (such as Frame Semantics) and take meaning to be the result of cognitive construal and not truth-conditional constraints (though see below for differences concerning the prominence of verbal semantics). CCG and RCG are therefore closely related to each other and are also the most widely used Construction Grammar frameworks. This is particularly true for usage-based studies that adopt a corpus-based approach. In theory, results from corpus studies; that is, the analysis of the documented authentic use, type and token frequency of constructions, are highly relevant for any usage-based approach. Take, for example, collostructional analyses (for an overview; cf. Stefanowitsch 2013; also Section 5.1.2), the family of quantitative corpus-linguistics methods that aim to statistically identify significant associations of word constructions and phrasal/clausal constructions or significant co-occurrence patterns of two slots in a construction. Virtually all major publications using these methods are framed in a CCG/RCG framework (inter alia, Colleman 2009a, 2009b; Gilquin 2006; Gries and Stefanowitsch 2004a, 2004b, 2010; Hilpert 2008; Mukherjee and Gries 2009; Schönefeld 2006; Stefanowitsch 2006; Stefanowitsch and Gries 2003, 2005, 2008; Wulff et al. 2009). Still, important differences between CCG and RCG can nevertheless be found: while CCG has a stronger focus on trying to capture and motivate language-specific generalizations (Goldberg 2006: 226), RCG, due to its strong typological background, is reductionist: it emphasizes that all grammatical categories are language-specific and construction-specific and consequently assumes no formal syntactic structure other than the part–whole structure of constructions and the grammatical roles that occur in constructions. Moreover, RCG advocates an exemplar semantics model of the syntax–semantics mapping in which specific situation types are organized in a multidimensional conceptual space. Formal construction types are then said to have a frequency distribution over that conceptual space.

The format of our representation (7.1) is heavily influenced by CCG, so the CCG constructional template of the Caused Motion construction should not be too difficult for you to interpret. Since the representation of Arguments Structure constructions in CCG has changed considerably over the years, however, I will present the initial template (7.8) as well as the most recent version (7.10):

(7.8)   Initial CCG Caused Motion construction. (Adapted from Goldberg 1995: 52)

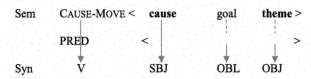

The construction in (7.8) shows that, originally, CCG like (7.1) employed semantic roles such as 'cause', 'goal' and 'theme' as well as semantic primitives like 'CAUSE-MOVE'. These Sem(antic) properties were then linked to Syn(actic) ones (the same functional slots we have in (7.1), with the only difference that (7.8) does not specify linear order). In Section 5.1.2, we already saw that CCG distinguishes SBJ and OBJ slots (which are considered to encode 'profiled' argument roles) from other syntactic slots such as OBL (which are said to host 'non-profiled argument roles'). On the semantic pole, profiled arguments are furthermore highlighted by boldface. The PRED slot together with the empty list < > is reserved for the semantic frame of the verb that merges with the argument structure construction. Example (7.9) illustrates this for *sneeze*:

(7.9)   Initial CCG Caused Motion construction with SNEEZE (adapted from Goldberg 1995: 54)

Sneeze is an intransitive verb and only contributes the semantic role 'sneezer' to *She sneezed the napkin off the table*. All other slots and roles are added by the construction (7.8).

Recently, Goldberg has significantly simplified the constructional template for argument structure constructions:

(7.10)   Current CCG Caused Motion construction
                (adapted from Goldberg 2019: 34)
                Form: Subj, V, Obj, Oblique$_{path}$
                Meaning: X causes Y to move (to/from) Z

The construction in (7.10) dispenses with the PRED level and the Meaning pole no longer draws on semantic primitives, but is only given as a semantic paraphrase, instead. The Form pole is similar to our description in (7.1), but the comma notation is supposed to indicate that the construction imposes no linear order of the various syntactic slots. This allows the template to cover active transitive declarative constructs (*She*$_{X=Subj}$ *sneezed* [*the napkin*]$_{Y=Obj}$ [*off the table*]$_{Z=Oblique\_path}$) as well as, for example, relative clauses (*the napkin which*$_{Y=Obj}$ *she*$_{X=Subj}$ *sneezed* [*off the table*]$_{Z=Oblique\_path}$). It cannot, however, explain other valency patterns such as passive sentences ([*the napkin*]$_{Y=Subj}$ *was sneezed* [*off the table*]$_{Z=Oblique\_path}$; see Section 5.1.3).

In Section 5.1.2, we discussed Croft's criticism of Goldberg's approach. As you will remember, he noted that in many instances completely schematic argument structure constructions overgeneralize. In contrast to this, his RCG approach advocates a more fine-grained constructional network that includes Verb-Class-Specific as well as Verb-Specific meso-constructions. In RCG, these meso-constructions are considered to 'represent a force-dynamic (in the broad sense) construal of an event' and 'a verb in a particular tense-aspect construction represents an aspectual construal of an event' (Croft 2012: 392). Recently, he started to advocate the following geometric representation of constructions that combines information on the involved semantic frames, the causal force-dynamic chain as well as temporal and aspectual properties of Verb-Specific meso-constructions. Figure 7.2 illustrates this for the past tense Verb-Specific-*wiped*-construction:

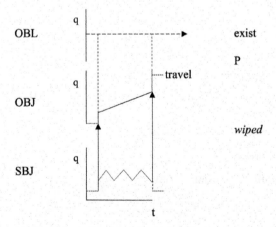

Figure 7.2 *RCG representation of past tense wiped in Caused Motion construction (adapted from Croft 2012: 338–9)*

First of all, note that in geometric representations such as Figure 7.2 all dashed lines represent backgrounded information, so only the solid lines are supposed to convey information that is activated or foregrounded by a construction. Now, as expected, Figure 7.2 has syntactic slots for subject (SBJ), object (OBJ) and the oblique (OBL) argument. Each of these elements has an individual graph that shows how it is affected over time ('t' = x-axis) and whether it experiences any qualitative changes ('q' = y-axis). First, look at the graph for the SBJ slot. Over time you see a zigzag line that is supposed to represent an activity of a participant that goes on for a certain amount of time, but after which the participant has not changed. This makes sense since the subject in *She wiped the polish onto the table.* is not affected by the event (and thus ends at the same qualitative level as before the action). The object on the other hand, here *the polish*, is in a different state after the event (it moved onto the table), which is why in its graph segment there is a straight line going up (which indicates that the OBJ is in a different qualitative state after the event). Moreover, as we signalled by the features 'CAUSE(EVENT$_2$(AGENT$_1$), MOVE(THEME=FIGURE$_3$ ...)' in our template of (7.1), the SBJ is the agent causing this movement of the OBJ. In Figure 7.2, this is expressed by vertical, directed arrows from the SBJ graph to the OBJ graph. These vertical arrows express the causal FORCE-DYNAMIC construal of the SBJ action affecting the qualitative state of the OBJ. The P slot then is for the preposition that will specify the direction of movement of the OBJ (e.g., *to* or *off the table*). Finally, the OBL slot is backgrounded (hence the dashed lines) and only has a straight line, since in the Caused Motion construal it is not seen as qualitatively affected by the action (in contrast to the Causative *with* construction in *She wiped the table with polish.*, see Section 5.1.1).

The RCG representation showcased in Figure 7.2 probably offers the most comprehensive constructional analysis of the interaction of verb meaning, argument structure and tense/aspect. Yet, so far, it does not seem to have been adopted widely. In fact, most CCG and RCG publications only offer a shorthand notation of constructions of the type used by Traugott and Trousdale (2013: 8): they directly link FORM and MEANING using a bidirectional arrow: [[F]↔[M]]. Along these lines, the Caused Motion construction would be rendered as [[SBJ$_1$ [V$_2$ OBJ$_3$ OBL$_4$]$_{VP}$]$_5$ ↔ 'agent$_1$ causes theme$_3$ to move along path$_4$ by doing V$_5$'].

7.5   Summary of Construction Grammar Approaches

This concludes our short introduction to the various Construction Grammars. Table 7.1 summarizes the properties of the seven Construction Grammar approaches presented above:

As Table 7.1 shows, Construction Grammar approaches still disagree on important theoretical and empirical points. It will therefore be interesting to see whether the various approaches will converge on these issues in the next couple of years or not. Still, from a cognitive linguistic point of view, a clear positive

Table 7.1. *Summary of properties of Construction Grammars*

Property	BCG	SBCG	PA	FCG	ECG	CCG	RCG
Constructional storage	complete inheritance	complete inheritance	usage-based	usage-based	usage-based	usage-based	usage-based
Formalization	yes	yes	yes	yes	yes	no	no
Processing-oriented	no	no	yes	yes	yes	no	no
Defective constructions	yes	yes	yes	yes	no	no	no
Theory of meaning	Frame Semantics	Frame Semantics	Conceptual Semantics	Model Theoretic	Embodied Simulation	Frame Semantics	Frame Semantics

trend towards more cognitively-oriented approaches to the meaning pole of constructions can already be observed – something that should be highlighted more explicitly by future constructionist research and which I tried to account for by the constructional representation format chosen for the present project.

Construction Grammars are a family of cognitive linguistic approaches that provide a psychologically plausible theory of human language. Over the past thirty years, the notion of constructions as cognitive pairings of form-meaning has spawned a large body of research. Construction Grammars offer a cognitive syntactic framework that has successfully provided an explanatory account of first as well as second language acquisition and has received support from psycho- as well as neuro-linguistic studies. Considering their empirical success, it is somewhat surprising that so far only a handful of authoritative summaries of Construction Grammars exist. There are numerous research articles, monographs and edited volumes and even two journals specifically dedicated to construction-ist research (*Constructions and Frames* and the open access online journal *Constructions* www.constructions-journal.com). Yet, so far only one handbook (Hoffmann and Trousdale 2013b) and two textbooks have been published (Hilpert 2019; Ziem and Lasch 2013, both mostly focusing on CCG/RCG approaches). The major reason for this is that so far one cannot identify one single Construction Grammar theory. As the present chapter has shown, despite important shared theoretical commitments, the various constructionist approaches still differ with respect to important empirical and theoretical points. Moreover, the notational systems vary greatly, which is why the present book has tried to equip you with a notational system that allows you to read and understand constructional templates from all these different approaches.

It will be interesting to see whether the various approaches converge on certain assumptions within the next couple of years (concerning, for example, the lexical vs phrasal construction controversy or the question of defective constructions; see also Section 8.4). Despite these controversies, however, it is important to point out again the empirical descriptive and explanatory success that Construction Grammars have already had as cognitive theories of language and that future constructionist research will undoubtedly contribute to a deeper understanding of human language and the mind.

Exercises

7.1 What are the main parameters along which the various Construction Grammar approaches differ?

7.2 Which constructionist approach do you think is best suited for language variation and change? Which constructionist approach do you think is best suited for language processing?

8 Outlook: Emerging Research Topics in Construction Grammar

In this book, we have explored the view that there is ample empirical evidence to suggest that the full range of mental grammatical knowledge, from morphemes to abstract syntactic patterns, can best be described as constructions. We have seen that Construction Grammar can explain how children acquire English and that it provides a cognitively plausible account of the synchronic variation of Englishes across the globe as well as the diachronic changes that affected the English language over the centuries. In this final chapter, I will show you how we can bring together everything that we have learnt so far to analyse authentic constructs. As you know, outside of textbooks, constructs are often going to be fairly complex and will involve the activation a multitude of constructions. I will, therefore, introduce you to a representation system (Constructional Approach to Syntactic Analysis; Herbst and Hoffmann 2018) that allows us to illustrate the various constructions that combine to produce complex utterances. Then, I will conclude the book by briefly discussing some phenomena that I, personally, think are currently emerging as 'hot topics' in constructionist research.

8.1   Constructional Approach to Syntactic Analysis

Take a look at the following authentic sentence from a travel documentary:

(8.1)   This rendered him speechless with laughter and he tottered helplessly out of the room and was not seen again for hours.   (From Douglas Adams and Mark Carwardine, *Last Chance to See*, 1990)

Example (8.1) has twenty-one words, only one of which appears twice (*and*). So just counting the number of word constructions gives you a first idea of how complex actual utterances are – and so far we have not even taken into account the various clausal and phrasal constructions or argument structure constructions that are also part of (8.1)! How can we even begin to visualize the interaction of all the constructions underlying such a complex sentence?

In order to address this issue, Herbst and Hoffmann (2018) developed what they call a 'Constructional Approach to Syntactic Analysis' (CASA). They use constructional grids to break down constructs into all their component constructions. Figure 8.1 illustrates such a CASA analysis for the first clause of (8.1) (*This rendered him speechless with laughter*):

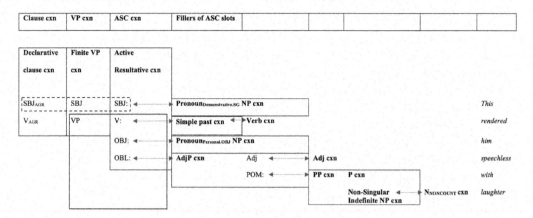

Figure 8.1 *CASA analysis of* This rendered him speechless

The first thing you will note in Figure 8.1 is that CASA grids only provide the names of 'cxns' (i.e., constructions such as the 'Declarative clause cxn' or the 'Active Resultative cxn') as well as their MORPHOSYNTAX slots (e.g., 'SBJ' or 'POM'). This does, of course, not mean that MEANING plays no role in CASA. However, as you can already see, the analysis of constructs using these limited pieces of information is already complicated enough as it is. When you see a CASA grid such as Figure 8.1, then you have to understand that the label of a construction (e.g., 'Active Resultative cxn') is only a placeholder for a complex FORM-MEANING pairing that requires a much more detailed description elsewhere in your constructicon (see our template (5.2) in Section 5.1.1).

What the CASA approach allows us to see at one glance is how constructions combine to produce complex constructions. In CASA, double arrows are used to indicate which elements fill the slots of abstract constructions. Let me illustrate this by focusing on the Active Resultative construction (see (5.2), Section 5.1.1):

- the Pronoun$_{Demonstrative.SG}$ NP cxn *This* (see (4.21), Section 4.2.1.1) fills the SBJ slot;
- the Pronoun$_{Personal.OBJ}$ NP cxn *him* (see (4.20), Section 4.2.1.1) fills the OBJ slot;
- the AdJP cxn *speechless with laughter* (see (4.70), Section 4.2.2) fills the OBL slot; and
- the V slot is filled by the Simple Past construction *rendered* (see (5.51), Section 5.2).

In addition to this, some constructions will also overlap: the clause in Figure 8.1 is an instance of the Declarative clause cxn (see (5.75), Section 5.3), a construction that, inter alia, ensures subject–verb agreement. This abstract clausal construction overlaps with the Finite VP cxn (see (4.113), Section 4.2.3.3) and the Active Resultative cxn, since all three have a slot for the SBJ. In CASA, such an overlap of slots shared by several constructions is indicated by boxes (see the dashed box in Figure 8.1). Similarly, the Finite VP cxn will overlap with all non-SBJ elements of the Active Resultative cxn (thus grouping these as the 'predicate constituent').

The internal analysis of the ADJP *speechless with laughter* is fairly straightforward (with the Non-Singular Indefinite NP constructioncxn *laughter* (see (4.38), Section 4.2.1.1) appearing in a POM slot). In contrast to this, the verb *rendered* probably needs a bit more explanation. As you can see in Figure 8.1, *rendered* fills the slots required by the Simple past cxn (see (5.51), Section 5.2). Now, this is, obviously, a shorthand representation for the more complex interaction of word, inflection and tense-aspect constructions (namely, a RENDER Lexeme construction (Section 4.1), the V-Past Tense cxn (see (3.29), Section 3.2.1) and the Simple Past cxn). When you see a CASA representation, you will therefore have to remember that it will always represent the result of the complex interaction of lexical and tense/aspect constructions.

Returning to the full sentence (8.1), you will have noticed that the clause in Figure 8.1 is coordinated with another Declarative clause construction using the *And* Coordination construction (see (4.153), Section 4.2.5):

(8.2)   [This rendered him speechless with laughter]Declarative clause construction
and [he tottered helplessly out of the room and
was not seen again for hours]Declarative clause construction

We will explore the CASA analysis of the *And* Coordination construction shortly. For the sake of exposition, Figure 8.2 therefore only provides a CASA analysis of the second Declarative clause construction of the sentence:

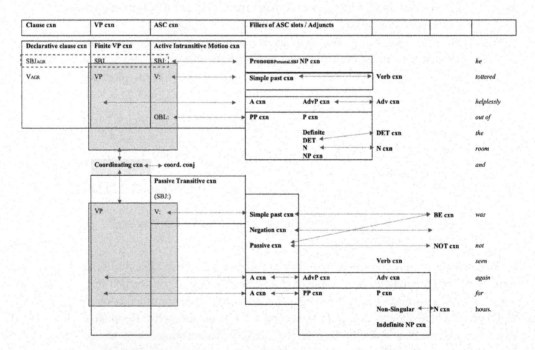

Figure 8.2 *CASA analysis of* he tottered helplessly out of the room and was not seen again for hours

The full figure might be a bit overwhelming, but if you focus on the individual constructions, then it should be easier to read. Start with the top left corner: there we see that the construct, similar to Figure 8.1, is again licensed by the Declarative clause cxn and the Finite VP construction. The main difference between the two figures lies in the *And* Coordination construction that combines the two VPs (VP1: *he tottered helplessly out of the room* | VP2: *was not seen again for hours*). In Figure 8.2, the coordinated VPs are highlighted by boxes with light grey shading. Due to this coordination, the two VPs share the same SBJ (*he*), which explains why the second VP has no overt filler for its SBJ slot (indicated by '(SBJ:)' in Figure 8.2). Moreover, while the argument structure construction associated with the first VP is an Active Intransitive Motion cxn (see (5.16), Section 5.1.1), the second VP is linked to a Passive Transitive construction (see Figure 5.3, Section 5.1.3). Another important difference between Figure 8.1 and Figure 8.2 is that the latter contains adjuncts/adverbials ('A') that are not selected for by the argument structure constructions. As we discussed in Section 4.2.3.3, adjuncts/adverbials are modifiers that select for the constituent that they modify. In Figure 8.2, all adjuncts/adverbials (*helplessly, again, for hours*) modify a VP and all are therefore linked to a VP via a bidirectional arrow in the figure above. Finally, the analysis of *was not seen* might at first sight also appear a bit complex. As you will remember, however, from our discussion of passive and tense/aspect constructions, BE can simultaneously fill the tense slot of the construction as well as the AUX slot of the passive construction (the latter also requiring the past participle *seen*), which explains why there are two arrows to and from *was*.

I hope the above figures and their discussion were not too intimidating or too difficult to follow. In the exercises, I will give you a couple of easier sentences with which to practice the CASA analysis. For now, it is only important that you see that our constructionist approach can also fully analyse complex sentences that appear in authentic spoken and written discourse.

8.2   Multimodal Constructs – Multimodal Constructions?

Let us, next, focus a bit on the relationship of spoken and written language for a second. For a long time, linguistics had a written language bias. Many analyses were based on the language of written texts – for various practical as well as ideological reasons (cf., e.g., Coulmas 2013: 225–43). In the twentieth century, however, the focus shifted to spoken language. After all, almost all children learn to speak way before they learn to write and while speaking seems to be picked up in a fast and natural way, writing is a skill that requires conscious effort and explicit teaching. Once linguists started to look more carefully at spoken data, however, they also realized that actual communication comprises much more than just verbal forms. In a conversation, it is not only important what people say but also how they say it. Take, for example, the construct in (8.3):

(8.3)   Well done!

Example (8.3) can be uttered with an excited intonation (with a high pitch on *well* and a fall of the voice on *done*) by someone who is wearing a genuine smile on their face and who is patting you on your back in a friendly way. Alternatively, it can be produced with an ironic intonation (with low pitch on *well* and hardly any pitch movement on *done*) by a speaker with a negative face expression, who is slowly and unenthusiastically applauding you. It seems pretty straightforward how you would interpret these two different constructs: in the first case, you would probably consider this as a genuine expression of congratulation, while in the second one, you would guess that the other person is rather unimpressed with your achievements. Yet, depending on the specific pragmatic context in which (8.3) is uttered, these interpretations might also change: most of us would find it very odd if a complete stranger produced the enthusiastic realization of (8.3) after you had just sneezed in the street, while the ironic realization might just be the kind of banter that you and your friends engage in as part of your daily routine.

Whenever we speak face-to-face, we thus do not just use language, that is, verbal constructions. We also use our hands, stance as well as varying facial expressions to communicate the complex semantic, social as well as emotional meanings we want to express (Steen and Turner 2013). Indeed, we tend to communicate multimodally even when it does not seem necessary: it has, for example, been shown that when talking over the phone, people often use gestures despite the fact that the hearers can obviously not see them (Cohen 1977; McNeill 2013b: 206). Moreover, when we become aware that our interlocuter cannot see us, for example, when composing text messages, we often feel the need to complement our written code with iconic emojis (such as ☺ or ☹) to express emotions that would otherwise be conveyed by our gestures, stance or facial expressions. In fact, gestures and verbal utterances can be seen 'as different sides of a single underlying mental process' (McNeill 1992: 1)

How can we interpret multimodal language use from a Construction Grammar perspective? Well, usage-based approaches claim that the input for mental entrenchment comprises rich 'social, physical and linguistic context' (Bybee 2010), which should include visual information as well. It is, for example, well-known that gestures (e.g., the thumbs-up sign 👍) that are repeatedly used with a constant meaning ('I agree!' or 'Good!') in a culture (also known as 'emblems'; McNeill 2000: 2–6) are stored as unimodal gesture constructions (cf. Hoffmann 2017c; Langacker 2005: 104; Zima 2017). A recent question in Construction Grammar is now whether in addition to unimodal gesture construc-tions, humans might also store multimodal constructions – constructions with verbal and gesture FORM elements that express a joint MEANING (Zima and Bergs 2017a).

Some researchers remain sceptical: Ningelgen and Auer (2017), for example, note that the gesture part of many speech-gesture combinations is only co-expressive (it appears to only emphasize a meaning already expressed by the verbal form elements) and, thus, optional. Under this view, gestures are only non-entrenched additives. For Ziem (2017), these multimodal constructs would not be evidence that speakers have an underlying multimodal construction in this case. He argues that one can only speak of a multimodal construction if both gesture and verbal FORM are obligatory: following this definition of multimodal constructions, gesture and verbal FORM-MEANING pairings are only considered to be entrenched if the absence of gesture or verbal FORM leads to the uninterpretability of an utterance.

On the other hand, a great number of authors have criticized this strict definition of multimodal constructions. As, Lanwer (2017), Schoonjans (2017) or Zima (2017), for example, pointed out, entrenchment is a gradual phenomenon. Consequently, we can expect a continuum of constructions ranging from those with an infrequent and loose gesture use, on the one end, and those with a frequent and systematic use of co-instantiated gesture-verbal pairs, on the other end. While the jury is still out on this issue, there are some first, interesting studies that seem to imply that speakers at least have some multimodal constructions: Bressem and Müller (2017), for example, showed that German speakers consistently use a Throwing Away Gesture with several verbal elements (namely, particles/negation/nouns, verbs and adverbs). In all of these uses, the gesture adds a meaning of dismissive quality or negative assessment to the construction. In the same vein, Zima (2017) argues that the English [*all the way from* X PREP Y]-construction is multimodal in nature: in her multimodal corpus data, around 80 per cent of all uses of the construction appear with a co-speech gesture. From a usage-based constructionist perspective, it is, thus, not unlikely that the mental grammars of speakers will also contain at least some multimodal constructions. Yet, clearly, more research is needed on this topic.

Beyond the question of whether a multimodal gesture and verbal pairing constitutes a multimodal construction, however, I argue that multimodal communication has other, equally important repercussions for Construction Grammar as a cognitive theory of language (Hoffmann 2017c). As mentioned throughout this book, constructions are FORM-MEANING pairings that are stored in the long-term memory. Constructs, on the other hand, are concrete utterances that are produced in the working memory (Cowan 2008; Diamond 2013). Only in rare cases, does a construct instantiate a single construction (e.g., when you produce a pre-fab greeting such as *Good morning!* or a saying such as *An apple a day keeps the doctor away*). Instead, in the working memory a construct will be 'constructed' by drawing on a number of constructions from the long-term memory. Just look at Figures 8.1 and 8.2 to see how many constructions are combined to give a sentence like (8.1).

Now, how is the combination of constructions into constructs normally modelled in Construction Grammar? As discussed in Section 7.4, more cognitively-oriented approaches remain vague on this, claiming, for example, that 'constructions [...] combine freely as long as there are no conflicts' (Goldberg 2006: 22).

Formal approaches (see Section 7.2 and 7.3), on the other hand, use 'constraint-satisfaction' to model construction combination. As mentioned in Chapter 7, these constraint-based approaches are highly successful at parsing natural language data. However, from a cognitive perspective the question arises whether constraint-satisfaction is really a useful metaphor for what the mind does. Do we only combine constructions into constructs in the working memory using constraint-satisfaction? And if so, is this a language-specific or domain-general process? Besides, how could multimodal information be created using constraint-satisfaction?

From a cognitive perspective, an alternative claim would be that Conceptual Blending drives constructional combination in the working memory (Fauconnier and Turner 2002; Hoffmann 2019b; Turner 2018). Conceptual Blending is a domain-general process that has been used to explain human behaviour across all domains of higher-order human cognition (http://blending.stanford.edu) – including mathematical invention, reasoning, categorization, art, music, dance, social cognition, advanced tool innovation and religion. It allows us to selectively combine two or more input spaces to create a conceptual structure that often has new, emergent meaning. This approach offers a straightforward account of how gesture and verbal information can become integrated into a single multimodal construct in the working memory (e.g., Steen and Turner 2013; Turner 2018). Again, however, this is an issue that is currently still hotly debated and requires much more constructionist research. Nevertheless, one research area where Conceptual Blending is emerging as particularly useful is the constructionist investigation of verbal creativity.

8.3   Construction Grammar and Creativity

Creativity is a crucial evolutionary adaptation capability that allows humans to think original thoughts and to find solutions to problems they have never encountered before. One area where humans are incredibly creative is language. Despite our large inventory of entrenched constructions, we regularly find new ways of saying novel things in innovative ways. Linguists from all types of theoretical approaches therefore claim that creativity is 'an essential property of language' (Chomsky 1965: 6) and the goal of linguistics itself, thus, is to account 'for the creative potential of language' (Goldberg 2006: 22). Yet, a closer look at linguistic research reveals that what linguists usually mean by 'creativity' does not necessarily coincide with how the term is used in other disciplines. In linguistics, 'creativity' is largely limited to productivity: i.e., how established abstract schemas of a language can be used to license novel utterances (Hoffmann 2018: 262; Sampson 2016). A case in point is Goldberg's latest monograph (2019): as she acknowledges, the primary question she addresses in her book is 'the partial productivity of grammatical constructions' (2019: 4). Consequently, she tries to uncover the cognitive principles that explain how native speakers can extend existing constructions. For example, speakers use the

Ditransitive construction (5.21) to produce novel utterances such as *somebody leaked me a focus group tape* (Goldberg 2019: 61), yet do not produce other utterances with it such as *explain me this* (Goldberg 2019: 1). As Goldberg argues, the acceptability of a novel construct crucially depends on the 'coverage' of a construction (i.e., the number and types of 'previously attested exemplars' 2019: 73, its exemplar cloud; see Section 2.1.3) as well as the 'competition' of existing alternative constructions. While both *leak* and *explain* can be linked to existing exemplars of the Ditransitive construction, such as *he slipped me the key*[1] or *tell me this* (Goldberg 2019: 1), the latter construct is blocked by a competing, strongly entrenched alternative (*explain this to me*).

Now, Goldberg's (2019) detailed account of constructional productivity can successfully explain the productive extensions of some constructions. Take, for example, the X BE NOT *the* Y-*est* Z *in the* Q construction, which licenses constructs such as *She's not the sharpest tool in the shed, Lilly* (COCA, *Trial Fire*, 2016) or *Poor Billy Frisk was not the quickest bunny in the warren.* (COCA, *South-west review*, 2009; both examples from Bergs 2018: 281). Normally, the adjective in the Y slot is a synonym of *intelligent* (cf. *She's sharp.* or *He's quick.*; Trousdale, personal communication) and the construction is consequently used to express that someone is not very clever. By the same token, an adjective like *shiny* is not a synonym of *intelligent* and therefore should not be within the coverage of the construction. It should therefore be precluded from being used in the X BE NOT *the* Y-*est* Z *in the* Q template. Nevertheless, (8.4) appears to be a perfectly acceptable (from Hoffmann 2019b):

(8.4)   I mean he's not the **brightest** lad is he?
           Not the shiniest penny in the piggy bank.[2]

In line with Goldberg's approach that multiple constructions are activated during production (2019: 140), we can see the steps that license the use of *shiny* in (8.4): in the preceding sentence *bright* is used as a synonym for *intelligent*, which due to its alternative meaning 'shining emitting, reflecting, or pervaded by much light' (OED[3]), primes *shiny*. This, in turn, acts as a scaffolding device that licenses the use of *shiny* in the X BE NOT *the* Y-*est* Z *in the* Q construction.

As you can see, Goldberg's account considerably extends our understanding of constructional creativity. At the same time, however, productivity; that is, making 'original use of the established possibilities of the language' (Leech 1969: 24), is just one type of creativity. What is missing in this model is a cognitive account of how a speaker can go beyond these possibilities: 'that is, if he creates new communicative possibilities which are not already in the language' (cf. also Sampson 2016 for a similar distinction of 'F(ixed)-creativity' and 'E(nlarging/extending)-creativity'; Hoffmann 2018: 262–3). Pressing questions for current constructionist approaches to creativity are therefore (Hoffmann

---

[1] Source: www.thefreedictionary.com/slip [last accessed 02 January 2021].
[2] Source: http://news.bbc.co.uk/sport2/hi/funny_old_game/2912483.stm [last accessed 02 January 2021].
[3] Source: www.oed.com/view/Entry/23303 [last accessed 02 January 2021].

2019b): how do speakers use their cognitive grammars to create 'E-creative utterances', which range from literary examples such as 'Bloom looked, unblessed to go. Got up to kill: on eighteen boob a week …' (from *Ulysses* by James Joyce) *or 'Thing-um-a-jig!'* (from *The Hunting of the Snark* by Lewis Carroll) to so-called 'Hashtag rhymes' (which consist of 'a metaphor, a pause and a one-word punchline, often placed at the end of a rhyme';[4] c.f., for instance, *'Swimming in the money, come and find me – Nemo'* from Drake's song *Forever*). As with multimodal constructs, it seems as if Conceptual Blending (Fauconnier and Turner 2002; Turner 2018) is the domain-general process that allows us to form E-creative constructs.

Conceptual Blending (Fauconnier and Turner 2002; Turner 2018) occurs when various input ideas, meanings or conceptual structures are selectively combined into a conceptual structure that is not identical to any of the inputs, often with emergent structure of its own. Let us illustrate how Conceptual Blending can account for the creative use of constructions:

(8.5)   Messi is the Mozart of football.   (Attributed to Zinédine Zidane)

(8.6)   Today is tomorrow!   (Groundhog Day 1993)

From a strictly computational point of view (8.5) and (8.6) should not be interpretable since they seem to contain contradictory information. Messi is not Mozart and today is not tomorrow! Yet, anyone who hears (8.5) immediately gets the intended meaning: Messi is a genius on the football pitch, just as Mozart was a musical genius. The way we get this meaning is via Conceptual Blending, which takes two (or more) input spaces (here FOOTBALL and CLASSICAL MUSIC) and blends them into a joint, new space that contains the creative, new meaning. Importantly, the blending process is highly selective: while you blend and compress the fact that Messi in his domain is as exceptional a skilled individual as Mozart was in his, you are not for a moment confused that Messi is Mozart, or that Messi lived in the eighteenth century, or that he composes music. Blending is thus a highly selective process and not the computational unification or constraint-satisfaction of all features of both input spaces.

Now, due to the great number of examples that work similarly to (8.5), such as *Vanity is the quicksand of reason.*, *Necessity is the mother of invention.* or *He's the Babe Ruth of Hungarian kayaking.* (Turner and Fauconnier 1999), it has been claimed that speakers of English have entrenched a X *is the* Y *of* Z construction that allows them to produce all these utterances. Nevertheless, even though this is a stored template, its various instantiations can only be explained by Conceptual Blending (and not by simple unification or constraint-satisfaction; cf. Chapter 7). Besides, even non-entrenched constructions such as (8.6) require a blending explanation: semantically, *today* is a concept that is crucially different to *tomorrow*. Yet, when Bill Murray's character Phil Connors utters (8.6) at the end of the movie *Groundhog Day* (1993), we immediately get what he is trying to say. In the

---

[4] Cf. www.houstonpress.com/music/a-brief-history-of-hashtag-rap-6529947 [last accessed on 02 January 2021].

fantasy film, Connors was caught in a time loop that forced him to relive the same day over and over again. Only once he has become a better person does the loop end and a new day finally break. When Connors realizes this, he exclaims (8.6). He does this by blending the meanings of two separate conceptual domains into a creative, new meaning (which we could be paraphrased by 'today is finally the day after the day that the character had to repeat in a time loop over and over again').

If we need Conceptual Blending to explain how speakers combine existing constructions into E-creative utterances as well as how they create multimodal constructs, then maybe this is also the only process we need for the combination of constructions into constructs? This would indeed be a very exciting finding, since blending is a domain-general process and we no longer would need to rely on language-specific versions of unification or constraint-satisfaction. Instead, it would turn out that 'the way we string sentences together is the way we think'! (Turner 2018, Hoffmann 2019b). Nevertheless, this claim is far from being a mainstream one in Construction Grammar. One particular problem is that so far no one has shown that Conceptual Blending is actually a falsifiable concept. (Gibbs 2000). But then again, is Construction Grammar a falsifiable theory?

8.4   Is Construction Grammar a Falsifiable Theory?

One of the hallmarks of scientific theories is their falsifiability; that is, the fact that they make predictions that can objectively be proven wrong (Hoffmann 2020b). So, can we actually falsify Construction Grammar? Is it a proper scientific theory?

In light of a large body of findings from empirical studies on first and second language acquisition as well as psycho- and neuro-linguistic evidence, we adopted a usage-based Construction Grammar approach in the present book. Such an approach argues that the human mind is not reductionist and not geared towards storage minimization (e.g., Bybee 2010, 2013). Instead, input (type and token) frequency is claimed to crucially affect how many constructions are entrenched in a speaker's mind. Now, usage-based approaches can claim greater psycholinguistic plausibility than complete inheritance approaches, yet the former also face important methodological problems: as Schmid (2020) high-lights, entrenchment is an individual process, yet a large body of evidence in usage-based studies comes from corpus data, which represent evidence for the conventionalization of structures across individuals. Since the linguistic input of speakers in a speech community will show considerable overlap, we can expect a considerable degree of convergence. Yet, even if, as suggested by Schmid (2020), we investigate performance data from single speakers in a corpus, we can never know the totality of linguistic input that these individual speakers have received. As a result, we can only use corpus data across individuals as a heuristic for getting at the passive constructional knowledge that speakers might have (and as with studies on active vs passive vocabulary, we can expect the passive constructional knowledge of speakers to be considerably greater than the number of constructions that they actively use). But is there any way that we could design tests that would allow us to falsify the number of constructions postulated by such a study?

Besides there is a theoretical issue that we have touched upon in passing in the previous chapters (particularly Chapter 7): Cognitive Construction Grammar as well as Radical Construction Grammar claim that constructions are always pairings of form and meaning. Hilpert even goes so far as to argue that:

> ... if Construction Grammar is to be seen as a veritable theory of linguistic knowledge, then this theory will make the strong claim that there should not be any constructions without meanings.   (Hilpert 2019: 57)

This statement represents the strictest and strongest constructionist hypothesis and appears to be falsifiable. Yet, things are unfortunately not that simple. As we saw in Chapter 7, even usage-based frameworks such as the Parallel Architecture postulate meaningless constructions to license sentences. Jackendoff (2013) argues that in addition to prototypical constructions with both FORM and MEANING pole, the mind will also generalize abstract syntactic principles without meaning (such as subject–verb agreement) or semantic principles without syntactic form, such as reference transfer in *I have read Shakespeare* (Shakespeare = 'books/ plays by the author Shakespeare', Hoffmann 2017b: 325).

In light of these methodological and theoretical issues, how can Construction Grammar become a falsifiable theory? As I put forward elsewhere (Hoffmann 2020b), any constructionist theory that wants to stand a chance at being falsifiable must meet at least the following requirements. It must have

(1)   **A psycholinguistic processing model**: as Chapter 7 showed, based on linguistic data alone, we are not able to decide whether all constructions must be meaningful or not. In order to make Construction Grammar falsifiable, we need a usage-based approach that is explicitly designed to model human language processing (Bencini 2013) and that can be subjected to psycholinguistic scrutiny. Currently, the major constructionist approaches that aim to model processing are Parallel Architecture, Fluid Construction Grammar and Embodied Construction Grammar. Whichever of these approaches is adopted, any constructionist processing model will have to offer, inter alia, an explanation for well-known linguistic event-related potential (ERP) effects: a negative spike in electrical brain activity is normally observed at around 400 ms after a semantically anomalous word (N400), while a positive spike at around 600 ms (P600) is associated with syntactic errors (Sharwood Smith 2017: 140). Recently, Delogu, Brouwer and Crocker (2019 and references therein) have argued that N400 is better interpreted as a context-sensitive retrieval effect (how easy it is to activate a word

considering the previous context), while P600 is indicative of integration into the context (how easily the word can be processed in the slot of a construction given the previous context). In contrast to the tenet that constructions exist on a lexicon-syntax cline (e.g., Croft and Cruse 2004: 255), these results in essence appear to support a processing dichotomy of substantive constructions (lexical retrieval) vs schematic constructions (integration of substantive constructions into the slots of schematic constructions). I do not think we have to abandon the tenet of a lexicon-syntax cline yet, but Construction Grammar should join forces with psycholinguistics to test whether the many partly substantive, partly schematic constructions that have been postulated actually differ categorically or gradually in their mental processing effects from fully lexical and fully syntactic constructions. A considerable body of constructionist psycholinguistic studies does already exist and continues to produce exciting results (e.g., Johnson and Goldberg 2013; Ziegler et al. 2019; see also Goldberg 2019: 31–3). To make Construction Grammar falsifiable, however, what we also need is a larger number of studies that take potentially problematic processing effects (such as, for example, the N400–P600) and ask whether these can be used to refute central claims of the theory.

(2)   **Neurolinguistic plausibility**: Construction Grammar approaches to language have also received important empirical support from neurobiological studies (Coulson 2017; Fedorenko et al. 2020; Pulvermüller, Cappelle and Shtyrov 2013). Nevertheless, this line of research has also presented evidence that calls into question the lexicon-syntax continuum (with distinct neurophysiological responses being elicited by lexical items and combinatorial, that is, schematic constructions; Pulvermüller, Cappelle and Shtyrov 2013: 412–14). Any falsifiable version of Construction Grammar must address this issue and also engage more self-critically with claims that neurobiological evidence suggests that 'language is an autonomous computational mechanism' (Bolhuis 2019: 571; see also Friederici 2017). Moreover, much more work is needed to see to what degree Construction Grammar can explain (Hatchard 2015) or be challenged (Boye and Bastiaanse 2018) by data from aphasia studies.

In essence, what I am suggesting is a constructionist version of the 'Derivational Theory of Complexity' (Sag and Wasow 2011; Müller 2019: 519): in the early days of Generative Grammar, transformations were considered to be cognitively real, which gave rise to the hypothesis that sentences that involve more transformational steps should also be more difficult to process. Once the experimental data failed to confirm this hypothesis, the Derivational Theory of Complexity was   abandoned,   and   generative   analyses   were   then   often   labelled 'representational' (i.e., not directly reflective of underlying mental processes and hence no longer falsifiable). I am arguing now that if we want to turn Construction Grammar into a falsifiable theory, we have to develop a 'Constructional Theory of Complexity': we have to design a processing-based version of the theory in a way that it becomes falsifiable by psycholinguistic and neurophysiological data. Obviously, a single experiment or data point cannot be taken as direct evidence that a theory is false. However, should psycholinguistic and neurophysiological evidence accumulate against Construction Grammar, we have to be prepared to consider it falsified (and not come up with a 'representational' version that is de facto not refutable).

8.5   Coda

In this book I presented a Usage-based Construction Grammar analysis to English that showed how this approach can account for all levels of description (from inflectional morphology and word-formation to information structure constructions and discourse patterns such as football chants). We have seen that this approach allows us to explain and understand language acquisition, variation and change. At the same time, the final chapter also indicated that there are still many exciting avenues for future constructionist research. I hope that the present book has motivated you to pursue some of these topics in your own studies and research. As you can see, there is still a lot of constructionist work in progress!

Glossary and List of Abbreviations

(X)+	one or more element of the type 'X'
1PS, 2PS, 3PS	grammatical categories: 1st person (e.g., *I*), 2nd person (e.g., *you*), 3rd person (e.g., *he, she, it*)
A	ADVERBIAL / ADJUNCT
ADJ	ADJECTIVE
ADJP	Adjective Phrase
ADV	ADVERB
ADVP	Adverb Phrase
agr	agreement (suffix)
AGR	subject–verb agreement
ARG-STR	ARGUMENT-STRUCTURE: a feature used by some Construction Grammar approaches (e.g., SBCG) to model syntactic valency. ARG-STR: $<NP_1, NP_2>$, e.g., means that a verb requires two NP arguments.
argument structure construction	abstract, schematic construction that encodes a basic human scene (someone moving in space, someone exerting force onto on an object, an object having a property, etc.)
AUX	auxiliary verb (BE, HAVE, DO and the MODAL verbs)
AVM	attribute-value-matrix
BCG	Berkeley Construction Grammar (a formal, complete inheritance approach to Construction Grammar)
BROWN	Brown Corpus of American English
CASA	Constructional Approach to Syntactic Analysis (a pedagogical approach to visualize how constructions combine into complex constructs)
CCG	Cognitive Construction Grammar (a non-formal, usage-based approach)
CG	Cognitive Grammar
CLAUSE$_{fin}$	finite clause
CLAUSE$_{nonfin}$	nonfinite clause

COCA	Corpus of Contemporary American English
COMPL	COMPLEMENT
collostructural analysis	family of statistical tests to examine the degree to which a word is attracted to the slot of a particular construction or how strongly two slots in the same construction are lexically associated.
complete-inheritance approach	an approach that only postulates the minimal number of constructions necessary to analyse a construct; only arbitrary FORM-MEANING pairings are stored as constructions, frequency of use plays no role in such an approach (unlike in usage-based approaches)
construal	mental perspective on a scene that finds its expression in linguistic utterances. The same situation (someone breaking a vase) can, e.g., be construed from a force-dynamic perspective (Transitive construction: *John broke the vase.*) or focus on the resulting state (Copulative Attribute construction: *The vase was broken.*).
construct-i-con/ constructicon	the mental network of all constructions (a term analogically formed on the 'lexicon')
construction	FORM-MEANING pairings that are stored in the long-term memory of speakers
constructs	FORM-MEANING pairings that are assembled in the working memory (very often entailing the simultaneous activation of several constructions)
Core Frame Elements	central participant roles that are evoked by a semantic frame (e.g., BUYER, GOODS, MONEY and SELLER are Core Frame Elements of the COMMERCE_SCENARIO)
DET	DETERMINER (e.g., *a* or *the*)
DNI	Definite Null Instantiation construction: construction that backgrounds a profiled participant of a verb that is not overtly expressed, but still contextually identifiable. *He cut and cut.*, e.g., backgrounds the ITEM role – but contextually it will be clear what is being cut. This is indicated by the fact that a question such as #*What did he cut?* is pragmatically odd in cases of DNI.
DTR	daughter node (SBCG)
ECG	Embodied Construction Grammar (a usage-based approach that models human processing)
E-creativity	Enlarging/extending-creativity

embodiment	the claim that meaning is embodied, i.e., that having a body and using it to interact with the world crucially affects your mental representation of meaning
entrenchment	mental storage of an item or construction
ERP	event-related potential
FCG	Fluid Construction Grammar (a usage-based approach that models human processing)
F-creativity	Fixed-creativity
FE	frame element
FEM	grammatical category (FEMININE, e.g., *she*)
FIGURE-GROUND relationship	in a spatial scene, the FIGURE is the focal element that is foregrounded while the GROUND provides the background location (cf. *A book*$_{\text{FIGURE}}$ *is on the table*$_{\text{GROUND}}$)
FLOB	Freiburg-LOB Corpus of British English
FORCE-DYNAMIC event	an event type in which force is being exerted by a source (agent / INSTIGATOR) onto a target (patient / ENDPOINT). The prototypical meaning of the Transitive construction (cf. *He*$_{\text{INSTIGATOR}}$ *peeled the banana*$_{\text{ENDPOINT}}$)
FORM	FORM pole of a construction (includes PHONOLOGY, ORTHOGRAPHY and MORPHOSYNTAX)
FRAME and Frame Semantics	a FRAME is a mental knowledge structure associated with scenes and events (such as the GIVING or the TAKING event). Frame Semantics is the theory that postulates these knowledge structure. FRAMES are part of the MEANING pole of constructions. They are encyclopaedic in nature (not just purely abstract, semantic knowledge). Online lexicographic databases for frames are currently being developed for many languages in the FrameNet project (for English, cf. https://framenet.icsi.berkeley.edu/fndrupal/)
FROWN	Freiburg-Brown Corpus of American English
Generative Grammar	a modular approach to grammar that argues for innate language-specific principles and parameters and denies the existence of grammatical constructions
GF	grammatical function
HPSG	Head-driven Phrase Structure Grammar (a constrained-based, formal approach to grammar)
ICE-GB	British English segment of the International Corpus of English

IDG	indigenous population in Dynamic Model
items-and-rules approaches	theories that postulate a strict lexicon-syntax division (with meaningful elements only being found in the lexicon, and syntactic rules making no reference to meaning)
L1	first Language
L2	second Language
lexeme construction	in a taxonomic network, due to their FORM-MEANING similarities, word constructions such *to kick*, *kick*, *kicks*, *kicked* (past tense), *kicked* (past participle), and *kicking* will be associated via horizontal correspondence links. If these similarities lead to a superordinate construction that unites the word constructions, the resulting superordinate node is called a 'lexeme construction' (which is represented by capital letters, e.g., KICK)
MASC	grammatical category (MASCULINE, e.g., *he*)
MEANING	the MEANING pole of a construction (includes meanings relevant to SEMANTICS, PRAGMATICS, SOCIAL, INFORMATION STRUCTURE and DISCOURSE-FUNCTION)
morpheme construction	partly substantive, partly schematic constructional templates that create word constructions
MTR	mother node
NEUT	grammatical category (NEUTER, e.g., *it*)
Nonnull Instantiation constructions	a construction that requires all Core Frame Elements of a lexeme construction to be overtly realized
NP	Noun Phrase
Null Instantiation	constructions that omit the realization of a foregrounded Core Frame Element (see also DNI).
OED	*Oxford English Dictionary*
OBJ	OBJECT
OBL	OBLIQUE: obligatory syntactic slots of argument structure constructions that is neither SUBJECT nor OBJECT (e.g., *He is **ill**.* or *They wiped the table **clean**.*)
P	PREPOSITION
PA	Parallel Architecture (a usage-based approach that models human processing)
PART	PARTICLE
PL	grammatical category (PLURAL, e.g., *we* or *they*)
POM	POSTMODIFIER, i.e., a slot for optional extra information in phrasal constructions that appears after

	the head of the phrase (e.g., *the man **that I went to school with*** or *the girl **from Ipanema***)
POSS	grammatical category (POSSESSIVE, e.g., *my* or *his*)
PP	Prepositional Phrase
pre-emption	an existing construction (e.g., *thief*) blocks a construct that could be licensed by another construction (e.g., *steal-er*)
PREM	PREMODIFIER, i.e., a slot for optional extra information in phrasal constructions that appears before the head of the phrase (e.g., *the **old** man* or *the **very happy** woman*)
PRON	PRONOUN
RCG	Radical Construction Grammar (a non-formal, usage-based approach)
SAI	subject–verb inversion
SBCG	Sign-Based Construction Grammar (a complete inheritance approach to Construction Grammar)
SBJ	SUBJECT
schematic construction	a construction with slots (un-ADJ construction: *untrue, unfriendly, unhappy*) that has high type frequency and, consequently, due to pattern detection leads to the creation of a construction with schematic slots. The basis for new, productive uses (e.g., *unGucci*).
SEM	SEMANTIC FEATURE
SG	grammatical category (SINGULAR, e.g., *I* or *she*)
STL	settler population in Dynamic Model
substantive construction	phonologically-specified construction (e.g., *That's the way the cookie crumbles.*), which is entrenched due to high token frequency (and/or salience)
usage-based approaches	approaches that assume that competence and performance crucially interact. Each token of use is registered and affects the mental constructicon. The information that is supposed to be stored is not just reductionist, it includes all sorts of contextual factors (including properties of the social, physical and linguistic context). The interaction of type and token frequency with domain-general processes (analogy, pattern-detection, schematization, etc.) plays a crucial role in these approaches
VP	Verb Phrase
word construction	smallest fully substantive constructions of a language

References

Aarts, Flor and Jan Aarts. 1988. *English Syntactic Structures*. 2nd ed. Oxford: Pergamon Press.

Aitchison, Jean. 2013. *Language Change: Progress or Decay?* 4th ed. Cambridge: Cambridge University Press.

Ambridge, Ben and Adele E. Goldberg. 2008. The island status of clausal complements: Evidence in favor of an information structure explanation. *Cognitive Linguistics* 19,3: 357–89.

Baker, Paul and Magnus Huber. 2000. Constructing new pronominal systems from the Atlantic to the Pacific. *Linguistics* 38,5: 833–66.

Barðdal, Jóhanna. 2008. *Productivity: Evidence from Case and Argument Structure in Icelandic*. Amsterdam: John Benjamins.

Barðdal, Jóhanna. 2011. Lexical vs. structural case: A false dichotomy. *Morphology* 21,1: 619–54.

Barðdal, Jóhanna, Elena Smirnova, Lotte Sommerer and Spike Gildea, eds, 2015. *Diachronic Construction Grammar*. (Constructional Approaches to Language 18.) Amsterdam/New York: John Benjamins.

Bauer, Laurie. 2001. *Morphological Productivity*. Cambridge: Cambridge University Press.

Bauer, Laurie. 2009. Typology of compounds. In: Rochelle Lieber and Pavol Stekauer, eds, *The Oxford Handbook of Compounding*. Oxford: Oxford University Press, 343–56.

Bauer, Laurie and Paul Warren. 2004. New Zealand English: Phonology. In: Edgar W. Schneider, Bernd Kortmann, Clive Upton, Rajend Mesthrie and Kate Burridge, eds, *A Handbook of Varieties of English. A Multimedia Reference Tool. Vol. 1: Phonology*. Berlin/New York: De Gruyter Mouton, 580–602.

Behaghel, Otto. 1909/1910. Beziehungen zwischen Umfang und Reihenfolge von Satzgliedern. *Indogermanische Forschungen* 25: 110–42.

Bell, Allan. 1984. Language style as audience design. *Language in Society* 13,2: 145–204.

Bencini, Giulia M.L. 2013. Psycholinguistics. In: Thomas Hoffmann and Graeme Trousdale, eds, *The Oxford Handbook of Construction Grammar*. Oxford: Oxford University Press, 379–96.

Bergen, Benjamin K. and Nancy Chang. 2005. Embodied Construction Grammar in simulation-based language understanding. In: Jan-Ola Ostman and Mirjam Fried, eds, *Construction Grammars: Cognitive Grounding and Theoretical Extensions*. Amsterdam: John Benjamins, 147–90.

Bergen, Benjamin K. and Nancy Chang. 2013. Embodied construction grammar. In: Thomas Hoffmann and Graeme Trousdale, eds, *The Oxford Handbook of Construction Grammar*. Oxford: Oxford University Press, 168–90.

Bergs, Alexander. 2010. Expressions of futurity in contemporary English: A constructional perspective. *English Language and Linguistics* 14,2: 217–38.

Bergs, Alexander. 2018. Learn the rules like a pro, so you can break them like an artist (Picasso): Linguistic aberrancy from a constructional perspective. *Zeitschrift für Anglistik und Amerikanistik* 66,3: 277–93.

Bergs, Alexander and Thomas Hoffmann. 2018. A Construction Grammar approach to genre. *CogniTextes* 18, https://doi.org/10.4000/cognitextes.1032

Berko, Jean. 1958. The child's learning of English morphology. *Word* 14: 150–77.

Blumenthal-Dramé, Alice. 2012. *Entrenchment in Usage-Based Theories: What Corpus Data do and do not Reveal about the Mind*. Berlin: De Gruyter Mouton.

Boas, Hans C. 2003. *A Constructional Approach to Resultatives*. Stanford: Center for the Study of Language and Information.

Boas, Hans C. 2005a. Determining the productivity of resultative constructions: A reply to Goldberg and Jackendoff. *Language* 81,2: 448–64.

Boas, Hans C. 2005b. From theory to practice: Frame Semantics and the design of FrameNet. In: Stefan Langer and Daniel Schnorbusch, eds, *Semantisches Wissen im Lexikon*. Tübingen: Narr, 129–60.

Boas, Hans C. 2006. A frame-semantic approach to identifying syntactically relevant elements of meaning. In: Petra Steiner, Hans C. Boas and Stefan Schierholz, eds, *Contrastive Studies and Valency: Studies in Honor of Hans Ulrich Boas*. Frankfurt/New York: Peter Lang, 119–49.

Boas, Hans C., ed. 2009. *Multilingual FrameNets in Computational Lexicography: Methods and Applications*. Berlin: De Gruyter Mouton.

Boas, Hans C., ed. 2010. *Contrastive Studies in Construction Grammar*. (Constructional Approaches to Language 10.) Amsterdam: John Benjamins.

Boas, Hans C. 2013. Cognitive Construction Grammar. In: Thomas Hoffmann and Graeme Trousdale, eds, *The Oxford Handbook of Construction Grammar*. Oxford: Oxford University Press, 233–52.

Boas, Hans C. and Ryan Dux. 2017. From the past into the present: From case frames to semantic frames. *Linguistics Vanguard* 3,1: 1–14.

Boas, Hans C. and Ivan Sag, eds, 2012. *Sign-Based Construction Grammar*. Stanford: CSLI Publications.

Bock, Kathryn. 1986a. Meaning, sound and syntax: Lexical priming in sentence production. *Journal of Experimental Psychology: Learning, Memory and Cognition* 12: 575–86.

Bock, Kathryn. 1986b. Syntactic persistence in language production. *Cognitive Psychology* 18: 355–87.

Bock, Kathryn and Zenzi Griffin. 2000. The persistence of structural priming: Transient activation or implicit learning? *Journal of Experimental Psychology* 129: 177–92.

Bock, Kathryn, Helga Loebell and Randel Morey. 1992. From conceptual roles to structural relations: Bridging the syntactic ceft. *Psychological Review* 99: 150–71.

Bolhuis, Johan J. 2019. Review of *Language in our Brain: The Origins of a Uniquely Human Capacity* by Angela D. Friederici. *Language* 95,3: 568–72.

Booij, Geert. 2010. *Construction Morphology*. Oxford: Oxford University Press.

Booij, Geert. 2013. Morphology in Construction Grammar. In: Thomas Hoffmann and Graeme Trousdale, eds, *The Oxford Handbook of Construction Grammar*. Oxford: Oxford University Press, 255–73.

Boyd, Jeremy K. and Adele E. Goldberg. 2011. Learning what not to say: The role of statistical preemption and categorization in 'a'-adjective production. *Language* 81,1: 1–29.

Boye, Kasper and Roelien Bastiaanse. 2018. Grammatical versus lexical words in theory and aphasia: Integrating linguistics and neurolinguistics. *Glossa: A Journal of General Linguistics* 3,1: Art. 29, 1–18.

Braine, Martin D.S. 1963. The ontogeny of English phrase structure: The first phrase. *Language* 39: 1–14.

Braine, Martin D. S. 1976. Children's first word combinations. *Monographs of the Society for Research in Child Development* 41,1: 1–104.

Bresnan, Joan and Marilyn Ford. 2010. Predicting syntax: Processing dative constructions in American and Australian varieties of English. *Language* 86: 186–213.

Bresnan, Joan and Jennifer Hay. 2008. Gradient grammar: An effect of animacy on the syntax of *give* in New Zealand and American English. *Lingua* 118: 245–59.

Bressem, Jana and Cornelia Müller. 2017. The 'Negative-Assessment-Construction' – A multimodal pattern based on a recurrent gesture? *Linguistics Vanguard 3*, s1: 1–9.

Broccias, Cristiano. 2013. Cognitive Grammar. In: Thomas Hoffmann and Graeme Trousdale, eds, *The Oxford Handbook of Construction Grammar*. Oxford: Oxford University Press, 191–210.

Brooks, Patricia and Michael Tomasello. 1999a. Young children learn to produce passives with nonce verbs. *Developmental Psychology* 35: 29–44.

Brooks, Patricia and Michael Tomasello. 1999b. How children constrain their argument structure constructions. *Language* 75: 720–38.

Brooks, Patricia, Michael Tomasello, Kelly Dodson and Lawrence B. Lewis. 1999. Young children's overgeneralizations with fixed transitivity verbs. *Child Development* 70,6: 1325–37.

Brown, Keith and Jim Miller. 1991. *Syntax: A Linguistic Introduction to Sentence Structure*. 2nd ed. London: Routledge.

Brunner, Thomas and Thomas Hoffmann. 2020. The *way* construction in World Englishes. *English World-Wide* 41,1: 1–36.

Butters, Ron. R. 2008. Trademarks and other proprietary terms. In: John Gibbons and M. Teresa Turell, eds, *Dimensions of Forensic Linguistics*. Amsterdam: John Benjamins, 231–47.

Bybee, Joan. 2006. From usage to grammar: The mind's response to repetition. *Language* 82: 711–33.

Bybee, Joan. 2010. *Language, Usage and Cognition*. Cambridge: Cambridge University Press.

Bybee, Joan. 2013. Usage-based theory and exemplar representations of constructions. In: Thomas Hoffmann and Graeme Trousdale, eds, *The Oxford Handbook of Construction Grammar*. Oxford: Oxford University Press, 49–69.

Bybee, Joan L. and Carol Lynn Moder. 1983. Morphological classes as natural categories. *Language: Journal of the Linguistic Society of America* 59,2: 251–70.

Bybee, Joan L. 1985. *Morphology: A Study into the Relation between Meaning and Form*. Amsterdam: John Benjamins.

Bybee, Joan L. 2000. The phonology of the lexicon: Evidence from lexical diffusion. In: Michael Barlow and Suzanne Kemmer, eds, *Usage-based Models of Language*. Stanford, CA: CSLI Publications, 65–85.

Cappelle, Bert. 2006. Particle placement and the case for 'allostructions'. *Constructions* SV 1-7: 1–28. www.constructions-journal.com.

Cappelle, Bert, Ilse Depraetere and Mégane Lesuisse. 2019. The necessity modals *have to*, *must*, *need to* and *should*: Using n-grams to help identify common and distinct semantic and pragmatic aspects. *Constructions and Frames* 11,2: 220–43.

Carpenter, Bob. 1992. *The Logic of Typed Feature Structures*. Cambridge: Cambridge University Press.

Casenhiser, Devin and Adele E. Goldberg. 2005. Fast mapping between a phrasal form and meaning. *Developmental Science* 8: 500–8.

Chambers, Jack K. 2008. *Sociolinguistic Theory: Language Variation and its Social Significance*. 3rd ed. Malden, MA: Blackwell.

Chomsky, Noam. 1965. *Aspects of the Theory of Syntax*. Cambridge, MA: MIT Press.

Chomsky, Noam. 1981. *Lectures on Government and Binding*. (Studies in Generative Grammar 9) Dordrecht, Holland: Foris Publication.

Chomsky, Noam. 1995. *The Minimalist Program*. Cambridge, MA: MIT Press.

Chomsky, Noam. 2000. Minimalist inquiries: The framework. In: Roger Martin, David Michaels and Juan Uriagereka, eds, *Step by Step: Essays on Minimalist Syntax in Honor of Howard Lasnik*. Cambridge, MA: MIT Press, 89–155.

Clark, Eve. 2009. *First Language Acquisition*. Cambridge: Cambridge University Press.

Clerck, Bernard de and Timothy Colleman. 2013. From noun to intensifier: *Massa* and *massa's* in Flemish varieties of Dutch. *Language Sciences* 36: 147–60.

Cohen, Akiba A. 1977. The communicative function of hand illustrators. *Journal of Communication* 27: 54–63.

Colleman, Timothy. 2009a. The semantic range of the Dutch double object construction: A collostructional perspective. *Constructions and Frames* 1: 190–221.

Colleman, Timothy. 2009b. Verb disposition in argument structure alternations: A corpus study of the dative alternation in Dutch. *Language Sciences* 31: 593–611

Colleman, Timothy. 2010. Lectal variation in constructional semantics: 'Benefactive' ditransitives in Dutch. In: Dirk Geeraerts, Gitte Kristiansen and Yves Peirsman, eds, 2010. *Advances in Cognitive Sociolinguistics*. Berlin/New York: De Gruyter Mouton, 191–221.

Cook, Vivian and Mark Newson. 1996. *Chomsky's Universal Grammar: An Introduction*. 2nd ed. Oxford: Wiley-Blackwell.

Coulmas, Florian. 2013. *Sociolinguistics: The Study of Speaker's Choices*. 2nd ed. Cambridge: Cambridge University Press.

Coulson, Seana. 2017. Language and the brain. In: Barbara Dancygier, ed. *The Cambridge Handbook of Cognitive Linguistics*. Cambridge: Cambridge University Press, 515–32.

Cowan, Nelson. 2008. What are the differences between long-term, short-term, and working memory? *Progress in Brain Research* 169: 323–33.

Croft, William. 2001. *Radical Construction Grammar: Syntactic Theory in Typological Perspective*. Oxford: Oxford University Press.

Croft, William. 2012. *Verbs: Aspect and Causal Structure*. Oxford. Oxford University Press.

Croft, William. 2013. Radical Construction Grammar. In: Thomas Hoffmann and Graeme Trousdale, eds. *The Oxford Handbook of Construction Grammar*. Oxford: Oxford University Press, 211–32.

Croft, William and Alan. D. Cruse. 2004. *Cognitive Linguistics*. Cambridge: Cambridge University Press.

Crystal, David. 2003. *English as a Global Language*. 2nd ed. Cambridge: Cambridge University Press.

Culicover, Peter W. and Ray Jackendoff. 1999. The view from the periphery: The English comparative correlative. *Linguistic Inquiry* 30: 543–71.

Culicover, Peter W. and Ray Jackendoff. 2005. *Simpler Syntax*. Oxford: Oxford University Press.

Drąbowska, Eva. 2000. From formula to schema: The acquisition of English questions. *Cognitive Linguistics* 11: 83–102.

Davidse, Kristin. 2004. The interaction of quantification and identification in English determiners. In: Michel Achard and Suzanne Kemmer, eds, *Language, Culture and Mind*. Stanford: CSLI, 507–33.

Declerck, Renaat. 1991. The origins of genericity. *Linguistics* 29,1: 79–102.

Declerck, Renaat. 2006. *Grammar of the English Verb Phrase, Vol 1: Grammar of the English Tense System*. (Topics in English Linguistics 60). Berlin: de Gryuter Mouton.

Deacon, Terrance. 1997. *The Symbolic Species: The Co-evolution of Language and the Human Brain*. London: Penguin.

Delin, Judy and Jon Oberlander. 1995. Syntactic constraints on discourse structure: The case of *it*-clefts. *Linguistics* 33: 465–500.

Delin, Judy and Jon Oberlander. 2006. Cleft constructions in context: Some suggestions for research methodology. www.fb10.uni-bremen.de/anglistik/langpro/projects/gem/delin-publications.html. Last accessed 06 January 2021.

Delogu, Francesca, Harm Brouwer and Matthew W. Crocker. 2019. Event-related potentials index lexical retrieval (N400) and integration (P600) during language comprehension. *Brain and Cognition* 135: Art. 103569, 1–14.

Diamond, Adele. 2013. Executive functions. *Annual Review of Psychology* 64: 135–68.

Diessel, Holger. 2006. Komplexe Konstruktionen im Erstspracherwerb. In: Kerstin Fischer und Anatol Stefanowitsch, eds, *Konstruktionsgrammatik – Von der Anwendung zur Theorie*. Tübingen: Stauffenberg, 36–51.

Diessel, Holger. 2013. Construction Grammar and first language acquisition. In: Thomas Hoffmann and Graeme Trousdale, eds, *The Oxford Handbook of Construction Grammar*. Oxford: Oxford University Press, 347–64.

Diessel, Holger. 2015. Usage-based construction grammar. In: Ewa Dabrowska and Dagmar Divjak, ed., *Handbook of Cognitive Linguistics*. Berlin: De Gruyter Mouton, 295–321.

Diessel, Holger. 2019. *The Grammar Network: How Linguistic Structure is Shaped by Language Use*. Cambridge: Cambridge University Press.

Diessel, Holger and Michael Tomasello. 2000. The development of relative clauses in English. *Cognitive Linguistics* 11: 131–51.

Dodge, Ellen K. and Miriam R. L. Petruck. 2014. Representing Caused Motion in Embodied Construction Grammar. *Proceedings of the ACL 2014 Workshop on Semantic Parsing*: 39–44.

Eckert, Penelope. 2004. Adolescent language. In: Edward Finegan and John Rickford, eds, *Language in the USA*. Cambridge: Cambridge University Press, 251–89.

Eckert, Penelope. 2012. Three waves of variation study: The emergence of meaning in the study of sociolinguistic variation. *Annual Review of Anthropology* 41: 87–100.

Ellis, Nick C. 2013. Construction Grammar and second language acquisition. In: Thomas Hoffmann and Graeme Trousdale, eds, *The Oxford Handbook of Construction Grammar*. Oxford: Oxford University Press, 365–78.

Eppler, Eva Duran and Gabriel Ozón. 2013. *English Words and Sentences: An Introduction*. Cambridge: Cambridge University Press.

Ernst, Thomas. 2002. *The Syntax of Adjuncts*. Cambridge: Cambridge University Press.

Erteschik-Shir, Nomi and Shalom Lappin. 1979. Dominance and the functional explanation of island phenomena. *Theoretical Linguistics* 6,1–3: 41–86.

Eysenck, Michael W. and Mark T. Keane. 2015. *Cognitive Psychology: A Student's Handbook*. 17th ed. London and New York: Psychology Press.

Evans, Nicholas and Stephen Levinson. 2009. The myth of language universals. *Brain and Behavioral Sciences* 32: 429–92.

Fauconnier, Gilles and Mark Turner. 2002. *The Way we Think: Conceptual Blending and the Mind's Hidden Complexities*. New York: Basic Books.

Fedorenko, Evelina, Idan Asher Blank, Matthew Siegelman and Zachary Mineroff. 2020. Lack of selectivity for syntax relative to word meanings throughout the language network. *Cognition* 203: Art. 104348, 1–24.

Fillmore, Charles J. 1977. Scenes-and-frames semantics. In: Antonio Zampolli, ed. *Linguistics Structures Processing*. Amsterdam: North Holland Publishing Company, 55–81.

Fillmore, Charles J. 1982. Frame semantics. In: The Linguistic Society of Korea, ed. *Linguistics in the Morning Calm*. Seoul: Hanshin, 111–37.

Fillmore, Charles J. 1985. Syntactic intrusions and the notion of grammatical construction. *Berkeley Linguistic Society* 11: 73–86.

Fillmore, Charles J. 1988. The mechanisms of 'Construction Grammar'. *Berkeley Linguistic Society* 14: 35–55.

Fillmore, Charles J. 2013. Berkeley Construction Grammar. In: Thomas Hoffmann and Graeme Trousdale, eds, *The Oxford Handbook of Construction Grammar*. Oxford: Oxford University Press, 111–32.

Fillmore, Charles J., Christopher R. Johnson and Miriam R. L. Petruck. 2003. Background to FrameNet. *International Journal of Lexicography* 16,3: 235–50.

Fillmore, Charles J. and Paul Kay. 1993. *Construction Grammar Coursebook*. Ms. Department of Linguistics, University of California: Berkeley.

Fillmore, Charles J. and Paul Kay. 1995. *Construction Grammar*. Ms. Department of Linguistics, University of California: Berkeley.

Fillmore, Charles J., Paul Kay and Mary C. O'Connor. 1988. Regularity and idiomaticity in grammatical constructions: The case of *let alone*. *Language* 64: 501–38.

Fillmore, Charles J., Russell R. Lee-Goldman and Russell Rhodes. 2012. The FrameNet construction. In: Hans C. Boas and Ivan Sag, eds, *Sign-Based Construction Grammar*. Stanford, CA: CSLI, 283–99.

Francis, W. Nelson and Henry Kučera. 1979. *BROWN Corpus Manual: Manual of Information to Accompany A Standard Corpus of Present-Day Edited American English, for Use with Digital Computers. Revised and Amplified version*. Providence, Rhode Island: Brown University, http://korpus.uib.no/icame/manuals/BROWN/INDEX.HTM. Last accessed 06 January 2021.

Fried, Miriam and Jan-Ola Östman. 2005. Construction Grammar and spoken language: The case of pragmatic particles. *Journal of Pragmatics* 37,11: 1752–78.

Friederici, Angelka D. 2017. *Language in our Brain: The Origins of a Uniquely Human Capacity*. Cambridge, MA: MIT Press.

Gentner, Dedre and Linsey A. Smith. 2013. Analogical learning and reasoning. In: Daniel Reisberg, ed., *The Oxford Handbook of Cognitive Psychology*. Oxford: Oxford University Press, 668–81.

Gerken, LouAnn. 2006. Decisions, decisions: Infant language learning when multiple generalizations are possible. *Cognition* 98,3: B67–B74.

Gibbs, Raymond W. Jr. 2000 Making good psychology out of blending theory. *Cognitive Linguistics* 11,3–4: 347–58.

Gilquin, Gaëtanelle. 2006. The verb slot in Causative Constructions: Finding the best fit. *Constructions* SV 1–3: 1–46. www.constructions-journal.com.

Ginzburg, Jonathan and Ivan A. Sag. 2000. *Interrogative Investigations: The Form, Meaning, and Use of English Interrogatives*. Stanford, CA: CSLI Publications.

Goldberg, Adele E. 1995. *Constructions: A Construction Grammar Approach to Argument Structure*. Chicago: University of Chicago Press.

Goldberg, Adele E. 2003. Constructions: A new theoretical approach to language. *Trends in Cognitive Sciences* 7,5: 219–24.

Goldberg, Adele E. 2006. *Constructions at Work: The Nature of Generalization in Language*. Oxford: Oxford University Press.

Goldberg, Adele E. 2011. Corpus evidence of the viability of statistical preemption. *Cognitive Linguistics* 22,1: 131–54.

Goldberg, Adele E. 2013. Constructionist approaches. In: Thomas Hoffmann and Graeme Trousdale, eds, *The Oxford Handbook of Construction Grammar*. Oxford: Oxford University Press, 15–31.

Goldberg, Adele E. 2019. *Explain Me this: Creativity, Competition and the Partial Productivity of Constructions*. Princeton: Princeton University Press.

Goldberg, Adele E., Devin Casenhiser and Nitya Sethuraman. 2004. Learning argument structure generalizations. *Cognitive Linguistics* 15: 289–316.

Goldberg, Adele E. and Ray Jackendoff. 2004. The English resultative as a family of constructions. *Language* 80: 532–68.

Gregory, Michelle L. and Laura A. Michaelis. 2001. Topicalization and left-dislocation: A functional opposition revisited. *Journal of Pragmatics* 33: 1665–706.

Gries, Stefan Th. 2013. Data in Construction Grammar. In: Thomas Hoffmann and Graeme Trousdale, eds, *The Oxford Handbook of Construction Grammar*. Oxford: Oxford University Press, 93–108.

Gries, Stefan Th. and Anatol Stefanowitsch. 2004a. Extending collostructional analysis: A corpus-based perspectives on 'alternations'. *International Journal of Corpus Linguistics* 9,1: 97–129.

Gries, Stefan Th. and Anatol Stefanowitsch. 2004b. Co-varying collexemes in the *into*-causative. In: Michel Achard and Suzanne Kemmer, eds, *Language, Culture and Mind*. Stanford, CA: CSLI, 225–36.

Gries, Stefan Th. and Anatol Stefanowitsch. 2010. Cluster analysis and the identification of collexeme classes. In: John Newman and Sally Rice, eds, *Empirical and Experimental Methods in Cognitive/Functional Research*. Stanford, CA: CSLI, 73–90.

Grondelaers, Stefan, Dirk Speelman and Dirk Geeraerts. 2007. A case for a cognitive corpus linguistics, In: Monica Gonzalez-Marquez, Irene Mittelberg, Seana Coulson and Michael J. Spivey, eds, *Methods in Cognitive Linguistics*. Amsterdam: John Benjamins, 149–69.

Grondelaers, Stefan, Dirk Speelman and Dirk Geeraerts. 2008. National variation in the use of *er* 'there'. Regional and diachronic constraints on cognitive explanations. In: Gitte Kristiansen and René Dirven, eds, *Cognitive Sociolinguistics: Language Variation, Cultural Models, Social Systems*. Berlin: De Gruyter Mouton, 153–203.

Haspelmath, Martin. 1997. *From Space to Time: Temporal Adverbials in the World's Languages*. München, Germany: Lincom Europa.

Haspelmath, Martin. 2008. Parametric versus functional explanation of syntactic universals. In: Theresa Biberauer, ed. *The Limits of Syntactic Variation*. Amsterdam: John Benjamins, 75–107.

Haspelmath, Martin and Andrea D Sims. 2010. *Understanding Morphology*. London: Hodder Education.

Hatchard, Rachel. 2015. *A Construction-based Approach to Spoken Language in Aphasia*. PhD thesis, University of Sheffield.

Hauser, Mark D., Noam Chomsky and W. Tecumseh Fitch. 2002. The faculty of language: What is it, who has it and how did it Evolve? *Science* 298: 1569–79.

Hawkins, John A. 1994. *A Performance Theory of Order and Constituency*. Cambridge: Cambridge University Press.

Hawkins, John A. 2004. *Efficiency and Complexity of Grammar*. Oxford: Oxford University Press.

Herbst, Thomas. 2018. Collo-Creativity and blending: Recognizing creativity requires lexical storage in constructional slots. *Zeitschrift für Anglistik und Amerikanistik* 66,3: 309-26.

Herbst, Thomas and Thomas Hoffmann. 2018. Construction Grammar for students: A Constructionist Approach to Syntactic Analysis (CASA). *Yearbook of the German Cognitive Linguistics Association* 6,1: 197–218.

Herbst, Thomas and Susen Schüller. 2008. *Introduction to Syntactic Analysis: A Valency Approach*. Tübingen: Gunter Narr.

Hilpert, Martin. 2008. *Germanic Future Constructions: A Usage-based Approach to Language Change*. Amsterdam/Philadelphia: John Benjamins.

Hilpert, Martin. 2013. *Constructional Change in English: Developments in Allomorphy, Word Formation, and Syntax*. (Studies in English Language.) Cambridge: Cambridge University Press.

Hilpert, Martin. 2019. *Construction Grammar and its Application to English*. 2nd ed. Edinburgh: Edinburgh University Press.

Hilpert, Martin and Susanne Flach. 2020. Disentangling modal meanings with distributional semantics. *Digital Scholarship in the Humanities*: Art. fqaa014, 1–15.

Himmelmann, Nikolaus. 2004. Lexicalization and grammaticization: Opposite or orthogonal? In: Walter Bisang, Nikolaus P. Himmelmann and Björn Wiemer, eds. *What Makes Grammaticalization – A Look from its Components and its Fringes*. Berlin: De Gruyter Mouton, 21–42.

Hockett, Charles F. 1960. The origin of speech. *Scientific American* 203,3: 88–96.

Hoffmann, Thomas. 2011. *Preposition Placement in English: A Usage-based Approach*. Cambridge: Cambridge University Press.

Hoffmann, Thomas. 2013. Abstract phrasal and clausal constructions. In: Thomas Hoffmann and Graeme Trousdale, eds, *The Oxford Handbook of Construction Grammar*. Oxford: Oxford University Press, 307–28.

Hoffmann, Thomas. 2014. The cognitive evolution of Englishes: The role of constructions in the Dynamic Model. In: Sarah Buschfeld, Thomas Hoffmann, Magnus Huber and Alexander Kautzsch, eds. *The Evolution of Englishes The Dynamic Model and Beyond*. (Varieties of English Around the World G49.) Amsterdam: John Benjamins, 160–80.

Hoffmann, Thomas. 2015. Cognitive sociolinguistic aspects of football chants: The role of social and physical context in Usage-based Construction Grammar. *Zeitschrift für Anglistik und Amerikanistik* 63,3: 273–94.

Hoffmann, Thomas. 2017a. From constructions to construction grammar. In: Dancygier Barbara, ed. *The Cambridge Handbook of Cognitive Linguistics*. Cambridge: Cambridge University Press, 284–309.

Hoffmann, Thomas. 2017b. Construction grammars. In: Dancygier Barbara, ed. *The Cambridge Handbook of Cognitive Linguistics*. Cambridge: Cambridge University Press, 310–29.

Hoffmann, Thomas. 2017c. Multimodal constructs – multimodal constructions? The role of constructions in the working memory. *Linguistics Vanguard* 3,s1: 1–10.

Hoffmann, Thomas. 2018. Creativity and construction grammar: Cognitive and psychological issues. *Zeitschrift für Anglistik und Amerikanistik*, 66,3: 259–76.

Hoffmann, Thomas. 2019a. *English Comparative Correlatives: Diachronic and Synchronic Variation at the Lexicon-Syntax Interface*. Cambridge: Cambridge University Press.

Hoffmann, Thomas. 2019b. Language and creativity: A construction grammar approach to linguistic creativity. *Linguistics Vanguard* 5,1: 1–8.

Hoffmann, Thomas. 2020a. Construction Grammar and creativity: Evolution, psychology and cognitive science. *Cognitive Semiotics* 13,1: 1–11.

Hoffmann, Thomas. 2020b. What would it take for us to abandon Construction Grammar? Falsifiability, confirmation bias and the future of the Constructionist enterprise. *Belgian Journal of Linguistics* 34: 149–61.

Hoffmann, Thomas. 2021. *The Cognitive Foundation Of Post-colonial Englishes: Construction Grammar as the Cognitive Theory for the Dynamic Model.* Cambridge: Cambridge University Press.

Hoffmann, Thomas and Graeme Trousdale. 2013a. Construction Grammar: Introduction. In: Thomas Hoffmann and Graeme Trousdale, eds. *The Oxford Handbook of Construction Grammar.* Oxford: Oxford University Press, 1–12.

Hoffmann, Thomas and Graeme Trousdale, eds. 2013b. *The Oxford Handbook of Construction Grammar.* Oxford: Oxford University Press.

Hollmann, Willem. 2013. Constructions in Cognitive Sociolinguistics. In: Thomas Hoffmann and Graeme Trousdale, eds, *The Oxford Handbook of Construction Grammar.* Oxford: Oxford University Press, 491–509.

Hollmann, Willem and Anna Siewierska. 2007. A Construction Grammar account of possessive constructions in Lancashire Dialect: Some Advantages and challenges. *English Language and Linguistics* 11: 407–24.

Hollmann, Willem and Anna Siewierska. 2011. The Status of frequency, schemas and identity in Cognitive Sociolinguistics: A case study on definite article reduction. *Cognitive Linguistics* 22: 25–54.

Hopper, Paul J. 1987. Emergent grammar. *Berkeley Linguistics Society* 13: 139–57.

Hopper, Paul J. 2011. Emergent grammar and temporality in interactional linguistics. In: Peter Auer and Stefan Pfänder, eds, *Constructions: Emerging and Emergent.* (De Gruyter linguae & litterae / Publications of the School of Language and Literature Freiburg Institute for Advanced Studies 6). Berlin: De Gruyter Mouton, 22–44.

Huddleston, Rodney. 2002. The clause: Complements. In: Geoffrey K. Pullum and Rodney Huddleston, eds, 2002. *The Cambridge Grammar of the English Language.* Cambridge: Cambridge University Press, 213–321.

Hudson, Richard A. 1997. Inherent variability and linguistic theory. *Cognitive Linguistics* 8,1: 73–108.

Hudson, Richard A. 2007a. English dialect syntax in Word Grammar. *English Language and Linguistics* 11,2: 383–405.

Hudson, Richard A. 2007b. *Language Networks: The New Word Grammar.* Oxford: Oxford University Press.

Hudson, Richard A. 2010. *An Introduction to Word Grammar.* Cambridge: Cambridge University Press.

Hundt, Marianne, Andrea Sand and Paul Skandera. 1999. *Manual of Information to Accompany the Freiburg – Brown Corpus of American English ('Frown').* Freiburg: Albert-Ludwigs-Universität Freiburg. http://korpus.uib.no/icame/manuals/FROWN/INDEX.HTM. Last accessed 06 January 2021.

Hundt, Marianne, Andrea Sand and Rainer Siemund. 1998. *Manual of Information to Accompany the Freiburg – LOB Corpus of British English ('FLOB').* Freiburg: Albert-Ludwigs-Universität Freiburg. http://korpus.uib.no/icame/manuals/FLOB/INDEX.HTM. Last accessed 06 January 2021.

Iwata, Seizi. 2005. Locative alternation and two levels of verb meaning. *Cognitive Linguistics* 16: 355–407.

Iwata, Seizi. 2008. *Locative Alternation: A Lexical-constructional Account*. Amsterdam: John Benjamins.

Jackendoff, Ray. 2002. *Foundations of Language: Brain, Meaning, Grammar, Evolution*. Oxford: Oxford University Press.

Jackendoff, Ray. 2010. *Meaning and the Lexicon: The Parallel Architecture 1975–2010*. Oxford: Oxford University Press.

Jackendoff, Ray. 2013. Constructions in the parallel architecture. In: Thomas Hoffmann and Graeme Trousdale, eds, *The Oxford Handbook of Construction Grammar*. Oxford: Oxford University Press, 70–92.

Jackendoff, Ray S. and Jenny Audring. 2016. Morphological schemas. *The Mental Lexicon* 11: 467–93.

Jackendoff, Ray S. and Jenny Audring. 2020. *The Texture of the Lexicon: Relational Morphology and the Parallel Architecture*. Oxford: Oxford University Press.

Johansson, Stig, Geoffrey N. Leech and Helen Goodluck. 1978. *Manual Information to Accompany the LANCASTER-OSLO/BERGEN CORPUS of British English, for Use with Digital Computers*. Oslo: University of Oslo. http://korpus.uib .no/icame/manuals/LOB/INDEX.HTM. Last accessed 06 January 2021.

Johnson, Matt A. and Adele E. Goldberg. 2013. Evidence for automatic accessing of constructional meaning: Jabberwocky sentences prime associated verbs. *Language and Cognitive Processes* 28,10: 1439–52.

Jurafsky, Daniel. 1992. An on-line computational model of human sentence interpretation. *Proceedings of the National Conference on Artificial Intelligence* AAAI-92: 302–8.

Kay, Paul. 1973 On the form of dictionary entries: English kinship semantics. In: Roger Shuy and Charles-James N. Bailey, eds, *Toward Tomorrow's Linguistics*. Georgetown. Georgetown University Press, 120–38.

Kay, Paul. 2013. The limits of (Construction) Grammar. In: Thomas Hoffmann and Graeme Trousdale, eds, *The Oxford Handbook of Construction Grammar*. Oxford: Oxford University Press, 32–48.

Kim, Jong-Bok and Laura Michaelis. 2020. *Syntactic Constructions in English*. Cambridge: Cambridge University Press.

Kristiansen, Gitte. 2008. Style-shifting and shifting styles: A socio-cognitive approach to lectal variation. In: Gitte Kristiansen and René Dirven, eds, 2008. *Cognitive Sociolinguistics: Language Variation, Cultural Models, Social Systems*. Berlin: De Gruyter Mouton, 45–88.

Labov, William. 1972. *Sociolinguistics Patterns*. Philadelphia: University of Pennsylvania press.

Labov, William. 1990. The intersection of sex and social class in the course of linguistic change. *Language Variation and Change* 2: 205–54.

Labov, William. 2001. *Principles of Linguistic Change. Volume II: Social Factors*. Oxford: Blackwell.

Lakoff, George. 1987. *Women, Fire and Dangerous Things: What Categories Reveal about the Mind*. Chicago: Chicago University Press.

Lakoff, George and Mark Johnson. 1980. Conceptual metaphor in everyday language. *The Journal of Philosophy* 77: 453–86.

Lambrecht, Knut. 1994. *Information Structure and Sentence Form: Topic, Focus, and the Mental Representations of Discourse Referents.* Cambridge: Cambridge University Press.

Lambrecht, Knut. 2001a. A framework for the analysis of cleft constructions. *Linguistics* 39,3: 463–516.

Lambrecht, Knud. 2001b. Dislocation. In: Martin Haspelmath, Ekkehard König, Wulf Oesterreicher and Wolfgang Raible, eds, *Language Typology and Language Universals: An International Handbook.* Vol. 2. Berlin and New York: de Gruyter, 1050–78.

Lambrecht, Knut and Kevin Lemoine. 2005. Definite null objects in (spoken) French: A construction-grammar account. In: Mirjam Fried and Hans C. Boas, eds. *Grammatical Constructions: Back to the Roots.* Amsterdam: John Benjamins, 13–55.

Langacker, Ronald W. 1987. *Foundations of Cognitive Grammar. Vol. I: Theoretical Prerequisites.* Stanford, CA: Stanford University Press.

Langacker, Ronald W. 1991. *Foundations of Cognitive Grammar. Vol. 2: Descriptive Application.* Stanford, CA: Stanford University Press.

Langacker, Ronald W. 2000. *Concept, Image and Symbol: The Cognitive Basis of Grammar.* 2nd ed. Berlin: De Gruyter Mouton.

Langacker, Ronald W. 2005. Construction Grammars: Cognitive, radical and less so. In: Francisco José Ruiz de Mendoza Ibáñez and M. Sandra Peña Cervel, eds. *Cognitive Linguistics: Internal Dynamics and Interdisciplinary Interaction.* Berlin: De Gruyter Mouton, 101–59.

Langacker, Ronald W. 2008. *Cognitive Grammar: A Basic Introduction.* Oxford: Oxford University Press.

Langacker, Ronald W. 2009. *Investigations in Cognitive Grammar.* Berlin: De Gruyter Mouton.

Lange, Matthew K. 2004. British colonial legacies and political development. *World Development* 32,6: 905–22.

Lanwer, Jens Philipp. 2017. Apposition: A multimodal construction? The multimodality of linguistic constructions in the light of usage-based theory. *Linguistics Vanguard 3*,s1: 1–12.

Laporte, Samantha. 2019. *The Patterning of the High-frequency Verb* make *in Varieties of English: A Construction Grammar Approach.* PhD thesis, Catholic University Louvain-la-Neuve.

Lauwers, Peter and Dominique Willems. 2011. Coercion: Definition and challenges, current approaches, and new trends. *Linguistics* 49,6: 1219–35.

Le Page, R.B. and Andrée Tabouret-Keller. 1985. *Acts of Identity: Creole-based Approaches to Language and Ethnicity.* Cambridge: Cambridge University Press.

Leech, Geoffrey N. 1969. *A Linguistic Guide to English Poetry.* London/New York: Longman.

Lefebvre, Claire. 2004. *Issues in the Study of Pidgin and Creole Languages.* (Studies in Language Companion Series 70). Amsterdam: John Benjamins.

Leino, Jakko. 2013. Information structure. In: Thomas Hoffmann and Graeme Trousdale, eds, *The Oxford Handbook of Construction Grammar.* Oxford: Oxford University Press, 329–44.

Levine, Robert D. 2017. *Syntactic Analysis: An HPSG-based Approach*. Cambridge: Cambridge University Press.

Lieven, Elena V. M., Heike Behrens, Jennifer Speakers and Michael Tomasello. 2003. Early syntactic creativity: A usage-based approach. *Journal of Child Language* 30: 333–70.

Lieven, Elena V. M., Julian M Pine and Gillian Baldwin, 1997. Lexically-based learning and early grammatical development. *Journal of Child Language* 24: 187–219.

Mather, Patrick-André. 2012. The social stratification of /r/ in New York City: Labov's department store study revisited. *Journal of English Linguistics* 40,4: 338–56.

McCawley, James D. 1981. The syntax and semantics of English relative clauses. *Lingua* 53,2: 99–149.

McEnery, Tony and Andrew Wilson. 1996. *Corpus Linguistics*. Edinburgh: Edinburgh University Press.

McKercher, David A. 1996. *On the Syntax and Semantics of English Adverbials*. M.A. thesis, University of Victoria.

McNeill, David. 1992. *Hand and Mind: What Gestures Reveal about Thought*. Chicago: University of Chicago Press.

McNeill, David. 2000. Introduction. In: David McNeill, ed. *Language and Gesture*. Cambridge: Cambridge University Press, 1–10.

McNeill, David. 2013. Gestures as a medium of expression: The linguistic potential of gestures. In: Cornelia Müller, Alan Cienki, Ellen Fricke, Silva H. Ladewig, David McNeill and Sedinha Teåendorf, eds, 2013. *Body – Language – Communication: An International Handbook on Multimodality in Human Interaction. Vol. 1*. (Handbooks of Linguistics and Communication Science 38.1). Berlin: De Gruyter Mouton, 202–17.

Mikkelsen, Line. 2011. Copular clauses. In: Klaus von Heusinger, Claudia Maienborn and Paul Portner, eds, *Semantics: An International Handbook of Natural Language Meaning*. Volume 2. Berlin, Boston: De Gruyter Mouton, 1805–29.

Mesthrie, Rajend, Joan Swann, Ana Deumert and William L. Leap. 2000. *Introducing Sociolinguistics*. Edinburgh: Edinburgh University Press.

Meurers, Walt Detmar. 2001. On expressing lexical generalizations in HPSG. *Nordic Journal of Linguistics* 24,2: 161–217.

Meyerhoff, Miriam. 2019. *Introducing Sociolinguistics*. 3rd ed. London/New York: Routledge.

Michaelis, Laura A. 1994. A case of constructional polysemy in Latin. *Studies in Language* 18: 45–70.

Michaelis, Laura A. 2010. Sign-Based Construction Grammar. In: Bernd Heine and Heiko Narrog, eds, *The Oxford Handbook of Linguistic Analysis*. Oxford: Oxford University Press, 155–76.

Michaelis, Laura A. 2013. Sign-Based Construction Grammar. In: Thomas Hoffmann and Graeme Trousdale, eds, *The Oxford Handbook of Construction Grammar*. Oxford: Oxford University Press, 133–52.

Michaelis, Laura A. and Knud Lambrecht. 1996. Toward a construction-based model of language function: The case of nominal extraposition. *Language* 72: 215–47.

Michaelis, Laura A. and Josef Ruppenhofer. 2001. Beyond Alternations: A Constructional Model of the German Applicative Pattern. Stanford, CA: CSLI Publications.

Mohndorf, Britta. 2003. Support for *More*-Support. In: Günter Rohdenburg and Britta Mondorf, eds, *Determinants of Grammatical Variation in English*. (Topics in English Linguistics 43). Berlin: De Gruyter Mouton, 251–304.

Mohndorf, Britta. 2009. *More Support for More-Support: The Role of Processing Constraints on the Choice between Synthetic and Analytic Comparative Forms*. Amsterdam: John Benjamins.

Mufwene, Salikoko. 2001. *The Ecology of Language Evolution*. Cambridge: Cambridge University Press.

Mufwene, Salikoko. 2004. Language birth and death. *Annual Review of Anthropology* 33: 201–22.

Mukherjee, Joybrato and Stefan T. Gries. 2009. Collostructional nativisation in New Englishes: Verb-construction associations in the International Corpus of English. *English World-Wide* 30: 27–51.

Mukherjee, Joybrato and Sebastian Hoffmann. 2006. Describing verb-complementational profiles of New Englishes: A pilot study of Indian English. *English World-Wide* 27: 147–73.

Müller, Stefan. 2006. Phrasal or lexical constructions?. *Language* 82,4: 850–83.

Müller, Stefan. 2008. *Head-Driven Phrase Structure Grammar: Eine Einführung*. 2nd ed. Tübingen: Stauffenburg Verlag.

Müller, Stefan. 2010. *Grammatikteorie*. (Stauffenburg Einführungen 20). Tübingen: Stauffenburg Verlag.

Müller, Stefan. 2019. *Grammatical Theory: From Transformational Grammar to Constraint-based Approaches*, 3rd revised and extended ed. Berlin: Language Science Press.

Nemoto, Noriko. 1998. On the polysemy of ditransitive *save*: The role of Frame Semantics in Construction Grammar. *English Linguistics* 15: 219–42.

Nemoto, Noriko. 2005 Verbal polysemy and Frame Semantics in Construction Grammar: Some observations on the locative alternation. In: Mirjam Fried and Hans C. Boas, eds. *Grammatical Constructions: Back to the Roots*. Amsterdam: John Benjamins, 119–36.

Ningelgen, Jana and Peter Auer, P. 2017. Is there a multimodal construction based on non-deictic *so* in German? *Linguistics Vanguard 3*,s1: 1–15.

Nosofsky, Robert M. 1988. Similarity, frequency and category representations. *Journal of Experimental Psychology: Learning, Memory and Cognition* 14: 54–65.

Nosofsky, Robert M. 2011. The generalized context model: An exemplar model of classification. Emmanuel M. Pothos and Andy J. Wills, eds, *Formal Approaches in Categorization*. Cambridge: Cambridge University Press, 18–39.

Nunberg, Geoffrey, Ivan A. Sag, and Thomas Wasow. 1994. Idioms. *Language* 70: 491–538.

Núñez, Rafael and Kensy Cooperrider. 2013. The tangle of space and time in human cognition. *Trends in Cognitive Sciences* 17: 220–9.

Patrick, Peter L. 2008. Jamaican Creole: Morphology and syntax. In: Edgar W. Schneider, eds, *Varieties of English 2: The Americas and the Caribbean*. Berlin: De Gruyter Mouton, 609–43.

Payne, John and Rodney Huddleston. 2002. Nouns and noun phrases. In: Geoffrey K. Pullum and Rodney Huddleston, eds, 2002. *The Cambridge Grammar of the English Language*. Cambridge: Cambridge University Press, 323–524.

Perek, Florent. 2015. *Argument Structure in Usage-based Construction Grammar*. Amsterdam: John Benjamins.

Perek, Florent and Maarten Lemmens. 2010. Getting at the meaning of the English *at*-construction: The case of a constructional split. *CogniTextes* 5. http://cognitextes.revues.org/331.

Petré, Peter. 2017. The extravagant progressive: An experimental corpus study on the history of emphatic [*be Ving*]. *English Language and Linguistics* 21,2: 227–50.

Petruck, Miriam R. L. 1996. Frame semantics. In: Jef Verschueren, Jan-Ola Östman, Jan Blommaert and Chris Bulcaen, eds, *Handbook of Pragmatics 1996*. Amsterdam: John Benjamins, 1–11.

Pickering, Martin J. and Guy Barry. 1991. Sentence processing without empty categories. *Cognition and Neuroscience* 6,3: 229–59.

Pinker, Steven. 1989. *Learnability and Cognition: The Acquisition of Argument Structure*. Cambridge, MA: MIT Press.

Pinker, Steven. 2002. *The Blank Slate: The Modern Denial of Human Nature*. New York: Viking.

Plag, Ingo. 2003. *Word-Formation in English*. Cambridge: Cambridge University Press.

Pollard, Carl and Ivan A. Sag. 1994. *Head-driven Phrase Structure Grammar*. Chicago: Chicago University Press.

Pope, Jennifer, Miriam Meyerhoff and D. Robert Ladd. 2007. Forty years of language change on Martha's Vineyard. *Language* 83,3: 615–27.

Prasada, Sandeep and Steven Pinker. 1993. Generalisation of regular and irregular morphological patterns. *Language and Cognitive Processes* 8,1: 1–56.

Prat-Sala, Mercè and Branigan, Holly. 2000. Discourse constraints on syntactic processing in language production: A cross-linguistic study in English and Spanish. *Journal of Memory and Language* 42: 168–82.

Preston, Dennis R. 1996. Variationist perspectives on second language acquisition. In: Robert Bayley and Dennis R. Preston, eds, *Second Language Acquisition and Linguistic Variation*. Amsterdam: John Benjamins, 1–45.

Prince, Ellen F. 1978. A comparison of IT-clefts and WH-clefts in discourse. *Language* 54: 883–906.

Pullum, Geoffrey K. and Barbara C. Scholz. 2002. Empirical assessment of stimulus poverty arguments. *The Linguistic Review* 19: 9–50.

Pulvermüller, Friedemann, Bert Capelle and Yury Shtyrov. 2013. Brain basis of meaning, words, constructions, and grammar. In: Thomas Hoffmann and Graeme Trousdale, eds, *The Oxford Handbook of Construction Grammar*. Oxford: Oxford University Press, 396–416.

Quirk, Randolph, Sidney Greenbaum, Geoffrey Leech and Jan Svartvik. 1985. *A Comprehensive Grammar of the English Language*. London: Longman.

Radford, Andrew. 1988. *Transformational Grammar: A First Course*. Cambridge: Cambridge University Press.

Radford, Andrew. 1997. *Syntax: A Minimalist Introduction*. Cambridge: Cambridge University Press.

Radford, Andrew. 2004. *Minimalist Syntax: Exploring the Structure of English*. Cambridge: Cambridge University Press.

Radford, Andrew, Martin Atkinson, David Britain, Harald Clahsen and Andrew Spencer. 2009. *Linguistics: An Introduction*. 2nd ed. Cambridge: Cambridge University Press.

Rakison, David H. and Chris A. Lawson. 2013. Categorization. In: Philip David Zelazo, ed. *The Oxford Handbook of Developmental Psychology. Vol. 1: Body and Mind*. Oxford: Oxford University Press, 591–627.

Reichenbach, Hans. 1947. *Elements of Symbolic Logic*. New York: The Macmillan Company.

Ross, John R. 1986. *Infinite Syntax!* Norwood, NJ: Ablex Publishing Corporation.

Ruppenhofer, Josef and Laura A. Michaelis. 2010. A constructional account of genre-based argument omissions. *Constructions and Frames* 2,2: 158–84.

Saeed, John I. 2003. *Semantics*. Oxford, UK: Blackwell.

Sag, Ivan A. 1997. English relative clause constructions. *Journal of Linguistics* 33: 431–84.

Sag, Ivan A. 2010. English filler-gap constructions. *Language* 86,3: 486–545.

Sag, Ivan A. 2012. Sign-Based Construction Grammar: An informal synopsis. In: Hans C. Boas and Ivan Sag, eds, *Sign-Based Construction Grammar*. Stanford: CSLI Publications, 39–170.

Sag, Ivan A., Hans C. Boas, and Paul Kay. 2012. Introducing Sign-Based Construction Grammar. In: Hans C. Boas and Ivan Sag, eds. *Sign-Based Construction Grammar*. Stanford: CSLI Publications, 1–30.

Sag, Ivan A., Thomas Wasow and Emily M. Bender. 2003. *Syntactic Theory: A Formal Introduction*. Stanford, CA: CSLI Publications.

Sag, Ivan A. and Thomas Wasow. 2011. Performance-compatible competence grammar. In: Robert D. Borsley and Kersti Börjars, eds, *Non-transformational Syntax: Formal and Explicit Models of Grammar*. Oxford, UK/Cambridge, MA: Blackwell Publishers Ltd, 359–77.

Sampson, Geoffrey. 2016. Two ideas of creativity. In: Martin Hinton, ed. *Evidence, Experiment and Argument in Linguistics and Philosophy of Language*. Bern: Peter Lang, 15–26.

Saussure, Ferdinand de. 1916. *Course in General Linguistics*. New York: Philosophical Library.

Schmid, Hans-Jörg. 2000. *English Abstract Nouns as Conceptual Shells: From Corpus to Cognition*. Berlin: Mouton de Gruyter.

Schmid, Hans-Jörg. 2020. *The Dynamics of the Linguistic System: Usage, Conventionalization, and Entrenchment*. Oxford: Oxford University Press.

Schneider, Edgar W. 2003. The dynamics of New Englishes: From identity construction to dialect birth. *Language* 79,2: 233–81.

Schneider, Edgar W. 2007. *Postcolonial English: Varieties around the World.* Cambridge: Cambridge University Press.

Schneider, Edgar W. 2011. *English Around the World.* (Cambridge Introductions to the English Language.). Cambridge: Cambridge University Press.

Schönefeld, Doris. 2006. From conceptualization to linguistic expression: Where languages diversify. In: Stefan Th. Gries and Anatol Stefanowitsch, eds, *Corpora in Cognitive Linguistics: The Syntax-Lexis Interface.* Berlin/New York: De Gruyter Mouton, 297–344.

Schoonjans, Steven. 2017. Multimodal construction grammar issues are construction grammar issues. *Linguistics Vanguard 3*,s1: 1–8.

Sharwood Smith, Michael. 2017. *Introducing Language and Cognition: A Map of the Mind.* Cambridge: Cambridge University Press.

Shaw, Alex. 2010. *Shall We Sing a Song for You? The Good, the Bad and the Downright Offensive – Britain's Favourite Football Chants.* London: John Blake.

Slobin, Dan I. 1985. Crosslinguistic evidence for the language-making capacity. In: Dan I. Slobin, ed. *The Crosslinguistic Study of Language Acquisition. Vol. 2: Theoretical Issues.* Hillsdale, NJ: Lawrence Erlbaum, 1157–256.

Steels, Luc and Joachim De Beule. 2006. Unify and merge in Fluid Construction Grammar. In: Paul Vogt, Yuuga Sugita, Elio Tuci, and Chrystopher Nehaniv, eds, *Symbol Grounding and Beyond: Proceedings of the Third International Workshop on the Emergence and Evolution of Linguistic Communication, LNAI 4211.* Berlin: Springer, 197–223.

Steels, Luc, ed. 2011. *Design Patterns in Fluid Construction Grammar.* Amsterdam: John Benjamins.

Steels, Luc. 2013. Fluid Construction Grammar. In: Thomas Hoffmann and Graeme Trousdale, eds, *The Oxford Handbook of Construction Grammar.* Oxford: Oxford University Press, 153–67.

Steen, Francis and Mark Turner. 2013. Multimodal construction grammar. In: Mike Borkent, Barbara Dancygier and Jennifer Hinnell, eds, *Language and the Creative Mind.* Stanford, CA: CSLI Publications, 255–74.

Stefanowitsch, Anatol. 2006. Distinctive collexeme analysis and diachrony: A comment. *Corpus Linguistics and Linguistic Theory* 2,2: 257–62.

Stefanowitsch, Anatol. 2013. Collostructional Analysis. In: Thomas Hoffmann and Graeme Trousdale, eds. *The Oxford Handbook of Construction Grammar.* Oxford: Oxford University Press, 290–306.

Stefanowitsch, Anatol and Susanne Flach. 2017. The corpus-based perspective on entrenchment. In: Hans-Jörg Schmid, ed. *Entrenchment and the Psychology of Language Learning: How We Reorganize and Adapt Linguistic Knowledge.* Berlin: de Gruyter, 101–27.

Stefanowitsch, Anatol and Stefan Th. Gries. 2003. Collostructions: Investigating the interaction of words and constructions. *International Journal of Corpus Linguistics* 8,2: 209–43.

Stefanowitsch, Anatol and Stefan Th. Gries. 2005. Co-varying collexemes. *Corpus Linguistics and Linguistic Theory* 1,1: 1–43.

Stefanowitsch, Anatol and Stefan Th. Gries. 2008. Channel and constructional meaning: A collostructional case study. In: Gitte Kristiansen and René Dirven, eds,

Cognitive Sociolinguistics: Language Variation, Cultural Models, Social Systems. Berlin/New York: De Gruyter Mouton, 129–52.

Sternberger, Joseph Paul and Brian MacWhinney. 1988. Are inflected forms stored in the lexicon? In: Michael Hammond and Michael Noonan, eds, *Theoretical Morphology: Approaches in Modern Linguistics*. San Diego, CA: Academic Press, 101–16.

Szmrecsanyi, Benedikt and Bernd Kortmann. 2009. Between simplification and complexification: Nonstandard varieties of English around the world. In: Geoffrey Sampson, David Gil and Peter Trudgill, eds, *Language Complexity as an Evolving Variable*. Oxford: Oxford University Press, 64–79.

Szmrecsanyi, Benedikt. 2010. The English genitive alternation in a cognitive sociolinguistics perspective. In: Dirk Geeraerts, Gitte Kristiansen and Yves Peirsman, eds, 2010. *Advances in Cognitive Sociolinguistics*. Berlin: De Gruyter Mouton, 141–66.

Taylor, John R. 2002. *Cognitive Grammar*. Oxford: Oxford University Press.

Thomason, Sarah G. 2001. *Language Contact: An Introduction*. Washington, DC: Georgetown University Press.

Tomasello, Michael. 1992. *First Verbs: A Case Study of Early Grammatical Development*. Cambridge: Cambridge University Press.

Tomasello, Michael. 1999. *The Cultural Origins of Human Cognition: An Essay*. Cambridge, MA: Harvard University Press.

Tomasello, Michael. 2000. The item-based nature of children's early syntactic development. *Trends in Cognitive Sciences* 4: 156–63.

Tomasello, Michael. 2003. *Constructing a Language: A Usage-Based Theory of Language Acquisition*. Cambridge, MA: Harvard University Press.

Tomasello, Michael. 2006. Construction Grammar for kids. *Constructions SV* 1–11: 1–23. www.constructions-journal.com.

Tomasello, Michael. 2009. The usage-based theory of language acquisition. In: Edith L. Bavin, ed. *The Cambridge Handbook of Child Language*. Cambridge: Cambridge University Press, 69–88.

Tomasello, Michael. 2014. The ultra-social animal. *European Journal of Social Psychology* 44: 187–94.

Traugott, Elizabeth Closs. 2008a. Grammaticalization, constructions and the incremental development of language: Suggestions from the development of degree modifiers in English. In: Regine Eckhardt, Gerhard Jäger and Tonjes Veenstra, eds. *Variation, Selection, Development: Probing the Evolutionary Model of Language Change* (Trends in Linguistics. Studies and Monographs 197). Berlin/New York: De Gruyter Mouton, 219–50.

Traugott, Elizabeth Closs. 2008b. The grammaticalization of *NP of NP* patterns. In: Alexander Bergs and Gabriele Diewald, eds, *Constructions and Language Change* (Trends in Linguistics. Studies and Monographs 194). Berlin: De Gruyter Mouton, 21–43.

Traugott, Elizabeth Closs. 2015. Toward a coherent account of grammatical constructionalization. In: Jóhanna Barðdal, Elena Smirnova, Lotte Sommerer and Spike Gildea, eds, 2015. *Diachronic Construction Grammar*. (Constructional Approaches to Language 18). Amsterdam: John Benjamins, 51–79.

Traugott, Elizabeth Closs and Graeme Trousdale. 2013. *Constructionalization and Constructional Changes*. (Oxford Studies in Diachronic and Historical Linguistics 6.) Oxford: Oxford University Press.

Trotta, Joe. 2000. *Wh-clauses in English: Aspects of Theory and Description*. Amsterdam and Philadelphia, GA: Rodopi.

Trousdale, Graeme and Jan-Ola Östman. 2013. Dialects, discourse and Construction Grammar. In: Thomas Hoffmann and Graeme Trousdale, eds. *The Oxford Handbook of Construction Grammar*. Oxford: Oxford University Press, 476–90.

Trudgill, Peter. 1974. *The Social Differentiation of English in Norwich*. Cambridge: Cambridge University Press.

Trudgill, Peter. 2004. *New-Dialect Formation: The Inevitability of Colonial Englishes*. Edinburgh: Edinburgh University Press.

Turner, Mark. 2018. The role of creativity in multimodal construction grammar. *Zeitschrift für Anglistik und Amerikanistik* 66,3: 357–70.

Turner, Mark and Gilles Fauconnier 1999. A mechanism of creativity. *Poetics Today* 20,3: 397–418.

Ungerer, Friedrich and Hans-Jörg Schmid. 2006. *An Introduction to Cognitive Linguistics*. London: Routledge.

Van Rooy, Bertus. 2010. Social and linguistic perspectives on variability in World Englishes. *World Englishes* 29,1: 3–20.

Van Trijp, Remi. 2014. Cognitive vs. generative Construction Grammar: The case of coercion and argument structure. *Cognitive Linguistics* 26,4: 613–32.

Velupillai, Viveka. 2015. *Pidgins, Creoles and Mixed Languages: An Introduction*. Amsterdam/Philadelphia: John Benjamins.

Vogelaer, Gunther de 2010. (Not) acquiring grammatical gender in two varieties of Dutch. In: Dirk Geeraerts, Gitte Kristiansen and YvesPeirsman, eds, 2010. *Advances in Cognitive Sociolinguistics*. Berlin: De Gruyter Mouton, 167–90.

von Sobbe, Linda, Edith Scheifele, Claudia Maienborn and Rolf Ulrich. 2019. The space–time congruency effect: A meta-analysis. *Cognitive Science* 43,1: 1–23.

Wasow, Thomas. 2002. *Postverbal Behavior*. Stanford, CA: CSLI Publications.

Wells, John C. 2006. *English Intonation: An Introduction*. Cambridge: Cambridge University Press.

Weinreich, Uriel, William Labov and Marvin I. Herzog. 1968. Empirical foundations for a theory of language change. In: Winfred P. Lehmann and Yakov Malkiel, eds, *Directions for Historical Linguistics*. Austin: University of Texas Press, 95–189.

Wierzbicka, Anna. 1988. *The Semantics of Grammar*. Amsterdam: John Benjamins.

Winford, Donald. 2003. *An Introduction to Contact Linguistics*. Malden MA: Blackwell.

Wulff, Stefanie, Nick C. Ellis, Ute Römer, Kathleen Bardovi-Harlig and Chelsea LeBlanc. 2009. The acquisition of tense-aspect: Converging evidence from corpora, cognition and learner constructions. *Modern Language Journal* 93: 354–69.

Ziegler, Jayden, Giulia Bencini, Adele Goldberg and Jesse Snedeker. 2019. How abstract is syntax? Evidence from structural priming. *Cognition* 193: Art. 104045, 1–13.

Ziem, Alexander. 2017. Do we really need a multimodal construction grammar? *Linguistics Vanguard 3*,s1: 1–9.

Ziem, Alexander and Alexander Lasch. 2013. *Konstruktionsgrammatik: Konzepte und Grundlagen gebrauchsbasierter Ansätze*. Berlin: de Gruyter.

Zima, Elisabeth. 2017. On the multimodality of [*all the way from X PREP Y*]. *Linguistics Vanguard 3*,s1: 1–12.

Zima, Elisabeth and Alexander Bergs. 2017. Multimodality and construction grammar. *Linguistics Vanguard 3*,s1: 1–9.

Index of Constructions

General Index

Printed by Printforce, United Kingdom